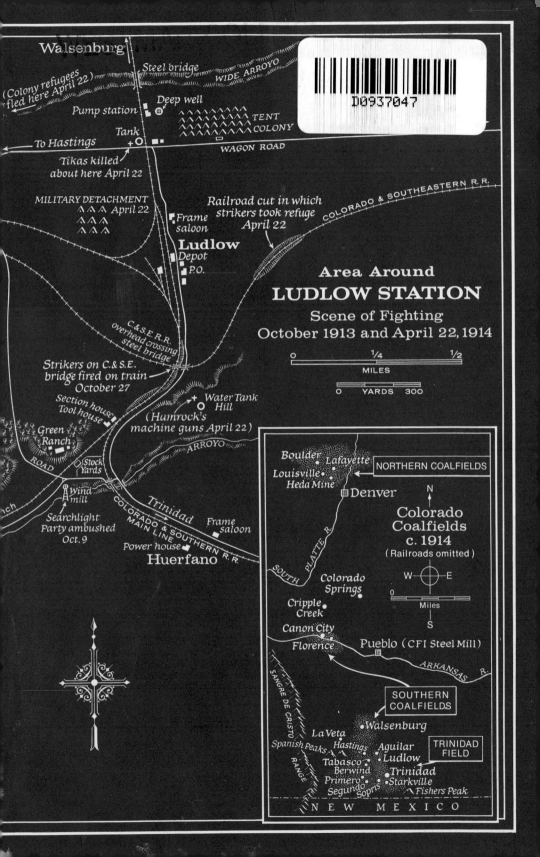

LEONARD F. GUTTRIDGE was born in Cardiff and as a boy witnessed the blight of the Depression in the Welsh coal valleys. He has made his home in the United States since 1947 and is co-author of *The Commodores.*

GEORGE S. McGOVERN, U.S. Senator from South Dakota, received his Ph.D. degree from Northwestern University, where his doctoral dissertation dealt with the Colorado coal strike of 1913–1914. His other books include *War Against Want* and *A Time of War, A Time of Peace.*

THE GREAT
COALFIELD WAR

Books by George S. McGovern

WAR AGAINST WANT

AGRICULTURAL THOUGHT IN THE
TWENTIETH CENTURY

A TIME OF WAR / A TIME OF PEACE

Books by Leonard F. Guttridge
(with Jay D. Smith)

JACK TEAGARDEN: JAZZ MAVERICK

THE COMMODORES: U.S. NAVY
IN THE AGE OF SAIL

THE GREAT
COALFIELD WAR

GEORGE S. McGOVERN

and

LEONARD F. GUTTRIDGE

ILLUSTRATED WITH PHOTOGRAPHS
AND WITH MAPS BY SAMUEL H. BRYANT

HOUGHTON MIFFLIN COMPANY BOSTON
1972

First Printing w

ISBN: 0-395-13649-0
Library of Congress Catalog Card Number: 72-177532
Printed in the United States of America

To the American
Coal Miner

▰▰▰

PREFACE

THIS IS AN ACCOUNT of the most ferocious conflict in the history
of American labor and industry. The battleground was bleakly
scenic: the coal-bearing foothills of the Rocky Mountains. The
story's essentials are uncomplicated: intolerable work conditions
fomenting labor insurgence, capitalist resistance followed by
strike culminating in strife. The United States had experienced
no domestic bitterness of comparable intensity since the Civil
War.

For reasons at first glance as mutually unrelated as the disappearance of frontier outlawry, modifications in the immigrant
flow from Europe, and the establishment of the principle of collective bargaining, important elements producing Colorado's agony
in 1913 and 1914 were afterward made impossible to develop,
either in that state or anywhere else in the nation. And in an age
all too familiar with violence and massacre the convulsion in the
western coalfields six decades ago might seem remote and irrele-
vant. It is neither. Nothing contributed more mischievously to
the grief and martyrdom in Colorado than the same unexorcised
demons that haunt us today, that deprive us of the will to communicate with one another, the instinct for compassion, and the
courage to abandon a stubbornly held belief found to violate
common sense and humanity.

The authors wish to thank the many institutions and individuals
that gave generously of their time and patient effort during
preparation of this book. The material used is described in the

viii   *Preface*

section dealing with sources, but it may be noted here that a considerable amount heretofore unseen by researchers or historians
was made available; and an extra degree of gratitude is due to
the several persons who assisted the task of research fully aware
of the possibility that the documentation unfolded might cast
friends or relatives of precious memory in an unfavorable light.
Theirs was a special kindness.

CONTENTS

Contents

National Guard officers at Ludlow, April 1914

The militia mans a machine-gun post with mine-guard allies at the foot of Water Tank Hill

Ludlow tent colony on the eve of its destruction

The death pit, where women and children perished

Ruins of the tent colony at Ludlow, April 1914

Funeral for the martyred Louis Tikas

"Ludlow, Colorado, 1914" by John Sloan

Balkan-born miners like these guerrilla strikers attacked Forbes on April 30, 1914

Mining property at Forbes, still burning after the attack

Frank Walsh, Chairman of the Industrial Relations Commission, 1915

Frank Snyder, slain at Ludlow

John D. Rockefeller, Jr., after appearing before Frank Walsh

Mackenzie King, Canada's future prime minister, and the young Rockefeller during their tour of the properties in the fall of 1915

The United Mine Workers' monument to the Ludlow dead, shortly after its construction in 1915

MAPS

.■.■.

ILLUSTRATIONS

(following page 242)

United Mine Workers' leaders Frank Hayes and Ed Doyle, 1915

John Lawson, Mother Jones, the aggressive matriarch of the miners' union, and Horace Hawkins, United Mine Workers' attorney

General John Chase, Commander of the Colorado National Guard

Jeff "King" Farr, long-time sheriff of Huerfano County and protector of the CFI's interests

The saber charge along Main Street, Trinidad, January 22, 1914

John C. Osgood testifying before the Congressional investigating committee, Denver, February 10, 1914

L. M. Bowers, Chairman of the Board, CFI, during the strike

"Black Hand" letter of warning received by John McQuarrie, who testified on behalf of the strikers before the Congressional group

The crude armored car feared as the Death Special

Miners' houses in the town of Primero, about 1910

Elias Ammons, Governor of Colorado

John Lawson, strikers' leader, and the Greek interpreter Louis Tikas

Strikers' tent colony near Walsenburg after the great blizzard, December 3, 1913

National Guard militiamen en route to a battle near Ludlow

Coal company guard and two militiamen wait on a loaded car for the approach of union pickets

MAPS

THE GREAT
COALFIELD WAR

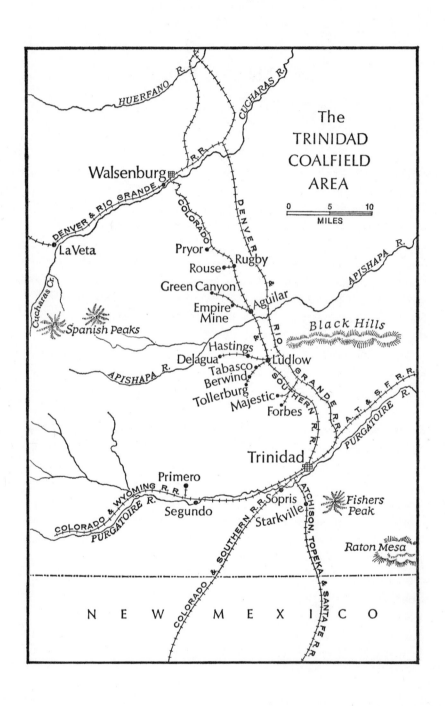

The
TRINIDAD
COALFIELD
AREA

0   5   10
MILES

HUERFANO R.

CUCHARAS R.

R. R.

COLORADO

DENVER

APISHAPA R.

Walsenburg

La Veta

DENVER & RIO GRANDE

Cucharas Cr.

Spanish Peaks

APISHAPA R.

Pryor

Rouse

Green Canyon

Empire
Mine

Rugby

Aguilar

Black Hills

Hastings

Delagua

Tabasco

Berwind

Tollerburg

Majestic

Forbes

Ludlow

RIO GRANDE R. R.

SOUTHERN R. R.

A. T. & S. F. R. R.

PURGATOIRE R.

Trinidad

Primero

COLORADO & WYOMING R. R.

PURGATOIRE R.

Segundo

COLORADO & SOUTHERN R. R.

Sopris

Starkville

ATCHISON, TOPEKA & SANTA FE R. R.

Fishers
Peak

Raton Mesa

N   E   W   M   E   X   I   C   O

THE COAL BARONS' DOMAIN

THE EXPLOITERS HAVE COME AND GONE. The last industrialists abandoned the region three decades ago. Time and natural growth are softening or effacing vestigial scars and ruins. Without further modern encroachment the landscape has returned to its former barren serenity. Once far enough westward to escape sight of Interstate 25, it is possible to stand anywhere within the 600-square-mile tract of lonely foothills and flat plain and exercise the imagination undisturbed.

The distant pair of snow-dappled massifs commanding the west horizon are identified as Spanish Peaks for the comparatively few tourists venturing this far south of Colorado's principal resort routes. One's own inclination is to prefer their older Indian designation of *Huajatolla*, "Breasts of the Earth." They stand in splendid isolation although they are twin members of the state's easternmost family of mountain chains, created by the same crustal cataclysm among whose by-products was the Trinidad coalfield.

The convulsion, a late Mesozoic series of seismic throes, folded and tilted vast granite and sedimentary strata, generating enormous pressures until the entire area burst above the surrounding plains. The permanent results, affording bold relief from the regional desolation of south-central Colorado, are most dramatically exemplified by such separately intrusive bodies as the Spanish Peaks, the lava-capped Raton Mesa, and the Sangre de Cristo's glittering belt of mountaintops curving like a bejeweled cutlass from the Arkansas River south to Santa Fe.

Just as awesome, were they visible, are the dikes and sills that radiate several miles from the eruptive center far below Spanish Peaks — the long vertical masses of igneous rock that cut across the coal-bearing strata following the intrusion of the Peaks, and the lateral sheets of molten rock that were forced into and between the strata. Their molten heat metamorphosed coal beds into natural coke. The dikes often petrified into barriers that were to balk and exasperate coal miners sixty thousand millennia later. But although, in addition, coal near the center of the molten disturbances was completely destroyed, the heat spreading elsewhere converted vast quantities of subbituminous coal into high-grade bituminous and coking coals.

A few traces left by the industry and society involved in tapping the rich veins linger yet: slag pits, crumbling coke ovens, the concrete pillars of a tipple, here and there the shell of a company-owned church or school. But whether amid these ghostly relics in the piñon-clad foothills, or on the green and khaki prairie that begins so abruptly at their base and unrolls to the eastern horizon, it matters little where one pauses to meditate. The profound igneous turbulence of the geological past defies adequate comprehension.

Equally beyond all scope of measurement is the violence of human emotion for which this now-silent terrain was the setting at a time infinitely nearer the present.

❋

There were other coalfields. Perhaps once, before disturbances and erosion separated them into widely spread, detached areas, they had formed a single rich bed. At any rate, they totaled some 25,000 square miles, approximately one quarter of Colorado, and assured the state the distinction of possessing the nation's largest bituminous coal reserve, one half of it, however, too deeply buried for profitable mining. In the Trinidad field, not only were the coal measures generally accessible, but the type of coal, peculiarly adapted to making coke, promised the highest industrial profit.

The natural coke left by the marked metamorphosis that occurred when the coal came in contact with the igneous rock had a hardness and specific gravity noticeably greater than unaltered coal, and to the coal-mining operators it was worthless. The usable product of the Trinidad field was a high-grade bituminous coal readily identified by its rich blackness, shiny luster, and cubicle fracture. Moreover, although the field extended scarcely more than fifty miles from Walsenburg in the north to Trinidad in the south, the coal extracted was conveniently adaptable to a variety of domestic and industrial purposes.

Shortly after the turn of the century, 60 per cent of Colorado's coal output came from the Trinidad field's two counties, Las Animas and Huerfano. They constituted the chief production area for coking coal west of the Mississippi.

Flanked by mountain grandeur to the west and monotonous flatland eastward, this roughly rectangular strip of Colorado was to become, thanks to its seemingly limitless profit potential, the dominion of distant industrial barons. What they were enabled to create, largely through development of localized political machinery and the maintenance of a form of serfdom or feudal autocracy, was a domestic imperialism unique in American history. Brutal or benevolent (it could be either), this imperialism was to flourish for nearly two decades until exposed and checked in the wake of dreadful tragedy. And it seems somehow appropriate that the events took place where they did, in a region already haunted by tales and myths of savagery and woe.

These legends are the legacy of Indians and explorers. The Spanish priest Valverde is credited with having named the principal range of peaks when he beheld them bathed in the deep red glow of dawn and was moved to exclaim, *"Sangre de Cristo!"* — Blood of Christ. The nearer Spanish Peaks served as landmarks for explorers and fur traders but were shunned by the Utes, who believed them to be the abode of demons appointed by a jealous god to guard Huajatolla's gold from the priests and monks seeking its treasure for the supplication of rival deities. To the south of

Spanish Peaks, above the foothills, looms the 13,000-foot range of the Sangre de Cristo called Culebra — "snake" — snowcapped most of the year, shimmering on windless days in purple and silver, its eastern slopes providing the springs and melting snows to feed the forks of the Purgatoire.

Like that of the county which it traverses, the river's name is derived from the fate of a band of conquistadores who, late in the sixteenth century, left Mexico on a northward exploration for fabled gold. Their two leaders quarreled, one killed the other, and the expedition's priest, refusing to continue under the leadership of a murderer, turned back with a handful of followers. The others carried on, to die or be massacred by Indians near the headwaters of the stream. The expedition that discovered their bones along the riverbank, aware that the souls, in the absence of a priest to administer last rites, were doomed to wander in eternal purgatory, named the stream El Rio de las Animas Perdidas en Purgatorio.

Scarcely wider than a creek except when the snows melt, the Purgatoire (French traders Gallicized the name) flows eastward through foothills covered with juniper or piñon as far as Segundo, Sopris, and Trinidad, when black slag enters the contest for possession of the slopes.

Trinidad, in the shadow of the dissected tablelands of the Raton Mesa, has altered so little in three quarters of a century that today it retains a curiously alien aspect. Here began the long ascent to Raton Pass that faced merchants and army units following the mountain branch of the Santa Fe Trail. In 1880 the first train reached Santa Fe and the trail faded into folklore. It had been Trinidad's main reason for existence and source of wealth, but far from vanishing with the mule wagons and the overland stage, the town achieved yet greater importance as a busy railroad junction and the seat of Las Animas County. The coal-mining decades accelerated its growth and prosperity. Afterward Trinidad quietly declined, its population rarely exceeding 12,000. Today, sod-roofed adobe dwellings still survive in its environs, and parts of the town display much of the original architecture, in the style of the late frontier period, that existed when Ute peddlers, Mexican sheepherders, railroad construction workers, fur trappers, cowboys, and coal miners strolled and brawled in the deviously angled streets. There are no passenger trains now between Denver and Trinidad and the highway into New Mexico skirts the town along an aloof overpass. The setting for some novel history, Trinidad has suffered an odd neglect and seems in consequence to have retreated into private contemplation of its unadvertised past.

Northward out of Trinidad as far as Walsenburg, the all-but-abandoned Colorado and Southern Railroad track marks the eastern border of what was the Trinidad coalfield. Commencing a few miles beyond Simpson's Rest, a sandstone bluff named for the pioneer who sought refuge in its honeycomb of caves from a Ute war party, the track runs past an occasional cluster of weather-beaten ruins, some scarcely more than heaps of weed-choked debris, all that remains of the depots where railroad spurs branched off the main line westward into the coal canyons. At one such deserted station about fifteen miles from Trinidad, the wind blows steadily through windows long without panes, but the stone walls of saloon, post office, and store remain intact, and equally upright is the signpost alongside the railroad track that says LUDLOW. Six miles further the track passes Aguilar and crosses the Apishapa, another creek whose source is in the Sangre de Cristo, its Indian name roughly translated as "Stinking Water." Before Walsenburg is reached a final abandoned spur points toward La Veta Pass at the foot of the Spanish Peaks, a valley described in Indian legend as once a paradise where pain and suffering were unknown until the white man invaded it, whereupon the angry gods of Huajatolla made La Veta as prone to grief as the rest of the world.

Walsenburg was a trading post before furious coal mining in its north, west, and south approaches brought it a population of some 4000 and distinction as the seat of Huerfano County. The area got its name from an isolated volcanic butte whose forlorn aspect brought to the imaginative Spanish mind *huerfano* — orphan.

Although some industrial mining of coal had occurred in Colorado as early as the Civil War years, there was no important production until the coming of the railroad. When Colorado achieved statehood in 1876 its coal output exceeded 100,000 tons for the first time and that same year the Colorado Coal and Iron Company, founded by the entrepeneurs of the Denver and Rio Grande Railroad, opened up mines below Trinidad on the old Santa Fe Trail at Engleville and Starkville, while constructing the first big coke ovens at nearby El Moro. For Colorado the 1870s and 1880s were decades of industrial bonanza marked by frenetic gold and silver mine rushes, irrigation and canal expansion, and fiercely competitive railroad construction. This last development gave emphasis to the manufacture of iron and steel, which in turn firmly established the importance of coal production in the state-wide boom. In 1882 Colorado's miners extracted more than a million tons of it.

Yet in retrospect the coal industry appears as a mineral enterprise somehow apart. It had few if any of the ingredients that made gold and silver mining a fabulous hazard of intoxicating strikes and disastrous failures. No millionaires were made overnight. Neither were any paupers. Silver and gold prospectors, whether experienced and professionally geared for their expeditions or tyros equipped with little more than audacity and zeal, shared in common a profound gambler's instinct. By contrast the coal operators were circumspect and sure-footed, intensely ambitious but planners rather than plungers, given to realistic assessment before investment, and once committed, merciless in the management and growth of their business. Such a man was John Cleveland Osgood.

Born in Brooklyn, New York, and orphaned at an early age, Osgood moved west while still young to settle in Ottumwa, Iowa. As bookkeeper for a coal mining company he noted the attractive tallies on its balance sheets, and in 1879 he bought into the White-breast Coal and Mining Company with properties in southern Iowa. Before reaching thirty Osgood was its president. He had also acquired a post with the Chicago, Burlington & Quincy Railroad and on behalf of this concern toured Colorado in 1883 to investigate the state's coal resources. Six years later he had organized the Colorado Fuel Company with three close associates: Julian A. Kebler, an engineering graduate from the Massachusetts Institute of Technology and formerly in charge of the C. B. & Q.'s Missouri coal interests; Alfred C. Cass, Whitebreast's agent in Nebraska; and John Lathrop Jerome, a prominent Denver lawyer. Soon the Colorado Fuel Company had expanded rapidly enough for this foursome to liquidate its Iowa enterprises in favor of more exciting prospects in Colorado. For a hectic decade thereafter the "Iowa Crowd" — none of them had in fact been born there — were feared or admired throughout Colorado's business world.

In Colorado coal-mining speculation at that time centered on two principal regions yielding the mineral in high quality: the southern field at the foot of the Raton Mesa, and the Grand Mesa counties of Pitkin, Garfield, and Gunnison west of the Continental Divide. Osgood and his colleagues set out to control both. Consolidation, cunningly engineered, was their favored reaction to competition. After four years the Colorado Fuel Company had absorbed several coal firms operating on the western slopes as well as mines near Trinidad and Walsenburg. To exploit effectively the company's coal and iron resources Osgood in 1890 developed plans for a steel works in Denver. And if the Iowa Crowd dreamed of acquiring the same industrial power west of the Mississippi that Andrew Carnegie had secured in the East, its next step was a big one toward realization. The Colorado Coal and Iron Company, founded to supply the West with steel rails and wire fences, operated the only blast furnace and converter between the Missouri River and the Pacific Coast. Faced now with determined competition in manufacturing, in addition to fuel pro-

duction, the company found itself with no alternative but to negotiate a merger. Osgood dictated the terms. In October 1892 the
Colorado Fuel Company and the Colorado Coal and Iron Company were consolidated as the Colorado Fuel and Iron Company,
with a capital of $3 million.

By the turn of the century the CFI was the most powerful coal
and steel enterprise in the West. Besides control of an open-
hearth steel plant at Minnequa, on the south fringe of Pueblo, and
properties in the state's richest coal beds, the Osgood forces had
established a hold in southern Wyoming with the acquisition of
some 8000 acres of coal lands in Carbon County, and by opening
up the massive iron strata at Sunrise. In southern Colorado the
greater part of the state's section of the Maxwell Land Grant had
become the company's property, thus enabling it to build its own
railroad system, the Colorado and Wyoming, up the Purgatoire
Valley from Trinidad to the foot of Culebra Peak for development
of iron ore lands and the cluster of valuable coal mines at Sopris,
Segundo, Primero, and Tercio.

Osgood detested having his picture taken. This may account
for the flinty or intimidating glare with which, when cornered, he
confronted the photographer's lens. From his known views one
could infer that the expression also signified avarice and ruthless-
ness. He believed in the sanctity of profit, duty to stockholders,
and the laborer's right to no other prime liberty than to go elsewhere if he found the terms imposed by his employer unacceptable. On the subject of a coal operator's obligations to his workers, Osgood could sound callous: Accident at work was usually
the fault of careless miners. He had no objection to laws determining a company's liability but could envisage few if any instances where its officers might be blameworthy. Osgood was
presumably serious when he suggested that miners living in crumbling shacks they had themselves assembled were probably
healthier than fellow workers living in sturdier, company-built
houses without the benefit of fresh air pouring through cracks in
the wall. He regarded the growth of unionism as a monstrous

threat and would sacrifice all his business fortunes if necessary to avoid dealing with a single representative of organized labor.

In the Denver Club, where Colorado's business cliques gathered, such convictions would not have sounded remotely out of place. Osgood probably expressed them more forcibly than most. Yet he also had the acumen to realize that a discontented worker is usually an unproductive one. He was not the only businessman to understand this either, but among the coal capitalists it was Osgood who pioneered the translation of the concept into an active program of employee welfare that in retrospect provides a novel example of industrial paternalism.

In Osgood's vision no business enterprise was likely to founder if run as an orderly family. Twin prerequisites to maximum production were a company officer's parental solicitude and the employee's filial subservience. Had the phrase "labor-management relations" been in vogue at the time, Osgood might have defined it as essentially an ideal of masters and toilers bound by mutual respect and common allegiance to the company. It made no sense to neglect the worker's physical health and mental tranquillity. To sustain both was to secure his loyalty and thereby avail the company of his maximum usefulness. To the extent by which a company fell short of this ideal, it not only ran the risk of declining production due to dissatisfied labor but increased that hazard by turning the workers into easy marks for outsiders peddling dangerous philosophies. "We do not ask credit as philanthropists," Osgood once said. "We are aiming to carry out common-sense business ideas."

On this basis Osgood theorized that particular care was necessary to make the workingman's surroundings as pleasant as possible. Few coal operators bothered to wonder whether the bleak appearance of most coal-mining sites would not dispirit the miners in permanent residence. Fewer still considered plans for environmental improvement. Osgood, a fastidious man by some accounts, regarded the average coal camp as an eyesore. Whether he was motivated principally by his attachment for neatness and good order or apprehensions lest depressing precincts produce a corresponding decline in production figures, the fact remains that he set about the creation of a model company town.

As a prototype for other operators to copy, Redstone was an unfair choice. Even Osgood's plans for stylish landscaping could have made little headway in the dusty desolation of Las Animas and Huerfano counties. But the setting for his experiment was the mountain magnificence of west-central Colorado, where, in the Crystal River Valley, the CFI operated a coke plant. In this wonderland of aspen forest and scarlet cliffs that Osgood had earmarked as his personal scenic retreat, he built a million-dollar mansion for himself and neatly spaced cottages painted in a variety of colors for his miners and their families. A school, church, and opera house were added. Since liquor was a prevalent cause of lowered work capacity, a company-controlled saloon, designated "club-house" and built in Swiss-German architectural style, was opened in 1900 with a grand ball and the imposition of a permanent "no treating" rule.

There was only one Redstone. But elsewhere throughout the CFI mining empire, a similar program of innovation was necessary to safeguard the worker, and his output, from boredom, indignity, drink, and disgust. In July 1901 Osgood and Julian Kebler, the company president, together set up a Sociological Department entrusted with the establishment and maintenance of free kindergartens, night schools, cookery schools, libraries, musical societies, and the organization of parties, Fourth of July picnics, religious events, band concerts, and balls. December 1901 saw the first issue of the weekly *Camp and Plant*. Selling at ten cents a copy, this professionally printed and illustrated company magazine was intended to serve as a safe alternative to the kind of popular periodical in whose pages the unwary worker might chance upon the latest piece of muckraking journalism. *Camp and Plant* featured prose, poetry, travel articles, and halftone photoengravings, and chronicled in three languages the CFI laborer's rewarding life-style, one wherein education and culture were prized, religion and patriotism accorded due reverence, and a family spirit fostered under the company banner. As *Camp and Plant* announced in an initial statement of aims:

> There are 38 camps, rolling mills and steelworks of the CFI in Colorado, Wyoming and New Mexico, at which 15,000 men are employed digging coal and iron ore and making it into coke, iron and steel. At present, one camp knows but little of the other. Through this weekly, it is intended to make Fierro, New Mexico, and Sunrise, Wyoming, although separated by 1000 miles, as well acquainted with one another as Sopris and Starkville, Colorado, two camps but five miles apart.

The text was unfailingly optimistic. Sopris reports that "Thanksgiving found our bright little camp full of good cheer and happiness . . . Nature was never sunnier and the dear old flag on school and storehouse carried joy to all . . ." Company cottages are "neat and comfortable . . . One who has gleaned his ideas of a coal camp from the yellow journals would look in vain for the hovels and squalor so often depicted." The Engle coal camp on the slopes south of Trinidad is a blissful haven: ". . . lace curtains . . . sweet tones of a piano . . . peace, plenty, prosperity abound . . ." — notwithstanding that an accompanying illustration is a gloomy vista of drab dwellings and treeless terrain overshadowed by the coal tipple, railroad tracks, and laden cars. With gentle insistence the social notes contain reminders of the benefactor's virtues. Mrs. John Osgood's servant suffers apoplexy and is taken to hospital by her mistress "with that beautiful sympathy for the distress and suffering of others that has always characterized her." The Osgoods provide 500 volumes as the nucleus of a camp library and a 1600-pound bell is installed in the Osgood Public School, Rouse. At Christmas each camp child receives a doll or drum with candies and fruit from the Colorado Supply Company, the CFI's subsidiary, a chain of company stores located in camps and nearly every town where the company's workers live or gather. A circulating art collection — 360 photographs on subjects ranging from Michelangelo's sculpture to the Barbizon school of painting — is purchased and sent around the schools.

The dead are laconically saluted, and restored patients congratulated, all in the same column. "Mrs. Smith and her son Herbert returned from the CFI Hospital at Pueblo. Little Herbert is trotting off to school as usual. 'Glad to see you again, Herbert' . . . The funeral of Pietro Filippi, who suffocated in the slack bin . . . took place on Tuesday. The Redstone band played a dirge . . ." And Utopia has its foes. From time to time *Camp and Plant* urged constant vigilance against those who lurked just beyond company precincts seeking to subvert the simple coal miner. Readers were reinforced with complete texts of inspirational or watchful affirmation, such as the latest sermon against socialism by Bishop Matz of Denver and the widely printed exhortation to fidelity and enterprise, Elbert Hubbard's "Message to Garcia," enormously popular among businessmen.

What finally curtailed Osgood's grandiose essays in industrial paternalism was neither socialism nor unionism but the complex feuds and maneuvers of capitalists like himself. Devious and substantially clandestine, they are not easy to trace. One initial factor, by all accounts, was the obsessive desire of John Warne Gates, the notorious Chicago plunger, to outwit J. P. Morgan, who had just completed the organization of the first billion-dollar trust: United States Steel Corporation. The situation had possibilities for exploitation that John Osgood found attractive, and in the summer of 1901 he was engaged in preliminary discussions for the sale of the CFI to United States Steel while simultaneously jockeying to keep control of the company from Gates, who was furthering his own schemes by steadily gathering up CFI stock.

Osgood conducted most of his business in New York. His Denver colleagues, particularly John L. Jerome, the company treasurer, retained their faith in his power and professed determination to prevent any eastern bloc from taking over the company. But the endless dealing and speculation, relayed westward in coded telegrams or reported as breathtaking intelligence in the financial columns of newspapers, served only to intensify their apprehensions. Osgood's attempted reassurances promised ultimate benefit for all. By the end of the year the possibility of United States Steel absorbing the CFI had vanished because the Morgan interests thought the asking price too high. The following year Gates made his bid for complete control. His repeated offers to buy the company were rejected. Statements issuing from the Boston Building, the CFI's headquarters on Seventeenth Street, Denver, emphasized the management's determination to preserve the company's independence. It was a policy apparently justified by good health. The CFI had weathered the stock market panic precipitated in 1901 by a battle among railroad magnates for control of the Northern Pacific system, and its net profit for the year 1902 exceeded $2 million, permitting investment in long overdue improvements at the Minnequa Steelworks.

Gates's next move to oust the unyielding Osgood was scheduled for the annual meeting of stockholders. For weeks in advance the struggle was measurable in wild fluctuations on the New York Stock Exchange. After the closing of the stock books on July 31, 1902, the Gates syndicate secured large blocks of CFI stock by purchase of the proxies, with the intention of voting on these at the meeting. So the contest was shifted to Denver. Here Osgood was a master technician on his home ground, uplifted by local popular sympathy and equipped with a superior grasp of Colorado laws. There was another factor. Unmentioned in Colorado newspapers, rumored along Wall Street, the John D. Rockefeller interests were waiting in the wings, and about now the men in command at the CFI privately solicited their intervention.

The power struggles of what President Theodore Roosevelt had recently called "the malefactors of great wealth" were waged with flamboyance and reported as daily melodrama, yet their preliminaries were conducted with intense secrecy. When George Jay Gould's enthusiasm won the attention of his banker, John D. Rockefeller, to Colorado's natural resources and the CFI's attractive potentials, Rockefeller sent Frederick T. Gates on an unpublicized reconnaissance. Gates (no relation to the Chicago financier) was a former Baptist pastor endowed with a rare blend of canny business sense and evangelical zeal, qualities so captivating to the cool and taciturn Rockefeller when the two met during a project connected with the Baptist Theological Union that the multimillionaire hired him as associate and counsellor. In the fall of 1902 Gates inspected the Minnequa plant and toured the Trinidad coalfield escorted by Julian Kebler. The visit was kept out of the papers and Gates even turned down an invitation to Denver on grounds that he cared nothing for the operating department but was interested only in properties.

One week after Gates returned to New York, where he explained his absence as a health trip, Rockefeller set forth on what was also announced as a westerly journey for purposes of salubrity. Without fanfare he visited Pueblo and the Trinidad region. It was during this time that he decided to invest $6 million in CFI stock.

Meanwhile John Gates and his henchmen had arrived in Denver on their special train for what the local press heralded as the biggest battle of financial giants the West had ever seen. The Gates forces flung charges of stock jobbery. Osgood countered with allegations of proxy fraud. The stockholders' meeting was set for August 20. On the eve of it a plea in the federal court to declare Gates's proxies legal was thrown out. Also denied was an application for a district court order compelling Osgood to open up the company stock book for inspection by the Gates syndicate. Osgood took the position that any transfer of stock that did not have his signature and approval was invalid under Colorado law. The new owners were therefore not entitled to attend the stockholders' meeting, and with only hours to spare Osgood obtained an injunction preventing them from so doing. To enforce it, troops of sheriff's deputies stationed themselves at the Boston Building and Gates, learning of the injunction as he left the Brown Palace Hotel for the meeting, headed furiously for the Denver railroad station instead. The struggle was resumed on the New

York Stock Exchange. It lasted only a few more weeks before the Chicago gambler tired of it and sold his shares to George Jay Gould.

The CFI's annual stockholders' meeting, postponed by the injunction, took place December 9 on the seventh floor of the Boston Building. This time the event was billed as the first round between warring railroad interests for possession of the company, but immediately at issue was John Osgood's continued control. Unlike the raucous acrimony during the Gates onslaught, the election of directors now proceeded under conditions of intense calm and deceptive cordiality. The new board of directors announced at midnight was heavily dominated by men of Wall Street.

The company management was left unchanged: Kebler, president, A. C. Cass, vice president, Osgood, chairman of the board, and John Jerome, treasurer. The outcome was officially labeled a compromise and rather anxiously interpreted by Osgood's friends in Denver as a personal triumph. From the same pens responsible for *Camp and Plant* came reports of wild celebration in the Trinidad coalfield, of torchlight parades and dynamite explosions, of a "spontaneous outburst of approval participated in by all the foreign and native population, showing they are a happy people, proud to continue their labors under the Osgood management." And still the name of Rockefeller was scarcely whispered. Not until the following spring, in a series of swift developments, was his control of the company publicly affirmed, to the angry dismay of countless citizens convinced that Colorado had been secretly "sold out" to Wall Street.

The management of the CFI, already uncomfortable because of failure to complete new mills at Pueblo as scheduled, had found itself faced with heavier embarrassment. The CFI payroll now approximated $1 million a month. As indicated by telegrams from John Jerome to Osgood in early spring 1903, the company lacked the ready cash not only to pay its workers but to meet other maturing obligations as well. At one point Osgood questioned

Jerome's estimates, drawing the treasurer's tart comment that it was beyond him to figure to the day the CFI's enormous expenses. Meanwhile the Denver banks would make no more loans and the company was rapidly going broke.

As news of the CFI's mysterious nonpayment of some $600,000 in debts preoccupied Wall Street gossip, and in the face of agitated communiqués from Denver, Osgood registered calm. Privately he assured Jerome of his confidence that the Rockefeller-Gould interests would bail the company out. This proved all too true. In June came simultaneous announcements of soaring CFI stock and further heavy investment by Rockefeller and Gould, while it was also said that the $600,000 worth of notes delayed in payment had been cashed in Rockefeller's office. Osgood was now reported vowing to resign as chairman of the board if forced to yield any further remnant of a control already diminished since the meeting of the previous December. This he did on June 24 at a board meeting in the company's New York office. Cass and Jerome also resigned as directors. Osgood explained the afternoon's "deal" as meaning that property worth some $50 million had passed into control of interests with ample resources to meet the company's growing responsibilities. This evidently suited Osgood as compensation for whatever the damage done to his pride.

The art of business speculation in this era was largely a matter of feints and intrigue. Manifest feelings and stated motives were best taken with a grain of salt. The proportion of honesty to double-dealing in all the transactions coming after the first evidences of Rockefeller's designs on Colorado's mineral wealth is unknown. Coups were undoubtedly engineered and stocks manipulated. Whether or not the course of events was planned or merely fortuitous, Osgood professed final satisfaction. He was the only member of the original founders of the company who did. A sense of betrayal haunted others and Denver newspapers reported that the state of Colorado had at last been "annexed" by eastern capitalists.

To soften this reaction the new board of directors, weighted with New York directors including Frederick Gates and John D. Rockefeller, Jr., signified willingness for the Denver-based titular heads to continue in office. Osgood stated positively that the distinctive character of the company as a Colorado enterprise would be preserved. Unconvinced, Kebler and Jerome resigned their positions. And whatever the private emotions of all but Osgood of the old Iowa Crowd, chillingly short time was left for their disclosure.

On July 4, ten days after his resignation from the company, Alfred Cass died suddenly at his home near Osgood's Redstone retreat. Strain of overwork was blamed. Just then, John Jerome, loyal to Osgood but long unhappy over his business tactics, prepared a suit against him for legal claims. It never came to court, neither did the details get into the newspapers, and snubbing his old friend and partner, Osgood left for Europe on an extended trip. Jerome was a sorely distressed man. In addition to his responsibilities with the CFI he had been principal owner of a cotton mill headlined as an inhumane "Misery Hollow" during a prolonged campaign conducted by the Denver *Post* against child labor. To keep the mill operating, Jerome had drawn heavily on personal resources. Labor troubles forced him to shut it down. His private burdens became intolerable. Less than five months after Cass's death Julian Kebler suffered a fatal stroke, and only thirty hours later John Jerome swallowed an overdose of sleeping pills.

The coincidental deaths of three long-time business associates, none of them elderly men, set tongues wagging. Jerome's funeral had yet to take place when the CFI's attorney was obliged to defend the new regime with a press statement. The three former chieftains had not died because of "the relentless pursuit of Rockefeller agents for control of the CFI . . . each of the deceased gentlemen was undermined by unceasing labor in the interests of the company long before Gould and Rockefeller had any interest there."

That interest was now certainly dominant. John D. Rockefeller's stock holdings totaled approximately 40 per cent of both the common and preferred stock of the company and in addition he held about 43 per cent of its bonds. He had secured control of properties in three counties of Wyoming, eight of Colorado, the huge steel works at Pueblo, anthracite and bituminous mines in three New Mexico counties, and a manganese mine and iron claims in Utah.

Colorado had by no means heard the last of John Osgood, the surviving member of the Iowa Crowd. In short order, he left the CFI a wealthy magnate, secured control of 90 per cent of the stock of the Victor-American Fuel Company, and reorganized it into his former company's principal competitor. As for his brand of paternalism among the CFI workers, under the new management it was allowed to dissipate. Within a year following Osgood's departure *Camp and Plant* ceased publication. The emphasis in company concern for its laborers shifted from their social and cultural well-being to their physical soundness, a trend not unconnected with a rise in the rate of mine accidents. As its activities diminished the CFI's Sociological Department became subordinate to the Medical Department based in Pueblo and consisting of about forty doctors and a $250,000 hospital occupying thirteen acres. The CFI's hospital facilities, justifiably described as "second to none in the west," were available to the company's 60,000 miners and steelworkers and their relatives. Each worker was charged one dollar a month for his medical insurance.

It became a favorite conviction of John Osgood's that the abandonment of the forms of company paternalism which he and Julian Kebler had pioneered and encouraged was much to blame for the terrible events which occurred a decade later. No one else seemed to think so.

⁂ 2 ⁂

LIFE AND DEATH IN THE PROPERTIES

THERE WERE TWO PRINCIPAL METHODS of getting the coal out: long wall and room and pillar. In the first, the roof was allowed to subside as coal was taken out. While this way had its advantages — for one thing there would be no loss of coal left in pillars — room and pillar was the general practice in Colorado coal mines. The room was driven off the entries with pillars of coal left to keep the roof from caving in as the men moved on. After the required number of rooms had been worked, when all the coal had been mined, the pillars were pulled out.

Coal diggers usually worked in pairs, often kneeling or prone, to "undermine" by pick and get at the foot of the vein. Timbermen would be sawing logs into props and crossbars, notching them, fitting them together to brace roofs as the miners advanced. Some of the diggers might be drilling holes for the "shot," an explosive of "permissible powder," so-called because it contained a limited portion of nitroglycerine and was legally approved for detonation underground. Shot firers were a specialized group who, entering the mine only after the diggers and timbermen had gone home, tamped a "shot" or charge of powder into the shot holes and ignited it with an electric battery. The next morning the diggers found their coal broken up and loosened from the face for them to continue their pick mining. Mules hauled the coal from the rooms to the main haulage ways through which most of the traffic flowed; coal from all parts of the labyrinth traveled in electric trolleys to the outside tipple, where it was weighed and dumped for shipping.

The bituminous diggers labored in conditions familiar to miners everywhere: cramping confinement, suffocating dust, and near-total darkness. But unlike the "day workers" — truck layers, timbermen, pumpmen, electricians, and blacksmiths — who were paid by the day, the diggers' salary was determined by the amount of commercially marketable coal they brought out. They were thus obliged to wash the coal before it left the mine, to remove the "boney" — rock, slate, and impurities. Any labor but that which directly produced usable coal was "dead work" for which, in most cases, the miners received no pay. Dead work also included the displacement of rock layered above and below the coal veins, "brushing" (clearing rock to allow the passage of mine cars), and often timbering, usually where the roof was bad and sagged, dangerously squeezing props and crossbars. Debris fallen overnight must be cleared away. Sometimes a shot firer would "overcharge" — put too much powder in — with the possible result of concussion bringing the roof down. The diggers paid for the shot firers' excesses by having to clear up before they could resume digging. Dead work, unprofitable and heartbreaking, was a source of deep frustration.

In the opinion of most operators, these things were as they should be. John Osgood was one who professed inability to understand why miners demanded pay for dead work. As Osgood once argued, was not the coal miner, after all, a contractor with duties to perform for which he must expect no reward? "He agrees to lay track in his run, timber his run, drill holes for the shot firer and when the coal is broken down, to load and send it out. If through his carelessness there is a fall in the roof, he has to clean that up. He has also to make his breakthrough from one room to another . . . some of these things are the dead work they want us to pay for . . ."

Since a coal digger's livelihood depended upon the tonnage of coal he mined, coal weighing practices were of intense emotional concern. As each car rolled to the tipple, the size of his earnings hung momentarily on factors beyond his control, a stranger's honesty and judgment and the fallibility of the scales over which the pit car rattled, often at a speed considered by many an anxious miner as too fast for accurate weighing. Accidental or deliberate, short weighing was widespread. Sometimes the scales were faulty. State inspectors time and again filed reports of scales in error by as much as several hundred pounds. Colorado legislators had responded to miners' complaints of short weighing with passage of a law allowing them to elect a check-weighman from their own ranks who would have access to tipples, scales, and record books.

Despite operators' denials of violating the law, check-weighmen in the Trinidad field were few and far between. Miners believed that they courted dismissal by asking for any. Operators blamed the failure of the system on the mistrust prevailing among workers of varied nationality. John Osgood had some additional theories. "A man cannot tell, even if he thinks he can, what weight he loads on a car in the mine. If there is a great deal of fine coal, it is heavier than if there are many chunks and coarse interstices . . . A weighman can, if dishonest, when a car weighs 3000 pounds, credit the man only 2500 and credit the extra to a friend." Some operators were accused of robbing their own employees by paying mine officials to credit miners with less tonnage than they had produced. But whether the trouble was faulty equipment, dishonest mine officials, or unscrupulous company operators, it made no difference to the average miner. As much a part of him as the pick he wielded was the tormenting conviction that he could never be sure of being fully paid for what he had sweated to produce. There was no means of knowing. He had no trustworthy check-weighman. Daily he felt cheated.

A miner's workday was without standard length. Coal mining was a seasonal business. There were times of the year when, as Osgood put it, "demand is urgent and by working a little additional time, men could make better wages and the company sell more coal." For twenty years Osgood led the operators' fight against an eight-hour day. Their lobbying was effective. A law passed in 1905 limiting the hours of toil for underground workers was weak and loopholed, and the coal companies paid little attention to it.

The miner's salary was not significantly different from wage scales elsewhere in the land, perhaps slightly below those of the unionized state of Wyoming, a little higher than those of other competing unionized states like Kansas, Oklahoma, and Missouri. Colorado operators boasted of the "astonishingly large" wages their miners enjoyed, an average of $4.00 a day. In fact, by 1913 the average gross wage for the state's coal miners was no higher than $3.50 per working day. Few miners worked more than 200 days each year. Thus in 1911 when the average mine was in operation only 174 days, the most favored miner, even by the operators' own salary estimates, had an annual income of $696.00. From this were deducted fixed charges for blacksmithing, explosive powder, and medical expenses, the latter usually $1.00 levied monthly on each miner entitling him and his family to the services of the camp doctor or, in the case of CFI employees, treatment at the company's Minnequa Hospital. In short, it was difficult to compute a coal miner's average daily take-home pay for a complete year. In 1912 the Colorado Bureau of Labor Statistics put the figure at $1.68.

The miner lost some of it to the "pluck me" stores, well-stocked retail outlets maintained at most big coal camps ostensibly for his purchasing convenience. The CFI, for example, established the Colorado Supply Company to handle its retail trade with the miners, and with $700,000 capital stock and no competition in over half of the camps, the chain of stores returned a profit of 20 per cent. A similar merchandising system brought roughly the same returns to John Osgood's Victor-American Fuel Company.

The success of the company store was due in part to its diversified and reasonably priced stock. In coal regions where rival retail outlets were accessible to miners, intimidation became another necessary factor. The worker patronized conventional stores at risk of displeasing the superintendent and perhaps losing his job. Bound up with the company store was the scrip or truck system: payment of wages in the form of scrip or draft redeemable only at the company outlets. Colorado outlawed the use of scrip in 1899 and at the same time banned "any requirement or understanding whatsoever by the employer with the employee that does not permit the employee to purchase the necessaries of life where and of whom he likes, without interference, coercion, let or hindrance." This was legislation running counter to the interests of the autonomous coal baronies and therefore it went long disregarded. Ten years after passage of the law thousands of Colorado miners were still compelled by policy or circumstance to trade at the company store, with scrip their indispensable currency.

❋

The camps or coal towns were "open" or "closed." An open camp had a public highway leading to it, and a few were incorporated towns, their mayors and councils usually officers or employees of the company. But without any sham of municipal democracy, most properties were closed and unincorporated. The closed camp was fenced, often with barbed wire, and the access road was company property. The canyon approaches were policed by armed camp marshals, paid by the company but deputized by the local sheriff and therefore empowered to make arrests. The camp marshals were the sentinels of the isolated canyon compounds and the properties they patrolled and protected contained the all-important mining installations and their adjunctive growth of workers' homes, church, company store, school, saloon, and streets.

The miner's dwelling might be the frame hovel he built himself — the only way to keep some of the foreigners, declared an attorney for the CFI, was to let them build their own shacks — or a four-room cement-block cottage built by the company for $700 and rented to him at $2 per room per month, bringing the company, by its own estimate, "a fair return of 6 to 8 per cent." The CFI maintained some 1500 to 2000 of these houses, and the lease under which employees were permitted occupancy contained a clause providing for its termination by the company on three days' notice and dispossession of the tenant. A similar provision appeared in the leases of other companies.

Within the confines of the company town then, the miner made the best of his limited freedom. He possessed no rights. He was prevented by language barrier as well as company edict from gathering with other miners to discuss social welfare, wages, physical safety, or politics. He was provided with no machinery for the redress of real or fancied grievances. His value to the company consisted of his labor and an unprotesting compliance, on which depended shelter no less than livelihood, for to offend his employer was to antagonize his landlord.

Trespassers ventured near the closed camps at their own risk. But suitably equipped with signed authority from company headquarters in Denver, one might have found a tour of the CFI's properties in the Trinidad coalfield during their control by the Rockefeller interests to be a moving experience.

The Roman Catholic Church at Sopris, one of the company's oldest camps, held monthly services, and a Methodist minister doubling as superintendent of Osgood and Kebler's legacy, the Sociological Department, conducted Protestant meetings in the company school, where on schooldays some 200 children jammed four ill-heated, poorly lighted classrooms and whose primary teacher was forever hopeful of introducing the Montessori system.

A motion picture was shown once a week on the camp for ten cents admission, children five cents. The miners' homes were all frame, some sturdy and in good repair, but about fifty set apart in a squalid cluster farther up the canyon were built of dry-goods crates, scrap boxes, corrugated iron, and powder cans by the Italian coke pullers who first populated the camp and paid ground rent of a dollar a month. Most of these shacks became uninhabitable during heavy rains. Once the Methodist minister was obliged to carry a mother in labor from flooded premises to a dry patch outdoors for her delivery.

Each privy was a few boards and a gunny sack tacked together around a hole in the ground not two feet deep. The water supply for Sopris was pumped from the Purgatoire River into a reservoir close to the mine and, testified the minister, "Its utility for drinking purposes is prohibitive unless the user wants to get full of mud — not only full of mud half the year but also black with coal and coke dust, as during storms the stuff is washed into the river by water running through the arroyos. The families fill one or more barrels from the hydrants, depending on their needs . . . about half an ounce of pulverized alum is thrown into each barrel to settle the water before exposure to the broiling sun." The minister considered it a miracle that there were no more than the 157 reported cases of typhoid fever on CFI properties in 1912.

Farther west the Purgatoire was also the water source for Primero, the biggest producer in the Trinidad field, yielding more than 2000 tons a day by undercutting and shooting down. Mules drew the coal to the main partings for haulage to the surface by 20-ton electric motors, steam locomotives towed it from the openings to a giant, 300-yard-long tipple spanning the canyon, and the waiting gondolas were loaded six at a time, roar of falling coal drowning the patriotic hymns from the company-owned school, an afterpall of black dust settling on the monotonous rows of company-built cottages that parallel the two-mile spur of the company's railroad, the Colorado and Wyoming. The coal was taken down the spur to Segundo, where in the shadow of slag piles and refuse heaps the Mexicans held a dance every fortnight and the Italians played a ball game in which the losing team bought everyone a bucket of beer.

The coal camps in Berwind Canyon comprised a particularly rich development. When mining first began here in 1888 very little prospecting was necessary, thanks to the prominence of a six-foot vein outcropping at the foot of the canyon wall. In 1912 some 300 miners at Berwind digging coal for 55 cents a ton wrenched out 362,939 tons for the CFI and, after deductions for powder, smithing, house rent, and medical insurance, a miner's net wage for the year scarcely exceeded $600. The children of Berwind and nearby Tabasco attended an overcrowded school — sixty-five pupils in the intermediate class — which was, however, electrically lighted, steam-heated, and provided with drinking fountains of pure mountain water. In other respects the sanitation was deplorable. "Refuse from kitchen, sick chamber, laundry room, stable, is dumped promiscuously in and near the camp . . . the outside water closets are moved every two years, at other times we disinfect with chloride of lime."

The people made their purchases from a general store at Ludlow, from the company store, or from a visiting huckster wagon. And whether at home, at school, or in one of Berwind's four saloons, no one could escape the soot mists and unburned gases from the long rows of coke ovens at Tabasco.

A circulating library operated in the CFI's camps, the selection of titles subject to the supervision and censorship of the Sociological Department's management board, consisting of the general managers of the Fuel Department and the Iron Department, the traffic manager, and two company vice presidents. Darwin's *On the Origin of Species* was banned from the library stock as anti-scriptural," the *Rubáiyát* of Omar Khayyám, inadmissible unedited, might have qualified "if expurgated." The only newspapers allowed on the properties were local publications of emphatically antiunion flavor and, while miners were permitted the *Saturday Evening Post, Puck, Life,* and *Judge,* no socialist magazines were allowed and *Harper's Weekly,* its recent pages significantly hospitable to the nation's most clamorous muckrakers, no longer welcome.

To charges that their employees' children were ill schooled, operators quickly pointed out that although the companies built the schools and "indirectly" assisted them toward higher standards, they were conducted under the same public-school laws applicable elsewhere in the state. All eight grades were taught in every big camp, by teachers who were often graduates from state normal schools or universities. For the children of the coal camps there was spiritual succor in the challenge of even a company-controlled classroom and in the imaginative, as yet uncrushed, hopes of youth. Their mothers had no escape. Cooped up day on day in her mineral-red boxcar house, a miner's wife was prey to a dismal boredom relieved only by religious devotions, private dreams, and the inevitable onrush of terror that accompanied each report of mishap in the mine.

The miners found their balm and companionship in the always available saloon, which thus became not only an institution of recreation and sociability, but an espionage post where company "spotters" listened for dissident talk, a labor-recruitment bureau, and especially when the saloon stood on ground rented from the company, a convenient center for political manipulation.

The circumstances were appropriate for an unholy alliance between coal operators and politicians. Colorado had not advanced very far from a period of frontier lawlessness. Its newspaper columns in the years before the First World War told of aviation feats, advances in wireless telegraphy, feminist emancipation, sophisticated thought, motion pictures, and twentieth-century prospects in art and fashion. They could also be relied upon for almost regular accounts of cattle rustling, train holdups, sheriff's posses in pursuit of outlaws. For all the talk of Colorado's destiny in the exciting new age, the state's general stance and mood owed much to a sense of the recent past. The elements of conflict against overwhelming odds in a land barren of law and authority still lingered, detectable in the boisterous affrays which enlivened Colorado's early politics. Frontier attitudes and traditions were naturally in sharpest focus on the county level. And it happened to be there, in mountainous hinterlands where survival might yet depend upon dexterity with a six-shooter, where the nuances of law meant less than the thrust of private initiative and were lost entirely on hosts of immigrants, that the state's great mineral riches were locked. The circumstances were altogether compatible for exploitation by industrial barons who were anarchists for profit, scornful of political authority, and imbued with less respect for legislated principles than for the unwritten laws of competitive capitalism.

The practice of the coal companies as seen by Edward P. Costigan, a notable Colorado attorney and political reformer, became "to assert ownership of courts, executive and legislative officials, of coroners' and other juries, of the churches, of the saloons, of the schools, of the lands, of the houses upon the lands, and eventually a certain ownership of the men who toil upon the lands." Costigan spoke from close observation, and also in the rueful aftermath of personal conflict with coal companies. But no bias robbed his words of truth. The counties of Huerfano and Las Animas were geographically part of Colorado. Industrially and politically they were, in the first years of the century, the barony or principality of the Colorado Fuel and Iron Company.

As early as August 14, 1903, the Rocky Mountain *News* of Denver assumed that its readers were well aware that "as the Colorado Fuel and Iron Company goes, so goes the [Republican] Party. It has always been the dominating influence in party affairs, for it controls enough votes in the various counties in which it operates to hold the balance of power."

Few enjoyed a more detailed insight into the CFI's political intriguery than Jesse G. Northcutt, a Trinidad jurist who had safeguarded its interests locally for several years. In 1907, as a result of a dispute with an Italian liquor dealer over rental payments, the CFI obtained a court injunction which closed up his saloon. Since the Italian was a client of Northcutt's and a millionaire who had handsomely contributed to county Republicans, the judge turned on the company and charged it with folly and ingratitude. He dissociated himself from it and delivered one or two speeches that, so revelatory were they, his foes would use to embarrass him in later years after he had returned to the company fold. One in particular, which he gave at the Lamar Opera House on October 12, 1912, detailed the corruption of which the company had been guilty and concluded, "The candidates [for political conventions] are selected not with a view to their fitness, not with a view to their ability to discharge their duty, not with a view to their integrity, but how they conform to the question: 'are they satisfactory to the company?'" His remarks were supported by the declaration of another speaker that no delegate to a convention to nominate so much as a justice of the peace could be named until someone in the party telephoned Denver for the approval of Cass Herrington, chief attorney for the CFI and, as was widely known, the company's political manager.

No one bothered to investigate just how such political malpractice may have looked to immigrants who had read enough about America to have arrived with a simple-hearted belief in the purity of her democratic canons.

But company participation in political affairs was so devious and intricate as to have taxed the understanding of the native-born no less than the immigrant. Coercion of votes, fixing of nominations, improper appointment of county clerks and judges, ballot stuffing, convenient rearrangement of precinct boundaries, everything needed was done in Las Animas and Huerfano counties to secure ownership of all public officials from deputy sheriffs on up to judges of the bench, and done with such efficiency that an attorney general of Colorado, closely allied with business interests, was to talk almost with state pride of a "very perfect political machine, just as much a machine as Tammany in New York," and the company's own chairman of the board from 1907, LaMont Montgomery Bowers, would admit that the CFI, "a mighty power in the entire state," voted every man and woman in its employ without any regard to their status of naturalization and would, he had heard it jocularly said, register even the mules. "A political department was maintained at a heavy expense. The decent newspapers everlastingly lampooned the CFI at every election and I am forced to say the company merited, from a moral standpoint, every shot that was fired into their camp." Bowers, of whom much more will be heard, made this admission when the affairs of the company were undergoing public exposure.

In Las Animas County the events of 1912 provided an excellent display of the system at work. The Democratic candidate for the state legislature was defeated in the election by an illegal conspiracy. The Committee on Privileges and Elections of the state legislative assembly was to prove as much during subsequent extensive hearings. A good deal of its findings conformed to the traditional pattern of local political machines. Municipal officials at Trinidad, trading their official power for votes and contributions, offered protection to gamblers and saloonkeepers. At least 100 town prostitutes paid six or seven dollars a month to the Republican organization for freedom to practice their trade. In the precincts which fell within the confines of mining camps, the committee found that the election was "wholly under the control of officers and agents and employees of the coal companies." Company representatives helped the illiterate miners mark the ballots, whiskey flowed freely around the voting booths, one of which was presided over by "a noted self-confessed criminal who pretended to act as constable of the election," and at Sopris a company marshal carefully told each miner how the boss wished him to vote. The Committee on Privileges and Elections, deciding in favor of the complainant, expressed hopes that "in no other place in the United States could be found a condition so degraded, so corrupt or so infamous as this."

The committee had only to look at the neighboring county of Huerfano, where the courthouse at Walsenburg was in effect a branch office of the CFI and full political control on behalf of the company was exercised through the powerful and willing services of Sheriff Jefferson "King" Farr.

Unknown outside Colorado, no particular name to conjure with in Denver, Farr comported himself around Walsenburg and vicinity with despotic self-assurance, safe in the knowledge that when necessary for the ratification of his questionable tenure and tactics, he could draw upon both political influence in the capital and some of the wealth of Wall Street. Farr's interests were indistinguishable from those of the CFI and the county Republican organization. Local businessmen and lawyers opposed them at professional and physical risk. Under Farr's domain district attorneys were impotent. "His word was a command to voters," one attorney testified. "In criminal cases where he took an interest I have never known [one] where the verdict was not in accordance with his wishes. If he desired a man convicted, there was no lawyer powerful enough to acquit. I have never known or read of any man who had such complete and absolute control over the destinies of the people where their rights and liberties were involved as had Sheriff Jefferson Farr of Huerfano County."

Jeff Farr was one of three sons who left their native Texas to become the biggest cattle dealers in southern Colorado. At the height of their prosperity Edwin Farr was elected sheriff of Huerfano County and was into his second term when, in July 1899, a train robbers' syndicate formed by ex-members of two notorious outlaw bands, Black Jack Ketchum's and Butch Cassidy's, held up a Colorado and Southern train near Folsom, New Mexico. Posses mustered at Walsenburg and Trinidad, crossed the mountains, cornered the bandits west of Cimarron, and in the ensuing gun battle Sheriff Ed Farr was shot dead. Jefferson Farr succeeded his late brother as sheriff, swearing vengeance against evildoers, and as his subsequent career made plain, these he was quick to identify as union organizers, labor agitators, and all foes of the county Republican Party. During the course of three successive terms the political machine Farr created ran elections and law courts for the benefit of the Party and the Colorado Fuel and Iron Company. To his cattle interests he added real estate and wholesale liquor, thereby gaining control of saloons and brothels. A prominent citizen of Walsenburg whose sheer survival as a critic of the Farr machine owed much to his advanced age and distinguished Civil

War service charged that virtually all of the county's forty-five saloons belonged to the Spanish Peaks Mercantile Company of which Jeff Farr was president.

It was largely in the saloons that miners' votes were canvassed and bought. One of Farr's favorite boasts was that his county machine could always come up with at least a 2200-vote majority to the state Republican organization, and indeed when the Democratic candidate won the state governorship in 1908 by a narrow margin, with county results throughout Colorado correspondingly close, the exception was Huerfano County, where 3064 votes to 774 were counted in favor of the Republicans.

The quality of local justice in the coal counties was measurable by a sheriff's incorruptibility. Jury lists for district courts, compiled by the county commissioners from the tax roll, were supposed to be revised at intervals by the court. They rarely were. When a jury was required, the deputy clerk of the court and the sheriff drew from the jury list a panel of twenty-four jurors, half of whom were finally selected as the given jury. If twelve acceptable men were not found, the court issued a special venire to the sheriff and he proceeded to secure the needed jurors from the townspeople in general, without regard to the jury list. In cases of inquest the coroner was legally required to name the jury but in actual practice this too was done by the sheriff. Having a sheriff like Farr to pick coroner's juries enabled the coal companies to avoid responsibility for deaths in their mines. Blame went to the victims.

One of Farr's deputies described how he accompanied the coroner to a mine for the investigation of a fatal accident. They first went to the superintendent and asked whom he wished summoned to the jury. This was regular practice, and things were hardly different in adjoining Las Animas County, where in twenty-four of thirty cases of violent death accorded a coroner's inquest in 1910, the foreman was always the same man, a Trinidad bartender, gambler, and secretary of the Republican County Committee.

The most sordid evidence of miscarried justice following deaths in the mine appears in the judgments rendered. Available records for Huerfano County in the period 1905–1914 show ninety coroner's verdicts related to coal-mine fatalities and only one casts blame upon the management. The others repeat the same callous refrain: ". . . fall of rock, accident unavoidable . . ."; "fall of rock, due to his own negligence"; "broken neck, accident unavoidable . . ."; "rock fall in the third south entry, Walsen slope . . . unavoidable accident . . . we further exonerate the company . . ."; "K. Natokan came to his death by a fall of rock . . . his own carelessness in failing to take the rock down on timbering it"; "David Ferguson, died in the Rugby mine . . . due to his own negligence"; "death by neglect on his part and no other"; "run over by a car . . . death due to the negligence of deceased." An inquest on Joe Odarizzi, July 24, 1906, finds that he "came to his death by a fall of rock . . . he was warned of its condition . . . is solely to blame. We hereby exonerate the company . . ." D. L. Vigil died "by a car running over him and his own carelessness." One Shumway owes his death to "disobedience of orders"; Anton Pak killed himself because of his "gross neglect in not timbering"; and no one but the dead man is censurable for having lost his life in the Caddell mine on October 16, 1912, when he tried to rescue a workmate trapped by a fall.

Verdicts adverse to the victim relieved his employer of any moral obligation to furnish the surviving family with anything more appreciable than pious compassion or a cheap casket for the breadwinner's burial. There existed no legal obligation. Unlike more than a score of other states undergoing the same process of industrialization, Colorado had no compensation law. In 1911 the state general assembly set up a four-man commission to consider one. It consisted of two state senators, James Dalrymple, a former Scots mineworker and Colorado's chief coal-mine inspector, and John Osgood, who stood opposed to anything other than a token compensation plan. The commission's report was predictably ineffectual.

The absence of a strong workmen's compensation law delayed the introduction of maximum safety precautions. In states where compensation laws were in effect, having to award the dependents of a dead miner an amount perhaps equal to three years' earnings acted as an incentive upon employers to adopt proper safety devices and techniques. Colorado did have a mild liability law. To circumvent it, as well as to stave off costly compensation schemes, discourage lawsuits, preserve an image of concern, and perhaps assuage the personal conscience, Colorado coal operators followed an informal policy of paying the survivors of their dead a sum determined, as one of them put it, by "the facts and circumstances of each case." That they were not legally required to pay a cent was emphasized by them as proof of their fairness and charity.

In 1913 a total of 464 men were killed or severely injured in the state's coal mines. A total of $33,593.63 was paid to their kin. The detailed disbursement is not known. Forgetting the injured, no matter how badly disabled, and assuming the entire compensatory amount went to the relatives of the 110 men killed (they included 51 widows and 108 children), the average payment was $305.40, enough to insure a respectable funeral with a little left over but still scarcely more than half a year's net earnings.

Personal-injury suits against the large companies were next to impossible. The widow of a man killed by a falling roof in a CFI mine ignored advice that she should be satisfied with the $25 coffin the company had paid for and sought a $1000 settlement in court. Her unsuccessful efforts left her destitute and snapped her mother's mind. The coroner's records concerning the accident were "lost" and the only juror she could recall as having sat on the inquest turned out to be a former superintendent of the company who still held substantial stock in it and, not irrelevantly, in a Trinidad undertaking establishment. According to John J. Hendricks, long an attorney for the third judicial district comprising Las Animas, Huerfano, and three other counties, the district judge did not permit a single personal-injury suit to go before a jury in the six years that he sat on the bench. Hendricks confessed that neither he nor his predecessors had been able to prosecute personal-injury cases before any jury in the district.

Some attorneys found the courage to defy corporate power by taking cases out of the district and prosecuting them in Denver or Pueblo. Most were afraid to incur corporate enmity. Judge North-cutt, during one of his periodic estrangements from the CFI, de-scribed Hendricks as the only lawyer in the Trinidad coalfield not cowed by the coal barons. The others were in fear of professional blacklisting and political persecution. Lawyers, no less than crip-pled miners and poverty-crushed widows and orphans, realized the futility of pressing suits in the courts of Huerfano and Las Animas. From 1890 to 1913 only six damage suits were brought against coal companies in Huerfano County. In not one were damages awarded against the company involved and during the same period of almost a quarter-century not a single damage suit was advanced against the Colorado Fuel and Iron Company in Las Animas County.

···· 3 ····

LABOR TAKES THE OFFENSIVE

ON AUGUST 14, 1903, Governor James H. Peabody's incoming mail contained a registered letter that began "We, the United Mine Workers of America of District 15 . . ." It listed the alleged grievances of Colorado's coal miners and declared that the time had come to set things right. Peabody bridled at the hint of a threat but was not unsympathetic, and he responded to further overtures from the union officials by inviting the principal coal managers to confer with them in his presence. To the Colorado coal operators the phrase "rights of labor" was an absurdity or sedition, and almost to a man they rejected Governor Peabody's invitation.

Some operators were members of the Colorado Mineowners Association. Others belonged to the Citizens' Alliance, a Denver-based organization founded with the help of the chamber of commerce and sprouting branches all over the state. Businessmen everywhere were forming themselves into protective groups with such haste that for all their accumulative wealth and political pull it could have been diagnosed as a symptom of insecurity. Yet their self-confidence seemed as genuine as their self-esteem, and they were prepared to resist the inroads of organized labor with an assortment of means, including the hiring of gunmen and the withdrawal of their advertising when necessary to blackmail newspaper publishers who lost sight of their interests.

❋

Though trade unionism in the United States got off to a bold start, its growth thereafter was a slow and painful process. By the time of the Civil War there were at least twenty large unions, including those of printers, molders, stonecutters, machinists, blacksmiths, and locomotive engineers. "Labor is prior to and independent of capital," Abraham Lincoln had said. "Capital is only the fruit of labor, and could never have existed if labor had not first existed. Labor is the superior of capital and deserves much the higher consideration." But half a century after these fine words were uttered scarcely a capitalist could have been found to agree, and any union challenging private enterprise to regard labor as more than a cost-of-production figure courted trouble. Of necessity many labor unions were born in stealth and survived as mystical orders. The first truly national organization, the Knights of Labor, was a secret society with exclusive rites and mysterious symbols. Some of these were discarded with safety and in 1885, after sixteen years of its existence, the membership exceeded 700,000 (it had begun with just eleven tailors).

But the Knights of Labor never developed an effective structure for collective bargaining, its hierarchy split into conservative and radical factions, and the rank and file, impatient with disputes and ineffectual leadership, swung to the American Federation of Labor, newly formed and modeled after the world's sovereign labor trust, the British Trades Union. The Knights of Labor disintegrated. At Columbus, Ohio, January 22, 1890, its miners' division amalgamated with another miners' group called the National Progressive Union. The new organization called itself the United Mine Workers of America.

During subsequent years it was to dawn on the men of organized labor that they could expect no more sympathy from law courts, politicians, at times even the public, than from oppressive businessmen. When the Amalgamated Association of Iron and Steel Workers defied Carnegie and Frick at the Homestead plant in 1892, state troops as well as the Pinkerton Detective Agency were mobilized against it and in the end destroyed the nation's best organized union. Following the intervention of federal troops in the Pullman strike three years later, the United States Supreme Court affirmed that the Sherman Anti-Trust Act, by expressly forbidding combinations in the restraint of trade, could be used against labor unions where they were engaged in a "conspiracy to hinder and obstruct interstate commerce." (It was 1914 before passage of the Clayton Act exempted unions from antitrust legislation.)

Against the spread of unionism employers resorted to fear and intimidation, the use of spies, strikebreakers, blacklists and "yellow dog" contracts, obliging an applicant for work to repudiate all unionist affiliation or intent before he could get a job. Nevertheless, unions gained ground. When in April 1894 the United Mine Workers issued its first call for a strike, more than three quarters of the nation's 193,000 bituminous coal miners obeyed.

They did not include the miners of Colorado, where, as in other western states, unionism was slower taking hold because of apathetic workers, difficulties of communication in remote regions, and an instinctive suspicion of politically sophisticated organizers from the East. It is also plausible that western coal miners, no less than silver prospectors and western stock-market speculators, were affected by frontier traditions of self-reliance and individualism. What scattered stoppages had occurred, mostly for higher wages, since 1875 were localized gestures, usually unsuccessful. The first strike to involve the entire Colorado coal industry began in June 1894, with the company store added to inadequate wages as a grievance.

Except for this walkout, which also failed to budge the operators, the only major strikes in Colorado until the turn of the century had to do with metals. In the wake of rich discoveries of silver, lead, and iron deposits in 1876, miners struck repeatedly for higher wages and shorter hours. The discovery of gold at Cripple Creek in 1881 opened another chapter of labor turbulence, and as the UMW continued to make negligible headway west of the Mississippi, the initiative in the drive to organize miners of every description was seized by the Western Federation of Miners.

This union was founded at Butte, Montana, in May 1893 with a fairly orthodox set of objectives. Politically it adhered to nothing more subversive than moderate socialism. But its outspoken militancy and radical tactics gave western businessmen the shivers. In 1893 the Federation unionized Cripple Creek's gold miners, who struck the next year. The same pattern of unionization followed by a strike for higher pay was repeated in the silver lands around Leadville, this time with violence added. Two mines came under attack. The state militia went into action. An attorney defending union officials charged with inciting a riot was kidnaped, taken out on the prairie, and tarred and feathered. The strike collapsed in 1897.

At Telluride four years later strikebreakers hired under the same terms that men had gone on strike to gain were set upon with fatalities on both sides. Settlement was arranged by what was then an innovation on Colorado's labor scene: a state government investigating commission. But the semblance of respect that this implied on the part of state officials toward the rights of labor was a signal for mine operators to intensify efforts they had begun to control or influence the instruments of government. That same year the WFM moved its headquarters to Denver. No doubt existed that it had become the most powerful labor organization in the Rocky Mountain region. It was about now that the Mineowners Association and other antiunion combinations were developed by businessmen who read danger signals in the WFM's motto: "Labor produces all wealth; wealth belongs to the producer thereof."

As a slogan this also reflected the convictions of the rank and file of the United Mine Workers, whose leaders, however, tended to veer at crucial moments in the direction of compromise. The initiative for bold action usually came from below. The course of each succeeding administration in the coal miners' union was too relentlessly dogged by dissension. The malady of factional strife destined to infect the union power structure well into the twenti-

eth century had already taken root. Moreover, no amount of loyalty or valor in the field could compensate for a chronic shortage
of funds, in those early decades, with which to wage prolonged
campaigns.

That wresting the rights of labor from men of enormous wealth
required financial resources of comparable magnitude was one of
the ironies of an age for which the gross extravagances of the rich
earned the epithet "gilded." The strike of 1894 collapsed because
of the coal miners' necessity to eat, and a second stoppage in the
bituminous fields called three years later found the union all but
bankrupt. Yet now for the first time coal operators were made to
see reason and agree to new wage scales. This was victory of a
sort, although gall to the taste of miners impatient with compromise and sensitive to betrayal. But these were temporarily silenced by an outpouring of praise for John Mitchell, the young
former miner who, as a member of the executive board, had
largely engineered the settlement and in consequence was swept
into power as the United Mine Workers' fifth president.

At the turn of the century the organization was strong in Illinois, Indiana, Ohio, and western Pennsylvania, maturing in Kansas, Iowa, Arkansas, and the Indian Territory (Oklahoma). A
meager, bloodied brotherhood in West Virginia attested to that
state's obdurate resistance to unionism at whatever cost. Some
5000 union cards had been issued in Kentucky, Tennessee, and
Alabama. In the fall of 1900 Mitchell led a brief strike against the
stubborn eastern Pennsylvania coal interests that ended without
unionization of their mines but brought it noticeably closer.
Mitchell's popularity with his miners was further enhanced, not
enough however to banish suspicions that his conservatism, likable personality, and well-known convivial habits were nudging
him into a perilous fraternity with the capitalist class.

Unionists worried over Mitchell's exchange of miner's cap for
silk hat and apparent lack of interest in labor's revolutionary future found confirmation for their fears in his espousal of the Na-

tional Civic Federation, a newly formed group that lumped socialists together with reactionary employers as enemies of industrial
peace. In the spring of 1902 the Socialist Labor Party weekly
People jeered at Mitchell as one whose "mission is to prove to the
companies that his union is dollars and cents in their pockets."
Before the year ended, his direction of a strike against the anthracite bosses nettled even some of his devoted followers into accusing him of a double-cross. Mitchell was in fact beset by real fears
of what a possible coal famine might do to the store of favorable
public opinion he had carefully built up for himself and his union.
And indeed this esteem began to evaporate with the approach of
winter and diminishing coal supplies in the eastern United States.
The union's funds dwindled at the same time.

President Theodore Roosevelt intervened. The operators softened, pledging as did Mitchell to abide by the decisions of a commission. Militants in the union perceived the moment as one of
victory within grasp, the operators obviously whipped, submission now to arbitration the utmost folly. Thus Mitchell was pic-
tured as naive and pliable, a victim of capitalist seduction, White
House patronage, and his own self-indulgence. But he could
hardly go back on his word, and the great strike ended, with
promises for the miners and nationwide relief transformed into
popular admiration for the miners' leader. Within the movement
itself he had made new enemies, and from their denunciation,
from ill health and exhaustion, Mitchell sought his own private
relief in bouts of heavier drinking. When he made speeches now,
they usually contained reiterations of his staple belief, notwithstanding the ominous growth of contrary evidence, that "there
should be no irreconcilable conflict between capital and labor."

In making plans to organize the coal miners of Colorado,
Mitchell played less of a role than his vice president, Thomas L.
Lewis, to whom he had entrusted supervision of the union's sixty-
five field organizers. A former coal miner from Ohio credited by
some with a brilliant knowledge of the coal industry, Lewis was a

coldly unappealing intriguer whose plotting and personality were ultimately to be forged into a weapon whereby he would destroy himself in the labor movement.

As it happened, neither Mitchell nor Tom Lewis attended the important convention of UMW District 15 at Pueblo in September 1903 to discuss the Colorado operators' rejection of Governor Peabody's invitation. But the Western Federation of Miners exhibited its characteristically strident concern and sent its president, Charles H. Moyer, to exhort the coal miners to a strike. The Federation was always ready to champion the cause of the laboring class, whatever category, but right then, in the latest of its struggles with the metalliferous-mine operators of Telluride and Cripple Creek, implications of solidarity on a broad front would have been a welcome stimulant. On September 25 the UMW delegates (at least one of whom was a Pinkerton undercover agent) drew up a series of demands calling on the coal managers for an eight-hour day, semimonthly salaries, abolition of the scrip system, improved wage scales, and more modern methods of purifying air in the mines. Except for the eight-hour day and wage increases, these were provisions already embodied in Colorado law, and before anything further could be done in the affairs of Colorado's coal miners, the demands were overshadowed by stormy developments in the struggle of the hard-rock laborers.

In the Cripple Creek strike of a decade earlier the Western Federation of Miners had not been so self-reliant, its partial victory then was secured by a sympathetic state administration. In the present strike, called to demand the enforcement of an eight-hour day for smeltermen and an end to discrimination against union members, the power of the state was thrown on the side of the Mineowners Association and the Citizens' Alliance. Governor Peabody, despite the insistence of local merchants that the strikers were generally nonviolent, heeded instead the opinion of Brigadier General John Chase, a state National Guard officer of pronounced antiunion proclivities, that the militia was indeed required. Sherman Bell, Peabody's adjutant general, a former

Rough Rider palpably afire with memories of military dash, ordered the troops to Cripple Creek and Chase took command.

A prominent and kindly Denver ophthalmologist, a benign father, a gentleman farmer, and church organist, John Chase had only to put on the khaki and braid of a National Guard officer to become the state Napoleon, a battlefield overlord summoned in extremity to outwit socialists, anarchists, and other deadly foes. Chase's maternal uncle had helped to establish the U.S. Military Academy at West Point. All of his elder male relatives had fought in the Civil War. Chase himself had been denied opportunity for glory in the Spanish-American War when some impropriety was found in his appointment as major in the Third U.S. Volunteer Cavalry. All these factors doubtless contributed to the dreams of military grandeur and epical command that abundant evidence shows him to have nursed and which were granted fulfillment only in the series of campaigns he directed against Colorado's motley forces of hard-rock and bituminous miners on strike, native and foreign-born. But if there is an antic element about the figure General Chase cut during military performance, no humor softened the impact of the jackboot justice that he meted out to innocent and guilty alike, or mitigated the threat he thus posed to the judicial processes.

Chase's troops at Cripple Creek were virtually the hired men of the operators who had agreed to Governor Peabody's request that they put up the money for the militia campaign by accepting certificates of indebtedness payable in four years. No one seemed humiliated by this arrangement and judged from the contemporary standpoint of economic realities it was actually not that shameful. Colorado was a young state, her present and future fortunes apparently bound up with those of the mining concerns. Under these circumstances it had become only natural to identify the survival of the state with the profits and prosperity of private industry. So far as is known no militia officer, certainly not General Chase, felt the slightest disgust over the fact that the mineowners were paying for his keep.

Some of the struck mines resumed operations as soon as Chase arrived on the scene, and while strikebreakers were protected, strikers were arrested without charge and herded into an old wooden jail immediately dubbed "Chase's bullpen." The Western Federation of Miners reacted by bringing a suit of habeas corpus, and on September 24 four prisoners for whom writs had been secured were brought into the courthouse.

Chase had surrounded the building with troops, mounted a gatling gun at the nearest intersection, and placed rifle squads in the National Hotel opposite the courthouse. Inside, he and thirty troopers sat prominently with the prisoners. Unintimidated by this display Judge W. P. Seeds of Teller County rejected the plea of "military necessity" offered in defense of the arrests and ordered the four men released. At once Chase was on his feet, speaking sharply: His instructions were to maintain the peace; he was unable to comply with the order of the court. He shouted commands at his men. They sprang upright, rifle butts crashing on the courthouse floor. Then they were marching their prisoners outside. A bugle sounded. The four were returned to the bullpen.

"I trust," Judge Seeds was saying to the stunned court, "that there will never again be such an unseeming and unnecessary intrusion of armed soldiers in the halls and about the entrances of American courts of justice."

During this impasse between civil jurisprudence and military rant Governor Peabody's mind was in confusion. He sided with Chase but had failed to positively declare martial law. Another governor of Colorado was to find himself in a predicament for the same reason. Now all Peabody could think of to do was hurry word to Sherman Bell in Cripple Creek advising that the judgment of the court had better be obeyed and the prisoners released. The message was passed on to Chase, who again, at first, refused to obey. His excuse later was that Bell, out of secret jealousy because Chase had grabbed all the military glory the strike had to offer, had deliberately concealed the fact that the advice from Denver bore Governor Peabody's signature. In a last fling before his recall to face a court-martial for willful disobedience, General Chase ordered the entire editorial staff of the prounion Victor *Daily Record* jailed in his bullpen.

"It is the intention of the mineowners to stamp out unionism," the general freely admitted once back in Denver. "The troops will remain there until this is done." Then he went before the court-martial, was found guilty on all counts, and sentenced to dismissal from the Colorado National Guard. Governor Peabody signed his formal approval, but an outcry from the general's supporters charging his administration with conspiracy to produce "an American Dreyfus" made him think again. Citing General Chase's services to the state, he set aside the verdict he had just approved and unwittingly stored up trouble for future governors by ordering the general restored to duty.

In the jittery wake of the labor unrest at Cripple Creek the temporarily eclipsed issue of the demands raised by the coal miners gathered at Pueblo reassumed significance almost as an ultimatum. But at UMW headquarters in the Merchants Bank Building, Indianapolis, the response to any talk of a strike was cool. District 15 officials came before the national executive board insisting that the time for a confrontation with Colorado's coal operators was now or never. President Mitchell dampened their ardor by putting off a decision pending further tries for peaceful negotiation, and on October 6 he requested a conference with the managers of the Colorado Fuel and Iron Company and the Victor-American Company. The rejections came swiftly, salted with warning. "We do not think your organization is authorized to represent our miners," wrote J. F. Welborn, the CFI vice president, "as very few of them belong to it. If you understand the situation as it really is, you no doubt regard the inciting of any further industrial disturbance in Colorado as ill-advised and criminal."

Welborn was more or less right about the size of union membership among his employees. It was a minority, although by no means fractional. So it came as a shock to the CFI and other companies when in Las Animas County alone about 6500 miners

obeyed the UMW's strike call on November 9 and the union
handed at least one third of them one-way train tickets to Illinois,
Missouri, Iowa, and the Indian Territory where new jobs awaited
them.

But the strike failed to pass the test of solidarity. Three thousand miners of the northern counties had also come out. When
the weaker northern operators offered them an eight-hour day and
slight wage increases the union's national officers persuaded them
to accept. They returned to work after less than a month's stoppage, their brethren in the south left to continue a strike against
powerful bosses who, though deigning to consider an upward
nudge of wages, refused to yield an inch on the issue of the eight-
hour day.

Again rose the cries of betrayal. None declaimed more strenuously against John Mitchell and the "ring of fools" in the Merchants Bank Building in Indianapolis than Mary Harris Jones, the
self-proclaimed mother of the United Mine Workers, the paid
union organizer in laced boots and pansied bonnet whose revolutionary billingsgate had shrilled above the doctrinaire oratory of
every major strike in the past dozen years. With a bustling personality that swept aside the speculations about her misty background, this sexagenarian firebrand had spared no effort to win for
herself the double image of fearless and endearing leader of labor
and vengeful virago to exploiters of the toiling masses. And
Mother Jones's very grip on the affections of miners made her on
occasion a source of embarrassment to the feud-ridden leadership
of the mine workers' union.

Meanwhile, confounding mine operators as well as the
UMW's national officers who presumed the southern strike
doomed by the settlement in the north, the men of the Trinidad
coalfield stayed out, some of them cherishing the belief that a coal-
hungry public in midwinter might force the bosses to come to
terms. This possibility vanished when arrangements were made
for coal shipments from eastern states, and the UMW leaders
gave soft-hearted assurances that in view of the onset of winter

nothing would be done to impede them. Anyway, it appeared that coal importation might not be necessary. The CFI was bringing in strikebreakers, Italian laborers at first, transferred from the steel plant at Pueblo. At the same time, striking miners were invited back to work and offered the protection of newly hired mine guards, many of them former gunmen and cowboys attracted to the steady pay of five dollars a day.

Evicted from their company homes, shivering in tents, harassed by the mine guards, and sustained by little more than local charity and the histrionic visitations of Mother Jones, the band of strikers in southern Colorado grew ever more forlorn. On December 2 John Mitchell arrived in Denver to confer with Governor Peabody. He also accepted an invitation to address the chamber of commerce, affording fresh ammunition to his critical brothers in the union.

Had the miners of the northern field stayed out with the southern strikers, metal workers and coal miners alike would have reaped the benefit. This argument was loudly promoted by Robert Randall, a vociferous UMW official in the northern field who had ties with the Western Federation of Miners. He was not the only one convinced that John Mitchell had handed victory on a platter to the Denver Citizens' Alliance, the CFI and Victor-American, condemning Colorado's coal miners to "a state of abject peonage for years to come." At the UMW convention of 1905 Randall insulted John Mitchell to his face. "Nineteen thousand men, women and children, cold, hungry and dressed in gunny sacks . . . encamped on the barren hills and in desolate canyons . . . while you discussed the labor question over the banquet board . . ." And he went on to compare the union president, "the little tin labor god of the capitalist class" with the valiant field work of Mother Jones "whose white-haired head will soon be laid to rest."

Mother Jones, who had a long way to go before that end, managed to survive each interunion conflict with her popularity intact. She had also shrugged off, without bothering to deny them, the slanders based on material allegedly in the Denver office of the Pinkerton Agency purporting to fill the gaps in her early chronology with managerial assignments in the red-light districts of Denver, Chicago, Omaha, and San Francisco. Wherever she went the capitalist targets of her own vituperative arrows made sure that the scurrilities preceded her. And she could not count on her beloved union for good references. She had irritated too many in the UMW's upper echelons with her jeering allusions before miners' assemblies to the "cowards" and "weaklings" supposed to lead but subverting the struggle. The profanities she hurled at union officialdom for feebleness or inaction matched her venom for the rich bosses, and only she could have got away with it.

Besides her phenomenal hold on the rank and file, her services in the field had been valuable. John Mitchell had showed little compunction about sending her into some of the bloodiest sectors of the first campaign to organize West Virginia in 1901. Now her many admirers expected the union to show its gratitude by defending her character against defamation. There is evidence that a libel suit was considered until the union's attorney in Denver, blaming the nature of Colorado laws and the weakness of the case, advised against it. Privately, requests were made to Mitchell for at the minimum a public rebuttal and the union's testimonial of confidence. They were coolly turned down. "I never heard of her prior to 1894," Mitchell wrote in one reply. The charges, regrettably, concerned her life before that date, ". . . so I am unable to speak on the subject." And to a New Hampshire cleric seeking to nail the rumors before lecturing about Mother Jones at a women's social club, Mitchell answered, "I can give you little information . . . except the fact that she has been more or less prominently identified with the labor movement for some years."

When official and vigilante elements in Colorado renewed their counterattack against organized labor with the melting of the snows in 1904, that identification was warrant enough for Mother Jones's deportation from the southern strike zone. Governor Peabody, heeding the combined alarums of Adjutant General Bell

and the sheriff of Las Animas County, had once more decided on
military force to police a strike zone. In Trinidad on March 26 an
armed squad arrested Mother Jones, a striker, and two editors of
Il Trovatore Italiano, a local paper for Italian miners that had recently accused the CFI and Victor-American along with the Citizens' Alliance of paying out $200,000 to keep the troops in the strike
zone. The paper had also reminded striking miners of their duty
to shop only in stores whose windows or counters displayed the
union label. Mother Jones and her companions were put on an
eastbound Santa Fe train and ordered not to come back.

"The socialists and anarchists of the United States have selected
Colorado as the best field in which to exploit their peculiar ideas."
All efforts should be made to "resist their political encroach-
ments." Statements like this one from the Citizens' Alliance in
Denver typified the rationale employed to persecute or suppress
insurgent labor, and one of the most effective efforts was found to
be deportation. In Telluride more than 100 armed men, symbolic
white caps identifying them as vigilantes of the Citizens' Alliance,
had seized some 80 members of the WFM, hustled them aboard
a special train, and celebrated its departure with a shooting spree.
A final tally of deportations from the metalliferous region during
the strike of 1903-4 approximated 300. Trinidad's ten weeks of
military rule that same spring saw 100 persons deported because,
said Major Zeph Hill, the militia commander, "I believe their absence is better for the people than their presence." Like General
Chase in the hard-rock mining fields, Major Hill had his bullpen
and before he was finished had filled it with 164 "military prisoners."

Colorado's industrialists and their political menials could now
afford to relax. The threat to their interests was being crushed or
beginning to crumble. The day Mother Jones was deported from
Trinidad, militiamen arrested Charles Moyer, the leader of the
Western Federation of Miners, near Telluride on charges of dese-
crating the American flag by mailing copies of it inscribed with
unionist propaganda. There ensued another show of military defi-

ance as officers refused to produce Moyer in court on a writ of
habeas corpus. This case reached the state Supreme Court, which
avoided the question of whether such writs could be suspended
during periods of martial law and merely decided that Moyer's
arrest and detention were justified.

Sympathy for the Western Federation of Miners was in any
event dissolving in the roar and flash of train derailments and
dynamite blasts, like the powerful explosion at the Independence
railroad depot near Victor, Colorado, on June 6, 1904, which
killed twenty-five nonunion miners. At least some of the outrages
were the work of professional saboteurs in the pay of detective
agencies. Without much doubt, the Independence explosion was
traceable to the depraved free-lance bomber Harry Orchard. But
hardly had the echoes faded from each thunderous blast when
obloquy was hurled upon the WFM.

As for the Trinidad coalfield, its striking miners had come to
realize that their self-imposed hardship was for a deserted cause.
Yet even though the national officers of the UMW notified them
on June 2 that strike funds would be cut off, and while coal operators not only refused to negotiate with them but to all appearances had totally forgotten their existence, still the men of District
15 voted in convention to continue the strike. But now it was all
bravura and doomed not to survive the fall. By then the coal
mines were being operated at almost full capacity with the labor
of strikebreakers. What had been a boldly launched crusade was
no more than meaningless delusion, and only now did the miners
abandon it.

There were comparatively few left. Thousands had gone to
other states. Those who remained and returned to work found
themselves in a minority with men of continental European stock.
On the streets of Walsenburg, Trinidad, Aguilar, and around the
coal camps, Scots burr and Welsh lilt were no longer dominant
vocal tones.

John Osgood had once asked the Commissioner of Immigration
in Washington, D.C., whether it would be a violation of labor laws

to send a recruiting agent to Europe with enticing pictures of coal camps and pamphlets listing wage scales. He was informed that it would. However, Osgood paid at least one visit to Europe to study the possibilities of foreign recruitment and Upton Sinclair in 1914 would claim to have seen "lying advertisements with bright colored pictures . . ." printed by the CFI and posted at railroad stations in southern Europe. The developing myth that coal operators deliberately planned a work force of ethnic variety was based on reliable reports that in many mines Italians were placed alongside Serbs, Croatians next to Austrians, and so on down a line of perhaps a score of different nationalities, a deployment that foreclosed the discussion of grievances. In the rhetoric of a future labor mediator, Ethelbert Stewart, when told of a company where twenty-one languages were spoken, "The purpose was, of course, to produce in advance a condition of confusion of tongues, so that no tower upon which they might ascend into the heavens, could be erected."

An 1888 estimate that four fifths of Colorado's coal miners were English-speaking had remained constant until the labor struggles of 1903–4. Deportations, the UMW's policy of depopulating the coal counties, an exodus of the disillusioned — all this would have produced a ruinous labor vacuum had not Italians, Austrians, Slavs, Serbs, Poles, and Montenegrans "drifted from the sea coast and through the different mining states to Colorado," said E. H. Weitzel, general manager for the CFI, "without any effort on our part, except to create such conditions as would draw labor."

Within a few short years this immigratory phenomenon established a settlement of southern and eastern Europeans, all but isolated in a western environment itself in convulsive transition from frontier primitivity to modern competitive industrialism. The last to arrive in significant numbers were the Greeks, their departure from the motherland compelled by circumstances that paralleled, on a smaller scale, the Irish potato famine with its historic consequences in the pattern of American immigration.

A disease infested French currants and ruined a generation's crop, forcing French wine makers to import from Greece. By the end of the nineteenth century Greek prosperity largely depended upon the export of currants, but in the meantime France had begun to control the blight. The Greek economy shook. It collapsed entirely in 1907 when the currant crop failed. The spread of poverty produced a surge in emigration and the Greek government did nothing to discourage it.

Greeks who had earlier emigrated wrote home exaggerated letters with photos enclosed showing themselves decked out in American finery. Greeks serving as labor agents in the New World composed glowing advertisements for newspapers in Crete and mainland Greece. Steamship agents roamed the towns and mountain villages with tall tales of abundant employment in the United States. Whole families clamored for steerage space.

Most of those arriving on American shores in 1907 and following years were immediately worse off than ever. The United States was in the middle of a slump. From 1906 to 1914 a yearly average of 31,000 Greeks, men and youths, left for America and their flight from privation did not end when they made port. For most it was necessary to carry on the westward movement, far into an alien desolation of bleak plains and mountain slopes where they did not, picturesque though it might have been, set about indulging their homesickness with dances, mandolins, and trumpets. Embittered and quarrelsome, disdained by immigrants of other European stock, they searched and struggled and fought for survival. And for many hundreds the end of the journey was absorption into the polyglot communities of exploitable labor, more than 70 per cent non-English speaking by 1910, that tore 100,000 tons of coal every year from each of the twenty-two big mines driven deep into the Trinidad coalfield.

··· 4 ···

BIBLE CLASS AND DUSTY SEPULCHERS

ON JANUARY 20, 1907, a worker in the Colorado Fuel and Iron Company mine at Primero informed the fire boss, whose responsibility was mine safety, of a dangerous accumulation of gas. He was ordered back to his job and warned not to alarm the other miners. There would have been little time. The explosion took place as he was collecting his tools. It left him mangled. Three days later in the same mine a bigger blast killed twenty-four men. Since dust greatly aggravated the danger of gas explosions the law required that gaseous mines be thoroughly and regularly sprinkled. Except for hasty precautions should word from Trinidad warn of the approach of a state mine inspector, Primero was sprinkled only when the dust became so thick it interfered with the passage of the mules. On January 31, 1910, Primero exploded again and this time took seventy-nine lives.

The Las Animas political machinery reacted as expected. A jury of six, five of them employees of the CFI, ascribed the deaths to an explosion, cause unknown. In less than twenty-four hours of the disaster and without leaving Denver, the chairman of the company's board of directors, LaMont Montgomery Bowers, had formed his own conclusions, which he outlined in a letter to his nephew, Frederick T. Gates, a company stockholder and the confidant and mentor to both Rockefellers, sire and son. Some miner had probably broken the rule against carrying pipes and matches into the mine. The men were prone to be careless. The mine was thoroughly ventilated but like most soft-coal mines contained concentrations of gas. The dust ignites, Bowers explained, "and then havoc follows." He had recently been assured by a state mine inspector that the CFI was taking satisfactory steps to prevent disasters. "But they will happen and we have to make the best of it." The mine was reported to be undamaged. "Work will be resumed as soon as the miners get over the excitement."

As a matter of fact, the official opinion of the state mine inspectors printed in the Twelfth Biennial Report of the Colorado Bureau of Labor Statistics charged the company with willful neglect in failing to have the mines sprinkled or to apply other safety measures since previous accidents, and that by compelling men to work under those conditions it was guilty of "cold-blooded barbarism."

Gates relayed Bowers' theories to John D. Rockefeller, Jr., slightly misquoting his uncle to put the blame more squarely on careless or disobedient miners. His reference to the disaster was but two or three lines, in an otherwise typical letter between business intimates habitually sensitive to the fluctuations of the stock market and not remotely familiar with the subterranean perils of roof falls and bituminous gas. And when the younger Rockefeller, to whom the senior had entrusted supervision of his Colorado interests, wrote to Denver only a few days after the tragedy, he made not the slightest mention of it.

In due course national puzzlement would focus on an apparent incongruity between Rockefeller's well-publicized Christian philanthropy and active interest in social uplift, and on the other hand a well-nigh total ignorance, willful or otherwise, of the plight of those whose blood and brawn contributed to the family's enormous fortunes. The contradictions were never cleared up to everyone's satisfaction, even after public outcry and official inquiry forced Rockefeller into making the attempt. His claim then of being wholly appreciative of the conditions which surrounded wage earners and full of sympathy for every endeavor to better them rang quite out of harmony with the almost simultaneous admission that he knew nothing of the Colorado coal miners' wage scales, was unable to name the counties where the CFI mines were located, was unaware of any grievances among the miners, had only the vaguest impression of their housing facilities, was in utter ignorance of the company's influence in regional and state politics, could not say if the steelworkers at Pueblo worked twelve hours a day or seven days a week, and was not in the habit of reading government reports about labor conditions in the properties his company owned.

Rockefeller's explanation for all this would be that such matters were best left to the officers of tested competence on the scene. This was a policy which accommodated the dictates of his conscience, the obligations of duty as he saw it, and a convention of modern corporate business that limited the responsibility of stockholders to little more than the election of directors. Rockefeller was to add that a large stockholder could, however, exercise considerable moral influence over the directors and indeed should properly do so.

The Rockefellers, unlike most of the money monarchs with whom they competed or conspired, detested flamboyance and had cultivated no taste for publicity. One reason for this was the austere regimen imposed by their stern adherence to the Baptist church. Also, according to his sympathetic biographer, the young Rockefeller was handicapped from having been born into a stifling volume of wealth. The all-round impression conveyed of him is of an essentially simple man whose genuine modesty and courtesy masked a life-long drive to find ways and means of employing the great family fortune for the betterment of mankind. Before he died in 1960 this philanthropic obsession had caused him to give away nearly $475 million.

He did so without desire for fanfare, tending to shun public notice except where publicity aided one or other of his humanitarian causes. The reticence was noticed at an early age, and from the time he left college he avoided a first-name basis with even intimate associates, although, as one of his sons was to remark, when he wanted to he could "charm the birds out of the trees."

His childhood was restricted but not unhappy. In college he mastered an acute shyness and did very well scholastically. Not the athletic type, he managed the football team's ailing finances instead of playing in its ranks and put it decisively in the black. Not until he entered his father's office, a step so taken for granted that it was never discussed in advance, did Rockefeller feel lonely and out of place. Some of the shyness returned and he suffered fits of self-deprecation. Those who knew him at this time portray a morose and anxious youth unnecessarily troubled by a sense of distance between his own inadequacy and his father's towering skills. The elder Rockefeller had indoctrinated him with principles of thrift and industry, and burning convictions of duty. Now duty demanded that the son gradually take on the burdens of business long shouldered by the father. And in short order young Rockefeller's self-doubts were cruelly confirmed. Using money loaned him by his father to open a margin account, he bought stock from a financier of subsequent slippery reputation on Wall Street and as a result involved himself in losses totaling at least $1 million.

In the privacy of his office on the fourteenth floor at No. 26 Broadway he suffered a remorse which he described to his father as "bitter and humiliating." But his recovery was remarkably swift and aglow with promise for his future in big business. It reflected a strong personal rededication and the probably tougher tutelage he was now receiving from the astute and outspoken Frederick T. Gates. He began to exhibit a mastery of detail in a variety of business and domestic projects entrusted to his supervision, often haggling over even small bills in what might have struck mortals of lesser means as inscrutable penny-pinching, but from a different standpoint has been interpreted as a militant assertion of the wickedness of waste and "rooted in an axiom of stewardship." Always preferring to measure things for himself, he took to carrying a four-foot rule in his hip pocket, a convenient symbol of his "increasing passion for exactness." He was largely instrumental, with Gates, in the sale of his father's Mesabi iron interests to J. P. Morgan, a transaction involving $75 million and which emphatically demonstrated the junior Rockefeller's firm grasp of business detail and his dauntlessness in the presence of more aggressive capitalists.

During that period Rockefeller was leader of the Men's Bible Class at the Fifth Avenue Baptist Church, a position he held eight years, weathering periodic storms of popular sarcasm, particularly after a discourse on the common principles of capitalism and Christianity in which he developed an analogy between business consolidation and the cultivation of an American Beauty Rose. But the theme was by no means universally ridiculed and the size of Rockefeller's Bible class grew from about fifty to two hundred.

These were the years when his father, still president of Standard Oil, seldom came to the office. More and more the administration of business and charity on the mammoth scale shifted to the son, who, however, seemed to accept the challenge with no trace now of his former lack of self-confidence. When he gained control of the Colorado Fuel and Iron Company, he was studying plans for the proposed Rockefeller Institute of Medical Research, and on the business front held directorships in Standard Oil, United States Steel, Federal Smelting and Refining, American Linseed, the Missouri Pacific, and the Delaware, Lackawanna and Western railroads, the Manhattan Railroad, Consolidated Coal, Virginia-Carolina Chemical, and any number of banks.

With all this he still found time for soul-searching, an activity which evidently entered an accelerated phase in 1908, the year that the journalistic drumfire against the listed villainies of Standard Oil was in a kind of crescendo. When the disclosures reappeared as evidence in the federal courts, Rockefeller's position as an instructor in the Scriptures lost considerable eminence and, pleading overwork, he gave up the job. Overworked or not, that same year he was elected vice president of Standard Oil. A new onslaught against the company was then being mounted by

Hearst's Magazine, which would expose intimacy between certain of its high officers and the Republican Party in Pennsylvania and Ohio.

As early as 1902 Rockefeller had resigned a bank directorship on the conscientious grounds that while having to answer to the public for the conduct of their business, bank or company directors could not possibly know much about it or dictate its management. Considering Rockefeller's swift accumulation of directorships, it might be supposed that his objections had evaporated. But in the following years his public transformation took three significant forms: an awareness of the difficulty of keeping up with the details of so many organizations, a vanishing zest for making money, and an all-consuming eagerness to invest in philanthropic experiments.

By 1909 the signs were unmistakable. Notwithstanding the skills he had displayed in the capitalist market, the relish with which he had mastered fiscal minutiae, the outbursts of parental pride touched off by his every accomplishment, after less than a decade in his father's footsteps John D. Rockefeller, Jr., was fed up with the world of Wall Street.

He faced a supreme decision. According to his later recollection, he weighed the options beset by a host of conflicting loyalties — to ideals, duties, conscience, parents, and stockholders. His father characteristically left him alone to make up his own mind. What he finally decided upon was an almost total break with big business. On March 1, 1910, he retired from the board of directors of United States Steel. Two days later his severance from the Standard Oil directorate was disclosed in an announcement which conveniently freed him from the odium about to envelop the company — two months hence the United States Supreme Court would order it dissolved under the Sherman Anti-Trust Act. And now Rockefeller was elevated in the public vision as a business leader humanitarian enough to abandon the lists of competitive finance for a life wholly dedicated to philanthropy. The newly conceived Rockefeller Foundation would be the means through which he determined to apply his enormous wealth to the succor of society. "This does not mean that Rockefeller is to be a less important man," *Current Literature*'s April 1910 issue reminded its readers. "It means that he is to be hereafter a much more important man than he ever would have become as a financial magnate."

True, false, or merely premature, the new and praiseworthy personification of John D. Rockefeller, Jr., accepted by the public at large in the early months of 1910 bore slight resemblance to the private Rockefeller writing to L. M. Bowers in Denver on February 7 that same year. Silent on the subject of Primero, where the bodies were still being brought out, he sounded, if not exactly like a financial magnate, certainly like an acquisitive and calculating financier riled by reports of sought-after business contracts going to the competitor closest on his heels. The Victor-American Fuel Company, he had been informed, was showing profit and other rival companies were starting up in the West. The CFI's rate of growth, on the other hand, had failed to increase in the last three and a half years. What was wrong? Why could not the CFI have captured the business going to Osgood? Bowers had cut operational costs, a good way of making money, but the important thing, Rockefeller stressed, was to increase the output.

Unaccustomed to tart strictures from the Rockefellers, whom he had so long and devotedly served, Bowers responded with a vilification of the company's principal rivals and a stiff defense of his own performance. "We have positive proof that these two coal companies [Victor-American and Rocky Mountain Fuel] have been systematically robbing their miners by underweight." Bowers professed astonishment that men like Osgood were able to hoodwink and swindle the public. As for the CFI, it had been on the verge of bankruptcy when he arrived in Denver but at risk of personal health and comfort and, although unfamiliar with the iron industry and while totally ignorant of coal mining, he had imposed economies, eliminated the expendables, and restored the company to a firm footing.

LaMont Montgomery Bowers got many a fellow businessman's back up because of an unaccommodating and contentious personality. Even the younger Rockefeller once noted that Bowers could be a very unpleasant enemy. But his worth in business was formidable. Thoroughly schooled in nineteenth-century fundamentals of profit making, Bowers also possessed a rare facility for instinctively grasping the essentials in areas of industry where he was a perfect stranger.

Born near Binghamton, New York, in 1847 he began his business career selling soap and was soon into wholesale grocery. Later he founded a land agency in Omaha, Nebraska, where he had gone for his health, and in 1895 Frederick T. Gates, two years after his own appointment as confidential adviser to John D. Rockefeller, Sr., maneuvered his uncle into a similar position on the oil magnate's staff. The chance arose out of Rockefeller's need for vessels big enough to ship his Mesabi ore from Duluth to the ports on Lake Erie. Gates knew the very man that the situation called for, one "who was never on a ship in his life, and who would not know the stern from the bow or an anchor from an umbrella, but he has a good sense, is honest, enterprising, keen and thrifty . . . has the art of quickly mastering a subject."

Under Gates's direction Rockefeller had built great ore docks at the head of Lake Superior and got Samuel Mather, a Great Lake shipping mogul, to spend $3 million on ore-carrying vessels. But it was L. M. Bowers, the landsman totally unschooled in marine engineering, who became inspiration and architect for the creation of Rockefeller's iron-ore fleet. He designed the first 500-foot vessels ever seen on the Lakes, equipped some of them with his own inventions, including a stockless anchor, and when Rockefeller sold the fleet to U.S. Steel in 1901 it numbered fifty-eight huge ships. By that time the amazing Mr. Bowers had become one of the capitalist's most prized agents.

Bowers later affirmed his personal creed in public. He made the customary boast of faith in rugged individualism and unfettered endeavor, recalled early sympathies with striking miners in the Pennsylvania anthracite fields where he ran his grocery — "They were largely Welshmen . . . a splendid lot" — and declared his lifelong affection for the common people. He was a hard man. "If I were a chap of putty I could not have handled millions as I have for years." As a youth he had worked twelve hours a day for thirty cents an hour. "I know what work is, the same as any man that goes down in a coal mine."

In 1907 Bowers, preparing to take his consumptive wife to Colorado for the benefit of the mountain air, asked the Rockefellers for something to do in the West. (Bowers often spoke of his own health as unstable although he rarely appeared other than crisply energetic and lived to be ninety-six.) He was then aged sixty but in no disposition, he told the young Rockefeller, "to lay down and rust out." He was forthwith directed to look into the affairs of the then faltering CFI.

He found an insufficiently exploited concern hamstrung with debts and such extravagances as Political and Detective departments. Bowers conducted an unobtrusive surveillance of the top personnel and structure, played an ill-defined role in its reorganization, and by the end of the year had come into the open as its vice president, chairman of the executive committee, and treasurer. In a private memoir prepared long afterward, Bowers asserted that prior to his taking over, the CFI was a detriment to the state of Colorado. No more "outrageous political debauchery" was ever practiced than had been for years by the company's Political Department. More or less single-handedly he strove to get the company "out of politics — body, boots and breeches." The actual results of Bowers' housecleaning rather suggested a change to more sophisticated methods instead of outright reform, with an impact less ethical than economic. Bowers' own most decisive claim was that through wholesale renovation and the elimination of deadwood (250 salaried men were reduced to 175) the firm showed gains of more than $1 million in the first half of 1908 and was able to meet its every obligation.

At the head office in the Boston Building, L. M. Bowers worked in association with Jesse Floyd Welborn, president of the firm, whom he privately sized up as honest and intelligent but without the necessary degree of "spunk" for standing up to business competitors. Bowers also harbored initial suspicions that Welborn was secretly jealous of "the real force in the concern" but he took this in his stride, confident that "I can whip him." The question of rank among the executives in the Boston Building and its bearing upon areas of responsibility were to acquire significance in the years ahead.

What Bowers meant by a lack of spunk was that Welborn had none of his bombast, although the company president belonged to the same breed of industrial officers opposed to unions and the concept of collective bargaining, whose affluent homes and country-club habitat were so remote from the shacks and saloons of their labor force as to preclude any profound comprehension of its lot or welfare needs. Born in Nebraska in 1870, Welborn had been with the CFI from its infancy. A bookkeeper in 1893, he was chief salesman six plodding years later, vice president when A. C. Cass died in 1903, and in the president's chair in 1907, eight months before Bowers established himself in authority. Hardworking and intensely loyal to the firm, Welborn was said to conceal genuine likability behind his standoffishness. He may have had no great love for the rough and tumble of business life and whenever possible he escaped the Denver ferment for the pastures and feedlots of his cattle farm.

Salvaging the CFI was probably as irresistable a challenge to L. M. Bowers as floating the Great Lakes iron-ore fleet had been. In February 1908 he reported to the younger Rockefeller that he had everybody from executives to office boys shortening their lunch periods and working harder. They no longer looked upon him as "a tenderfoot from the east." But much was yet to be done. Bowers was expressly desirous of cleaning out the detectives, spies and "secret service" agents that the company had employed since the 1903–4 strike at a cost of $20,000 a year. Bowers considered most detectives "grafters," an opinion not shared by E. H.

Weitzel, the company fuel manager and a fan of the Pinkerton Agency who had hired its operatives to spy on District 15 of the UMW and who kept a photograph of William A. Pinkerton, the founder, hanging over his desk in the CFI's general office at Pueblo.

At the close of his first year with the CFI, Bowers reported a new springiness in Welborn's step brought about by the firm's revival for which he, Bowers, invited the credit. Probably for the first time in Welborn's eighteen years with the company, Bowers told his nephew, the president could base his ambitions on rock, not sand. Welborn's buoyancy was indeed so marked it made Bowers himself feel young again.

Whether or not he knew of it, the chairman's own conduct was exciting whispers. To the Reverend Eugene Gaddis, the Methodist minister appointed to run the Sociological Department, Bowers was "a man of Louis the Fourteenth airs" whose "poses and poises were enough to make a burro laugh." The comment was not unprejudiced — Gaddis had been piqued by the withering effects of Bowers' economies upon his programs for sustaining morale in the coal camps. Welborn's opinions of Bowers are unrecorded. They may be inferred from Gaddis' plausible assertion that Bowers, through his connections with the Rockefellers, suspended a sword of Damocles over the executives' heads in the Boston Building that reduced them all to "manikins and office boys."

L. M. Bowers' instinctive reaction to Rockefeller's complaint about laggard business may have been to apply himself more ruthlessly to improving the company's health with results guaranteed to make Rockefeller or any other disgruntled stockholder in New York swallow his bile. Perhaps he and Welborn dutifully bent themselves to intensified efforts to widen the CFI's lead over Victor-American. Already the company produced one third of the state's entire coal output. But at any rate, more and more of their attention was taken up by the recurrence of fatalities in their mines and the ammunition such misfortunes provided for the unionists, radicals, and muckraking journalists.

The Starkville mine was thirty years old. Long before the foundation of the company now operating it, men had dug coal from this rich seam running beneath the Raton Mesa. A honeycomb of workings stretched eastward to the Engleville system under Fisher's Peak. Said to be nongaseous and relatively safe, Starkville was an easy mine to work. Shooting or blasting was forbidden as unnecessary. The coal could be knocked down with a pick. After the last Primero disaster the state labor commissioner investigating mine safety in southern Colorado had emphasized the dangers of dust and warned that sprinkling roadbeds was not enough, that the sides and ceilings of mines should also be kept thoroughly saturated. According to the same commissioner in a subsequent report, not even the floor at Starkville had been sprinkled. The majority of miners were Polish, men and boys with limited mining experience. On October 9, 1910, many of them were four miles deep in the mountainside when the mine exploded with such force the timbers flew from the entrance.

"With gunny sacking spread upon the greasy floor and with tubs and tables ready, the coroner of Las Animas waits in a grimy machine shop for the pitiful procession that must soon come filing out of the dismal hole in the hillside," wrote Damon Runyon, then a beginning reporter for the Rocky Mountain *News.*

E. H. Weitzel, the fuel manager, arrived in Trinidad from Pueblo and with other CFI officials oversaw the rescue operations from the company's private rail car *Sunrise,* parked on the Sante Fe siding. Runyon reported that men with experience in previous calamities were rushed to Starkville from other camps and entering the stricken mine "they all believe they are working toward a sepulchre." That was about as far as Runyon and the rest of the press corps got in terms of direct reporting. Orders from the *Sunrise* stipulated that when the bodies came out no reporter or photographer would be allowed within a quarter of a mile of the entrance. The intimidating squad mustered to enforce this order, if necessary by smashing cameras or other rough methods, included County Sheriff Jim Grisham, Billy Reno, chief of detectives for the CFI, the sheriff's deputy, George Titsworth, and the Segundo camp marshal, Bob Lee — all of them destined to figure in the coalfield's gathering agony. Now they were performing their customary function of shielding the operations of the CFI as far as possible from the critical scrutiny of outsiders.

For further assurance of concealment the officers in the *Sunrise* took recourse in darkness. Rescuers had been instructed not to talk with reporters. It leaked out nevertheless that they were under orders to remove none of the victims during daylight hours for fear the grisly sight would cause panic or riot. This was vigorously denied. All the same, prolonging the audible anguish at the mine entrance, the first eleven bodies were not brought out until nightfall and the coroner, refusing to allow relatives near because of the victims' "horrible" condition, ordered a hurried burial. But then forty or more dead miners were found unblemished with their food buckets empty, indicating that they had survived the explosion by hours, possibly days — four had elapsed — before suffocating in the afterdamp. And it was immediately speculated that better ventilation of the inner workings or a speedier rescue system might have saved them.

Jesse Welborn, who had arrived from Denver, stationed himself at the mine entrance and, with shirt sleeves rolled, prepared sandwiches and coffee for the rescue party, a display of concern that, even when reported sympathetically in terms like "millionaire's grit" and "democratic human interest," did nothing to silence the whispers that the tragedy was caused by the company's negligence.

It could hardly have helped when a spokesman for the CFI who insisted that Starkville was nongaseous and would be in operation before the end of the month practically extolled the disaster as a godsend to mining science, historic evidence that under certain conditions dust may explode without the agencies of gas or fire. By the same token the cause of mining science received another bonus four weeks later when the Victor-American mine at Delagua exploded and killed eighty-two.

Even *Coal Age,* an operators' periodical, acknowledged and deplored the sorry standards of U.S. coal-mine safety when compared with those of Great Britain and other European countries. In 1913, a year when 434 men died in a catastrophic Welsh explosion, total British fatalities numbered 1742. That same year 2785 died in American mines. And Colorado's record was the worst. In the twenty-eight years from 1886 to 1913 statistics for the state showed an annual average of 7.14 deaths per 1000 employed miners, double the national figure in the industry and four times that for Illinois, Iowa, and Missouri where the mines were unionized.

There were understandable reasons for Colorado's woeful record. The geological upheaval of the Rocky Mountains in this region had badly broken the strata of coal and rock overlaying the Trinidad sandstone. As coal was removed in a room, treacherously hidden faults and fractures allowed rock to slip and sag, straining timbers until they broke and the roof collapsed. Due to the comparatively high altitudes where southern Colorado's coal properties were situated, mines tended to dry out, aggravating the dust problem as coal of highly friable quality floated in pulverized form through the dry atmosphere. And wetting down, even in otherwise well-supervised mines, might be neglected as uneconomical when the mine was so remote from a water source that all available labor was utilized to haul enough supplies uphill for drinking purposes.

Yet natural causes could not wholly account for Colorado's bloody mine toll, more than half of which James Dalrymple, the state's mine inspector in these years, believed was avoidable. Aside from the moral question of the operators' responsibility, two foremost practical reasons were inadequate enforcement of the state's mining code and the general incompetence of miners, foremen, and superintendents. One coal mine inspector reported that not a single mine in the state was properly timbered. As late as October 1913 another noted excessive dust in a mine owned by a Rocky Mountain Fuel subsidiary and recommended daily sprinkling. This was not done. In less than two months the mine exploded, killing thirty-seven men.

Dalrymple, though empowered to bring prosecutions against operators who flouted the law, admitted soft-pedaling the whole thing because the coalfields were so scattered, his staff of inspectors so small, there was little enough scope for proper study, recommendations and follow-up inspections, much less time to prepare lawsuits.

Since the mineowners stood to profit from improved safety, their search for stratagems to forestall appropriate legislation was an exercise in misplaced cunning. And they persisted in their obtuseness. At first L. M. Bowers zealously promoted the theory that mine accidents were due to the workers' own carelessness. Later, as organized labor increased its activity in Colorado, he advanced speculation that such disasters as at Primero and Starkville were the deliberate work of anarchists who smuggled dynamite into the mines. Even Bowers felt constrained to abandon this line after Dalrymple cut it to shreds with the professional opinions of his office. Then Bowers reported that "our own experts" agreed with the state authorities: at Starkville an electric train in the mine had snapped in half, knocking out mine props and collapsing timbers coated with a quarter-century's accumulation of dust which sparks from the derailed locomotive immediately ignited.

No two experts could agree on what to do about dust, Bowers told Rockefeller and his fellow directors, their anxiety aroused by newspaper charges that the disaster would not have occurred had the mine been regularly sprinkled or $10,000 been spent on a good airshaft. Bowers would not deal with the charges publicly. To dispute with agitators was to fall into their trap. "Drive out one devil and seven come in . . . we have found it wise to say nothing."

But it was becoming harder. An article in *Pearson's Magazine* called "How Coal Owners Sacrifice Workers" was in Bowers' view a muckracker's rehash. A letter from a former employee of the

Pueblo plant about child labor in the steel shops was "all bun-combe," the writer a dreamer, a liar, a socialist. The boys at the plant had a "soft snap" compared with his, Bowers', childhood. Bowers' reply, written to Frederick Gates, was forwarded to Rockefeller with Gates's scribbled comment: "I expected this breezy letter. There is nothing to which he is more acutely sensitive than neglect in such a matter."

Still Bowers thought it prudent to investigate. He was not displeased with the findings. They revealed that of the 114 boys in the Minnequa shops only 4 were aged 14, the majority were 16 or 17. No more than half of them worked occasional twelve-hour days. Their daily rates were $1.32 to $2.00. Three quarters of them were foreign-born, 44 per cent orphaned or fatherless.

But the tide of bad publicity crept higher. Apprehensive letters sped from New York to Denver and Bowers continued to fret on the defensive. An article in *Survey* had given the company credit for its hospital and sociological work but asked awkward questions about the Pueblo plant and the Starkville inquest. Bowers reminded the men in New York that the author, John A. Fitch, was a notorious muckraker and Edwin Brake, the Colorado secretary of labor to whom Fitch had mostly talked, a political shyster. But, while brushing off critics in this fashion served to ease minds in the Boston Building, it did not work so well at 26 Broadway, and Bowers was obliged to furnish specifics.

Low salaries? Pueblo got the westerly overflow of "foreigners"; many of the CFI's workers were inferior to men employed in the eastern mills, yet were paid "practically" the same wages. Excessive work? No steel mill anywhere could be run in all its departments on an eight- or ten-hour basis. To "shift" men thus in furnace work would be as senseless as changing surgeons in the middle of an appendectomy. The uproar over hours was only raised by "muckrakers, labor disturbers and the milk and water preachers and professors." Sunday work? Two thirds of the men were alien-born, and for them Sunday was no different from any other day and would only be spent in sloth, waste, or drinking.

Bowers dealt with Fitch's other charges. No inquests were held when the cause of death was "openly known" unless someone asked for them. Anyway, not a word of complaint had been heard from the bereaved families of Starkville or Primero. The company, legally liable or not, took good care of them. Bowers did not add that when amounts were paid to the next of kin the company's attorneys got their signatures or marks on forms releasing the company of all liability.

Hoping to exorcise the specter of labor unrest nourished by the muckrakers and "trust-busting political shysters" he raged against, Bowers emphasized the positive. Business was good, he told his nephew Fred Gates in November 1911. The company's profits had gained over $500,000 in four months and, providing the coal trade held up, the boom should continue. He was expecting an order for 20,000 rails from Northern Pacific, whose executives were saying that the CFI's rails were second to none. The following year Bowers reported a continuing business ascent and improved safety precautions in the mines. This time he added a bulletin about the men. They were well paid, well housed and, as far as the officers could learn, they were contented. But the enemy was constantly "dogging of their heels . . . we are always fearful of strikes . . . we can never tell when trouble will come."

Bowers pinpointed the source of it as being the strong influence that agitators wielded over the "ignorant foreigners who make up the great mass of our ten thousand miners." The foreigners he spoke of were made up of thirty-two assorted nationalities. Twenty-seven different languages were heard. At best these people were judged by native-born Americans as quaint and simple-minded. Some of them, questioned by the Reverend Eugene Gaddis for one or other of his sociological notions, answered that the President of the United States was John D. Rockefeller. Mine operators and muckrakers alike spoke of them as uneducated, an estimation that was statistically supportable: In 1912 one eighteenth of Colorado's population lived in the southern coalfield, yet that region contained more than one third of the state's illiterate.

The criteria for literacy that stigmatized the coal diggers as ignorant foreigners were produced by bureaucratic minds liable to be affronted by a simple inability to sign one's name in English. Still, the miners were obviously limited in self-expression and showed only the barest traces of a formal education. The difficulties impaired their efficiency in the mines. The Sociological Department struggled to improve the situation with night-school programs.

Perhaps the time might have been more profitably spent in teaching the foreign-born something about the odious turns American democracy could take in remote hinterlands subjugated by absentee masters of wealth and power. But in this regard they were soon to get an education, harsher and more trenchant than anything to be learned in Eugene Gaddis' company classrooms.

5

THE OPERATORS RESIST

ALTHOUGH ITS MEMBERSHIP FIGURE of 260,000 in 1906 represented a 10 per cent reduction compared with that of the previous year, the United Mine Workers remained the country's biggest union. But while wresting sizable concessions from mineowners in eastern and central states, it unwittingly encouraged the continuing obduracy of operators elsewhere who heard via newspapers and from the furtive intelligence of labor spies that the union was in deep trouble. To some it must have appeared that in no time at all the UMW must founder under drunken and disputatious leadership.

Their confidence was not all that deluded. In January 1907 only 500 delegates attended the convention at Indianapolis, less than half the usual number. They heard John Mitchell renew his opposition to the belief that "the interests of the working man are to be advanced and promoted by my standing up and calling every employer an exploiter and a robber and a thief." But the fire had gone out of him. He was in no shape to fence simultaneously with unyielding coal bosses, treacherous union officers, and socialist miners ideologically sworn to a militant class struggle. The recent death of a second child and the loss of all his savings in a bank failure had driven him deeper into alcoholism.

He clung to union leadership for the best part of another year, stepping down in the midst of emotional farewells and a rancorous contest for the president's chair. In the end it was won by the man who had so long coveted it. During the next three years under Thomas L. Lewis' administration, new intrigue and rebellion would split and shake the union structure, but it was also during this period that the campaign to organize Colorado's coal miners gained momentum and became more and more identified with the brooding figure of John R. Lawson.

Eight years after his birth in 1871 to Scots parents, Lawson was a breaker boy at Mount Carmel, Pennsylvania, straddling a chute as the coal tumbled down between his legs, snatching out the slate as fast as he could pump his little arms. At nine he was a door boy, opening and shutting the bulkhead door that regulated the mine's air current, and at thirteen he drove a mule hauling the loaded cars. After a correspondence course with the Scranton School of Mines, he followed his father across the continent to Oregon and when the elder Lawson's venture into mine management failed the two moved south to work side by side digging Colorado's coal. Lawson worked briefly for the Colorado Fuel and Iron Company. After his father returned East he married a rancher's daughter, who quickly came to terms with the realization that the quiet miner with the pugilist's frame and gravely aquiline face courted risks beyond those accepted by every man who toils in coal mines.

Lawson had inherited instincts for unionism from his father, a former member of the Knights of Labor, but developed his own restless compulsion to translate them into action. Unimpressed with doctrinaire socialism and disdainful of compromise, Lawson, said to crave peace, pursued a course which tempted violence. Perhaps he could have avoided it only in another time or place, or had he confined his furtherance of unionism to motions and resolutions at District 15's local meetings. Instead he preached unionism at every opportunity, and, worse from the standpoint of mine operators, he won an instant following. Thus he became a menace. During the unsuccessful strike of 1903 a dynamite explosion wrecked his home and almost killed his wife and infant daughter. Five months later the suspected dynamiter, owner of a small mining company in Garfield County, where Lawson then lived, shot and wounded him on a New Castle street. In the spring of 1907 Lawson, now an international organizer for the UMW and a member of its executive board, began plans for an organizing campaign in the Walsenburg area. Huerfano County's overlord, Sheriff Jeff Farr, had been previously notified. Lawson was jailed on a trumped-up charge of carrying a concealed weapon and threatened with Farr's unrelenting harassment should he remain in the county. Lawson then transferred his office to Trinidad, but here, too, sidewalk assaults and death threats were an organizer's lot. And, meanwhile, no great enthusiasm for organizing southern Colorado's coalfield flourished in the Merchants Bank Building at Indianapolis.

Lawson had a crusader's impatience with executive caution and was all for continuing the effort. But the financial panic afflicting industry in 1907, the drop in union membership, a depleted treasury, and a corrosion of rank-and-file morale through factionalism had the effect of forcing the UMW into a period of retrenchment and self-examination. Not for anything would Lawson have abandoned his determination to organize the southern Colorado field and the work was in fact carried on in secrecy. But covert activity shifted to the northern mines, which were relatively unimportant in production and number of miners employed and where the task of union recruitment entailed less risk to life and limb. Here the miners lived under more civilized conditions than those in the Trinidad field. Many owned their own homes in Lafayette, Louisville, and Frederick, sent their children to moderately decent schools, and participated in a democratic community life. They were mostly English-speaking, generally intelligent and industrious men, and although forbidden even the crudest system of redress for discontents at work, their dignity had not been warped by the kind of merciless feudalism that trapped the immigrant colonies 200 miles to the south. The weak hold of the operators upon the economic and social life of the area likewise reduced their political influence. In contrast to those wretched camps all but sealed within the canyons east of the Sangre de

Cristo, the mining towns of Boulder, Weld, and Jefferson counties had no company-controlled sheriffs or brutalized corps of camp marshals and were in consequence more accessible to union organizers. It took Lawson and his associates but a short time to unionize the northern field and only a little longer to wear down the resistance of operators to negotiation. On July 14, 1908, the UMW, primarily through Lawson's endeavors, won its first major contract in Colorado, affecting seventeen companies in the northern field.

The gains were not all that spectacular. They included an eight-hour day, semimonthly paydays, the checkoff of union dues and fees, positive payment for dead work, improved safety measures, and the settlement of disputes through grievance committees. Some of those concessions were already provided for by state law. But the real significance extended beyond the letter of the agreement. It had a political consequence: the welding of union support for John Shafroth, the Democratic candidate who went on to win Colorado's gubernatorial election. The establishment of a bridgehead in Colorado also put fresh heart into those union leaders discouraged by the failure so far to organize that state. And the southern organizers, few in number and operating in perilous stealth, were inspired by the news, although it remained necessary for safety's sake to hide out in the hills by day and, nocturnal missionaries in hostile territory, creep into the coal camps after dark.

Internal strife still tortured the union. Its convention of January 1910 in Tomlinson Hall, Indianapolis, proceeded in an atmosphere of tension broken by repeated uproar. Discussion and decisions were tainted with bitterness. At the center of the most heated controversies stood Tom Lewis, the miners' president, regarded by men ostensibly his lieutenants as crooked and power hungry. Even Frank Hayes, the ordinarily good-humored young socialist from Illinois who was cut out more for wine and balladry than ideological dogma or the bureaucracy of labor organization, clashed vehemently with Lewis and, like others in the near riot on the floor of Tomlinson Hall, had to be silenced by comrades serving uncomfortably as sergeants at arms. The miners assumed a semblance of unity under Mother Jones's annual harangue, laughing or weeping in concert and on cue to her anecdotal pathos and profanity, stamping applause as she ripped into "Morgan, Belmont, Harriman and Oily John." But when Mother Jones left to catch her train, as she seems so often to have been on the point of doing, the convention resumed its rough passage.

The delegates would have been more usefully employed discussing ways and means of countering the efforts begun by the operators of southern Colorado to sabotage the new detente between the northern mineowners and organized labor. Price agreements, improved markets, and other inducements were offered the northern operators by the CFI and other companies if they would only pull free from the UMW. The severance was to come anyway. Just before March 31, 1910, the contractual expiry date in accordance with the national union scale agreements, the union held a special convention in Turner Hall, Cincinnati, to decide on new wage scales and working schedules. There was argument in favor of limiting action to the consolidation of recent gains. Delegates from Colorado were mindful of the intense pressure the CFI and Victor-American companies had brought to bear on the northern field, pressure best offset at this stage by conservative union proposals for nothing more upsetting than a renewal of the northern contract. Instead the convention voted that each district demand a 5½ per cent wage boost and improved working conditions, including a half-holiday on Saturdays.

The demands were rejected outright by the operators in northern Colorado and in accordance with the ruling of the Cincinnati convention a strike was called. It is a wry indication of the disunity with which the UMW committed itself to the fatal campaign in Colorado that even as some 3000 miners in the northern counties of that state flung aside their picks on April 4, 1910, members of the union's board of executives in Indianapolis were secretly conspiring to hamstring its now-intolerable president by confronting him with evidence exposing him as an adulterer.

Tom Lewis was finally ousted in 1911. Despite an unsolicited promise he gave not to sell his services to the other side, after an unsuccessful bid in 1912 to regain power in the union, he did just that by serving as adviser to operators fighting the cause of unionism in West Virginia. Lewis went on to publish *Coal Mining Review*, a trade organ, and was instrumental in the formation of the National Coal Association. Thus did this oddly execrable man who had started in the mines as a breaker boy and was a bona fide founding father of the UMW earn the title of a Benedict Arnold of labor.

His successor at the union's helm, the dignified, handsome John P. White, inherited a divided body, elements of whose factions all but came to blows in convention. Indeed, this was a time when the Pinkertons and other traditional foes of insurgent labor could have had little difficulty recruiting spies or planting agents in the UMW's quarrelsome ranks — while the strike in northern Colorado continued.

The companies were hiring armed guards and importing strikebreakers from the East. In July 1910 the Northern Coal and Coke Company engaged the services of the Baldwin-Felts Agency. They also tried and failed to win the aid of MP Capp, a sheriff whose adamant incorruptibility was as rare in the coal counties as the conjoint capitals he is said to have substituted for a first name somehow missed at birth.

Capp refused to issue deputy sheriff's commissions to the hired guards or heed the operators' demand that he send an appeal for the state militia. His claim that he and other civil authorities were quite capable of maintaining peace locally was endorsed by state investigators from Denver, and accordingly Governor Shafroth dispatched no troops. His Secretary of State, James B. Pearce, reported continuing tranquillity in the area early in 1912 and added: "Certain interests have for so many years been accustomed to break strikes with the militia that it is a difficult thing to discontinue the habit. It is much the cheapest and speediest method for them, as the taxpayers of the state pay the bills. A striking illustration of this is given in the bond issue of over $950,-000 to settle the Cripple Creek war debt."

Getting nowhere with Sheriff MP Capp, the operators washed their hands of him and turned to the courts. On November 30, 1911, they secured an injunction from a friendly judge, Greely W. Whitford of the district court at Denver, to restrain the strikers from gathering in groups, posting notices, or interfering with the nonunion operation of the mines. The week before Christmas sixteen strike leaders were arrested for congregating on the streets of Lafayette. Judge Whitford ordered them to jail for a year, but street demonstrations and talk of impeachment by a number of Denver legislators with an eye on labor's nascent voting power altered the judge's mind for him and all sixteen strikers were released.

A second attempt to intimidate the miners by law took place the following summer when the Rocky Mountain Fuel Company, which had just bought out the properties of Northern Coal and Coke, obtained a dissolution of the ineffective Whitford injunction and petitioned for another on grounds that neither Governor Shafroth nor any other state or county authority could keep the peace. The decision of a federal district judge named Robert Lewis to deny the petition preserved the rights of strikers to picket and assemble and lifted the hearts of unionists north and south of Denver.

It had a sobering effect on Colorado's major coal operators. After all, great profits were at stake. The CFI, Victor-American, and the Rocky Mountain Fuel companies were together producing well over half the state's total coal output. The CFI led the way with 32 per cent, almost double the production of its closest competitor, Osgood's Victor-American. Nothing must hinder company expansion. The upward curve of annual profits must be maintained. New strategies were required on more than one front.

The retention of influence in the state legislature and county courthouse hung in the balance as 1912 developed into a year of shifting political sands and unprecedented public disquiet over the growth of corporate power. That November Woodrow Wilson carried Colorado by a handsome majority. The Democrat, Elias Ammons, won the governorship with comfortable pluralities. What worried the southern coal operators was so big a reduction in the Republican majorities in Las Animas and Huerfano that no longer could those counties be complacently regarded as strongholds. Elsewhere in the nation the control of politics by corporate industry reaped scandalous publicity.

So adjustments were called for. Some of the more obvious crudities of the system had perforce to be eliminated, more subtle means cultivated. On November 1, 1912, circulars sent out by J. F. Welborn to mine superintendents ordered adherence to "the company policy of non-participation in politics and its desire that every one of its employees should be and feel free to vote as he sees fit." On face value this was commendable. But just how the company was in fact participating in politics could have been deduced from a letter that L. M. Bowers wrote to the junior Rockefeller three days after Welborn's announcement. Rockefeller had asked why the CFI's surplus finances were deposited exclusively in Colorado banks when the possibility existed of larger rates of interest at banks in other states.

Bowers told him why. Colorado was overpopulated with foreigners under the heel of labor agitators and shysters elected to the legislature or appointed by the governor to responsible posts like mine inspector and commissioner of labor. Laws were introduced which, if enacted, "would hamper and cripple our operations and reduce profits to zero." There were two ways of overcoming this: by direct graft under cover or the securement of important men in the state whose influence could defeat the obnoxious measures or induce the governor to veto them. "Without our direct solicitation, we are able to secure the cordial cooperation of the wealthy officers and stockholders of several influential banks who, for self-interest or for the common good, or both, will give us their support." Each of the four largest banks in Denver had twelve or fifteen directors who "play a mighty important part in this state in dictating its laws, notwithstanding the enormous majority of the laboring class. Our money is a very important matter to them and they will go to great lengths to prevent assaults upon us . . ." It behooved the company to give the banks maximum business and support "so that we may have their influence to protect us from hostile legislation." This barefaced admission of the use of Rockefeller's wealth to exert control of the Colorado state legislature drew not the slightest token of displeasure from 26 Broadway.

Equally essential to the company's prosperity as the defeat of "obnoxious measures" in the statehouse was the continued loyalty of its simple-minded coal miners and their immunity to the blandishments of union organizers. On this front, brute force and intimidation were acceptable weapons.

Company officers who bothered to pay this disagreeable side to their enterprise any more than brief regard found justification in the assumption that the victims had to be dangerous criminals and anarchists. For this self-delusion news accounts provided ample nourishment. In 1906 Clarence Darrow had won acquittal for the three leaders of the Western Federation of Miners accused of implication in the assassination of former Governor Frank Steunenberg of Idaho. Five years later when twenty persons died in the explosion that wrecked the Los Angeles Times Building — a crime the William Burns Detective Agency hung on the brothers MacNamara, both union men — not even Darrow could confound the foes of labor with a verdict of not guilty. In March 1912, fifty-four officers and smelters of the Structural Iron Workers Association were indicted for participation in dynamite outrages that had taken more than a hundred lives in six years. It made no difference how strenuously labor's moderate spokesmen, led by Samuel Gompers, objected that bomb planters like the MacNamaras did not typify labor but were traitors to the working class. Labor's still-maturing public image was badly disfigured by violence.

The extremists saw no need to apologize. "You cannot view the class struggle through the stained glass windows of a cathedral or through the eyes of capitalist-made laws," declared Big Bill Haywood, president of the WFM and one of the defendants in the Steunenberg trial. The concept of labor's crusade as unremitting war between irreconcilable classes was never out of place among militant unionists, but it also came in handy for those capitalists in need of a rationale to condone tough and arbitrary reaction. This was particularly true of the men who controlled Colorado's coal mines. For all the dignity and worthiness with which John Mitchell had fought mineowners, dissidents in his circle, and his own personal insobriety for the UMW, few Colorado operators, at least in the beginning, drew much distinction between that union and the Western Federation of Miners. Incredibly, many labeled the moderate Mitchell himself a scoundrel, "a greater tyrant and autocrat than the Czar of Russia" in John Osgood's words. In his early correspondence from Denver, L. M. Bowers tended to confuse the UMW with the WFM and even after he had learned to tell the difference he preferred to equate them when denouncing their threat to business and the nation.

The system of camp marshals or mine guards, as they were usually called, evolved as the companies' private police forces and was enlarged in response to the appearance of union organizers in the vicinity of coal properties. The principal qualifications for the job were an eye for recognizing outside agitators and malcontents on the company payroll and the willing ability to "run them down the canyon." Detectives and spies were also hired, their job being to keep mine guards and property officials suitably informed and maintain surveillance on such hotbeds of plotting as the 29th of July, an Aguilar saloon frequented by Italians whose name celebrated the date on which an anarchist assassinated King Humbert of Italy in 1900.

Spies and sleuths for the Colorado Fuel and Iron Company were hired and supervised by William Hiram ("Billy") Reno, who before transferring his detective and espionage talents to the coal business had been successively employed as a private operative for the Thiel Detective Agency, an officer on the Denver Police Force, and an agent for the Colorado and Southern Railway. In this latter capacity he had helped chase the Black Jack Ketchum train robbers in 1899. Dispute still lingered over his premature retreat from the gun battle that cost Sheriff Ed Farr his life, but as chief of detectives for the CFI, Reno collaborated closely with the dead lawman's brother and successor. It was Reno who informed Jefferson Farr of the purpose behind John Lawson's arrival in Walsenburg in 1907 and the necessity of making things hot for him. Reno had good cause to boast of himself as the labor organizers' nemesis.

Hounded off trains, driven from hotels, messengers of the night risking pain and death for small pay and out of stubborn conviction, the union organizers had to be a hardy breed. The experiences of a Croat named Michael Livoda give a good idea. No sooner had he arrived in Walsenburg during the first weeks of 1912 for a campaign among the Slavic miners, than he was arrested by Jeff Farr's deputies and hauled before the sheriff for a customary bout of abuse and warning. Then Livoda was hustled to the railroad track and ordered to keep traveling. For weeks thereafter men in the saddle trailed him. Yet he managed to sign up miners after dark at mountainside rendezvous around a piñon fire and slip past mine guards for whispered recruiting on the company's property, and he utilized the aid of sympathetic saloonkeepers in Aguilar who were paid a commission for their cooperation. Livoda returned to the Walsenburg area early the next summer and hid out at the CFI's Ravenwood mine, only to be tracked down by a deputy sheriff and two or three mine officials who beat him savagely about the head and face, afterward kicking him so hard that for two months he could neither stand up nor seat himself without assistance.

Strong-arm methods were all very well, but no matter how optimistic and self-glorifying the reports from Detective Billy Reno and his agents, they could not conceal the fact from the CFI executives that intimidation alone was not enough to discourage the union movement in the south. In April 1912 the CFI announced wage increases of 10 per cent to all its miners. And that this was no dispensation inspired by generosity but coldly calculated to calm a turbulence of exploitable advantage to union organizers was made clear a week later in a letter Bowers wrote to Fred Gates: ". . . I know of no better way than to anticipate demands and do a little better by the men than they would receive if they belonged to the unions. This keeps them in line and reasonably happy." Early in 1913 the company abolished the scrip system, adopted a semimonthly payday, and implemented the eight-hour workday with effect from March 1. The changes were accredited to J. F. Welborn, the company president, and publicly said to be "not influenced in any way by the activities of union organizers."

But again Bowers' private correspondence with New York suggests evidence to the contrary. "We studied the eight hour day problem, which we knew would come up in the form of bills in the legislature and would be pushed through by agitators . . ." The company experimented with eight-hour day labor and found that while saving on "overhead expenses" the same work output resulted. "After this had been settled in our mines we established an eight-hour day for all our coal miners." The adoption of semimonthly paydays was also "wholly unsolicited . . . done as a matter of policy, anticipating that these questions might arise sooner or later . . ."

Following the CFI's lead, as they usually did, the other companies took similar steps. And about a month after the CFI's latest concessions the state of Colorado passed new mining laws requiring the inspection of mines at least once every ninety days, the certification of mine foremen and mine bosses, and a staff of five deputy mine inspectors to assist the chief in his efforts to conduct statewide supervision.

As things turned out only three deputy inspectors could be maintained, not enough to inspect mines everywhere in the state more than once in four months. And when a dangerous condition was discovered, the office lacked the personnel to recheck the mine and determine if its recommendations had been followed. In another subsequent development, the companies' self-serving ruse of granting pay raises backfired somewhat, because many of the beneficiaries gave credit to the UMW and the result was a sharp increase in the union's secret membership. Still, the passage of legislation designed to safeguard the lives of coal miners, along with the more charitable attitude that the companies were now apparently disposed to take, suggested a trend toward removing at least some of the miners' grievances. The significance was not lost on the union officials. The coal operators' favors were perhaps no more than token, and if a trend at all, it was a cautious one, but if it continued there was no telling how the union's struggle to assert its relevance in the Colorado coalfields might be affected or how far back might be set its fundamental goal of recognition.

A year before, on April 30, 1912, when Edward Doyle, secretary-treasurer of District 15, wrote from Denver that "the southern coalfield is the key to the situation," John White, the UMW president, had acknowledged as much but regretted that the union was in no position to wage an intensified organizing campaign in that area. The treasury was half-empty. Between 1900 and 1910 nearly $9 million had been paid out to finance strikes alone, and prospects for substantial recoupment had been shattered by the economic depression of 1911, which idled thousands of union members. But now the Indianapolis office was in receipt of frequent intelligence that the present strike in northern Colorado, itself a drain of the union's resources, dragged on only because the intransigence of the operators was sustained by a flow of money and even arms from southern operators. President White was essentially a moderate with inclinations to compromise reminiscent of John Mitchell, but his very distaste for expensive and acrimonious strikes was good reason for no longer postponing decisive action in Colorado's southern counties.

In a way his efforts had made it easier. He had achieved some success in fulfilling his vow to unify the union's discordant elements and at the end of his first two years' leadership it was experiencing a modest revival. The latest membership figures exceeded 300,000. Detectable too among this swelling rank and file in dealings with the coal operators was a skepticism toward the concept of an ultimate partnership between labor and capital preached by the National Civic Federation and indeed a cornerstone of union policy left in place by Mitchell.

Critics cited the new restlessness as proof that socialists had "captured" the union, and although John White was not remotely a socialist, his vice president, the convivial young redhead Frank J. Hayes, rejoiced in his reputation as one. At the annual convention of 1912 some of the hardest-hitting rhetoric had come from activists led by Adolph Germer in favor of UMW endorsement of the Socialist Party as the political party of the working class.

The symptoms of a new offensive by militants in the UMW to gain the upper hand coincided with the eroding effects that concessions granted by the Colorado managers threatened to have on the argument that their workers needed the union. All of a sudden then, the time seemed right for sterner union action in that state. President John White showed plainly that he leaned toward the notion but he was not the type to be rushed. He summoned John Lawson to a meeting of the union executive board for a discussion of the prospects. Lawson acknowledged that $800,-000 had already been spent on Colorado and added bluntly that many times that amount would be needed to finish the task. This threw a little cold water on recently rekindled fires at union headquarters but failed to douse them entirely, and they were soon fanned anew by Lawson's persuasive personality. Also, some of the officers may have quietly told themselves that Lawson's estimate could be wrong. John White, for one, banked hopefully on the achievement of a strong union in Colorado without prolonged strife. At all events, the gamble was worth taking. Success would put an end once and for all to the state's costly and interminable disputes. When Lawson reboarded the train for Denver, he carried the UMW's mandate for leading a full-scale southern drive in the early months of 1913.

Twenty-one pairs of organizers trained in the Denver office were sent to the Trinidad coalfield. One of each pair was the "active organizer" who moved in the open, his partner an undercover man who posed as a miner looking for work and feigned antiunion bias once hired in order to secure the best position for espionage or secret recruitment. If he won the right amount of confidence of his foreman or superintendent he was also able to point out genuine antiunionists as unionists. When this idea worked well, the scabs and strikebreakers were run down the canyon in the belief that they were union men, while carefully coached men with union affiliation showed up at the mines to apply for the vacant jobs.

John Lawson arranged the office in Trinidad on a permanent basis. Adolph Germer was also in the area for field work and under earnest advice from union moderates to watch his language. Germer, an orthodox socialist notable in the party through his efforts to rid it of the unruly Bill Haywood, had himself an intemperate tongue, so much so that his appointment as a UMW organizer in Colorado loosed a new round of bickering in the union's executive circle. Lawson, meanwhile, was parrying questions about the size of increased labor activity with soft words. To a reporter from the Trinidad *Chronicle-News,* owned by the company attorney, Judge Jesse Northcutt, he said, "There is no cause for alarm. The organization I represent is not contemplating a strike as conditions at this time do not call for action of that kind." The coal operators were unbeguiled. Thanks to intelligence systems like Billy Reno's, they were quite aware of the union's toughened campaign plans and were casting about for ways to neutralize them.

Detective agencies, warned a former Scotland Yard chief inspector visiting the United States, constituted an evil of great potential menace to American society. "We shudder when we hear of the system of espionage maintained in Russia, while in the great American cities, unnoticed, are organizations of spies and informers." The heavy participation of private detective agencies in labor and industrial struggles was a uniquely American phenomenon, for some three or four decades a thriving business of which the otherwise well-informed knew next to nothing. Yet phone directories listed them quite plainly, sometimes employing the euphemistic "industrial engineer" to convey their specialty, and the largest agencies like Pinkerton, W. J. Burns, and Waddell-Mahon, had offices in most big cities. They used clipping services or other means to keep abreast of developments in industry and labor and were prepared at the first approach of a storm to dispatch salesmen or introductory sales literature to prospectively embattled employers. Once at bay before rebellious labor, the industrialists could count on the agencies to supply on contract every kind of need from spies and strikebreakers to high-powered machine guns cranking out 120 shots a minute.

In 1914 a federal investigator was to compile a list of no fewer than 275 active detective agencies in the United States, most of them busily engaged in areas of labor conflict:

> We found that private detectives are not merely guards of the property of the companies who hire them and subservient to local law and order forces, but are rather the entire law and order force themselves and bend the local authorities to their will . . . the caliber of the men engaged . . . is of the lowest kind, hoboes, thugs, ex-convicts, gunmen, and when they know they have the authority of the law behind them, there is no telling to what extremes they will go.

Having founded the first private detective agency in the Western world and furnished the Union with a secret service during the Civil War, it was Alan Pinkerton who drew the attention of rich businessmen to the benefits derivable from a system of espionage and surveillance maintained among the workers. That this would involve penetration of any organization the laborers formed for their own ends became notoriously plain when the news got out that a Pinkerton agent named James MacParlan had ingratiated himself with the secret band of Pennsylvania coal miners calling themselves the Molly Maguires and in due course betrayed them to the law and the hangman. MacParlan was rewarded for his services with the management of the agency's Denver office and while in this post, one he held for over thirty years, was retained by the Mineowners Association in their determined effort to smash the Western Federation of Miners.

When the focal point of conflict between capital and labor in Colorado shifted from the metallurgical to the bituminous fields, the services were sought of a detective agency with specific, recent, and successful experience in combating organized or striking coal miners.

The Baldwin-Felts Agency, an accredited corporation with main offices in Roanoke, Virginia, and Bluefield, West Virginia, concentrated its activities in the industrial East and had operatives in at least five states. The firm specialized at first in railroad disputes — Walter Belk, an agent whose subsequent reputation was odious even for a private detective, had been involved in a strike of workers for the Seaboard Air Line Railroad — but the agency made its first real strides in the somber coalfields of West Virginia. In the Cabin Creek district a local association of mineowners paid the firm $500 a day to supply them with weapons and agents. Eight years later, in February 1913, Baldwin-Felts men armed with Winchesters rode a special train from Charleston to Paint Creek and shot up a tent colony housing the sleeping families of striking miners.

They had made their Colorado debut as camp guards soon after the strike opened in the northern counties, and as events now quickened in the south they were seen on the streets of Walsenburg, Aguilar, and Trinidad, strolling and coldly staring and taking no great trouble to conceal their firearms. Engaged by the apprehensive operators of the CFI, Victor-American, and Rocky Mountain Fuel, they included the elite of the agency as well as its three-dollar-a-day gunmen and on arrival were immediately deputized by the county sheriffs, who in anticipation of trouble were in the process of raising an army of deputies. Between January and September 1913 Jefferson Farr, who boasted of holding daily conferences with CFI officials, indiscriminately recruited 326 applicants. Walter Belk was deputized on January 16 and Albert C. Felts, a director of the agency, a month later. According to Felts's vague estimate, about forty to seventy-five operatives were assigned to southern Colorado.

One supposes them to have been a hard lot, the sinister riffraff they were said to be, although the mean look of old-time motion-picture heavies that some of them wore was doubtless affected to intimidate. Certainly, more than half a century later, in 1971, the mere mention of Baldwin-Felts thugs to some of the forgotten band of veterans of the West Virginia and Colorado coalfield wars was all that it required to make gnarled flesh crawl and wasted limbs tremble in a fit of consuming rage.

On July 24, 1913, John Lawson announced in Denver that unionization of all coal miners in the state was to be pushed rapidly to completion. Frank J. Hayes arrived four days later to take command of the accelerated campaign. The vice president had only recently directed an arduous drive in West Virginia. Born in What Cheer, Iowa, Hayes had worked in coal mines at age thirteen, was a breezy orator before reaching twenty, and after a hasty self-education in Marxism, he ran for governor in Illinois on a socialist ticket in 1912. He celebrated his arrival in Colorado with a speech emphasizing the destiny of his organization as a force for emancipation. Without its help the miners of Colorado could never throw off their shackles. "No serf or slave ever freed himself." He was an exuberant speaker and many an immigrant who learned to understand his words, not to mention perhaps more than one uneasy mineowner, came to look upon Hayes rather than the dour John Lawson as a youthful silver-tongued Moses bent on liberating the oppressed of the coalfields from industrial bondage.

Hayes's first step was to organize a policy committee to speak for the miners. Composed of himself, Lawson, Ed Doyle, and

John McLennan, District 15's president, this quartet of self-assertive former miners, fated to hold together as a team for only a limited crucial period, was empowered by headquarters in Indianapolis to organize, bargain, or call a strike.

At one of their first meetings in the union's office on the third floor of the German-American Trust Building in Denver, the four drafted a call for common sense and conciliation. Economics if nothing else dictated a policy of avoiding costly strikes. Hopes were pinned upon the practical acumen of the opposition. Hayes honestly thought that if the operators were sensible businessmen they would rather meet the situation around a conference table than square off on an industrial battlefield. But he left no one in doubt of the alternatives. "We prefer to reach an agreement of some kind with the mineowners. But the men have been clamoring for a strike and I am empowered to call them out if their efforts to unionize are resisted."

Circulars went off to the miners.

GREETINGS:

This is the day of your emancipation. This is the day when liberty and progress come to abide in your midst. We call upon you to enroll as a member . . .

Organizers followed in the wake of the circulars and opened branch offices in Aguilar, Walsenburg, and Florence in Fremont County.

On August 6 the policy committee tried to obtain a conference with the operators and the new governor, Elias Ammons, served as a go-between. The effort failed. Ammons was much disturbed by rumors of industrial storms ahead, but he had come to office without any clear notions of how best to weather them. Now J. F. Welborn told him that a meeting with UMW officials might be interpreted as recognition of the union and from John Osgood and David W. Brown, vice president of Rocky Mountain Fuel, came substantially the same response. The following week Ammons ordered Edwin Brake, the state labor commissioner, to study personally ways and means of heading off a strike. Brake took the noon train out of Denver on August 15 and arrived in Trinidad shortly before 8 P.M.

It was a Saturday; the songs of the Salvation Army circle in front of the Coronado Hotel blended in the summer dusk with a loud variety of European accents. Baldwin-Felts men moved among the crowd. At about 8:30 two of them, George Belcher and Walter Belk, sauntered down Commercial Street and at the intersection with Elm, near the Packer Building, which housed UMW organizers on the upper floor, they brushed past Gerald Lippiatt.

An Italian organizer for the northern field, Lippiatt had come to Trinidad for the annual convention of the State Federation of Labor, opening the following Monday. Some slight evidence suggests that he had been shadowed since getting off the train. At all events, epithets now flew between the organizer and the Baldwin-Felts men. Lippiatt disappeared into the Packer Building, emerged after a few minutes, and the detectives were waiting. According to eyewitnesses Lippiatt drew a .45 pistol and dared the pair to repeat what they had called him earlier. Instead the detectives produced their own guns. All the weapons fired. A bullet entered Belcher's leg above the knee. Six of the eight shots fired by the detectives struck Lippiatt, killing him instantly.

Edwin Brake had just checked into the Toltec Hotel when he heard the shooting. A coroner's jury of six Trinidad businessmen dismissed the slaying as "justifiable homicide." The verdict kindled emotions in the West Theater, as 150 delegates to the labor convention, each wearing a bow of mourning, stared at an empty black-draped chair while John McLennan served notice that organized labor in Colorado would not sit idly by while comrades were shot down. Frank Hayes roused the delegates to their feet with an electric speech. And about the same time in Denver a statement issued from J. F. Welborn's office: "We will never accede to union recognition. That is the absolute, determined and certain ultimatum of the operators — strike or no strike." Governor Ammons received Brake's report from the Toltec Hotel in Trinidad. It told of "a terrible unrest." Unrest burdened the atmosphere in the state capital and the southern coalfields, and the threats and obstinacies of these late August days foreshadowed tragedy piling on tragedy.

"THE BATTLE CRY OF UNION"

ELIAS AMMONS IS not the only figure in gubernatorial history to have run the risks of an instinctive disposition to be fair to everybody, but rarely did the characteristic bring more grief than in his case. Veteran observers of Colorado politics summed him up as a weak-kneed executive irresolute in crisis, yet there is contrary evidence from a period before his unhappy governorship when he exhibited a brand of fortitude noteworthy even in an environment where the quality, often essential to survival, was not uncommon.

Eleven years old when he came to Colorado from North Carolina, the eldest of six children in an impoverished family, Elias Ammons had received little schooling; because of his father's chronic ill health he was required to work from the age of five. He spent the greatest part of his boyhood outdoors in all weathers — ranching, lumbering, skidding railroad ties, hauling cordwood to limekilns — and at fourteen was sawing wood to earn money for the purchase of schoolbooks. The next year at high school age, he was assigned to the fourth grade but still had to assist his family. In summer he worked on a ranch. During the school year he lighted and turned off the city's gas lamps, dogtrotting along seven miles of Denver streets losing precious sleep. Since the income was never enough, he even dug up tin cans to melt the solder for sale. And while still a youth, Ammons went nearly blind.

His eyesight was weakened by an early attack of measles.

Then, shooting game for a livelihood — these were days when a deer brought $1.50, antelopes $1.00 — he suffered an accidental gunshot wound in the head on the last day of the hunting season. This left his sight even more seriously impaired, but with great effort he took up newspaper work and at twenty-five was associate editor of the Denver *Times*. When he could no longer see well enough he left the newspaper business and bought about twenty head of cattle. Once able to expand as a rancher, Ammons at last began to prosper. He entered politics and community service, became president of the Colorado Cattle and Home Growers Association, acquired interests in Denver banks, and in 1890 took office in the state assembly, where among other things he authored legislation providing for the adoption of the columbine as Colorado's state flower.

Defeated twice as a candidate for lieutenant governor, Ammons, a Democrat, won office as governor in the same landslide of 1912 that put Woodrow Wilson in the White House. Although Ammons' greatest support came from the rural classes whose interests he held most dear, he had no reason to expect other than cooperation from the state's industrial laborers, for whom he professed a keen sympathy rooted in the struggles of his own youth. He had employed the well-liked John Lawson as his campaign adviser on labor affairs.

Ammons also felt entitled to count on the understanding of mineowners and other businessmen who shared his love for Colorado and his abiding faith in the state's future, feelings he displayed at least once in the form of a published poem about forests of balsam and pine, flowers of lavender hue, the public weal, and the spirit of the West. Ammons' wedge-shaped features were grained and leathery, but he was not robust. Among private papers left by an acquaintance is a reference to the governor's inability, caused by his enfeebled sight, to look directly into the eyes of those with whom he had to deal, a handicap that, it was suggested, might have accounted for his intimidation on certain important occasions.

Under Ammons' administration agricultural schools were set up and a more equitable system of state taxation was prepared. But his time was ruthlessly consumed by labor strife and if indeed Elias Ammons had so much as a dozen hours of peace while governor of Colorado it had to be during his last day in office.

The inevitability of a strike in the southern coalfield — with the cardinal issue that of recognition of the United Mine Workers union — confronted Governor Ammons in late summer 1913. Assisted by the state labor commissioner, Edwin Brake, he had drafted a proposal for a three-point compromise offering the miners, union and nonunion alike, freedom to work in the mines, freedom to trade at outlets other than the company store, and the use of check-weighmen. This got nowhere. "Nothing less than full recognition of the union will satisfy us," declared Frank Hayes on August 24. Hayes could afford to be bold. Pledges of support for the union's drive were coming in from labor groups and zealots all over the country. Fred D. Warren, editor of the socialist *Appeal to Reason*, anticipated "a hot story for the next issue." Hayes had advised Warren to keep out of the situation until all peaceful resources were exhausted, a contingency which the editor now eagerly assumed had been reached. "I am clearing the decks for action. I want to make this the crowning crusade of the *Appeal's* career." What Warren planned was a monster edition exposing the plight of the coal miners in southern Colorado, and he dreamed of distributing from 3 to 5 million copies, which, had the *Appeal* gone that far beyond its customary figure of half a million, would assuredly have realized Warren's exultant wish to "break the world's record."

Actually the union's policy committee had not yet abandoned the path of calm conciliation, outwardly at least. "We are no more desirous of a strike than you are, and it seems to us that we owe it to our respective interests as well as the general public to make every honest endeavor to adjust our differences . . . The operators in [organized] states . . . are much pleased with the security and stability given to the industry through the medium of the trade agreement. Why oppose us here . . . ? Let us now meet as friends . . ." This letter from the policy committee to J. F. Welborn and other coal operators was dated August 26. No answer had been received from any of them when early in September Hayes left for Kansas City to confer with President John P. White, William Green, the union secretary-treasurer, and presidents of the largest union locals.

For John White and other cautious elements in the union leadership the intransigence of the operators in these tense days was only a part of the dilemma. Strikes were a costly means of securing recognition, often defeated the object, and even their threat as a method of coercion was a strategy to be pursued with the utmost care. Too precipitous or aggressive a pose could harden and unify the foe. On the other hand, any signs of faltering initiative on the national executive level might demoralize the members in the field and increase the influence of socialists and militants within the union. "The men are eager for the word to be issued," Adolph Germer had written to White from Trinidad on September 2. "In fact they are getting restless . . . unless something is done within the next week or ten days the men will come out of their own accord." Germer's own warmth was unmistakable. "We have the chance of a lifetime to do something for the Colorado miners . . . the barons and their gang are more worried than we."

The socialist organizer was speaking for himself. John White had enough worries and compounding the tension now were reports that the detestable Thomas L. Lewis had shown up in Colorado and persuaded John Lawson to publish an offer withdrawing the union's demand for recognition if some small points were conceded by the other side. This was not the first instance in high union circles of unhappiness over possible connivance between John Lawson and Lewis. There was little more to go on than the fact that Lawson had never been counted among those openly hostile to Lewis, but with or without good reason many unionists had come to regard Lawson as Tom Lewis' former henchman. By no stretch of the imagination could Lewis be henceforth considered as a union man. He now owned and managed the *Coal Mining Review and Industrial Index,* which was kept afloat by the businessmen who bought his advertising space; he showed his gratitude to the coal operators by editorially complimenting them on their sound sense and humanity. Only recently, in his June 1913 issue, had Lewis insulted the sacrifices of strikers in the unorganized West Virginia coalfields by describing the properties in terms more appropriate to the promotional pamphlets of a travel agency. Yet Lewis was still believed to have secret adherents within the miners' union, and officials at headquarters in Indianapolis went through a brief period of apprehension lest the unspeakable renegade usurp their leadership in the Colorado field.

It was at least impolitic of Lawson to allow any appearance of renewed association with Lewis under the present sensitive circumstances in Colorado, and Hayes, Germer, and others lost no time in telling him so. Hayes issued a statement to the effect that Lewis had no authority to represent the interests of the miners or speak for them. Lewis withdrew from the picture. The union leaders breathed easier. But that perilous interlude left them less disposed to dilly-dally. Besides, it was obvious to the conferees in Kansas City at the beginning of September that the policy committee's reasonably phrased appeal to the mineowners would never be answered. Hesitation vanished. Agreement was swift and unanimous that the Colorado campaign must take precedence over all others. The districts represented at the meeting pledged $600,000 in the event of a strike. Combined with a $1 assessment on each union member, the total figure would reach $1 million. At the same time, the labor policy committee scheduled a convention for September 15 in Trinidad and instructed each United Mine Workers local in Colorado to send a delegate. Invitations were also sent to the principal coal operators, who, to nobody's surprise at this point, refused to extend the courtesy of a reply.

"We are very much concerned and on the anxious seat," Jesse

Welborn wrote to one of the New York directors on September 6, "yet there is nothing to do but wait." That the president of the CFI would not have to wait very long was borne out by all the fervid signs.

Mother Jones had arrived in Denver after duty in the Michigan copper strike and accommodated reporters with a bouncy impression of a grandmotherly amazon summoned from one hard-pressed war front to another. She was followed three days later by John White, who revealed that all summer long the union's agents had been secretly engaging large tracts of land to be used as camps for strikers and shipping in tents used by West Virginia's miners. As a final warning to the obstinately silent operators, White challenged them to attend the forthcoming convention and settle differences amicably or face a union determined on a strike battle "to the limit of its resources." The miners' president went on to confer privately with Governor Ammons, who, however, believed that he had done all his office would permit to avert a strike.

White still clung to dwindling hopes of securing recognition without an expensive work stoppage. The nation's first Secretary of Labor, William B. Wilson, had been installed in office the previous March. Coal miners everywhere felt they had been given a sympathetic pipeline right into the White House, because Wilson had been their union's secretary-treasurer during John Mitchell's administration, and despite his cabinet status in the national government, he still loyally addressed members of the United Mine Workers as "brothers." White had requested the secretary to appoint a mediator in the Colorado dispute. Wilson wrote back promising to "press the New York end of it as rapidly as we can . . . before your convention meets." He sent Ethelbert Stewart, the knowledgeable chief clerk of the Bureau of Labor Statistics, to that city for a personal conference with John D. Rockefeller, Jr.

The multimillionaire was on vacation in Seal Harbor, Maine, until September 15, and when back in the city on that date, he was still unavailable to the federal emissary. But he instructed Starr J. Murphy, his closest legal adviser, to talk with him.

After presenting his credentials at Rockefeller's headquarters, Stewart asked whether the Rockefeller interests might be enlisted to intervene and ward off a strike. Stewart was immediately confronted with an attitude which was thereafter to typify the policy of the New York seat of CFI power and, rigidly adhered to, would contribute as much as anything to eventual conflict. Labor policies, insisted Murphy, were determined wholly by the mine managers on the basis of their firsthand knowledge. According to Murphy's own account of the "very pleasant" meeting to Bowers, the visitor from Washington was told that "we here in the east knew nothing about the conditions and would be unwilling to make any suggestions to the executive officers." And if anything were needed to show with harrowing precision how irrevocably that interview Stewart held with Murphy on September 16 at 26 Broadway had set the stage nearly 2000 miles distant for catastrophe, it would have been LaMont M. Bowers' gratified reply, complimenting Murphy on the way he had handled the hopeful mediator, because it "leaves us unhandicapped in the event there is a strike."

It was in this same letter that Bowers explained the company's tactic of heading off trouble by anticipating miners' demands with doled-out concessions, in this case with respect to the eight-hour day, check-weighmen, and shopping at company stores. Now there was a "trumped-up demand of a 10 per cent [wage] advance which is entirely buncombe . . . The main question and in fact the only matter up between the United Mine Workers of America and the Colorado Fuel and Iron Company is recognition of the union, which we flatly refuse to even meet with these agitators to discuss . . ."

John Osgood joined in the same theme: Recognition was the central issue and other demands only afterthoughts. Now the operators were conferring frequently, often in Osgood's office at the Victor-American Company. Sometimes the smaller mineowners attended but the dominant voices on each occasion were those of Welborn, Osgood, and David W. Brown, vice president of Rocky

Mountain Fuel. They swore practically in solemn compact to resist unionization and never to sign a contract with the United Mine Workers. Any operator who found himself mulling over the union's inducements had better show good cause for doing so. It was also decided that all expenses incurred through publicity and other antiunion activities should be prorated among the companies according to the amount of coal mined by each concern. As things turned out, the three largest companies footed the entire bill for the war against organized labor with the most powerful, CFI, assuming the generalship.

The powder keg could still be defused. The governor, for instance, might have heeded Edwin Brake's warning that frictions were bound to blaze if arrogant detectives and resentful miners rubbed shoulders in the streets. Brake suggested that Ammons order the sheriffs of Las Animas and Huerfano counties to disarm every man in the area and replace labor-baiting deputies and Baldwin-Felts gunmen with law enforcers selected on the basis of their impartiality. The governor took no action. Perhaps there was something to be said for his subsequent complaints that he had not received the cooperation he looked for from the state's labor department. Brake and his staff were undoubtedly sympathetic to the miners' cause. But Ammons exaggerated their prejudice. The trouble was that as the strike wore on he fell more and more under the influence of the operators while presumably deluding himself that he was charting a middle course. The most charitable explanation is that he wearied too soon of the preliminary bouts and was deficient in stamina for the main event.

And now little time remained. The union's leaders made a last-minute bid to play down the issue of recognition but it was too late for that also. The CFI officers, convinced of the righteousness of their motives, assured of no interference from New York, confident of their ability to outlast the adversary in terms of sheer dollar power, vowed a fight to the finish. For its part, the union declared its readiness to spend a million dollars on the struggle. Hope was derived from superiority in manpower. "We have more than 400,000 soldiers in our industrial army against millions of dollars of the 'plutes,' " Adolph Germer wrote to Eugene Debs's brother Theo in the week of the miners' convention. And incontestably, the union had Mother Jones.

To a eulogist who knew Mary Harris Jones for most of the hectic last third of her life, she was a "soft-spoken, fastidiously dressed little old lady with a white fichu and silver hair, such as Cecil B. de Mille might have picked for *Way Down East*." Someone else at a public meeting was introducing her as a great humanitarian when she interrupted with a peppery command to "Get it right, I'm not a humanitarian, I'm a hell-raiser." One would like her for a neighbor, thought Mrs. J. Borden Harriman on first encounter, an impression hastily amended to one of "a firebrand, foul-mouthed and partisan, a camp-follower and a comforter in the industrial war." Mother Jones insisted on being taken for what she was, adding little or nothing to the meager details presumed of her distant past: Dublin birth, schooling in Toronto, deaths of her husband and all their children in a yellow-fever epidemic in Memphis; dressmaking in Chicago until the Fire; the Workingman's Party of California fighting the importation of Chinese labor; the first big Pennsylvania coal stoppages of the 1890s. All added up to a forceful debut on the industrial battlefield as the old century waned. Yet when the questions began to circulate in the first years of the new, not a single notable in the labor movement could have said precisely when she appeared or from where. There is fairly reliable evidence that a prominent Roman Catholic priest and educator in Canada was her brother. She showed no public awareness of any such relationship. Neither did she bother to deny the talk that she had been a procuress. By her words and deeds Mother Jones lived exclusively for the class conflict and as self-revealing as anything else she ever said was her instinctive reply to a congressman who had asked where she lived: "Wherever there is a fight," she snapped.

The effects of her oratory upon the simple emotions of miners who adored her is best conveyed by samples of it.

I went into the state of West Virginia, [she recalled for the spell-bound delegates at the miners' special convention in the West Theater, Trinidad] and I knew those boys of old . . . There I saw women who had been beaten to death . . . and the babes of the coming generation . . . murdered by Baldwin-Felts thugs in the womb . . . This is America, my friends . . . Three thousand men assembled in Charlestown and we marched into the statehouse grounds, for they are ours and we have a right to take possession of them if we want to [laughter]. I called a committee and I said, "Boys, take this document into the governor's office . . . don't get on your knees . . . and don't say 'Your Honor' because very few of those fellows . . . know what it is" [laughter] . . . I says, "We will protect ourselves and buy every gun in Charlestown . . . the man that won't protect his home and fireside against the Baldwins has no right on the soil of America" [applause] . . . When I was about to close that meeting I said, "Boys, let Mother tell you one thing . . . Liberty is not dead, she is only quietly resting . . ." And that voice of fifteen hundred men rang in the air . . . "Oh, God, Mother, call her, call her now." There was a gang of those guards with a Gatling gun going up the creek in a buggy and they said, "Take your hand off that gun," and I said, "Oh, no, sir, my men made that gun, sir" [laughter]. Never did I see a man so bloodthirsty . . . his lips quivered, he thirsted for . . . the blood of those miners, and I said, "Don't you dare to move a bullet out of that gun" . . . Fear is the greatest curse you have got. I don't fear anybody . . . I am going to tell the governor of Colorado, I am going to stay here and by God, we will win . . . [applause]. If you are too cowardly to fight, there are enough women to come in and beat the hell out of you [laughter and applause] . . . Strike and stay with it . . .

As soon as they had recovered, the delegates stood up one by one to recite an assortment of grievances. There were complaints of being short-changed on payment of tons of coal dug, of salaries paid in company scrip worth ninety cents on the dollar and honored only in a company store or saloon, of forced voting for company-approved candidates, of blacklisting miners who had joined the union, and of being chased "down the canyon" for daring to ask for a check-weighman. This phase of the convention rattled the operators afterward into charging that the proceedings had been counterfeit. But if the authority and spontaneity of certain speakers were questionable, beyond doubt the mood of the miners was confident, determined, and ominously hostile to everything the coal operators stood for.

A scale committee was named composed of one delegate from each coal county. It drew up the following demands:

First — We demand recognition of the union.

Second — We demand a ten per cent advance in wages on the tonnage rates.

Third — We demand an eight hour workday for all classes of labor in or around the coal mines and at coke ovens.

Fourth — We demand pay for all narrow work and dead work, which includes brushing, timbering, removing falls, handling impurities, etc.

Fifth — We demand a check-weighman at all mines to be elected by the miners, without any interference by company officials in said election.

Sixth — We demand the right to trade in any store we please, and the right to choose our own boarding place and our own doctor.

Seventh — We demand the enforcement of the Colorado mining laws and the abolition of the notorious and criminal guard system which has prevailed in the mining camps of Colorado for many years.

The demands were unanimously approved and John Lawson read the policy committee's instructions for a strike. The door was not yet tightly closed. Mother Jones had been willing to grant the operators forty-eight hours to consider — "twenty-four hours is not enough because they might have a champagne jag on." The policy committee went further and gave them a week. Preparations for a strike went forward.

Ed Doyle, secretary-treasurer of District 15, was in charge of strike expenditures. The principal task was to insure adequate housing for the miners and their families, who, of course, would have to leave voluntarily the company property or face eviction. Doyle leased land near the mouths of the coal canyons, a feasible choice to reduce as much as possible the distance to be traveled by the exiting miners and families. The locations were also strategically ideal for the interception and harassment of scab labor. The positions staked out at Walsenburg, Rugby, Aguilar, Ludlow, Forbes, Suffield, and Sopris controlled the approaches to practically all the mines in the Trinidad coalfield. The largest and most important tent colony, close to the railroad spur serving the coalfield's most valuable properties, was earmarked for a forty-acre plot at Ludlow.

The operators had no intention of softening their stand during the week's grace period. According to L. M. Bowers, many of them took it for granted that the union officials, anticipating defeat, "will undertake to sneak out if they can secure even an interview with the operators . . . thus boasting before the public that they have secured the principal point, namely, recognition of the union." A meeting with union officials would scarcely of itself have represented a surrender of managerial power, but the fear that it might be so construed was enough to make the operators court the inevitability of a strike. Decisions were made to satisfy that predominant need, the avoidance of anything resembling even token recognition, and comfort was drawn from the reports of property superintendents and spies that the miners were so satisfied with working conditions they would neither join the union nor heed the strike call.

Misinformation and self-delusion were critically influential at this point. J. F. Welborn, who a fortnight earlier had privately notified the Rockefeller office of his apprehensions that the majority of men would walk off their jobs, now told the public that only 10 per cent of the miners were union and an even smaller number would put down their tools. Bowers advised the New York office similarly, adding that in reality the union possessed not even this small toehold in the CFI's mines because the few members were old unionists from the East hanging on to their union cards "as a matter of sentiment." All in all, the private correspondence of the Colorado operators on the eve of the strike reflected a willingness to trust their own propaganda and an eagerness to rationalize their steadfast position to each other, to the absentee directors, to themselves. The effort succeeded all too well. As the scheduled date of the walkout drew closer, no one connected with the companies registered the slightest disposition toward serious steps for avoiding it.

The official call went out on September 17: ". . . all mineworkers are hereby notified that a strike of all the coal miners and coke oven workers in Colorado will begin on Tuesday, September 23, 1913 . . . We are striking for improved conditions, better wages, and union recognition. We are sure to win." The call was signed by Hayes, Lawson, McLennan, and Doyle.

It was unnecessary to wait until September 23 for signs that the union officials had more accurately gauged the response of the miners than had the managers. The mass exodus got under way within hours of the strike call. In Fremont County 95 per cent of the coal diggers were idle by September 22. At Coal Creek on the previous day, a Sunday, E. H. Weitzel, the CFI's fuel manager, had waited at the Odd Fellows Hall to address employees of the nearby Radiant mine. The mine force of 135 marched in a body to the hall, filed upstairs to the United Mine Workers office on the floor above the one where they were supposed to hear Weitzel speak, and joined the union instead.

The Fourth Annual Trinidad–Las Animas Fair had been planned for the same week. Defying labor unrest and gloomy weather, the town went ahead with the opening ceremonies. Bands played and a tense community tried to assume a festive air. On the following day, September 23, clouds obscured Fishers Peak, rain poured and, as the temperature fell, changed to sleet and snow. Frank Hayes would recall the day as the most miserable he had ever known. Out of the canyons and across prairie flats crept long lines of pushcarts and mule wagons carrying unsmiling families, their old furniture, and personal treasures. The pathetic caravans crawled and swayed through the frozen downpour, wheels bogging in ice-encrusted mud, to be freed by the husband hauling and the wife pushing while shivering infants stared mutely from their perch on the domestic load. "An exodus of woe," reported Don MacGregor, whose uninhibited sympathy for the strikers was to drive him from the Denver *Express* into their ranks, "of a people leaving known fears for new terrors, a hopeless people seeking new hope, a people born to suffering going forth to new suffering."

At the tent site most of them found no shelter. An expected shipment of 1000 tents from West Virginia had failed to arrive. Drenched and marooned on a friendless plain, the wives and children helped the men build makeshift shelters or huddled beneath wagons and their own sodden furniture.

The snow kept up the next day, forced the abandonment of the Trinidad Fair, and worsened the plight of the strikers' families. Not until September 27 did the tents reach Ludlow and to the chilled and impatient miners it seemed that their unloading was preceded by an unnecessary amount of car-shunting from one siding to another, a cruel delay that looked to many as if planned deliberately by the Colorado and Southern Railroad at the behest of its profiteering allies in the coal industry.

The sun returned. Except for the crest of Fishers Peak and the eternally white summits of Huajatolla, the snow vanished. Just as rapidly pessimism at the tent colony sites melted before a brisk enthusiasm inspired by the warm and energetic presence of Frank Hayes and John Lawson. The tent floors were timbered, furniture was carefully arranged, heavy Excelsior stoves from Quincy, Illinois, were installed. Walls were partly wooded, fuel and water supplied, sanitary trenches and storage pits dug, and communication lines established with union headquarters in Trinidad. At Ludlow a wooden stage was erected for meetings and bedecked with the Stars and Stripes. A baseball diamond was marked out. Here too a large tent was set up for a school, assembly, and recreation. Lawson organized police squads to maintain discipline in the camps and committees were elected to deal with a variety of subjects from entertainment to sanitation.

Ludlow was blessed with several indefatigable young wives. An attractive Welsh redhead named Mary Hannah Thomas was appointed the colony's official greeter, and her melodic soprano was to be unfailingly heard when the occasion required the national anthem, Sunday School hymns, concert arias, or the strike song that Frank Hayes had just written, sung to the tune of "The Battle Cry of Freedom":

> . . . we will rally from the coal mines
> We'll battle to the end,
> Shouting the battle cry of union.
> The union forever! Hurrah, boys, hurrah!
> Down with the Baldwins, up with the law;
> For we're coming, Colorado, we're coming all the way,
> Shouting the battle cry of union!

7

CALIBAN MUST LEARN SOMETHING

THE UNION PAID WEEKLY BENEFITS of $3 to each striking miner, $1 for each wife, 50 cents each child. Headquarters for the strike remained in Trinidad, where rooms were rented and officials conferred. At the outset they had to deal with the important question of just how many miners had obeyed the call to strike.

Less than 30 per cent according to Frank Gove, an attorney representing the operators, and most of these were not in sympathy with the strike but forced by union terrorism to leave their jobs. Doyle reported to President White that 95 per cent of the miners were out and had "paralyzed" Colorado's coal industry. Doyle was an impulsive and voluble Irishman liable to blurt things without proof, but an impartial count by the Rocky Mountain *News* reached a figure not far short of this. The UMW's own records showed that 11,232 of the state's 13,980 coal miners were on strike at the end of September. Since about 2000 of these represented the northern properties, approximately 9000 men of the Trinidad field must have cast aside their picks. Finally J. F. Welborn himself privately admitted early in November that the largest companies had lost 70 per cent of their labor force while the more numerous smaller companies had lost virtually all their men. Weitzel, the fuel manager, wrote Welborn on September 26 that nearly all the Austrians, who had vowed to disregard any strike call, had left the Primero camp and if the "agitators" got to the Italians "we will lose all."

Shrewd, experienced corporation executives aided by an army

of detectives, guards, "spotters," and sundry surveillants had been utterly confounded. They had believed, or so they had said, that only an insignificant fraction of the coal diggers would obey the call. Ethelbert Stewart, in Denver as a hopeful federal mediator two weeks after the strike began, theorized to his superiors in the Department of Labor that "under a gunman's regime the company does not know whether their men are 10 per cent organized or 80 per cent . . . the sullen worker tells the gunman what he thinks he wants to know, lies about being satisfied, lies about belonging to the union . . ." Colorado miners had learned from experience to conceal their union allegiance and activities. In effect, the companies' antiunion policy was an ideal system for deceiving the officers, blindfolding them to the genuine feelings among the miners. Nothing the operators said about their employees, therefore, could be considered reliable.

When the operators repeatedly stated that less than 10 per cent of their men belonged to the union, its secret membership was hardly a factor in their calculations. But they were not that far out. Union officials themselves did not deny that shortly before the strike, and despite the risky work of the organizers, comparatively few miners had signed up in southern Colorado. It was safer not to do so, even secretly. This happened to knock apart the operators' argument that their workers were happy and contented. Unless the union, failing in its long campaign to organize, had suddenly terrorized this huge tranquil throng into subjection — a preposterous implication which the operators nevertheless kept reiterating — the men had struck of their own free will. And that they had done so, exchanging homes and jobs in the face of menacing guards and impossible weather conditions for an indefinite term of life under canvas supported by only a handful of dollars weekly, said precious little for the mass loyalty and high-salaried contentment that their masters boasted about to each other in the exclusive comfort of the Denver Club.

The circulars went up at every mine promising protection to men who remained on the job. "The only means," Weitzel would

say, "was to employ watchmen or others who could resist an attack force." William Reno hired fifty additional gunmen for the
CFI at an office rented for the purpose in the Dover Hotel in Denver and advertised for more. The situation also called for smooth
functioning of the well-oiled political machinery. Upon the company's request Sheriff Jeff Farr dispatched deputy sheriffs to guard
the CFI's properties in Huerfano County. The company furnished guns and paid the men $3.50 a day. Some were Baldwin-
Felts agents and the status of very few could have withstood legal
scrutiny. Qualifications for a man to be deputized under Colorado law included a year's residence in the county and sixty days
uninterrupted stay in the state immediately prior to the commission. Jefferson Farr confessed that he seldom considered the
background of the men he deputized — as far as he knew they
might have been "red-handed murderers." Some, indeed, were.

"There will be no violence if our union can prevent it." However well meant, these words of Frank Hayes at the start of the
strike had fast-diminishing relevance. The strategic proximity of
the tent colonies to railroad stations and canyon entrances was
itself a provocation to the operators' private army, while to the
sullen eyes of a striking miner the mere appearance of a mine
guard or Baldwin-Felts agent was an inflammatory affront. With
the walkout less than twenty-four hours old, Sheriff Jim Grisham
of Las Animas County was besieged with complaints that CFI
guards at Primero were refusing to let the miners return to collect
a second load of furniture from their tents. Grisham took action
only after the miners now encamped near the railroad depot at
Segundo threatened to attack the guards in a body and take their
belongings by force. The mood stayed ugly on the following evening when five Greeks damaging a company-built footbridge
across the Purgatoire were surprised by Robert Lee, deputy sheriff
and chief guard at the Segundo coking plants.

Bob Lee was a not unusual phenomenon in Colorado's coalfields, a freebooter from the state's lawless yesterday turned
security guard in the new industrialization. The CFI piously eulo-

gized him as a mild-mannered gentleman with roots in the honorable Virginian family of Robert E. Lee. By all other accounts Lee and his brothers, born in Kentucky, were a trio of vicious marauders who raided New Mexican villages and at one time owned a ranch that served as hideout for hunted outlaws, including Frank and Jesse James. At the turn of the century Bob Lee had moved to Colorado, where Billy Reno put him on the CFI payroll during the 1904 coal strike. With company status and a deputy's star Lee threw his considerable weight around more bullyingly than ever, his favorite victims now the foreign miners' wives or, when they resisted his advances, their unfortunate husbands. Even his fellow deputies and mine guards privately conceded that it was only a matter of time before Bob Lee got what was coming to him.

Lee was on horseback. As he rode down on the Greeks at the bridge, they fled toward a row of coke ovens. Lee drew a rifle from the scabbard at the side of his saddle, but a Greek hiding in an idle oven fired first and a load of buckshot ripped through Lee's throat killing him instantly.

The predictable newspaper comment that Bob Lee had lived and died by gun law would, in other circumstances, have served as adequate epitaph. But the strike gave his death a special notoriety and while unclassifiable by evidence as anything more than self-defense or an overdue act of vengeance, the dispatch of this long-hated bully was played up in the popular press and company propaganda as the first casualty of the coalfield war. (The union accorded this distinction to the slaying of Gerald Lippiatt in August.) The detailed facts about Lee's killing never came to light. A mounted posse and a carload of deputies raced into the hills and brought back a number of fugitive Greeks, none of them ever to be brought to trial, and when Governor Ammons, upset by news of the shooting, rang up Trinidad for full details, he got no coherent response. The CFI blamed Lee's death on "incendiary utterances" from Mother Jones, who with Frank Hayes had addressed 700 strikers in Starkville shortly before the shooting while company clerks spied on her audience, hiding their own faces when cameras were turned in their direction.

The initial effort by the new Department of Labor to mediate in an industrial dispute got nowhere. Ethelbert Stewart canvassed the situation well, studying the written statements of both sides and interviewing operators, miners, state labor officials, and Governor Ammons. But the operators distrusted him from the moment he arrived in Denver. L. M. Bowers, for one, was unable to see how it could possibly profit them to deal with an emissary of William Wilson, an acknowledged unionist whose cabinet presence "bespeaks a rough road ahead for our industrial enterprises." Stewart did too much "hobnobbing . . . with the most vicious of labor agitators." But Bowers and the other coal executives had made it bluntly clear to him that they would never encourage those who brewed strife and revolution, that they would cling to this principle until "our bones were bleached as white as chalk in these Rocky Mountains . . ."

Bowers' words were addressed to John D. Rockefeller, Jr., who forthwith signified that the men of 26 Broadway backed the Denver officers to the hilt. "We feel that what you have done is right and fair and that the position you have taken in regard to the unionizing of the mines is in the interest of the employees of the company. Whatever the outcome, we will stand by you to the end." A further communication from Rockefeller four days later conveyed the same assurance. "I realize that these are trying days for the management of the Fuel Company. Its actions are watched with great interest by this office, and its strong and just position will not lack backing at this end."

On the night of October 9 Stewart met Welborn, Osgood, and Brown at the governor's office in the statehouse. The operators had come prepared with a detailed interpretation of their side in the dispute but Stewart cut them off, saying in effect that he knew the whole affair inside out and was only interested in suggestions toward a settlement. This annoyed the operators intensely and

when Stewart next asked if they would meet union officials infor-
mally or propose some alternative their response was sulkily nega-
tive. As for Stewart, his own mind was already made up. The
problem in essence "is a strike of the twentieth century against the
tenth century mental attitude." Stewart reported the situation in
Colorado as extremely tense but advised his superiors that he
could be of no further service there.

In the Boston Building, L. M. Bowers was also disposed to report his views. "We find that Stewart has been for years connected with labor unions," he wrote to Rockefeller. "He came
here under false colors." Bowers ran on with rising temperature.
With Stewart and William Wilson in the government, "we are on
top of a volcano. When such men as these, together with the
cheap college professors and still cheaper writers in muck-raking
magazines, supplemented by a lot of milk-and-water preachers
. . . are permitted to assault the businessmen who have built up
the great industries and . . . done more to make this country
what it is than all other agencies combined, it is time that vigorous measures are taken to put a stop to these vicious teach-
ings . . ."

Bowers made it plain that the unionists were threatening the
company's profits: "Our net earnings would have been the largest
in the history of the company by $200,000," he told the young
Rockefeller on October 21, "but for the increase in wages paid the
employees during the last few months. With everything running
so smoothly and with an excellent outlook for 1914, it is mighty
discouraging to have this vicious gang come into our state and not
only destroy our profit but eat into that which has heretofore been
saved."

As Bowers assuredly knew, one of the remedial measures he
hoped for was already under way. On October 3 the United
States attorney general in Washington had received partly coded
intelligence from Harry E. Kelly, U.S. district attorney in southern Colorado, that the coal operators through Judge Northcutt,
their mouthpiece in Trinidad, were pressing him vigorously to

present their complaints against UMW officers before a grand jury convening in three days' time. The operators alleged violations of the Anti-Trust Act, charging that union officials were preventing the coal companies from fulfilling interstate contracts. The situation was politically sensitive and Harry Kelly uncertain what to do. He was forthwith given enlightenment. The Justice Department did not prosecute such alleged violations on mere *ex parte* evidence. A special agent would be assigned to the task of developing all the facts.

It was impossible to keep the agent's presence in the coalfield a secret. Within and outside Colorado there was an anxious reaction among Democratic ward politicians who had successfully wooed a big-city labor vote and now apprehended large defections to the Progressive Party should federal cooperation with the company-sponsored grand jury result in indictments against the union leaders. So with a weather eye on the political storm signals, Woodrow Wilson's attorney general warned Harry Kelly to have as little to do with the proposed investigation as possible. At the same time Ethelbert Stewart tried to have it called off on grounds that the conflict was industrial, not criminal. The jury hesitated, but Jesse Northcutt shoved it back into action and persuaded the foreman to telephone Denver for Governor Ammons' endorsement. This was secured and the investigation proceeded. And meanwhile, Ammons was under even more insistent pressure to order out the state militia.

On the eve of the strike the mineowners had adopted a position that, while many of their men might quit work under union intimidation, most would return to their jobs if the state guaranteed protection. A week later Welborn had announced that commitment of state troops to the strike zone would mean "a complete resumption of coal operations." In other words, Cripple Creek 1903–4 all over again, with the Colorado National Guard as strikebreakers. The coal operators' gadfly attorney, Northcutt, circulated a petition among Trinidad merchants demanding the mobilization of the militia, and the county sheriffs of Las Animas and Huerfano, also dancing to the companies' tune, wired Governor Ammons for troops right away.

The violence looked at first to be all on one side. Nothing infuriated striking miners more than the sight of scabs and strikebreakers heading into the canyons for work. The same day that Bob Lee was slain, a mob of strikers' wives and children manhandled a nonunion track layer at the Walsen mine. Next day about a hundred strikers dragged a strikebreaker from a public stage near the Ludlow tent colony. These were isolated incidents, nowhere serious enough to warrant troops. But subsequent clashes, spontaneous or deliberately provoked by mine guards as the unionists bitterly charged, furthered the operators' aim. Buildings were dynamited at the Primrose mine near Rugby, a hundred rifle shots were fired at the Oakview mine in the La Veta valley. A shack frequented by Bulgar strikebreakers at the Rocky Mountain Fuel Company's properties in Boulder County blew up. The local mayor swore that the mine guards themselves had set the dynamite for this one. And the first pitched battle at Ludlow was suspiciously like the planned-for outcome to a positive errand of provocation.

The atmosphere was explosive enough. John Lawson and Mother Jones had been in the Berwind Canyon that morning, October 7, and delivered fighting speeches. There was some string music afterward and Mary Thomas sang, but more than entertainment was needed to quench the bellicose ardor of some of the Greeks. Only a clash could dissipate it. Lawson and Mother Jones were repeating their performance at Aguilar in the afternoon when an urgent phone message brought them hurrying back to Ludlow.

To be asked along on a joy ride in a CFI company car with George Belcher and Walter Belk would have struck some as a macabre invitation. But the three who accepted outside the Toltec Hotel, Trinidad, that afternoon were local officials of coal companies with presumably no need to be scared of the Baldwin-Felts pair. The mission was supposed to reconnoiter the union colonies, and to some of the watchers in the tents the carload of hostiles presented an irresistibly tempting moving target. The first rifle volleys flew as the vehicle approached the cutoff to the Berwind Canyon. Each side was to claim the other fired first. Belcher ordered the car halted, took aim with his rifle, and fired twice. The driver ran around front, cranked the engine into life again, and they drove off at top speed for the Victor-American mine at Hastings. On their report of an ambush, seventeen mounted mine guards galloped to the Ludlow colony and opened up on the strikers now crouching behind a string of freight cars along the Colorado and Southern track.

A telegrapher at the depot, almost hit in the crossfire, tapped out news of the shooting to Trinidad. Sheriff Grisham took it upon himself to summon the local troop of the Colorado National Guard and sent it on a special train to subdue what the operators in Denver told Governor Ammons were "forty Greek and Montenegran sharpshooters from the Balkan War." The soldiers found nothing to do. John Lawson, arriving back at the Ludlow tents, had talked sense into his belligerent elements and, at least for the moment, had succeeded in pacifying them.

Lawson's personal dilemma was now taking shape. While not a socialist — he had worked for Elias Ammons' election — he interpreted the situation as a state of war forced upon the miners by the coal bosses. Unlike the ideological militants, he would not accept the theory of permanent and inevitable class conflict, but its present reality was inescapable. Seeing no alternative to victory, Lawson, a family man, was prepared to sacrifice every domestic concern to achieve it. His wife played no part at all in his involvement with the Colorado struggle, during which he saw little of their home and children.

Profoundly committed to the cause of labor unionism, Lawson was ill-cast as a bureaucratic politician within the organization and by no comparison was he a tub-thumping agitator in the Mother Jones mold. His manner of address was earnest and exciting without being excitable, and he spoke of the foe with pity or contempt more often than with hot rancor. No one ever denied his humanitarianism, which, as indicated in the United Mine Workers' final and ironic assessment of him, proved costly to himself and the cause to which he was devoted. "He was more of a crusader than an executive and often drifted from the orthodox path of unionism." Written long after the strike, the words betray the union's ultimate disenchantment with John Lawson, which, traceable back to his defense of Tom Lewis' policies, had set in before the stoppage and was to intensify during it.

The problem of his relations with the union was compounded by difficulties in the field. No pacifist, he looked by no means out of place in the foothills and arroyos dressed in blue sweater and overalls, a cloth cap tugged over his ears, a .45-caliber pistol strapped at his waist, and around his throat the red bandanna, worn now as a proud badge since the mine guards vilipended strikers as "rednecks." But the colonies under his command contained a heavy quota of hot-headed immigrants whose thirst for battle or more often simple revenge could lead them into situations cunningly set up by the opposition. Lawson's job was to control this element, predominantly Greek and wholly foreign in tongue and custom, without betraying anything which could be mistaken for timidity or indecision.

Perhaps there was more than a grain of truth in the impression other unionists formed of him as a publicity-seeker masquerading as a lone crusader. If so, Lawson is still best imagined as an anxious field marshal of the coalfield war, loved but scarcely understood by the majority in his command, denied the unlimited confidence of those he represented, yet allowing not one of these considerations to alter the course along which his principles compelled him.

Two days after the opening skirmish with the Baldwin-Felts detectives and in the same setting of black-scarred, piñon-studded hillsides, sparse ranch pasture, arroyo and railroad track, there occurred the first innocent bloodshed. To keep an eye on troublemakers, as Bowers explained it to John D. Rockefeller, Jr., the company was about to install eight large searchlights, each with a beam range of five or six miles. In the chairman's opinion, "this is a mighty fine scheme." One of the searchlights arrived at the Ludlow depot on October 9. In the afternoon a wagon train escorted by a dozen or more mine guards set out from the CFI mine and coke ovens at Tabasco to collect it. At about the same time, 1:30 P.M., Mack Powell finished his dinner and rode off to herd cattle.

Powell was himself a miner on strike with union affiliation until signing on as a cowpuncher for the Green ranch three quarters of a mile south of Ludlow. As Powell's three children watched him mount the bay, his wife felt a foreboding of danger, but he soothed her spoken fears, insisting that he must see to the cattle. The Powells waved good-bye to each other at the gate.

He was in the pasture, circling his cattle, as the foremost Tabasco wagon passed beneath the Colorado and Southern Railroad bridge. Gunfire broke out from the flats to the east, from hills to the west, and from about 800 yards north, where a high steel bridge carried the Colorado and Southeastern rails over the Colorado and Southern. The mine guards dismounted and sprang for cover, and the leading wagon driver, in the split second before leaping from his seat, saw Powell half turn in the saddle while bullets kicked up brown dust puffs about the horse's hoofs. Over a hundred shots were exchanged. Shortly before sundown Powell's bullet-pierced body was found in the pasture; any possibility of identifying the cowboy's killer vanished in the subsequent confusion of testimony, as did the widow's hopes of compensation from any source.

Now both sides stockpiled arms. The day of Mack Powell's death and the abortive meeting between Ethelbert Stewart and the coal operators in Governor Ammons' office, John Lawson sent the governor word that "four pieces of rapid fire artillery" had been bought by one of the companies. Albert Felts, functioning as a kind of military overseer for the mineowners, arranged the importation of at least eight machine guns from West Virginia, where some of them had recently seen service against striking miners. As J. F. Welborn afterward explained it, the coal operators had been left with no choice, since local law enforcement officers were unable to guarantee protection for the coal properties and the governor appeared oblivious to all necessity of mobilizing the state militia.

Even for Trinidad, the run on guns was phenomenal. Claude Shy, managing one of the town's three hardware firms (second-hand stores also sold guns) was subsequently asked if his duty as a town councilman was to preserve order and his business to sell guns and dynamite to anybody who came along. He answered both questions affirmatively. In the first week of October, Shy profited hugely by selling his entire stock of weapons, ammunition, and dynamite to agents of the operators and union alike.

On October 11 an automobile entered the alleyway behind Commercial Street and halted at the rear of Brown's Hardware, the establishment Shy managed. William Diamond, Robert Uhlich, one-eyed Sam Carter, and Anthony McGary were among the locally notable unionists who went into Brown's and came out with large boxes. Don MacGregor was also present, his role undergoing transition from Denver *Express* newspaperman to active labor militant. The automobile was the union's familiar all-red tourer. The boxes swung aboard it were unmarked and tightly closed, but it made no difference because the group included an undercover agent paid $3.50 a day by Billy Reno to spy on the strikers and make regular reports to the CFI's branch office in the First National Bank Building at the intersection of Commercial and Main. In due course his intelligence reached L. M. Bowers, who relayed it to John D. Rockefeller, Jr., in New York: ". . . beyond question that Winchester rifles and revolvers with large quantities of ammunition are being supplied to the sluggers . . . brought in from the other states, together with the bloodthirsty Greeks who have just returned from the Turkish war." There is no evidence that anybody in the Boston Building told Rockefeller during this period that the CFI and other companies were also storing up guns.

In the middle of the month Adolph Germer visited a wholesale hardware store in Pueblo with E. L. Neelly, a politically ambitious Huerfano County hardware retailer consolidating labor support in preparation for the attempted overthrow of Jefferson Farr's machine. Germer ordered about twenty high-powered Winchesters and Savages. Shipped express that same afternoon, the rifles were handed over to Germer, who still kept his membership on the executive committee of the Socialist Party and from time to time provided tindery copy for the columns of the *United Mine Workers Journal.* "Capitalism has run mad in Colorado," his article in the October 27 issue began. "The sheriffs of Huerfano and Las Animas counties have made their offices an adjunct to the CFI and the Baldwin-Felts Agency, called deputy sheriffs, rob and murder at will . . . Respectable people are no longer safe in the presence of these human hyenas." That same week Neelly's store shipped another twenty high-powered rifles and Germer collected these also.

The state government had more than an inkling of the arms race in the Trinidad coalfield but attempted no interference, aware that the operators, insisting on the right to protect their properties and employees, would have brooked none. As for the unionists, their justification for buying up weapons was the necessity of defending strikers' families and their canvas homes. All in all, a natural state of affairs, thought Ethelbert Stewart, who expressed his theory allegorically in a letter forwarded to President Wilson: ". . . if Caliban learns his master's language, and uses it to curse him, the blame can not be all Caliban's. For Caliban will and must learn something, and the only language common to all, and which all understand in southern Colorado, is the voice of the gun."

8

A TUMULT THREATENED

It was still mostly a war of nerves. When Adolph Germer was selecting the weapons in Pueblo he is said to have chosen one type as "the very gun to pull down those searchlights with." Few innovations on the part of the operators maddened the strikers more than the 18-inch and 32-inch lights whose 5000 candlepower beams swept their clustered tents throughout every night. The searchlight at Sopris was mounted on top of a coke washer. Two lights were installed at Oakview in the paradisiacal La Veta Pass. The Hastings light stood on the bluffs behind the Victor-American Company's Roman Catholic church. In a letter to Governor Ammons arguing that the United Mine Workers' violent conduct of the strike fully justified their refusal to deal with it, the operators scoffed at protests that the miners' families were robbed of rest by the probing searchlight beams, and suggested that if this was the case they had only to pitch their tents farther away from the coal properties.

This was rubbing it in with a vengeance, and the other side missed no opportunity to retaliate. Judge Northcutt had written to a crony on the New Mexico Supreme Court asking the loan of gunfighters to reinforce the coal counties' deputy sheriffs. Northcutt allegedly enclosed a check for their transport. On October 14 eighteen of them arrived at the Santa Fe railroad depot in Trinidad, were marched up Commercial Street to the offices of the Trinidad *Chronicle-News* and in Northcutt's presence were deputized and sworn in by Sheriff Grisham. They were then ordered to

Ludlow on a special train, but before they were halfway back down Commercial no fewer than 800 strikers and sympathizers closed in and detoured them to union headquarters instead. There must have been some fast and persuasive talking. When Grisham showed up to liberate his kidnaped deputies, they turned in their weapons and badges, protested that they had been hired under false pretenses, and the next day were on the train back to New Mexico.

The price of coal increased. There existed a statewide reservoir of conservative repugnance for labor stoppages. Utilizing both these circumstances, the operators secured the leverage of financial interests to try and force the governor's hand. As Bowers confided to the junior Rockefeller, "There probably has never been such pressure wrought upon any governor of this state by the strongest men in it as has been . . . upon Governor Ammons." The chamber of commerce and the real-estate exchange joined the clamor for militiamen to "drive the vicious agitators out of the state."

On October 15 Ammons conferred with John Chase, now Colorado's adjutant general, and the state attorney general, Fred Farrar, in order to satisfy himself of the military and legal basis for action. The important question was where the money was to come from. No state funds were available for what Ammons feared could develop into a million-dollar venture. It was an opportune occasion for the friendly bankers Bowers had once written Rockefeller about. From Ammons' standpoint the only practical recourse was to issue certificates of indebtedness. These the banks agreed to accept at 4 per cent interest, to cover an estimated $150,000 in expenses for the first month's military operations. Bowers reported the results to Rockefeller. "We have been able to secure the cooperation of all the banks in the city, who have had three or four conferences with our little cowboy governor, agreeing to back the state and lend it all the funds necessary to maintain the militia and afford ample protection . . ."

But Ammons had not yet made up his mind. He prayed that

the strike could still be settled without the need of troops. He had no wish to plunge his administration into heavy debt. Yet either troops or a settlement had better be provided before the violence got completely out of hand. The race to head off serious bloodshed ought now to have been emphasized to the worried governor by a fresh flurry of telegrams from the south announcing the debut of the Death Special.

Albert C. Felts claimed the dubious credit for its design and construction. He had an ordinary automobile shipped down from Denver, its tonneau removed, and its floor rebuilt of solid wood. The reconverted sides consisted of steel three eighths of an inch thick made on Felts's request at the CFI works in Pueblo. A shelter was built in the vehicle to house two machine guns. In photos this early version of an armored car looks somewhat less than terrifying. But the effect upon tented families each time it lumbered into view was the intended one of awe and apprehension. Its appearance on October 17 near the strikers' colony at Forbes, about halfway between Trinidad and Ludlow, was all the more frightening because it climaxed a series of nighttime sniping attacks that had forced the removal of women and children to a separate collection of tents.

A dozen deputies on horseback led by Zeke Martin, Grisham's undersheriff, showed up first, halting near the railroad embankment. In the rain that had begun to fall, one of them dismounted and headed for the grouped strikers with a handkerchief tied to his uplifted rifle. He announced that they had come to disarm anyone illegally carrying weapons. No impartial account of what then transpired exists. Northcutt's Trinidad *Chronicle-News* called it an unprovoked attack on the deputies. Marco Zamboni, an eighteen-year-old Austrian returning to the tents from a rabbit hunt cut short by the weather, charged that the miners were deliberately seduced into unwariness when the deputy engaged them in friendly conversation and passed a bottle of whiskey around. At any rate, suddenly the deputy was running from the tents and both sides were shooting. A Slav miner named Luke

Vahernik collapsed across a tent rope with a deputy's bullet in his brain. Old men in the tents crawled under their cots. Other strikers ran for their lives, and when they looked again from the cover of arroyos and scrub they gazed on the Death Special.

Belk and Belcher were in the contraption and both its machine guns were firing. Some 600 shots raked the tents, riddling canvas, bursting crockery, and shattering sticks of furniture. Marco Zamboni, nine wounds in his legs, sprawled all afternoon unattended in the drenching rain until the firing ceased at dusk. No effort was made by deputies or detectives to inspect the results of their shooting. As Judge Northcutt remarked drily, "The relations were not of that social character that demanded any such courtesies." Zamboni survived, permanently crippled.

In Denver the coal operators used the incident to intensify their pressure on Governor Ammons, who, however, even had he decided to turn out the National Guard, now faced another roadblock. Foremost among those in his administration whom he was to accuse of having betrayed or otherwise failed him in midcrisis was his state auditor, a colorful and muscular Irishman named Roady Kenehan. This former blacksmith and staunch unionist had already won himself a lively reputation by repeatedly holding up the payment of state expenditures, and there was scarcely an office or department in the administration that had escaped his charge of graft and jobbery. Now Kenehan withheld sanction for the governor's tentative arrangement with the Denver bankers. He aired loud doubts not only of its scrupulous legality but of any pressing need for militiamen, whose officers he regarded as either dolts or dissemblers.

On the question of whether troops were in fact required, Ammons, exasperated to the point of — for him — drastic action, now decided to satisfy himself. Early on October 21 he left Denver for Trinidad to make a personal tour of the strike zone.

That afternoon a huge demonstration organized by Mother Jones paraded outside the governor's hotel, the Cardenas, singing union battle songs and carrying banners saying WE REPRESENT CFI

SLAVES or, pointedly for the governor's benefit, DEMOCRATIC PARTY IS ON TRIAL. The Cardenas lobby just then provided a scene almost as interesting. Individuals waiting for Governor Ammons to come downstairs and begin his tour included agents of both sides in the strike war, each concerned lest Ammons form too favorable an opinion of the other. Lawson and John McLennan and the organizer William Diamond dashed forward to meet him at the same moment, as did the CFI fuel manager Weitzel and other coal company officials. And on the fringe of the group, endeavoring to appear as inconspicuous as his bullish frame would permit, hovered the one participant in the strike drama whose motivations for brutality are difficult to identify as either principle, ambition, greed, or stupidity.

What Karl E. Linderfelt was up to in Trinidad at this juncture, if not his entire role in the strike, would seem "clouded in mystery" to subsequent investigators whose time or inclinations to probe further had run out. The National Guard lieutenant was never specifically questioned about the nature of his instructions and the only thing resembling an explanation elicited during interrogation would be that General John Chase had sent him to Trinidad as an undercover man to help in determining whether or not troops were needed. Beyond question, Chase and Linderfelt had already privately made up their minds on this score. Both craved a renewal of active service in the defense of the state against agitators, wops, and rednecks.

The governor's tour, which doubtless fell within the scope of Linderfelt's surveillance, offered no better prospects that this would come about. Ammons complained to the press that no one on his trip had suggested how to end the strike. But the closest anything came to disturbing the peace that surrounded the governor wherever he went during two days of automobile travel occurred at the Victor-American properties near Walsenburg, when an armed mine guard refused to let him pass. Personally embarrassing, this could hardly qualify as an instance of public disorder and Ammons left the strike zone with no more noticeable intention of calling out the state militia than when he had entered it. The "pressure" Bowers had spoken of had not quite worked the trick. Nothing short of explosive circumstances would, it was evident, frighten the governor into the action which the coal operators so earnestly desired. And the events that now occurred, particularly those involving Karl Linderfelt, left a nagging possibility that they were fashioned to this end.

It was as if provocation waited for the governor's back to turn. On October 23 Ammons left the strike zone on a 1:30 P.M. train out of Walsenburg. At approximately the same hour Linderfelt, who had just accepted a deputy's commission from Sheriff Grisham, took a train from Trinidad to Ludlow. Also, that day Grisham and his undersheriff Zeke Martin threw a cordon around the tent colony at Forbes and ordered all the men out for questioning in connection with the previous week's shooting affray. The following day in Walsenburg, Sheriff Jeff Farr commissioned no fewer than fifty-five deputies and in short order blood flowed on Seventh Street.

The CFI's mine property began at the western end of the street. For a nonstriking German who lived there it was only a half-mile walk to and from work, but strikers' wives and children had made it a regular ordeal with their jeers and taunts. So he now boarded at the mine. His wife remained on Seventh Street and that morning she had found a note pinned to her door:

If you don't move out of this neighborhood within 24 hours we will blow you out. Your husband is scabbing. We mean business.

She telephoned the mine superintendent, who sent three wagons with an escort of mine guards to collect her and the furniture so she could join her husband at the mine. Shorty Martinez, Jeff Farr's undersheriff, and fifteen deputies augmented the escort. They pushed through hate-filled crowds to an alleyway behind the house. The shouting and catcalls echoed along Main Street to the courthouse, and Farr stepped out on the balcony above the entrance. He made a loud remark about the folly of interfering with his deputies and a lounger on the courthouse lawn "took a chill" from his tone.

The crowd on Seventh Street thickened. Miners' wives screamed insults and several children scooped dirt from the unpaved street and threw it at the guards. Then the furniture was loaded and the wagons moved off, reaching Seventh Street and Main when, without warning, Martinez's deputies swung their rifles up and fired into the crowd. Fifty rounds were discharged in five minutes. The demonstrators scattered, leaving three dead strikers in the rutted street — a Finn, an Italian, and a Slav.

Walsenburg grew quieter with the fall of dusk, but the county courthouse and the union headquarters both were barricaded as if for siege. Armed men thronged their rooftops. As night deepened, Farr, fearing an attack on his courthouse, telephoned Trinidad for help. Albert Felts boarded the northbound train with ten of Grisham's deputies and Judge Northcutt. There was a commotion before the train pulled out. A Colorado and Southern flagman had gone back to the rear car to put up the taillight. He found some of Felts's men maneuvering two machine guns aboard the sleeper. Before he could finish explaining that company regulations forbade that sort of thing, Felts and his men obeyed a nod from Northcutt and hustled him off his train.

At Walsenburg there was no further trouble for the rest of the night. But at daybreak demands to avenge the Seventh Street killings were voiced in every strikers' camp and nowhere more passionately than in the largest, Ludlow.

South of the colony mine guards and deputies were permanently stationed to guard the access routes to the CFI's Berwind and Tabasco properties and to protect arriving and departing train passengers. Karl Linderfelt now supervised them for $5 a day with expenses paid by the company. All night they had been tensed for action, alerted by reports that women and children were being sent from the Ludlow tents to Trinidad, Forbes, and Aguilar, and that autoloads of armed men were reinforcing the colony.

The strikers themselves expected trouble. What happened at Walsenburg appeared to signal a more warlike policy on the part of the other side now that the governor was gone. To frustrate a possible attack from Trinidad or by the mine guards and deputies returning from Walsenburg, strikers had that morning torn up portions of the Colorado and Southern railroad track north and south of Ludlow. After breakfast the railroad superintendent in Trinidad received a telephone message from an unidentified caller at Ludlow warning him not to let the Denver-bound passenger and mail train go through. It had already gone, but he managed to halt it at Forbes and afterward communicated with the colony again. John Lawson was there and told him that the track could be repaired, that his trains would not be interfered with providing he guaranteed that no deputies or mine guards were riding on the Colorado and Southern line. The superintendent gave his word. His trains rolled again but later that day, about 1:30 P.M., Adolph Germer in Walsenburg notified Ludlow that the deputies were coming down on the Denver and Rio Grande track, which ran roughly parallel with and two miles east of the Colorado and Southern. Lawson, directing operations from a deep arroyo north of the tent colony, sent a party of Greeks east to Barnes Station with orders not to let the train through, but it went by them anyway at 25 mph as they briskly fired upon it with rifles and six-shooters.

Linderfelt and a detachment of twenty men in the railroad section house half a mile below the Ludlow depot were under attack at about 3 P.M. Forty armed guards came down the canyon to Linderfelt's relief and the attacking miners withdrew from their firing positions along the crests and ridges. Fighting became scattered and desultory, ceasing altogether with the advent of night and a snowstorm. John Nimmo, a mine guard, was found face down in thickening snow south of the Colorado and Southeastern track. He had bled to death from stomach wounds.

Realizing that the section house would be untenable if the attack resumed next morning, Linderfelt's detachment abandoned it under cloak of darkness and the storm, and retreated along the canyon to Tabasco. At daybreak intermittent firing broke out again. Strikers seized the vacated section house and burned it to the ground. Bullets rained on the important mines at Hastings, Delagua, Berwind, and Tabasco. On the rocky slopes behind the coke washer at Tabasco a deputy sheriff named Tom Whitney died. This was Sunday morning, October 26.

A good deal of sleep was lost that weekend in Denver. The compulsion to settle the strike before taking the costly step of calling out the militia drove Governor Ammons to exhausting lengths. His last-ditch attempts to bring the operators and union leaders face to face involved, besides constant telephoning, an undignified amount of physical shuttling between the two parties, who never got closer to each other than when they briefly occupied adjoining offices under the same statehouse dome. As a precaution against any drain of the miners' trust in him, Ammons kept Thomas Patterson at his side, a venerable former U.S. senator and publisher of the Rocky Mountain *News*, whose reputation as a friend of organized labor was beyond question.

John White and Frank Hayes were in Denver and a discussion with these two union chiefs left the governor and Patterson in no doubt that they were prepared now to waive the issue of recognition if only the operators would meet them on equal terms. In fact the governor and Patterson gathered the impression that the United Mine Workers' president would call off the strike in exchange for a joint conference. This notion was conveyed to the operators in the next office and met with the now standard response that any meeting with the "interlopers" who had brought such a curse upon Colorado might be interpreted as recognition of the union. And indeed Welborn and his colleagues seemed to be physically poised for instant departure should a union official so much as thrust his foot into the same room with them.

The governor was being backed into a corner. Twenty representatives of Denver's five big banks borrowed his office for an executive meeting and afterward assured him that he could have the money he needed for the militia in thirty days. But Roady Kenehan was on hand too with a flat refusal to issue any warrants for military expenditures unless forced to by court order. The auditor professed to see no reason why the coal counties should not handle their own affairs. "The coal mine owners should be required to negotiate with their own employees," Kenehan declared. "If this is done the strike would undoubtedly be settled in a short time."

But the mineowners were too bent on toughening their squads of deputies and mine guards with the military power of the state to give up now. By Sunday night, as Welborn put it, "we had been pressuring the governor very hard for over twenty-four hours to save our mines." Near the end of his rope, Ammons telephoned Welborn that same night at the Denver Club, said he felt sure the strikers would waive both issues of union recognition and a pay raise and pleaded with the operators to do some small thing to help him out. According to Welborn, the governor revealed that he felt sick and worn out, and ought to be in bed. The CFI president replied that no concession would ever be made by the companies "to that murderous element" but that if the governor chose to write them a letter setting forth points in the strikers' demands already covered by law, the operators would gladly give an affirmative answer. Ammons, desperate for a glimmer of hope, suggested a meeting that very night. He was told that it could wait until morning.

The operators were in the governor's office at 8 A.M. sharp. Most of the day was then wasted on efforts to compose a letter addressed to them, over Ammons' signature, which would be acceptable to everybody. Former Senator Patterson took some of the initiative from the fatigued Ammons, but this was no help since the old man's contributions only added to the delay and confusion. Patterson was largely responsible for the first proposed letter, which dismissed the recognition issue in its first line, requested that the operators promise to abide by the statutes of law, then dealt with those features of the statutes which Patterson understood applied to the strikers' demands. The letter concluded with the provision that as soon as the strike was ended, the miners should be allowed back on their jobs without discrimination.

Presented to Welborn, Osgood, and Brown in the governor's office that afternoon, Patterson's draft touched off such a reaction that the executives' angry voices were audible in distant corners of the statehouse. The operators charged that words omitted from certain quoted statutes altered their meaning, and they emphasized that in any event, the provision about the men returning to work was quite unacceptable. The conference adjourned so that the operators might draft their own letter for the governor to sign and send them.

By then Welborn had been informed that his mines were under attack. He notified Albert Felts, who was in Denver, and the detective in turn spoke to General Chase before speeding south to Trinidad. Felts and Sheriff Grisham mustered a force of about fifty deputies and company guards and took it upon themselves to activate a dozen or so local militiamen. Chase meanwhile had sent a telegram to the beleaguered men in the Berwind Canyon estimating that Felts's relief force from Trinidad "should be in contact with the strikers at 10 A.M." Unknown to the general, however, the locomotive crew refused to scab and the special train — four steel cars and a caboose — still stood idle in the depot as noon approached.

In the superintendent's office at Tabasco, Linderfelt scribbled off a telegram to General Chase:

THERE HAS BEEN A CONTINUOUS BATTLE FOR 40 HOURS   WE HAVE NO EXPECTATION OF EVER RECEIVING ANY HELP FROM SHERIFF GRISHAM TOO MUCH DAMNED POLITICS . . . WE MUST HAVE AMMUNITION AND HIGH-POWER RIFLES TO HOLD THIS PLACE AND PROTECT WOMEN AND CHILDREN . . . THE ONLY SOLUTION IS TROOPS, AND AT ONCE

But in the meantime Felts had located a former railroad engineer among his own agents. He took over the throttle, the troopers and their allies entrained with their two machine guns, and at last the reinforcements moved out.

The strikers had ample warning from sympathetic telephone callers, but the impression received was not that the train would stop short of Ludlow for the relief of Linderfelt's force bottled up in Berwind Canyon. It was believed instead that the intention was to rake the colony with machine-gun fire, an easy accomplishment since the rails ran past the westerly fringe of the tents at no distance wider than thirty yards. That this was the understanding of the strikers who had been on edge since the shootings at Forbes and Walsenburg, Don MacGregor, for one, had no doubts. He acted on the same assumption. MacGregor had just filed an emotional story with his newspaper at Dawson, New Mexico, where a Phelps-Dodge coal mine, supposedly safe and modern, had exploded in two entries and entombed 206 men. Covering the disaster was MacGregor's last fling as a reporter and may well have accelerated his decision to join wholeheartedly in the labor war. When John Lawson's ambuscades had settled into their forward positions on knolls, slopes, and bridges commanding the railroad south of Ludlow, every man swearing that the Baldwin-Felts "steel train" would never reach their tents, MacGregor was on the firing line with a .30–30 Winchester, squinting along its barrel at the railroad track through still whirling snowflakes.

Five automobiles driven by local union officials and loaded with guns and ammunition for the strikers had left Trinidad about the same time as the deputies and militiamen. The autos overtook the train a mile or two beyond Forbes. It seemed to be crawling and was in fact right then under fire from the 300 or more strikers deployed in the hills. Bullets flattened themselves against the steel cars and splinters wounded five men. Albert Felts had no intention of taking the train farther north than the railroad switch to Tabasco. The switch was still some distance off but under the present gunfire to detrain even at this point would invite casualties. Felts issued orders and the scab engineer closed the throttle and threw the train into reverse. It rolled back four miles to Forbes Junction and was shunted in with such clumsy haste the last car sideswiped a telephone pole. The troops jumped down. Carrying their rifles and two machine guns, they marched over the hills through mud and ice in a southerly detour to avoid strikers' bullets. Not until well after dark did they reach Berwind and at 2 A.M. Linderfelt and Felts were holding a "council of war." Out in the freezing hills, meanwhile, the red-scarfed strikers dodged searchlight beams and crept to new vantage points in readiness for more sniping at dawn.

The opening volleys struck the Tabasco schoolhouse. Most of the women and children had been sent into Trinidad before the attack began but some workers' relatives stayed on, including the machinist's wife, who was preparing breakfast when bullets penetrated the frail wood home and wounded both of her two small children. Now scores of strikers were crowding the ridge above the Tabasco coke ovens. Linderfelt ordered his men to hold their fire while a party of mine guards scaled the snow-draped hillside to reach a machine-gun position. Once this was manned and the gun cranked, portions of the striker force melted away from the crest. They left two Greeks dead. Some of the strikers drifted west, to re-form along the heights above the Victor-American mine at Hastings.

At 6 A.M. a party of four mine guards had set out from Hastings intending to link up with a Berwind contingent. They were at the top of the canyon when a column of some seventy indefinable figures was glimpsed in the snow mists ahead. Three of the Hastings men paused. The fourth, Angus Alexander, carried on alone to make positive identification. He had not gone far when a single rifle shot from the advancing group killed him, and as he fell a powerful burst of Winchester rifle fire hurled rolling echoes into the canyons. The three mine guards bounded back down the canyon, one with a bullet in his foot.

Word that Greek snipers now besieged the Hastings mine was brought to Linderfelt by one of the scouts whose frequent reports and Linderfelt's own deductive imagination provided the material for agitated telegrams which were his contribution to the pressure on Governor Ammons for troops. One ran:

LARGE BODY OF MEN LEAVING AGUILAR TO REINFORCE   REBELS AT LUD-LOW MAKE STATEMENTS THEY ARE GOING TO CLEAN UP BERWIND AND HASTINGS   SITUATION LOOKS HOPELESS   NO HOPE CAN BE EXPECTED EXCEPT ONLY FROM TROOPS

And later:

UNABLE TO GET AMMUNITION IN   WHEN WILL TROOPS GET TO BERWIND PHONE LINE IN POSSESSION OF REBELS

Deference to the wishes of the coal company that had hired him may well have obliged Linderfelt to exaggerate the urgency if need be. But his talk of "rebels" evinced a professional conviction, one in which he probably exulted, that armed insurrection had indeed begun.

Linderfelt's alarums reached the governor through General Chase. Ammons was getting others from owners of small companies blaming his indecision for the violence and demanding to know how much more the situation had to deteriorate before he gave the signal for troops. But the governor hung on, waiting prayerfully for the operators of the big three companies to redraft the letter of settlement.

He and Patterson received the substitute draft at the governor's residence some time after 8 P.M. on Monday. It simply cited the numbers and titles of state mining laws, stated that the companies would continue to obey them, and replaced the offending provision with an offer to take back only those employees whose positions had not been filled and who could prove that they had not participated in any lawlessness. In other words, it was no more than a bland reiteration of the managers' claims to be scrupulously law-abiding and a demand that the union leaders voluntarily surrender the former jobs of miners to strikebreakers. Thomas Patterson knew the unionists would refuse to take the letter seriously and told the operators so. They did not appear concerned.

After they had left, Frank Hayes and John White were sent for. Their reaction to the letter as it now stood for Ammons to sign and the operators to accept surprised nobody. Dropping the recognition issue was one thing. To go this much further in pursuit of a strike settlement would be against all principle. As vehemently as the operators had rejected the first draft of the proposed letter, the union leaders rejected the second.

Now Ammons felt that he had no choice. It was after midnight but delaying the rest his frayed system needed he sent for his adjutant general. Senator Patterson assured him that he need not reproach himself, that he had done all any man could to bring the operators and the union leaders together. Beyond that Patterson had nothing more to offer save a reminder that the governor's order to Chase calling out state troops must make it plain that their only function would be the protection of property and of regular mine employees desiring to work. In no circumstances were they to aid in the installation of strikebreakers.

At 1:30 A.M. on October 28 a haggard Governor Ammons signed the executive order for Chase to police the strike field with such troops of the Colorado National Guard as he thought might be necessary to restore peace and enforce obedience to the law, "It having been made to appear to me," proclaimed the governor, "by the peace officers of Las Animas and Huerfano and other counties of the state of Colorado, by numerous civil officers and other good and reputable citizens . . . that there is a tumult threatened . . ."

9

MARTIAL LAW?

WHAT PRESIDENT WILSON THOUGHT of the Colorado coal miners' strike was indicated in a letter which left the White House for Denver on October 30, 1913. His views mirrored those expressed in Ethelbert Stewart's bluntly worded report pinpointing the cause of the trouble as the wooden intransigence of the operators. The President was "deeply disappointed" in the refusal of the executives to confer with the miners and "the attention of the whole country" had been focused on "the distressing situation in the mines of the Colorado Fuel and Iron Company." Since he was bound to hear from Congress about it, he would like "the responsible officers . . . [to] submit a full and frank statement of the reasons which had led them to reject counsels of peace and accommodation in a matter now grown so critical."

The President's letter was addressed to Jesse Welborn, but the first response it drew was a six-page tirade from LaMont Montgomery Bowers. The President had complained that Ethelbert Stewart was churlishly handled by the operators. According to Bowers, the reverse was true: Stewart was biased and opinionated. All that really bothered the unionists, Bowers went on, was recognition, and to this demand "we shall never consent, if every mine is closed, the equipment destroyed, and the investment made worthless." His company's record and his own motives were of such purity that his blood became overheated when the likes of "this vile woman" Mother Jones captured attention by her vulgar attacks. For the President's edification Bowers enclosed a complete reprint of the slanderous chronicle of Mother Jones's career in bawdyhouses, with certain words and phrases underlined in blue pencil.

Woodrow Wilson referred the letter to the Department of Labor for comment. It took the form of a lengthy and valuable analysis of the strike by the assistant Secretary of Labor, Louis Post. The basic grievances of the miners were interpreted, the antiquated labor policies of the companies exposed, and for good measure Post had something to say in defense of Mother Jones. Raking over references to a career of vice, which, if true, closed twenty-five years ago, was "shocking." Post had himself done a little investigating and learned, for one thing, that the Denver gossip writer who first put the story into print in 1904 was at that time a publicity agent for the Colorado and Fuel Iron Company. Post had only known Mother Jones since 1906. But Secretary Wilson's association with her dated from 1896, Terence Powderly introduced her to the Knights of Labor in 1877, and, like Post, neither of those distinguished labor leaders believed her capable of misconduct.

John D. Rockefeller, Jr.'s only documented reaction after reading a copy of what Bowers wrote to Woodrow Wilson is his own letter to the company chairman in praise of the "energetic, fair and firm way [that] this very trying matter" was being handled, and emphasizing that "we are with you to the end."

J. F. Welborn, at least, had the good taste to keep scurrility out of his correspondence with the White House. He wrote of Ethelbert Stewart's "unfriendliness" and made the usual claims about the well-paid lot of the miners and the infamy of the unionists, but his enclosures were nothing more lurid than copies of recent resolutions passed by the Denver chamber of commerce and the real-estate exchange absolving the coal companies of blame for rising fuel prices.

The comments on Welborn's letter were supplied by Ethelbert Stewart in a characteristically bold indictment of the mine executives: The Colorado struggle was a strike by modern labor against outdated and absentee ownership, the only fundamental issue being whether or not the operators would agree to some kind of negotiation. Their recalcitrance had frozen them into a position totally foreign to contemporary practices of industrial democracy and collective bargaining. Stewart denounced the contention that the workers were satisfied.

> Theoretically, perhaps, the case of having nothing to do in this world but work, ought to have made these men of many tongues, as happy and contented as the managers claim . . . To have a house assigned you to live in, at a rental determined for you, to have a store furnished you by your employer where you are to buy of him such foodstuffs as he has, at a price he fixes; to have a physician provided by your employer, and have his fees deducted from your pay, whether you are sick or not, or whether you want this particular doctor or not; to have churches, furnished ready-made, supplied by hand-picked preachers whose salary is paid by your employer; with schools ditto, and public halls free for you to use for any purpose except to discuss politics, religion, trade-unionism or industrial conditions; in other words, to have everything handed down to you from the top; to be . . . prohibited from having any thought, voice or care in anything in life but work, and to be assisted in this by gunmen whose function it was, principally, to see that you did not talk labor conditions with another man who might accidentally know your language — this was the contented, happy, prosperous condition out of which this strike grew . . . That men have rebelled grows out of the fact that they are men . . .

Stewart concluded by asserting that it must be impressed upon the coal managers that "feudalism is no longer acceptable." But on this score the likelihood of their improved vision dwindled with General Chase's annexation of the Trinidad coalfield. Karl Linderfelt right to the last minute played his part of a field commander holding a precarious position against imminent onslaught by overwhelming hordes. At 10:15 on the morning of November 1 a scout dashed into his headquarters with news that the "rebels" had halted 700 yards away and General Chase's infantry and cavalry were in sight, marching toward Berwind. When the troops arrived, Linderfelt was issued a lieutenant's uniform and given command of Company B, Second Infantry.

Under Colorado law the importation of miners during a strike was not prohibited so long as they were informed in advance of the existence of a strike. But Ammons, while empowering the militia to protect local miners who wished to return to their jobs, had ordered Chase to keep strikebreakers out. Thus the governor's policy went somewhat beyond his basic obligation to enforce the law and suppress violence. It reflected Thomas Patterson's influence and represented evidence that Ammons had not yet entirely truckled to the mineowners. But Patterson and similarly minded colleagues formed a relatively weak counterbalance to the powerful pressures that the mineowners could exert on the governor. His ban on strikebreakers would not be tolerated indefinitely.

Chase's military regime got off to a promising start with a show of fraternization and pageantry. He moved into the area with two partially mobilized infantry regiments, three troops of cavalry, a detachment of field artillery, the signal corps, and the hospital corps. Totaling 931 men, these units were divided into two base camps with one located on the outskirts of Trinidad and the other at Walsenburg. As directed by Governor Ammons, the general ordered all unauthorized persons in the strike zone disarmed. He drove out to Ludlow, met Lawson, who was accompanied by John McLennan, District 15 president, and Frank Hayes, and secured their promise to hand over all the colony's weapons.

Lawson had been having a difficult time of it. He felt no need to apologize for the shooting required to force the retreat of a train everybody had assumed was bringing gunmen to strafe the tents. But this success, not to mention the liquor some had got their hands on, had intoxicated many of the strikers, and for another tense twenty-four hours Lawson's leadership had teetered on a razor's edge. At the same time, news of the approaching militia had inflamed the tempers of those who remembered 1904, when striking miners were torn from their families, loaded in boxcars for

Kansas, Texas, and New Mexico, and dumped in the middle of prairies many miles from shelter.

It was no mean triumph for Lawson to have restored some stability to the colony in time for General Chase's arrival. And when the militia detail sent out from Trinidad concentrated on a plateau south of Ludlow, nothing more militant was registered on the strikers' part than an improvised brass band playing "Marching through Georgia" and "The Battle Cry of Freedom."

The occasion in fact developed into one of such picturesque appeal to Chase's fancy, suggesting a generous conqueror rewarding homage due from pacified aliens with a sophisticated show of military pomp and might, that he later described it as "memorable." He sent his infantry, cavalry, and field artillery parading in full regalia around the tents while "little children in white, as for a Sunday School picnic" sang and waved American flags and cheers rose from the colony's foreign-born, "many in strange Greek, Montenegran, Servian and Bulgar costume." The festive atmosphere soon evaporated when Chase's subordinates got down to business and ordered the surrender of anticipated hundreds of weapons. Just thirty-seven rusting rifles were brought out of the Ludlow tents; when the lieutenant in charge of the militia detail refused to believe they were all that the strikers had, someone stepped forward and gravely added a child's popgun to the pile.

That the honeymoon lasted for any measurable number of weeks again reflects credit on John Lawson, who before returning to Denver had sternly enjoined the strikers to refrain from provoking the militiamen or furnishing any pretext for misunderstanding. It was equally a tribute to the good sense of Captain Philip Van Cise, the Denver attorney in command of Company K, now bivouacked across the railroad track facing the Ludlow colony. Van Cise sent his occasional search parties into the tent city for hidden guns, but he also encouraged the best of terms between his men and the strikers, resulting in conferences, shared meals, and baseball games, in general a kind of peace that seemed too good to last.

It was, in any case, confined to Ludlow. The setting for the latest savagery was the former vale of paradise of Ute legend in the shadow of the Spanish Peaks. On November 8 an Oakview miner, William Gambling, in the town of La Veta to have an aching tooth treated, was pestered before and after his visit to the dentist by strikers seeking his membership in the union. He declared his wish to remain independent and begged them to leave him alone. At noon Gambling boarded the mail hack for Oakview. It was intercepted outside town and Gambling chased back by strikers brandishing guns and urging union membership, "only one dollar." Shaking them off, Gambling reached a telephone office and called the mine for an escort. Three mine guards and a chauffeur rode in to pick him up. The strikers left town first and settled in ambush behind a rude fort of railroad ties where the highway curved uphill three miles west of La Veta. Their fusillade struck the automobile as it rounded the bend. The driver, a youthful part-time employee working his way through college at Colorado Springs, died instantly. Leaping from the vehicle for cover, all three mine guards fell mortally wounded. Only Gambling survived, crawling with leg wounds to a distant ranch house.

Eight striking miners in the Walsenburg area, including four brothers, were arrested for the murders after militiamen found a pile of Winchester, Savage, and Remington rifles under a table in the brothers' house. The prisoners were handed over to Sheriff Jeff Farr.

The arrests did nothing to assuage Governor Ammons' alarm and for the first time he threatened to call for federal troops to suppress the lawlessness in his state. Somewhat anticlimactically, the governor charged Roady Kenehan with partial responsibility for the renewal of bloodshed because he had omitted to sign certificates of indebtedness for the militia, whose maintenance in the field was costing $4000 a day, before going off to the American Federation of Labor convention in Seattle as a delegate from the blacksmiths' union. "Kenehan is the one man whose stand threatens the crippling of our militiamen," Ammons declared, and called upon businessmen to furnish the state with the necessary credit until a mandamus against the watchdog of the treasury could be secured by the state Supreme Court.

At the same time Ammons wrote confidentially to General Chase quoting Ed Doyle's condemnation of the La Veta outrage as unjustifiable from every standpoint. This was Ammons' way of coaxing favorable response from the general to his anxious warnings against a show of partiality toward the coal companies and the military enlistment of mine guards and Baldwin-Felts gunmen, whose effect upon the miners was as a red rag before a bull. But Ammons was wasting words. Executive hints and advice were useless in curbing a general who, forever proud of his performance at Cripple Creek in 1903-4, now presumed the state to be in yet greater danger and himself called upon once more to save it. Touring his area of command on horseback or in transport furnished by the Colorado Fuel and Iron Company, issuing directives in battlefield jargon and signing them *Commanding General, Military District of Colorado*, John Chase was too happy in his element to heed anything less from Denver than firm, peremptory orders.

Chase was at nobody's bidding but the operators'. Circumstantial evidence at least supports the charge that their attorneys made deals with the militia virtually putting it at the companies' disposal. An unhealthy relationship between troops and mine management could not be missed by anyone with eyes. The miners had good cause to complain that the state militia's real function was the suppression of their activities, the protection of coal properties, and reinforcement of mine guards. Vehicles belonging to the CFI parked regularly outside the Columbian Hotel in Trinidad, where General Chase set up his command post. Troops were quartered in company buildings and furnished company supplies ranging from maps to mules. When Roady Kenehan held up their pay, the Colorado Fuel and Iron Company made loans to impoverished militiamen. The operators cashed the certificates of indebtedness issued to the militia and the CFI alone paid out up to $80,000, reimbursable with interest by the state.

It is almost tradition for merchants and businessmen to aid the comfort and convenience of troops billeted in their district. And it makes logistical sense for a field commander to court the local elements in possession of the most resources. But this was no conventional military situation. Even those militiamen sympathetic to the striking miners or without particular feelings either way had perforce to favor the mineowners who provided their sustenance. To the strikers, instances in broad daylight of intimate liaison between the troops and the mine management smacked of an open conspiracy against them. Where Chase was concerned, the suspicions were totally justified. The officially stated purpose of the militiamen in the strike zone — to disarm both sides and keep the peace — was in the general's mind merely a formal pretext. As far as he and his closest officers were concerned, this was a combat situation where businessmen were their rich and embattled allies against organized labor, the common foe.

Chase clashed almost immediately with the prounion district attorney of Las Animas County, John J. Hendricks. Four prisoners whom the militia had arrested were released by the civil authorities and Chase telephoned Hendricks demanding to know the reason. Before Hendricks could finish explaining, he was astonished to hear hysterical threats that a militia patrol would be on its way to arrest him and his staff. The general's point, once he had recovered enough self-control to state it, was that martial law invested him with supreme powers in the affected zone to arrest and release as he saw fit. This argument was to be employed frequently thereafter to justify promiscuous arrests, detention without charge, and other variations of trampled civil liberty, yet whether martial law actually existed was a mystery left unsolved.

The obvious place to seek clarification was the statehouse, but the governor's reply when Hendricks wired left him more mystified than ever:

GENERAL CHASE WAS DIRECTED TO ADOPT ALL LEGAL METHODS NECESSARY TO RESTORE ORDER AND MAINTAIN LAW   PLEASE CONSULT HIM

Hendricks tried again:

YOUR TELEGRAM FAILS TO GIVE THE DESIRED INFORMATION   HAVE YOU AS GOVERNOR PROCLAIMED MARTIAL LAW IN LAS ANIMAS AND HUERFANO COUNTIES

Ammons replied as before: consult the general. On November 15 Chase served the district attorney a peremptory notice announcing that all persons arrested as military prisoners would be subject to his pleasure. Five days later Hendricks was still wondering by what means he was supposed to know who were or were not military prisoners when Chase removed the necessity by creating his own tribunal to prosecute them.

The general had the remarkable gall later on to describe his "military commission" of seven officers including a judge advocate, Major Edward Boughton, an attorney for the metalliferous-mine owners of Crippled Creek, as no more than a "kindly and human device for the sole purpose of minimizing the possibility of error in judgment attaching to the incarceration of civilians." What it proved in effect was a dangerous infringement upon civil processes, and labor groups all over the state denounced the general's dictatorial assumption of judicial power and Elias Ammons' weak acquiescence.

In Denver, meanwhile, on November 13, a group of editors representing more than a dozen Colorado newspapers met at the Brown Palace Hotel on the invitation of John C. Shaffer, a Chicago publisher who had just bought out the Rocky Mountain *News* from Thomas Patterson. The announced purpose of the one-day session was to help the editors get a better view of the strike and with luck elicit from them some means of ending it. The big operators presented their usual formidably united front consisting of Osgood, Welborn, and Brown. L. M. Bowers, as Rockefeller's personal agent, had made it a rule to stay clear of such interviews and confrontations. The three striking miners picked almost at random from the coalfield to present the strikers' case to the editors lacked rhetorical eloquence — one had only just started to learn English — and their accounts of servitude and injustice were limited and undramatic. Osgood, elected perhaps by virtue of his seniority as the executives' spokesman, delivered a speech of enormous length that could without strain have been condensed into a simple confession of fear that recognition of the United Mine Workers would give the union control of the coal mining industry. When Osgood finally sat down, two or three editors drew attention to the unfair contrast between the brief and halting remarks of a trio of uneducated miners and the prolonged oratory of the experienced industrialist. They raised a motion that a more adequate and knowledgeable union spokesman be invited. This was adopted, and someone telephoned for John McLennan, District 15's president, at which point the operators stalked out.

After McLennan had arrived and made his speech, the editors named a resolution committee, which recommended the granting of strike demands for an eight-hour day, check-weighmen, the right to trade freely, and the general enforcement of state laws. These were the safe recommendations. Union recognition, a 10 per cent wage increase, and established rates of pay for dead work were brushed aside. Any miner could fix his own wage by the amount of work he accomplished, reasoned the committee, and consequently the wage issue was more or less an individual responsibility. The editors then called for an immediate end to the strike, with miners guiltless of law violations reinstated in their jobs. Participants in strike violence should face a military tribunal. The statement, with three editors dissenting, backed the militia and supported whatever police action Governor Ammons thought necessary.

Predictably, all this was embraced by the coal managers and rejected by union officials. The one useful result of the editors' conference was to reveal a tactic in the companies' campaign against the governor's prohibition of the importation of strikebreakers. Their joint reply to the editors ended: "When the operators . . . are not interfered with in employing men to replace those now on strike or who left before the strike . . . and are enabled to operate their mines under normal conditions . . . on the open shop principle, which has prevailed in Colorado for more than thirty years, we will put into effect the scale of prices for coal heretofore prevailing."

Ammons refused to take the hint and left the ban on strikebreakers undisturbed. As L. M. Bowers wrote testily to John D. Rockefeller, Jr., "The Governor hobnobs with Hayes, Lawson, McLennan and the rest of the gang, and either refuses or begs for more time to . . . protect the operators in bringing in outsiders to replace those who have left the state and those engaged in murderous assaults whom we refuse to take back under any circumstances."

The day of the editors' meeting, Governor Ammons filed a suit in the state Supreme Court for a mandamus to compel Roady Kenehan to audit and adjust claims for military expenses in the coalfield and approve certificates of indebtedness issued in payment of claims. Kenehan was back in Denver two days later amplifying his stand, or rather his admitted posture of "sitting on the lid." By no interpretation was it a challenge to the governor's authority. Instead, the auditor explained, it was based on a technical legality providing for the payment of the troops from the general fund except in certain cases, none of which was involved in the present strike.

This was one of those occasions when Ammons would have sworn that his auditor had a head as hard as the anvil he once hammered. The governor was in the middle of a nerve-wracking week. Reports from Washington of conferences between President Wilson and the Colorado delegation in the U.S. Capitol increased the likelihood of Congressional investigators invading the state, and the governor shuddered to think how Denver business-men would react. At the same time, despite his warnings to General Chase, strike leaders were bitterly complaining on November 16 that their old Baldwin-Felts enemies were being enlisted into the National Guard. But the administration's penury worried Ammons most of all. Though the banks had agreed to take certificates, someone in the state government whose identity remained unknown privately warned them that they would never be repaid. Some of the pledges were promptly canceled.

Things were becoming intolerable. "The coal strike must come to an end," desperation drove Ammons to declare. "I care not by what means." On November 19 he sent off telegrams simultaneously to President Wilson and the Secretary of Labor describing the strike situation as critical and "growing worse hourly," and he pleaded for the secretary's personal intervention. William Wilson was traveling, and Ammons' wire reached him on the Overland Limited at Wells, Nevada. His immediate message to the White House asking if he should go to Denver as requested crossed with the President's telegram advising him to do just that.

Secretary Wilson had no illusions about his ability to solve the governor's dilemma single-handedly. He wired John White, the union president, and John D. Rockefeller, Jr., inviting their cooperation. He also applied to the Standard Oil Company and ought not to have been surprised by its curt disclaimer of any concern or influence in the matter. Rockefeller's telegram ran to three pages and demolished any real hope the secretary entertained for help from that quarter. The affair was wholly in the hands of the executive officers who "have always been quite as solicitous for the well-being of employees as for the interest of stockholders." Their refusal to confer with strike leaders "meets with our cordial approval and we shall support them to the end." The men had left their jobs "due simply to their fear of assault and assassination" and Governor Ammons had only to "protect the lives of the bona fide miners to bring the strike to a speedy termination." It was a businesslike and unequivocal statement of the problem and solution and, if Rockefeller meant every word of it, spoke unhappy volumes for the credence which he gave to pronouncements from the Boston Building in Denver.

Secretary Wilson pressed forward with plans he had formed to get operators and strikers' leaders face to face almost the minute his train steamed into Denver's Union Station. That afternoon he made an agreeable impression with a luncheon address before the chamber of commerce, which from Ammons' standpoint, at least, was an encouraging augury. The governor happened to be breathing somewhat easier because Roady Kenehan had just been pried off the lid by a judgment of the Colorado Supreme Court ordering him to issue the certificates of indebtedness.

The operators had strong reservations about Wilson's visit. L. M. Bowers expected the worst because of the secretary's unionist past. Also, Bowers was smarting under a Presidential rebuke. "I can only say this," Woodrow Wilson had written him on November 18, "that a word from you would bring the strike to an end, as all that is asked is that you agree to an arbitration by an unbiased board." It was a request the President thought not unreasonable, "conceived in the spirit of the times," and which he backed with the "greatest earnestness and solemnity."

The President had no cause to doubt that his letter, which Bowers was privately to denounce for dodging the essentials, had been directed to the most appropriate quarter. When Bowers took occasion to notify the company officers in New York of the physical wear and tear on Jesse Welborn due to the strike, he alluded to Welborn as the acknowledged leader among the Denver operators. But according to prevalent opinion at the Department of Labor, based on reliable intelligence from Denver, the real force in the Boston Building was LaMont Montgomery Bowers, deferred to by Welborn, trusted devoutly by Rockefeller — "the one man," Louis Post had told the White House, whose "single word" could settle the strike. Bowers was to plea that sickness kept him on the sidelines throughout the trouble, although when questioned about his control over Welborn he bragged of how he could have made things "pretty hot" for him.

Instead of ruling out involvement in the strike, Bowers' ill-health was aggravated by it. Three months after the walkout he had told Rockefeller that only by quitting entirely could he anticipate a needed rest, that he was tormented by insomnia, indigestion, and nervous dyspepsia brought on by worry. The evidence materially suggests that if Bowers did not mastermind the operators' side of the coal strike his whims and prejudices swung a lot of weight in Denver and beyond question swayed willing minds at 26 Broadway. "We are profoundly distressed," wrote Rockefeller after reading a batch of one-sided accounts Bowers had sent him, "that such disorder, suffering and bloodshed should result from the action of the labor leaders."

One week after Rockefeller wrote that letter, and on the same day on which William Bauchop Wilson arrived in Denver with the President's mandate to restore industrial peace to Colorado, an outbreak of bloodshed in Trinidad had all the appearances of a planned execution.

FEDERAL INTERVENTION

GEORGE BELCHER, regarded as a likable fellow by his colleagues on the Baldwin-Felts payroll, was a detestable thug to the miners and, like Walter Belk, surely a marked man since the day the pair had shot down Gerald Lippiatt. The elimination of both detectives was often discussed among the strikers, not as murder but an act of war or retributive justice. It is unlikely that anybody at union headquarters in Indianapolis was involved in the planning and no serious evidence was offered in support of the attempted incrimination of Lawson, Doyle, and other prominent leaders in the strike field. The testimony provided by jail-cell confession, courtroom hearings, and in private documentation points to a rather clumsy plot on the lowest levels of the miners' organization.

Two Italian strikers named Louis Zancanelli and Mario Zeni were each given $25 in a Trinidad saloon and promised $1000 more if they killed the Baldwin-Felts pair. According to Zancanelli's subsequent confession, the men who offered them the job were two familiar local organizers, Anthony McGary and the one-eyed Sam Carter. The Italians were given a heavy revolver and five cartridges. Their dual target was narrowed to Belcher, and to assist them in deciding where the gun should be aimed, information was also vouchsafed that the detective went nowhere without wearing a steel bulletproof vest. For some reason Zeni backed out of the deal. Zancanelli shadowed Belcher for three days. About 7:30 P.M. on November 20 Belcher emerged from Hausman's Drug Store on Commercial and Main and started across the street toward the Coronado Hotel, where the Baldwin-Felts men roomed. Almost in the middle of the thronged intersection some-one crept behind the detective and fired. The bullet entered Belcher's brain, and as he fell his slayer threw the gun aside and ran, vanishing into an alley. Zancanelli was arrested that same evening and turned over to the militia.

While General Chase's cavalry swept through Trinidad's tilting streets, ostensibly to suppress any outbreak following George Belcher's murder, union officials moved fast to get Carter and Mc-Gary out of town. An automobile that would not be connected with the union was bought in a hurry and the two organizers were driven 130 miles east to Lamar, near the Kansas border, where they boarded an eastbound train at the Santa Fe depot. Carter and McGary were never arrested. Zancanelli meanwhile was vigorously questioned by Chase's judge advocate, Major Bough-ton. The interrogation lasted five days, at the end of which Boughton secured a confession by convincing Zancanelli that the union intended to abandon him. The militia also jailed Zeni and put him through forty-four days of sleeplessness, humiliation, and mental torture in an unavailing effort to extract corroboration of Zancanelli's story.

The sanguinary vendetta in the coalfield added fresh urgency to Secretary Wilson's labors in Denver. He had managed to per-suade the strike leaders to stop harping on union recognition in exchange for his promise to try and secure the operators' approval of an arbitrary committee to deal with miners' grievances at peri-odic intervals. On Governor Ammons' earnest request and under some newspaper pressure, the coal operators accepted Wilson's invitation to meet with three of their striking employees on the understanding that union recognition would not even be men-tioned. The conference was set for the morning of November 26 and if L. M. Bowers' words written that same week were anything to go by, the secretary could have saved himself further trouble and taken the next train back to Washington. Bowers described the United Mine Workers officials as now desperate, seeking escape from an untenable situation without disgracing themselves before their membership. By violating reason and common decency they had attracted public attention and this Bowers thought all to the good, for it aroused patriotic Americans against unions of every stripe. Bowers foresaw the open shop as a major political issue, with businessmen combining to make candidates for public office reveal where they stood on it, woe betiding anyone who wavered.

Having given the young Rockefeller the benefit of his political acumen, Bowers proceeded to educate President Wilson. Labor leaders were organizing everywhere to destroy the open shop and if their attacks were not resisted on the all-important Colorado front the way would be paved for national disaster. Writing thus, Bowers hoped Woodrow Wilson would read between the lines and perceive the real message: Federal intervention in the Colorado struggle giving the merest favorable nod to labor would be unwelcome and politically unwise.

The success of the meeting arranged by William Wilson was also threatened by developments in the strike zone. The hunt for Anthony McGary, wanted in connection with the murder of George Belcher, had spread beyond Colorado and Kansas into Iowa, McGary's native state. Because of a postman's confusion, a letter addressed to the wanted man had come into the possession of an attorney of the same name who lived in Des Moines. It was opened and read: ". . . just informed . . . that the accused in the Belcher killing had a meal ticket on him signed by you." The letter was signed *Ed Doyle*. It was turned in to the Colorado National Guard and Doyle was seized in Trinidad, hustled before General Chase's military commission, and asked about McGary's whereabouts or alleged complicity in the crime. When Doyle refused to answer, Major Boughton ordered him locked up until he decided to talk.

The meeting in Denver began at 10:30 A.M. in a room adjoining the governor's at the statehouse. "I hope to see the strike ended twenty-four hours after the sides get together," Governor Ammons said, a forlorn hope by noon when the news of Doyle's arrest was received. The strikers' representatives returned at 2 P.M. from a midday adjournment, during which union officials had got in touch with them, and refused to proceed until steps were taken to secure Doyle's release. Hurried calls were placed to Trinidad. Chase's first response was evasive and even after speaking with Governor Ammons the general professed to believe that he had convinced him of good grounds for Doyle's detention. In Denver the abrupt likelihood that Wilson's conference would fall apart before it could get started jolted Governor Ammons out of his ambiguous cast for once and his next telegram to Chase, while inexplicably short of a positive command, advised Doyle's immediate release. Only then did the meeting get under way.

It lasted fifteen hours. Facing the usual three operators, Welborn, Osgood, and Brown, were two former employees of the CFI and one who had worked for Osgood's Victor-American Company. Under Secretary Wilson's prompting, Governor Ammons drew up a proposal for settlement which acknowledged that recognition of the union was the only "insurmountable obstacle." The other difficulties were broadly covered by existing law. Ammons called for both sides to end the strike on the basis of complete acceptance of state mine laws and the reemployment of strikers "except where their places have been filled or where they have been guilty of violence or other unlawful acts." In other words, the miners were being asked to surrender the recognition issue and the demand for higher wages and expect nothing from their bosses but a promise to abide by the law. Ammons had tailored his proposals to the operators' views, which were known to have altered not one whit since the activation of the state militia. Inevitably, the miners rejected them. Very probably, the real purpose of the proposals had been to gain time while Wilson worked out his plan for an arbitration board.

What he envisaged was a panel of three men selected by the operators, three by the miners, and one by the six choices. Bearing his own and the governor's signature, the plan went to the operators, who immediately pointed out that the last word had yet to be said on the Ammons proposals since they had not been referred to the rank and file of the miners but only to three representatives acting, the managers charged, under furtive union direction. It followed therefore that Wilson's proposal was out of order.

There is evidence that duplicity was at work. J. F. Welborn confided to one of the CFI's New York directors later that the operators' minds were already made up on the subject of an arbitration board — it was the thin end of a wedge bringing union recognition closer. And they felt sure they knew why the secretary had thought up the idea. Their own tough letters to the White House and the junior Rockefeller's rejection of the secretary's request for cooperation had combined to make the Wilson administration work for any sort of a compromise, "to which we shall never consent," wrote L. M. Bowers. But it was decided to adopt, in Welborn's words, "a more effective way than by absolutely declining to consider arbitration." The more effective way was a stalling strategy. Secretary Wilson had no alternative but to suggest a poll of the striking miners on the first proposal, that put forward by Ammons, and temporarily withdraw his plan for an arbitration board until the results of the vote were known.

The United Mine Workers agreed to the referendum out of respect for its former secretary-treasurer. Massed meetings were called at the tent colonies and the governor's proposal read in English, Spanish, Italian, Slavic, and Greek. On November 30, while awaiting the results in Denver, Secretary Wilson wired the White House that he expected the miners to vote no. So it proved. The strikers were unanimously opposed to the original offer for settlement because of its omission of the recognition and wage issues. The operators then labeled the referendum a "farce" and charged "outside agitators" with telling the miners how to vote. It was made clear to Wilson that further ideas from his direction would be unwelcome. He was equally aware that, although the union was willing to shelve its bid for recognition and submit the entire matter to arbitration, all that the operators would concede was a pious pledge to heed state laws. The secretary packed for Washington. At about the same time, in the Boston Building, J. F. Welborn was composing his report on Wilson's visit for the directors in New York. "We reached no direct understanding; in fact we wanted none as we were almost sure that . . . an understanding between the miners and ourselves . . . would have received the stamp of approval of the officers of the organization and in that way been twisted into an arrangement between us and the organization."

The mineowners talked as if Woodrow Wilson's administration was up to its neck in conspiracy with organized labor to wreck the open shop in Colorado. Bowers claimed extravagantly that hundreds of previously neutral industrialists, editors, and politicians were applauding the coal operators' fight to a finish for industrial freedom against unionist tyranny. The strike was, Bowers now told Rockefeller, "unquestionably called with the approval of Secretary Wilson" and, a week later to Starr J. Murphy, Rockefeller's personal lawyer, he warned darkly that "behind the soft voice of Secretary Wilson is the hand of Esau . . . he is a cunning schemer who, while here, tried to trap the operators into some corner [so] that the labor leaders can claim . . . recognition."

Murphy, more attuned to public opinion in the eastern half of the country, hinted that it might be wise to go along with President Wilson's suggestion for a complete investigation of the dispute. If impartial, it could only convince the public that the operators were in the right. Reacting swiftly to the signs of weakness in the distant directors, Bowers wrote back that the Denver operators were too wide awake to swallow the possibility of an impartial committee named by President Wilson. Both Wilsons were working hand in glove with the United Mine Workers. The President could, if he wished, cease "whipping about the bush" and end the strike in twenty-four hours were he not so afraid of losing the labor vote.

Shortly after the secretary had returned to Washington with word that nothing could be done with the Colorado strike except systematically investigate it, President Wilson renewed his correspondence with L. M. Bowers and informed him of his recommendation for a Congressional investigation. Bowers told Rockefeller that, as a response to his own strong statements, the President's letter was "decidedly weak," one which "no shrewd businessman" would have written, and more or less a bluff because he knew that Congressman Edward Keating of Colorado and others "catering to labor" had failed to interest fellow legislators in holding an investigation and, Bowers concluded, "we are confidentially advised that President Wilson's recommendation . . . will be no more effective."

Bowers' unidentified informant was not reckoning with the resourcefulness of Edward Keating, whose principal campaign promise in 1912 had been to restore constitutional government to the counties of Las Animas and Huerfano. Keating's attempts so far to win approval of his resolution calling for a strike probe had been balked by failure to secure a quorum in the U.S. House of Representatives, where a freshman's image still hobbled him and the auspices for organized labor bloomed less markedly than the fear of radicalism and an infatuation with corporate business. But Keating gambled on a current of popular sympathy for coal miners, which his perception told him the mineowners would in their folly inevitably generate. Beyond this hunch and a lively faith in his ability to enlist White House support by riveting Woodrow Wilson's attention on the scandalous impasse in Colorado, Congressman Ed Keating had very little going for him. But by the end of November he had aroused new interest in the passage of his resolution and his spirited letters to union officials in Denver urged them optimistically to start lining up the witnesses.

Whether a Congressional investigation could get started before conditions in the Trinidad coalfield deteriorated became now a matter of touch and go. Without waiting for the results of the referendum to confirm the failure of the November 26–27 conference, Governor Ammons had yielded to the importunities of the coal managers and rescinded his policy against bringing in strikebreakers. Chase lost no time in issuing instructions for the protection of miners entering the military zone for work, and as if beyond caring about the possible appearances of a deal made with the companies, Ammons publicly hinted that the next move was up to them. "There is no excuse now for high prices," said the governor, "because the mines can be operated."

There has been no conflict of opinion that with this decision the downhill course of relations between strikers and state troops steepened dangerously. J. F. Welborn admitted that while general harmony had existed before the end of November, "As soon as the laborers from outside of the state commenced to arrive and the militia prevented the strikers from interfering with these men going to work, the feeling . . . immediately changed."

In retrospect the inexorable progression of tragedy appears relieved only by Roady Kenehan's irreverant tilts with the militia. Yet these were far from funny to the troops in Chase's command, and the blacksmith-auditor himself was never more serious. Undisguised sympathy for the strikers motivated his forays against the military no less than thrifty instincts. On November 29 a letter he wrote to the Rocky Mountain *News* explained his reluctance to authorize expenditures for the militia in convincing detail: He was determined never to "tolerate or connive in any schemes forcing taxpayers to pay $11 for a single gin fizz, $7 for a single cocktail" or vast sums for officers' shindigs attended by prostitutes for whom the militia furnished transport from and to their houses in "the land of the forbidden." Ten years of such extravagant depravities had left the taxpayers shouldered with debts totaling $1,500,000, the former state auditor having snored on the job. And Kenehan claimed abundant cause why *he* should stay awake: General Chase, now in supreme command, had sat on the military board auditing those outrageous bills.

This was all very well, but the men hurt most by past excesses

and Kenehan's consequent tight-fistedness were militiamen un-
blessed with officers' rank. As winter deepened, the lowly state
troopers on strike duty had a rough time of it. Their shoes wore
through and were not replaced, uniforms practically threadbare
when issued fell to pieces. "Breeches became so unsightly,"
recorded Colonel Edward Verdeckburg encamped near Walsenburg, "many men were compelled to buy overalls to cover their
nakedness." Kenehan's delaying tactics held up payment of their
salaries and, on Thanksgiving Day, 600 guardsmen at the San
Rafael camp outside Trinidad burned him in effigy while the militia band played "There'll Be a Hot Time in the Old Town To-
night." Next morning they sent a petition to Governor Ammons
demanding their pay. In reply he dangled hopes for a payday the
following Tuesday and with poignant truth placed responsibility
for their plight on "circumstances over which I have no control."

The payrolls were ready on December 3, Kenehan planning to
enter the militia camps and pay the troops in person with certificates of indebtedness, but the following day everything was
stalled by Colorado's worst blizzard in thirty years. Snow four
feet deep isolated the southern half of the state from the north.
Strikers' colonies were completely cut off and tents by the score
collapsed beneath the weight of snow and ice. Strikers' families
inured to hardship after ten weeks under canvas on a windswept
plain huddled around thier heavy stoves as the drifting snow
climbed to the ridge poles. A second storm followed the first and
J. F. Welborn wrote to the New York office, "This ought to cause a
good many of the strikers who are living in the tents provided by
the organization to seek comfortable houses and employment at
the mines." Yet it did not.

Perhaps because of the weather, Roady Kenehan got back on
the train for Denver while troops at two of the more remote National Guard outposts were reportedly still unpaid. General
Chase dispatched a sergeant to prevent the auditor from leaving
and there was an inevitable altercation in which other guardsmen

joined. One of them was leveling a pistol at the auditor and about to squeeze the trigger, when Captain W. C. Danks boarded the train in the nick of time and shoved himself between the two.

Kenehan had often accused the militiamen of wasting their earnings on liquor. This time, in a way, he was chiefly responsible. During the long wait for pay some of the soldiers had worked up quite a thirst. A gang of troopers broke into one shuttered saloon in Walsenburg after midnight and helped themselves to whiskey. When the saloonkeeper tried to stop them, they beat him.

The militiamen sobered up in time to escort the first batch of strikebreakers westward into the canyons. The companies had not waited for Governor Ammons to capitulate before initiating the enlistment of strikebreakers. Early in November a CFI sales agent had arrived in Joplin, Missouri, to establish an employment office, then continued east for the same purpose in Chicago, Cincinnati, Toledo, and Pittsburgh, where the recruiting was conducted in a bar. Some of the men who signed up had no idea they were headed for a strike zone. Others were unable to read the purported contracts between them and the companies. Guarantees of $3.08 per day and free railroad passage provided they worked at least thirty days were sometimes enhanced by promises of farmland they could rent for $1.00 a month per acre.

The CFI sales agent shipped more than 100 men from Joplin alone. At the other end of his itinerary the first Pittsburgh shipment left on December 15. Allowing for some who got drunk and vanished when the train stopped at Chicago, a sizable force entered the Trinidad coalfield and precautions were taken against any last-minute defections. Mine guards boarded the train, window blinds were drawn, and doors locked. The CFI admitted that about 800 strikebreakers came into the field. Very likely there were more. As the year ended, 9600 men were reported to be at work. According to the operators, the majority were old employees who had turned their backs on the strike. But in the German-

American Trust Building, Ed Doyle's payroll records still showed 19,300 men, women, and children on strike relief.

The central fact agreed on by the coal industrialists and the union, with separate reactions of hearty satisfaction and quiet dismay, was that there had been no general shut-down in the southern coalfield. Tension in the Boston Building had given way to optimism. "Since we commenced to ship men from the east," J. F. Welborn reported to the CFI executive committee on December 22, "our forces have increased rapidly, and unless some unforeseen interference develops, we should be able to take care of practically all demands on us for coal late in January." The strike and generally unfavorable business conditions had caused a reduction in railroad consumption of coal. Nebraska, Kansas, Oklahoma, and Texas, states that bought most of their coal from Colorado, had stocked up heavily on the eve of the strike and were now buying from the East and South. In sum, the normal demand for Colorado coal could not be expected before late 1914. "There has been no time since the coal strike of 1903–4 when such a strike as we are now experiencing would have injured the Colorado operators less than this season."

At the Merchants Bank Building in Indianapolis the mood was different. Disenchantment with the Colorado strike was setting in. William Green could see the treasury in his charge drained by a strike that apparently had less effect on coal production than the winter weather. Expenditures in the field, not always handled with economy, competence, or even honesty, appeared to be missing the target of financing a struggle to implement the ideals of trade unionism. There were traditional unionists with Scots, Welsh, or Anglo-Saxon names and points of view who had never felt at ease about subsidizing tented colonies of half-literate South Europeans and for whom a good many of the communiqués from Colorado had begun to acquire the flavor of Sicilian feuds and Balkan guerrilla battlefields. For the orderly bureaucrats in Indianapolis it was difficult to keep the Colorado campaign in any clear focus. Lawson's leadership appeared spasmodic. The initiative, at least according to newspaper accounts, often belonged to controversial members like Adolph Germer and Robert Uhlich, the rambunctious anarchist from Saxony whose transfer from the Western Federation of Miners to the United Mine Workers in 1907 had not been accompanied by any improved self-restraint. Stories portraying such "radicals" as union representatives, although in truth they were, gave officers who had inherited John Mitchell's brand of civilized moderation cause to wince.

Even Frank Hayes no longer made eloquent speeches about a fight to the finish and seemed, like others, inclined to pin his hopes instead to public inquiry. "We have a serious situation out here," he wrote to Mother Jones from Trinidad. "The operators are doing everything imaginable to break the spirit of the men." He discussed the effective methods of getting a Congressional investigation launched. "I feel sure it will produce results very favorable to our strike." Since he was writing to Mother Jones and dared not betray so much as a hint of defeatism, the union vice president did not elaborate. Hayes himself returned to Indianapolis after five months of steadily increasing disillusionment in the field.

The first week in December was marked by what the Denver *Express* announced as "the first attempt by capital to destroy all organized labor by means of the antitrust law." The federal grand jury which Judge Jesse Northcutt had demanded and neither Ethelbert Stewart nor the U.S. Department of Justice had been able to prevent, indicted twenty-five members of the United Mine Workers from John P. White on down for maintaining a monopoly of labor and conspiring in the restraint of trade. On the private instructions of the Department of Justice, U.S. District Attorney Harry E. Kelly tried to withhold the issue of arrest warrants. The request was denied. William Green, the union's secretary-treasurer and one of the indicted, hurried off a letter to the U.S. attorney general reminding him that he, Green, was also a Democratic state senator in Ohio and now faced acute embarrassment because of the indictments; by implication, so would the Wilson administration. Taking the view that the whole proceedings came under state rather than federal jurisdiction, all the attorney general could do to save political face was make it publicly plain that the government had no hand in calling the investigation, summoning witnesses, or presenting any of the evidence on which the indictments were based.

Actually, the findings of the grand jury were not all one-sided. They included significant legal confirmation of company malpractice, which was in itself tantamount to an indictment of the operators. State laws had been violated, county officers nominated, elected, and controlled by the companies. The scrip system remained in effect at some properties, miners were obliged to trade at company stores, and check-weighmen were denied. Despite all these charges, no action was leveled against the companies. But neither did the indictments against the unionists ever reach court. District Attorney Kelly, after a long delay, advised the Department of Justice that the indictments could not be sustained and almost two years later Kelly's successor entered a *nolle prosequi* and the indictments were no more.

As the year 1913 closed, plenty of unionists were already under lock and key as General John Chase's "military prisoners." Robert Uhlich, "vowing to change the established order of society," according to Major Boughton, was held in connection with the murder of a mine guard in the battle of late October. "Jim the Greek" Bicuvaris, facing a similar charge, had been brought into Trinidad jail personally by General Chase, who had discovered him wounded in a Denver hospital. Adolph Germer was held in Jeff Farr's jail at Walsenburg accused of buying guns for the union. Judge Northcutt's newspaper praised the Chase-Boughton commission as a fine body of officers and all but boasted of it being the first time in Colorado's history as a state that civil authority was superceded by a military tribunal. On December 6 the commission had passed recommendations on forty-three cases.

All jailed as a result were held incommunicado. Fear or complacency stilled whatever civic protests might have sounded in the
two coal counties, but in Denver the general's military dictator-
ship shocked officers of the State Federation of Labor into calling
a special convention for December 16. Invitations were sent to a
number of nationally famed labor personalities, to Samuel
Gompers, Clarence Darrow, John Mitchell, Eugene Debs. This
worried Governor Ammons all over again, yet still not enough to
destroy his reluctance to upset his adjutant general, and it was
with his customary vagueness that he cautioned Chase to turn
over to the civil authorities "any person found by you to be probably guilty of a criminal offense [and] not one who in your judgment ought to be detained further by you . . ." and only then
"provided it appears to you that the [civil authorities] are able to
cope with the situation." Even Chase could be excused for reading this as nothing but a renewal stamp on the general's carte
blanche.

Some 500 delegates representing nearly half as many unions
gathered in the Eagles Hall, Denver, for the State Federation of
Labor's special convention. High on its agenda were demands for
the recall of Governor Ammons and the retirement of General
Chase. But that morning's headlines gave miners in the audience
something else to think about. A disaster in Garfield County at
the Vulcan Mines, owned by a subsidiary of the Rocky Mountain
Fuel Company and largely manned by inexperienced strikebreakers, had just killed thirty-seven miners. Veteran coal diggers
talked bitterly about the Vulcan's poor safety record. The owners,
on the other hand, were to hint at union sabotage, but unfortu-
nately for such wishful theories Garfield was no company-
controlled county and a coroner's jury ruled the blast to have been
caused by the management's negligence. The Vulcan was to
claim an unexpected victim. Its owner, who had disgusted a number of people by notifying relatives of the dead within twenty-four
hours of the explosion that the company would allow $75 each
toward funeral expenses, was himself suddenly stricken, and

physicians disclosed that while in the mine soon after the accident he inhaled poison gas that affected a system already impaired by worry over the strike. He died in less than a month.

In the Eagles Hall the labor delegates accused General Chase of violating one of the most precious guarantees of the federal and state constitutions by assuming that the militia could supplant civil processes. On the speaker's platform the oratorical temperature fluctuated. There were echoes of moderation. Businessmen were asked "not to drive American workers into the hands of anarchists . . . We have no quarrel with the rich man . . ." But Mother Jones jumped up to make it rousingly clear that she for one despised the rich and would have it no other way, then crowned her performance by challenging the delegates to march with her on the statehouse. They did so early on December 16, over 2000 trudging through Denver's snowbanked streets, someone carrying a Ludlow banner in the lead and a strong Welsh contingent roaring hymns.

Governor Ammons heard them coming and braced himself. The moment he had been told of their intended march he had hastily promised to meet their delegates in the chamber of the state House of Representatives. The delegates in return had agreed not to bombard him with spoken questions. A list of written ones was handed him by Eli M. Gross, cigar maker, vice president of the State Federation of Labor, and a factory inspector in Ammons' administration. To those dealing with Chase, the governor protested that he could not dismiss any officers without legal proof of misconduct. Gross thrust more questions at him and the atmosphere in the chamber tightened. Did he personally agree with men being held incommunicado? It depended on the circumstances, he replied, and was immediately hissed.

"I want to give justice," the governor cried. "You seem to misconstrue what I say. I can tell from the questions." Gross retorted that justice was so rare a commodity in Colorado it could no longer be recognized. Ammons grew restive with the exchange and wanted it ended. With manifest agitation he whispered to

Gross that if the questioning persisted he would leave. The meeting broke up, and in the Eagles Hall that afternoon the very mention of the governor's name was a signal for catcalls and booing.

Resolutions were adopted characterizing Chase and Boughton as military despots and lickspittles for the coal companies, but Ammons had challenged them to present legal proof. A five-man investigation commission with John Lawson as chairman was elected and a letter of authority from the governor to insure the National Guard's aid and cooperation was secured. The commission left at once for the coalfield.

It was close to Christmas. So far, Denver's economy had not suffered significantly as a result of the strike, and its merchants, like those in most big cities across the land, anticipated that Christmas 1913 would be the most prosperous ever. The growth of science and industry was accelerating everywhere, promising abundant material benefits, but also confronting Americans with baffling new dilemmas. Theirs was the generation fated to get an early education in the twentieth century's matchless problems. One of the first harsh lessons was that business expansion and labor unification were potentially disastrous correlatives. On this Christmas Eve in Calumet, Michigan, where the Western Federation of Miners had called out the copper miners, a drunk or an antiunionist put his head into the hall where a concert had begun for strikers' families and screamed *"Fire!"* Seventy-two children died in the panicked rush for the exits.

Christmas was celebrated in the Colorado strike zone. The militia's mess hall at Trinidad was festooned with red and green bulbs donated by an electric light company. The officers ate turkey and pumpkin pie, the band played carols, and General Chase showed off the silver-mounted saddle that some of his officers had given him for Christmas. Fifteen miles away at Ludlow no holiday mood was evident. Many of the women had slipped into a permanent sullenness, a reaction to unfulfilled assurances that the strike would be over before the new year, the bosses beaten. Mary Thomas, who usually sang, was silent. On

Christmas Eve John Lawson drove into the colony with bags of fruit and candy for the children. Mothers made rag dolls out of old clothes. And as it had been on countless previous days, dinner on Christmas Day for the majority of strikers' families was rabbit stew.

Among John D. Rockefeller, Jr.'s Christmas mail was a letter from L. M. Bowers reviewing developments and touching on Governor Ammons' change of policy regarding strikebreakers. "We used every possible weapon to drive him into action." He was then as now hand in glove with the labor leaders "but the big men of affairs here have helped the operators in whipping the agitators, including the governor. Now these fellows [unionists] are cursing him without regard for common decency, so everybody is giving him more or less taffy . . ." Bowers still complained of indigestion and insomnia, but he managed to close on an optimistic note. "I have never known such wide approval by all classes of businessmen as we are getting in our fight for the 'open shop.'" He passed along news that the company was paying the 4 per cent dividends for the last half of the current year on the preferred stock. Then Bowers wished the multimillionaire a happy holiday season.

11

SABERS ON MAIN STREET

ON THE NIGHT of December 30, 1913, Corporal Cuthbertson of the Colorado National Guard set out from the Ludlow railroad depot with a detail and mules to extricate an automobile carrying medical corpsmen which had got stuck in deep snow near the strikers' colony. They had not proceeded far when the corporal's horse tripped over a length of taut double-stranded barbed wire half-hidden by snow and ice. The corporal was thrown and badly hurt. A youth hustled into the depot and brought before Lieutenant Linderfelt, commanding the troop, denied accusations of having set the wire deliberately and for an alibi he named Louis Tikas, leader of the Greeks at Ludlow. Tikas, not long released from solitary confinement in Trinidad jail, was next brought to the depot. Linderfelt declared that Tikas was responsible for the corporal's fall. The lieutenant afterward said he had several times heard Tikas utter threats against the militia. According to the Ludlow postmistress, who was present, Linderfelt struck both prisoners and shouted that he was "running this neck of the woods, not a lot of wops and dagoes."

On the following day a young couple strolling near the Colorado and Southern track was intercepted by "armed and half-drunk" soldiers and hauled before Linderfelt, who cursed them and allegedly identified himself and his officers as "Jesus Christs" who had to be obeyed.

The closest thing to a personal creed elicited from Karl E. Linderfelt was that to get results "you can't go at it with kid gloves." Whether his menacing self-aggrandizement was inborn or acquired during an active soldiering career in sordid wars must be speculated. He was born in Janesville, Wisconsin, in 1877 and at the age of seventeen dropped out of Beloit College, came to Colorado, and joined an uncle mining in Cripple Creek. Linderfelt's father, who apparently died in Paris, was said to have been a professor of anatomy in the Sorbonne. Linderfelt enlisted in the Fourth U.S. Cavalry, served in B Troop throughout the Philippine Insurrection of 1899–1900, and was later to boast that as a scout he participated in more fights and skirmishes than the rest of the troop.

The U.S. Army's expeditionary campaign against Aguinaldo's guerrillas was a frustrating and brutalizing experience. In retaliation for ambush raids, innocent Filipinos were massacred and mutilated in their jungle villages. In the Northern Luzon area, where Linderfelt is known to have seen action, few prisoners were taken and pacification usually meant burning down the primitive homes of the "niggers" and "googoos." It was an unconscionable war, soon forgotten, to be recalled seventy years later in the midst of national breast-beating over a similar unedifying conflict. The Philippine adventure may have been Vietnam's closest parallel in U.S. military history, a Victorian practice run with its own equivalents of body counts, search-and-destroy missions, and the dismemberment of the enemy dead by trophy-hunting victors. It is fair or even mandatory, when considering the odious role given Karl Linderfelt in the Colorado coalfields struggle, to reflect on the nature of the warfare he waged in the Philippine forests fourteen years earlier.

But in addition, Linderfelt joined the ragtag force of foreign mercenaries and Mexican insurgents who followed Francisco Madero across the Rio Grande in revolt against President Diaz. Captain of a handful calling itself the American Legion, Linderfelt engaged in and may have led the premature assault on Juarez, May 7, 1910, in disobedience of Madero's orders. Three days later Mexican provisional authorities in Juarez issued warrants for the arrest of five Americans, among them Linderfelt, on charges of robbery and looting. They were by then safely north of the border, where Linderfelt dismissed the allegations as lies, claimed credit for the fall of Juarez, and complained that he had been swindled of the ten dollars a day in gold promised by Madero for his services.

At the time of the horse-tripping incident, John Lawson and the State Federation of Labor's investigating commission, consisting of three other union officials besides himself, Eli Gross, and a University of Colorado law professor named James H. Brewster, were securing affidavits supporting charges against the militia that included robbery, drunkenness, assaults on children and females, intimidation of strikers, and the infliction of mental cruelty upon military prisoners. (As an admitted example of this last, some militiamen had derived hilarity out of terrorizing Italian and Greek captives by making them "dig their own graves" — actually privy vaults for the soldiers — and carried the prank so far that the victims wrote farewell letters to their wives and children.) Altogether, the interrogators questioned 163 witnesses and took 760 typewritten pages of testimony. Their report was of necessity one-sided since General Chase, in defiance of Governor Ammons' order to cooperate, had notified Lawson that the committee was forbidden to question the soldiers, whose point of view, if required, would have to be obtained from himself. The investigation was not completed when Lawson heard stories about Lieutenant Linderfelt's most recent misbehavior and so starkly were they in keeping with the evidence he had already collected that he wired Ammons right away:

WE HAVE REASON TO BELIEVE THAT IT IS [Linderfelt's] DELIBERATE PURPOSE TO PROVOKE THE STRIKERS TO BLOODSHED   HE HAS THREATENED TO KILL LOUIS TIKAS . . .

It later developed that Captain W. C. Danks, a relatively unobjectionable militia officer, was suggesting about the same time to

Judge Advocate Boughton that it might be prudent to separate Linderfelt from the Colorado National Guard altogether. No notice was taken either of Danks's or Lawson's advice. For that matter, nothing was done about the State Federation of Labor investigating committee's final report. Governor Ammons pigeonholed it with the single observation that the testimony on which it was based was not, after all, sworn.

The National Guard troops were by no means all a bad lot. A drab and unromantic assignment, uncertain pay and little recreation, inadequate clothing, and a set of bullying or stiff-necked officers were not likely to produce the most exemplary conduct in the field. Younger men in particular, many of them college graduates, had soon begun to acutely miss home, studies, jobs, and sweethearts, with foreseeable effects upon their morale. All endured the hostility of the strikers, traceable in many cases to the strike of 1903–4. During a tour of the tented colonies, state Senator Helen Ring Robinson was alarmed to find how wrathfully the deportations of a decade earlier were remembered. They had bred a special hatred, of a kind "that . . . does not die with the objects that caused it, but . . . gathers compound interest."

Some militiamen exulted in their traditional role as targets for the miners' dislike. These were the camp marshals or mine guards recruited into the state National Guard in spite of Governor Ammons' exhortations to Chase. One militia unit alone contained up to twenty-five enlisted mine guards who continued to draw pay from the company. E. H. Weitzel, CFI fuel manager, identified the traffic of militiamen to and from his office as former employees collecting not regular salary but small loans to tide them over until Roady Kenehan loosened his fist. General Chase professed no interest in the situation — "It has been customary for business houses to continue the pay of employees who are serving the state under orders of the governor." If this was not tantamount to contempt for Ammons' express anxieties about provocation in the strike zone, it certainly made manifest the general's total bias.

Not even Chase was so much of a buffoon as to fail to distinguish between payments to a soldier by private companies not involved in the strike and the continued employment of soldiers by the coal operators. Governor Ammons did in fact become aware of the recruitment of not only mine guards but the abominated Baldwin-Felts detectives as well. Yet he took no further action. The deadly liaison between the state militia and the mineowners was permitted to flourish openly.

The striking miners were now self-convinced or persuaded by their field leaders that the governor, defeated in his mediation efforts by the obstinacy of the operators, had escaped from his predicament by throwing in his lot with the forces that had frustrated him. In the union press Ammons became "a spineless tool of the operators." The miners despised him for his weakness while making no allowances for it. They did not know of the private scorn which coal operators also felt for the governor and could not reason that probably no state politician in history had to deal with a more inflexible and reactionary group of powerful capitalists, behind them the vast wealth of the Rockefellers. All that mattered to the miners was that Ammons had capitulated. Thus the presence of the troops symbolized the sway of the coal barons over the state executive. Colorado soldiers were making it easy for scabs and strikebreakers, were jailing friends and relatives, brazenly collaborating with managers and superintendents. The few traces of fraternization flickered out, and as the winter advanced, soldiers drawn from trades, professions, and colleges were released to go home. The quality of the troops, never high, further deteriorated.

Fate had effectively banked the incendiary elements. Almost in relief from contemplation of their miserable strike pay and depressing life in the crowded snowbound tents, strikers and their families lived out the winter nursing, even cherishing, a fatal animus for the militia.

❖

General Chase fancied himself a warlord in occupied territory. That he got away with his insolent harlequinade was because of the confusion over whether or not martial law existed. Even in his calm postgubernatorial years Elias Ammons could not say for sure that he had declared it, vaguely assuming that it obtained automatically with the arrival of the troops in the strike zone. As for Attorney General Fred Farrar, who seems not to have served as a fount of unequivocal advice, his idea was that although Ammons never officially invoked martial law, there was "something which approached it." In other circumstances General Chase's sweepingly no-nonsense approach would have afforded a welcome contrast. As things were, he had been directed by Ammons to use his own "judgment and discretion . . . in conjunction with, or independently of, the civil authorities." Never was there a more complete abdication of civil authority in peacetime to a military commander so temperamentally ill-suited for the sensitive particulars of a labor dispute.

"She seems to have . . . the facility of stirring up and inciting the more ignorant and criminally disposed to deeds of violence and crime . . . [her] speeches couched in coarse, vulgar and profane language . . . The fact that she is a woman and advanced in years she uses as a shield." Thus spoke General John Chase on Mother Jones, whose "shield" he proceeded to prove was no defense against his martial clout. On January 4, receiving word that she was en route to Trinidad, he ordered her arrested the moment she arrived. She got in about 8 A.M. on the Santa Fe line and at 9:30 the soldiers put her on a Denver-bound Colorado and Southern. An armed detail went along to prevent her from detraining at any of the stops.

In announcing the deportation, General Chase threatened to lock up Mother Jones incommunicado if she returned to the strike zone. He also took the formality of justifying his action as military duty, but this was purely for show. Certainly Chase felt no obligation to explain himself to Governor Ammons, who had not been told in advance of the plan to deport the elderly agitator but as expected declared quick support for the general's policy. Colorado was sinking under debt at a rate of $5000 a day, the cost of keeping peace in the coalfields. What Elias Ammons would have refused to condone against anyone disturbing it had become perilously marginal.

Telegrams protesting General Chase's action sped from the Merchants Bank Building in Indianapolis to Pass Christian, Mississippi, where the ailing President Wilson had isolated himself for an extended vacation. About the same time a letter arrived for the President from L. M. Bowers fulminating against "ignorant bloodthirsty anarchists . . . we are satisfied that more than 2000 guns are secreted in the mountains and that there is trouble enough ahead." Solicitous aides would have seen to it that none of these communications was allowed to disturb Wilson's rest and meditation, and in any event Mother Jones was endowed with more than enough cunning and audacity to fight her own battles. Shortly after midnight January 11 she slipped out of Denver and was off south again. She left the train at a stop before Trinidad and showed up at the Toltec Hotel for breakfast. This time Chase in person entered her room to arrest her. She was whirled through the streets in an automobile with cavalry escort and finally lodged under double guard in Mount San Rafael Hospital on the eastern outskirts of Trinidad.

This time there was no question. She had been seized on the flat order of Governor Ammons. It simply made no sense, in his opinion, to spend the state's money and effort on peace-keeping while letting an acknowledged firebrand run loose in the trouble zone. The requirements of humanity as well as logic appeared to be satisfied: She was unharmed, although confined without formal charge and denied visitors, and freedom would be hers the moment she promised to stay out of the strike district. As General Chase worded it, she was detained under "military surveillance" until willing to leave his area of command "permanently." Chase's military prisoners now totaled twenty-seven, most of them union officials.

Ten days after Mother Jones's arrest, miners' wives and sympathizers organized a protest demonstration. All morning the trains brought contingents of women from other parts of the state into Trinidad. Except for a scuffle with some nervous militiamen who ordered a banner reading HAS GOVERNOR AMMONS FORGOTTEN HE HAS A MOTHER? out of the parade, things got under way quietly enough at the railroad depot shortly after 2 P.M. More than a thousand women marched up Commercial Street, swung east on Main, then faltered near the post office. A dense cordon of National Guard cavalrymen, sabers drawn, blocked their path, General John Chase wheeling his horse to and fro before the front rank.

There may have been some initial misunderstanding about the parade route, perhaps a fear that the women were in reality bound for San Rafael Hospital to liberate Mother Jones. Northcutt's newspaper said afterward that they had been warned not to come near the hospital precincts. At any rate, Chase shouted for the women to stop; although slowed, they kept advancing. The general's horse brushed a sixteen-year-old girl and his spurred boot struck her in the breast. The blow was slight, the general's foot set in its stirrup, and it may not have been the vicious kick described afterward by the girl and countless union propagandists. But that was only the beginning. The horse stumbled, some said the animal bolted into a horse and buggy, but whatever the cause, General Chase swayed and fell off.

There was no shortage of witnesses to swear that above the outburst of derisive laughter the general bellowed, "Ride down the women!" His cavalry charged three times. A spectator reminded of Russia and Cossacks testified that Chase, once remounted, spurred his horse into the crowd swinging his pistol right and left. Militiamen tore the U.S. flag from the demonstrators and were promptly thumped by some using signs and banners as clubs. Sabers flashed. A woman was slashed across the forehead, another's ear was almost severed, a third's hands were cut as she spread them protectively before her face. The women retreated west along Main Street. A fifteen-year-old girl who had already felt the blows of a trooper's fists when she laughed at the unhorsed general had her instep smashed by a rifle butt. General Chase explained later that bringing the butt down hard across the toes was an approved and effective tactic in mob control.

The commotion rolled back to the First National Bank at Main and Commercial and the arrests began. Mary Hannah Thomas was grabbed as she made to enter a hairdressing salon in the Opera House blocks, but according to Major Boughton later, she was fomenting a riot. Certainly the tent colony's Welsh spitfire was never one to miss an opportunity for annoying the militia or "Rockefeller's thugs," and by her own admission would assemble Ludlow's children in the vicinity of troops or scabs at the mines for provocative renditions of "Union Forever." Even in more peaceful circumstances Mary Thomas' flaming red hair and good looks would have caused any trooper to give her a second glance. To soldiers ruefully familiar with her saucy hostility she was a most conspicuous target, and, however forcefully swung, a muff can do little against rifles and sabers. Mary Thomas was taken with seven other women to the county jail where, as she proudly recalled nearly sixty years later, she drove her jailors to distraction by singing in Welsh through the cell bars while her two infant children, confined along with her, vandalized the jailhouse bathroom. The Thomases were released after two weeks.

Imagination and the passage of time may have added spice to Mary Thomas' recollection of the cavalry charge along Main Street. If so, it could scarcely compare with what contemporary propagandists did with the incident, as if the bare facts were not enough to discredit General Chase and his troops. The Denver *Express* ran a double headline: GREAT CZAR FELL! AND IN FURY TOLD TROOPS TO TRAMPLE WOMEN. The story began, "A craven general tumbled from his nag in a street of Trinidad like Humpty Dumpty from the wall. In fifteen minutes . . . soldiers with swords were striking at fleeing women and children . . . Then there was bloodshed. The French Revolution, its history written upon crimson pages, carries no more cowardly episode than the attack of the gutter gamin soldiery on the crowd of unarmed and unprotected women . . ." None of this was helpful to strike leaders in the field. In Walsenburg, miners maddened by the accounts of women and children helpless under Chase's whirling sabers, were all for marching on Trinidad and sacking the Columbian Hotel, where Chase ran his headquarters, and Adolph Germer had a difficult time resisting demands that he reveal where the union's guns were hidden.

In Indianapolis the UMW's twenty-fourth consecutive convention had just started. Diminishing zeal for the Colorado strike was briefly revived, momentarily turning into a powerful rage when Frank Hayes leaped to the rostrum to read a telegram just received from John Lawson:

CAVALRY WITH DRAWN SWORDS RODE DOWN A THOUSAND WOMEN AND CHILDREN GENERAL CHASE WHO BECAME SO EXCITED HE FELL OFF HIS HORSE ISSUED ORDERS TO SHOOT THE WOMEN AND CHILDREN AND SHOOT TO KILL MILITIAMEN JAB SABERS AND BAYONETS INTO BACKS OF WOMEN WITH BABES IN ARMS AND TRAMPLE THEM UNDER THE FEET OF THEIR HORSES . . . FEELING IS INTENSE . . . UNION OFFICERS ARE DOING EVERYTHING TO PACIFY THE PEOPLE . . .

Distortions like those Lawson accepted in good faith from alleged eyewitnesses only worked toward opposite effect. Hundreds of strikers felt an overpowering urge to sweep upon the militiamen and, with or without guns, annihilate the lot. Indeed, miners of Segundo, Tercio, and Sopris filtered like a phantom army into Trinidad one night and quietly took up rooftop sniping positions. With General Chase's headquarters lined up in dozens of Winchester rifle sights, every passing hour increased the probability of a massacre.

As peace hung by a fragile thread in the coalfields, far to the east in Washington, D.C., Congressman Ed Keating's tireless efforts to win approval for a Congressional investigation were also at a critical juncture. The realization that not even President

Wilson's wholehearted endorsement of his resolution was enough to free it from limbo in the House Rules Committee had spurred Keating to a recourse, which, if not setting a precedent, certainly flouted tradition. He determined to call a caucus of Democratic members of the House for the purpose of considering the resolution and instructing the Rules Committee to make a favorable report on it. There was a good deal of furtive canvassing for signatures until Keating got the number he required. Members of the Rules Committee registered indignation but the caucus had to be called. Last-minute blocking tactics by Keating's foes came to naught, in part because one of his staunchest allies, Congressman David Lewis of Maryland, chairman of the House Committee on Labor, was a former coal miner since the age of nine, and he drew on his own emotionally gripping reminiscences to urge that the resolution be passed. And it was, on January 27, 1914.

News that the U.S. Congress would thoroughly investigate the situation in southern Colorado was flashed to Denver and relayed to the strikers positioned about Trinidad for attack. The threat receded. It is impossible to say for sure how real it had been, whether the intelligence had in fact narrowly averted a ghastly bloodletting. Only a percentage of the total strike force was involved. They were leaderless, had acted on blind impulse. Rational afterthought might have dispersed them as stealthily as they had assembled. There was, in any case, rebuilding to be done. The night before the news from Washington, a severe windstorm had swept the open prairie between the Spanish Peaks and the Black Hills, flattening scores of tents in every strikers' colony.

12

CONGRESS INVESTIGATES

THE HOUSE SUBCOMMITTEE ON MINES AND MINING began hearings in the senate chamber of the statehouse, Denver, February 9, 1914. Its chairman, Martin D. Foster, was a former physician from Olney, Illinois, and the members included a future Secretary of State, James F. Byrnes of South Carolina. Attorneys for the coal operators and the union were on hand. Major Boughton and Captain Danks represented the Colorado National Guard. Lawyers for both sides were allowed to cross-examine witnesses. At first the committee felt its way forward, as if to forestall any future charges that it had not been scrupulously fair and painstaking.

Russell D. George, the state geologist, gave the congressmen details on coal resources and the extent of their development in the state. James Dalrymple, chief state coal-mine inspector, reiterated a constant complaint that his office was too understaffed to function properly. Edwin Brake, the state labor commissioner, widened the gulf of mutual suspicion between himself and his governor by testifying that coal operators dominated the state politically and flouted state laws with impunity.

There were predictable interruptions from Fred Herrington, a CFI attorney (his brother Cass ran the company's Political Department), objecting to the drift of Brake's testimony when it reflected upon the coal management. Judge Northcutt, general attorney for all three major companies, conserved his cross-examination and causticity for the unionists. Opportunities came thick and fast after James H. Brewster, the legal professor serving as a union attorney, had drawn John Lawson's version of the history of the strike so far. Northcutt leaped at each one, but when he attempted to establish Lawson's presence on the scene of the battle in Berwind Canyon the judge made no headway. Each question coincided with sudden blanks in the union leader's memory. Northcutt abandoned this tack and had better luck when he fastened on Lawson's statement that union organizers in previous years were apt to be killed on the job. The judge challenged him to name a victim, and this time Lawson's memory really let him down. He could only recall one Oberinsky, a union organizer shot dead in a Rugby saloon in 1907 by a pair of Mexicans the saloonkeeper had just thrown out of the place for misbehaving. "On another occasion —" Lawson was about to continue but Northcutt interrupted.

"Just a minute. Are these all the facts that you can recall?"

When Lawson admitted they were, Northcutt struck an exaggerated pose of astonishment. Was this all the witness had on which to base his grave charge that Oberinsky died because he organized miners? The judge asked acidly if Lawson was in Rugby at the time, and the answer was no.

"And you did not see the man killed?"

"No, sir."

"All that you have told us here as to the murder . . . comes from hearsay?"

"Oh, yes. This is all hearsay." Under further questioning Lawson failed to produce the name of a single organizer killed. Northcutt later asked if the United Mine Workers had not been adjudged by a federal court in West Virginia as unlawful. Lawson replied, "I am not surprised at anything in West Virginia."

"You have a great lack of confidence in the courts of West Virginia?" And before Lawson could answer, Northcutt pressed on. "You don't have confidence in courts and officers of the law generally. You believe that you and your organization have a right . . . to take the law into your own hands, arm yourselves . . .

and go out and fight instead of appealing to the court. When did Mother Jones begin to work for the unions?"

"Probably before I was born."

"Have you heard her advise the men to use force in the strikes? Did you hear her at Starkville tell them to use their picks and knives?"

"No, I didn't."

"We will eliminate the word knives. Did you hear her tell them to use their picks?"

"No, I didn't . . . What else would a miner use but his pick?"

"Well, that depends on what he uses it for."

Testifying on the third day of the hearings, Albert C. Felts lifted the veil slightly on the viewpoints and modus operandi of strikebreaking detectives, a profession still as much of a mystery to the American government as to the general public. Felts told without blush how he provided the coal companies with mine guards of whose reputation he knew or cared little. Asked if it was the custom of detectives on coming into a strike field to obtain a deputy sheriff's commission, he said it was because of a necessity for the agents to work in the open with local authorities. He had never found but one sheriff in all the states where his agency operated who refused his detectives a commission. Felts admitted to the procurement of at least four machine guns, their shipment and maintenance financed by the coal operators, the actual remittance being paid him by W. C. Babcock, vice president of the Rocky Mountain Fuel Company, who, it transpired, had also turned over to Felts the automobile rebuilt as the Death Special.

John Osgood's contribution to the education of the congressmen was characteristically harsh and uncompromising. He would never dream of dealing with the UMW. None of his miners needed a wage increase. The eight-hour-day issue was a fraud, the fuss over check-weighmen caused by foreigners' distrust of one another, and the scrip system a harmless form of bookkeeping.

J. F. Welborn's manner in the witness chair was less brusque, but his views on conditions in the mining towns and camps ran along the same lines. He admitted employing Karl Linderfelt as a mine guard before the militia arrived in the strike zone, said he did not know what caused the disaster in the Primero mine in 1910, and told Professor Brewster that refusing to meet with union leaders had not burdened him with any sense of responsibility for subsequent violence and financial loss. He had no time for the miners' union.

"Your time is really taken up in making money, isn't it?"

"I am trying to make a living for myself."

"You . . . get a little more than four dollars a day, don't you?"

"Yes, but I've never enjoyed a salary equal to . . . four thousand or five thousand dollars for a few weeks as reported."

And when Brewster asked if in fact he got fully $5000 for nine weeks, Welborn rejected the question as immaterial. The professor shifted to the subject of safety. Welborn's confessed lack of knowledge of comparisons between fatality rates in the United States and those in mines of other countries led him to accuse the company president of disregarding "his great moral responsibilities and duties toward not merely his stockholders but . . . humanity." Unfortunately for the professor's attempt to focus culpability on Welborn and his company, a few observations from the congressmen's table inclined the discussion into a broader area where federal inquiry was long overdue: the dereliction or apathy of the nation as a whole including those elected to fashion its laws. The accident rate in American mines compared with those overseas was a disgrace, but there was more than enough blame to go around. Congress itself had so shirked its duty that not until four years before had it authorized the creation of a federal Bureau of Mines.

The committee's interval of self-reproach was brief. Its attention turned back to Colorado and Welborn's testimony closed with his emphatic assertion that "peonage does not now, and I am sure never has, existed in the CFI's camps during my connection with the company."

With fattening briefcases the committee transferred its activities to Trinidad, where almost immediately both sides in the conflict made maladroit attempts to intimidate witnesses.

On the day before he was due to testify, James Fyler, the local union secretary and tent-colony paymaster, had made up the payroll in his tent office and was taking a stroll with sixteen other strikers when some twenty-five National Guard troopers surrounded them. Herded up the canyon, they were treated to abusive insults from Lieutenant Karl Linderfelt, who then ordered them against a wall to face a firing squad. This turned out to be another of the militia's little jokes. The riflemen, after their order to fire, were grinningly dismissed and the strikers freed, to be chased down the canyon by soldiers wielding horsewhips and pickax handles. Next day in the West Theater, Trinidad, where the Congressional committee heard testimony, Fyler declared that the incident was definitely connected with his scheduled appearance. And the brutal but not entirely incomprehensible japes of bored and ill-educated soldiery paled in cruelty beside the sarcasm of Judge Northcutt, who, perfectly aware of the middle-aged miner's earlier proud claim to have dug coal since the age of ten, interrupted to ask if he had ever been hazed in college.

The operators' exhibit in the crossfire of charges of intimidation was an Austrian strikebreaker named Prako Burak, who had arrived from Pittsburgh on Christmas Eve and since worked at the Primero mine. One week before the Congressional hearings he was kidnaped near Segundo and ushered to the union office in Trinidad, where he was subjected to four days of harassment and attempted bribery by strikers telling him how he should testify. Their importunities were conducted through a Croat-speaking interpreter identified by the witness only as "Mike."

Names of the alleged abductors had been slipped to company attorneys. At 8 P.M. on February 6 in the West Theater four men in the audience were singled out for Burak's scrutiny. They included Mike Livoda, now District 15's vice president, and Jack McQuarrie, whose successive careers as a Pinkerton agent, Jeff

Farr's undersheriff, and detective for the Colorado and Southern Railroad had combined to make him a useful spy and informer for the UMW, since in 1911 his sympathies had swung to the unionists.

After some delay in the West Theater caused by a flurry of doubts over the credentials of the committee's interpreter, Fred Herrington asked Burak if the four men standing in the two front stalls were among those who had held him captive. Standing on the edge of the stage, Burak peered into the dimly lighted theater. When he shook his head, the company lawyers insisted that the four be brought to within eight feet of Burak and the parquet lights turned up. Still Burak could not positively identify. In the general hubbub that followed, loud hints were thrown that Burak had been mistreated by the other side, too, that his meals had been withheld to influence his testimony in favor of the operators. All that was finally established was Burak's loss of appetite, and the Austrian stepped down after asserting, conceivably with fervor, that he was anxious to get back to Pittsburgh.

Jack McQuarrie's public testimony ended his usefulness to the union as an undercover agent, and almost ended his life, judging by the "Black Hand" letters he received. But he survived and functioned openly thereafter as assistant to Horace Hawkins, Edward Costigan, and other union advocates.

In few other labor conflicts did spies ferret and swarm so busily. Tony Langowski, a member of the union local at Sopris, kept Billy Reno informed on what the strikers were up to from the first week of the work stoppage. A Polish cripple, Langowski had been hired for the job by Montgomery Massingdale, who as deputy sheriff, constable, militiaman, and mine guard had upheld law and order in the Trinidad area since the days when he had ridden posse with Reno in pursuit of train bandits. Massingdale received $3 a day from the CFI for his services. The company also paid Langowski and the other informers Massingdale hired. At the same time, Langowski appears to have done surveillance work for the union, for which he received $5 a day. It was not a case of his being a double spy, he told the subcommittee, but of saving lives on both sides. He had volunteered to testify after learning that his treachery was known to union officials. Evidently the union had not chosen to exploit the discovery as in the case of a former president of District 15, who, privately incriminated as a spy for a detective agency, remained on union rolls, unaware that he was being "used to the best advantage." After fearfully testifying, Tony Langowski vanished from the Trinidad coalfield.

Charles Snyder was a union man for fifteen years but at some point had defected to the company side. He worked as a mine guard for an undisclosed period prior to August 1912, and the following year he came to Ed Doyle in the German-American Trust Building with stories of how dastardly the operators had treated him and with what remorse he rued having been a scab. At length Snyder successfully pleaded the sincerity of his penitence. On Doyle's orders he bought a couple of automatic pistols and a box of shells on Larimer Street and headed south to Trinidad, where he attached himself to John Lawson as a bodyguard. Lawson seems not to have taken him seriously as one. Snyder was usually to be found performing routine chores, including gun-running. What the unionists never suspected was that after March 1914, and quite possibly for a time before, Snyder drew regular paychecks from the Baldwin-Felts agency.

Throughout the early months of 1914 spies and sundry agents were offering their services to both sides, often at the same time. One unsigned penciled note found in Ed Doyle's papers begins, "I can get a pass or letter of introduction to any of the superintendents or foremen any place from Linderfelt. He wants me to join his outfit and help him get rid of the Baldwin-Felts men in the [National] Guard and mines." This anonymous communicant also disclosed a proposition made by "the big three," presumably Osgood, Welborn, and Brown, to Linderfelt, inviting him to take charge of secret surveillance operations in the district, in which event they would fire all the Baldwin-Felts detectives. "The big three told Linderfelt that the Baldwin-Felts had not lived up to their contracts and that their notoriety was influencing public opinion against the operators." There is another "secret agent" letter to Doyle — "Reno says he is disgusted with the Baldwin-Felts work." But Linderfelt was undecided on the operators' offer because of the trouble brewing in Mexico and his wish, should the United States intervene, not to be tied up in Colorado. This intelligence was probably reliable. The lieutenant, by virtue of his experiences as an insurrectionary leader under Madero, regarded himself as an expert on that country and its problems. Doyle's informant was evidently someone in the company's inner offices trusted enough to socialize with the "big three" at the Denver Club, hence a request to Doyle for additional funds to meet the costs of "incidentals and drinks."

Even Governor Elias Ammons received information, solicited or not, from detective agencies. A letter to the governor dated March 21, 1914, written under the letterhead of the Globe Inspection Service ("Investigations conducted throughout the U.S., Canada and Europe") relays a report from an agent in Trinidad describing the operators' offer to Linderfelt "under a contract of $400 a month for four years and expenses after the troops are withdrawn." It is hardly coincidental that the sum exactly equaled General Chase's salary. Governor Ammons was also furnished details of arms bought by the union ("Mr. Doyle is purchasing Maxims Silencers"), informed that half a dozen Baldwin-Felts gunmen from West Virginia were serving under Lieutenant Linderfelt's command, and advised that further private communiqués would be sent to the governor "over our code signature 'Heron.'"

The prevalence of eager informants, hired or otherwise, the frequency of shifting loyalties, and a policy of continuing to employ and exploit known traitors rather than exposing or getting rid of them, must have made it extremely difficult for both sides to regard anyone with uninhibited trust.

The unfolding of somber events was enlivened by another performance from Roady Kenehan, like a jester dancing in and out of a funeral cortege. He reappeared in Trinidad late in February to investigate the National Guard's purchase of 270 horses at an approximate total cost of $25,000. Major Boughton advised his officers to ignore the auditor's subpoenas and was thereupon accosted by Kenehan, who "began to bellow like a wild animal and in general act insane." Boughton sarcastically reminded him that since the hall they were in was empty he ought to restrain himself until he could get an audience. Kenehan threatened to hold up payment on the contracts if he got no cooperation from the militia but this had no effect. The National Guard pointedly ignored Kenehan's presence with a show of business as usual. Displays of horsemanship, bayonet duels, and mounted drill at San Rafael were followed by a ball at the Columbian Hotel to which the blacksmith-auditor was not invited. He left for Denver on March 1 after a clash with the guard officer who had originally transacted the horse deal. They cursed each other and had got to the point of squaring off for blows when Kenehan remembered he had a train to catch.

In Denver the auditor refused to issue necessary warrants, and the horse traders were not the only merchants left empty-handed. Into Kenehan's office poured a stream of pitiful letters from near-bankrupt lodging-house keepers and laundry operators for payment of bills incurred by the soldiers, but these too Kenehan refused to settle, blaming General Chase for not having provided him with details of expenditures, and piously aghast at the thought of the enormities to be answered for by "whoever is responsible for this condition."

Kenehan reviewed his latest assault on the National Guard with characteristic heat: "They stalled the whole time I was down there . . . They dodged and crawled and finally insulted me." The militia were a bunch of lawless frauds, he told Ammons, and he warned the governor that unless he did his duty by making the National Guard toe the line then he, Kenehan, would do so. Experience had long trained Ammons into meeting his auditor's wrathful outbursts with soft words of admonition while seeking the facts of each case elsewhere. And anyway, these days Governor Ammons was paying less heed to his administrative officers than to his adjutant general, to all intents and purposes the person he now trusted the most.

General Chase was getting a salary of $400 a month and expense money up to $175 per week. He headed a state militia which military observers in other parts of the country looked upon as straight out of a comic opera. Its use of federal equipment in the suppression of strikes had already raised hackles in the War Department at Washington. The guards' field force of 695 men was commanded by no fewer than 397 officers. According to reports from the state treasury office, in a six-month period a total of $685,000 had been spent for guard duties at properties yielding an aggregate return of $12,378.67 to the state treasury in annual taxes.

At the close of February the governor withdrew all but 200 troops from the strike zone, but this step failed to diminish the drain on the treasury as much as he had anticipated. Maintaining the National Guard in the field was still an expensive undertaking. One group of twelve officers alone cost the state $5000 a month, and Chase, who remained in the field, continued to live like a warlord. He refused to be cross-examined by Martin Foster's Congressional committee, and when that same week the union attorney Horace Hawkins unsuccessfully sought release of Mother Jones through a petition to the Las Animas district court for a writ of habeas corpus, the general's sense of surrounding melodrama worked overtime.

> During the arguments [he wrote in his report to Governor Ammons] the courtroom was packed with a heterogeneous audience, the majority of which neither spoke nor understood the English language. The crowd . . . could not have been attracted by any desire to hear the proceedings, which it could not understand . . . I discovered a conspiracy among certain Italians in the audience to kill myself, the judge-advocate . . . and the district judge, who had incurred the hatred of the strikers by his decisions.

The conspiracy was not unusual since I have had military information of just such plots over and over again. On each of these occasions I have found it necessary to surround the courthouse with
soldiers. I have always been able to enforce order and prevent riot
or disperse mobs, but with all the force at my command I could
not prevent secret assassination, and assassination was impending
that day.

None was attempted, nor did Chase furnish proof that any was
contemplated. The next incident of bloodshed, occurring two
days later and almost immediately after the Congressional investigators had left Colorado, involved a mulatto named Neil Smith,
who applied for a job at the Forbes mine and later that evening
visited a friend in Bowen, three miles distant. Next morning he
was found dead alongside the Colorado and Southern track near
Suffield. According to a train crew, he had staggered drunk into
the path of their locomotive, but militiamen and sheriff's deputies
who recovered the body decided that he had been beaten to death
as a scab by strikers who then placed his corpse at the tracks to
give the look of an accident. A coroner's jury, which did not invite
the railroadmen to testify, blamed the death on "effects of wounds
by clubs and stones in the hands of parties unknown, after which
the body was placed on the track . . ."

Jesse Northcutt's antiunion paper, the Trinidad *Chronicle-
News,* admitted next day to the knowledge that Chase had long
favored breaking up the tent colonies — "hotbeds of dissension"
— as a means of restoring peace. The congressmen were gone.
Chase's military autocracy prevailed. The opportunity offered by
Smith's death was not to be resisted. Sheriff Grisham produced a
pair of bloodhounds and they led his posse straight to the strikers'
tent colony at Forbes. "In an effort to get the guilty, wholesale
arrests were made," explained the *Chronicle-News.* After the arrests a detachment of National Guard cavalry rode out to Forbes,
tore down the tents, and left more than fifty women and children
with their pathetic belongings exposed to the March weather.

"How long, oh God, how long?" lamented the union's local

newspaper, Trinidad *Free Press,* as it wondered which tent colony would next feel the weight of the general's "mailed fist." The paper vented most of its feelings on the "kow-towing executive . . . fully aware, in his puny heart, that the militia has got beyond his control." Conceivably the fact was also dawning on the governor, who in any case could scarcely avoid the implications in John Lawson's statement that now strikers would be advised to protect themselves. "A striking miner's tent is his home . . . as sacred to him as the mansion of the mineowner."

On Ammons' desk lay an invitation from General Chase to attend a ball given by the National Guard officers in Trinidad and set for March 10. This was the date of the Forbes evictions. The governor begged off at the last minute and sent his wife and daughter. The festivities were held in the Cardenas Hotel. The general and his lady led a grand march in full dress uniform and each of the dances that followed was heralded by a bugler sounding a familiar military call such as assembly, reveille, overcoats, tattoo, guard rout, fatigue, and sick. For a sentimental finale Major Boughton, who had organized the affair, had the band play "Home, Sweet Home," preceded by taps and audible to the union officials rushing about the Trinidad streets arranging shelter for the shivering homeless of Forbes.

In Denver, meanwhile, McLennan, Doyle, and Lawson confronted the governor with their protests. Ammons disclaimed responsibility for Chase's orders to his troops but assured the union leaders that no tents would be torn down elsewhere. More or less true to his word, and possibly embarrassed by the general's public statement that tent colonists deprived of a home could find adequate shelter in Trinidad jail, the governor sent him instructions to avoid getting mixed up in the dismantling of tents and to telephone him if he got the urge to do so again. In a strange move, ostensibly to offset reports believed to be reaching Washington, the governor also directed Chase to write President Wilson a letter explaining the Forbes incident.

General Chase took the occasion to banish any concern the

President might have had about Mother Jones. "[She] is, and always has been, at entire liberty to leave the strike district, but insists upon remaining, avowedly to make incendiary speeches. She is confined with comfort in a pleasant room in a large church hospital as a necessary peace precaution . . ." And on the other subject: ". . . a non-union miner was atrociously murdered near the union tent colony at Forbes . . . to which colony the murderers were easily tracked." The arrests were made at the urgent request of the sheriff and "the tents were ordered removed to forestall further outlawry." For good measure Chase reminded President Wilson that peace had been maintained and Colorado's laws and constitution preserved "with its own patriotic militia, thankless, self-sacrificing, patiently silent under abuse."

Governor Ammons was in accord with Chase at least on the necessity of keeping Mother Jones locked up. The governor honestly felt that she had given them no alternative. When Horace Hawkins told Ammons of his intention to liberate her through legal proceedings, the governor begged him to advise her to leave the area. Hawkins replied that she had a constitutional right to go where she pleased, and he might have added that anyway she would have ignored such advice. But that settled it as far as Ammons was concerned. Constitutional or not, the only sensible thing to do with outsiders bent on disrupting a peace so costly to maintain was impound them until they changed their minds. "I do not see," he was later to plead, "how anyone could have done any differently under the situation . . ."

The grounds cited by Judge A. W. McHendrie, an undisguised friend of the companies, for denying the writ of habeas corpus to free Mother Jones were that martial law prevailed in the section. Horace Hawkins next appealed to the state Supreme Court, not only on the old lady's behalf but that of other "military prisoners." Mother Jones's case was scheduled to be heard at 10 A.M. on Monday, March 16. Mother Jones had by then been imprisoned at San Rafael ten weeks incommunicado and to discourage rescue attempts her guard had been increased to six men day and night. It was obvious to Chase, if not Ammons as well, that consideration by the supreme bench was bound to reopen the question of whether or not the strike zone was actually under martial law. And an adverse opinion must inevitably circumscribe the powers with which Chase had so loftily invested himself. Thus there were good reasons, from the standpoint of both governor and adjutant general, for what developed next.

After a weekend of busy telephone calls between Denver and Trinidad, a National Guard colonel took Mother Jones out of San Rafael at 8 o'clock on Sunday night and boarded a northbound train with her. When they got off at Denver, she was spirited away to the Oxford Hotel and left there. She promptly let the union know that she was on the loose again and there occurred an immediate rush by different parties to publish conflicting versions of her release.

Mother Jones said she was told the governor wished to see her. Not so, retorted Ammons and Chase, she had wanted an audience with the governor and volunteered to leave the strike zone. Horace Hawkins was probably closest to the truth. "Her release was simply a tricky evasion of the test to determine the right of the National Guard to hold her."

Other releases quickly followed. Sixteen men held in connection with the death of Neil Smith were freed. They went straight to Forbes and began putting their tents back up. Lieutenant Karl Linderfelt arrived with a mounted detail. Again the tents were torn down and the militiamen camped on the ground to make sure they stayed down. There were no legalities sufficiently elastic to justify this and in Denver the state attorney general, Fred Farrar, felt obliged to advise Ammons that since the ground at Forbes was properly leased the strikers had every right to occupy it without molestation. More forcefully, Horace Hawkins called the militia's action an outrage and demanded an explanation from the governor at once. Judge Northcutt's press in Trinidad confidently assured its readers that to Hawkins' protest as well as others, Governor Ammons would pay no need And so it proved.

But now Ammons had a free-swinging Mother Jones to contend with again. On March 21 she bought a ticket for Trinidad and left Denver on the 11:30 P.M. train. Word of her coming sped south ahead of her. A militia captain boarded the train at Pueblo while she slept and waited until it pulled into Walsenburg. Mother Jones woke up under arrest. At daybreak she was handed over to Sheriff Jeff Farr, who padlocked her in a basement beneath Walsenburg courthouse.

"We are ready to meet any emergency" was how Governor Ammons bravely accounted for the old lady's latest incarceration. To some observers the governor appeared to be losing his grip. Perhaps he had reached the point where rational discussion over how best to contain Mother Jones lay beyond him. Helen Ring Robinson, a state senator who called on him about now, found the governor all cordiality until she brought up that subject at which he became agitated and launched into the old stories of Mother Jones's past "immorality." This in turn touched off the senator's excitement. "In some heat, I told him I was not at all concerned with the virtue of an eighty-two-year-old woman, but I was greatly concerned in the rights of habeas corpus." Like everybody else, including Mother Jones, who sought effect by stressing how old she was, Senator Helen Ring Robinson got the age wrong.

Ammons was deaf to such declarations, as he evidently also was by now to whatever scraps of sage advice issued from his attorney general, who, "tired of being the goat," indicated that henceforth the governor's strategy in dealing with Mother Jones would be without benefit of his counsel. These days the lawyer by whom Ammons felt himself badgered the most was the union's acidulous attorney Horace Hawkins, who in a series of sharp letters scoffed at Ammons' assertion that Mother Jones had returned south to show defiance of the authorities, challenged his right to dictate who shall go into Trinidad and who shall stay out, and suggested that "the best way to restore law and order is for the Governor himself to follow the law."

Mother Jones's reappearance in the strike zone and her fresh imprisonment coincided with the departure of troop contingents. Chase took no trouble to conceal his disfavor over the reduction of his command and tried to halt the process by warning Ammons that an army of strikers stood ready to attack isolated and depleted outposts. The strikers he described as financially exhausted with violence, now their last resort. Chase told the governor that his soldiers "would welcome an opportunity to demonstrate their efficiency."

That opportunity was still some time off. An uneasy quiet settled over General Chase's military domain. The soldiers left for home with a variety of memories of their service in the strike field. The "college boys" of Captain Philip Van Cise's Company K had stories to tell of baseball games with the miners, digging out snowbound trains after December's phenomenal blizzard, and the boredom of weeks without pay, thanks to Roady Kenehan. The detachment at Sopris celebrated the eve of their departure with a drunken brawl and a shooting spree. Mutiny haunted the outpost at Starkville and penniless soldiers begged loans from their officers to send home a pittance with which their families might stave off eviction. Colonel Verdeckburg concluded his report on the command at Walsenburg with a brand of parade-ground sentimentality. "As the tour of duty draws to a close there are mingled feelings. The bitterness of opposition and intimidation has softened in the thoughts of a real duty of a soldier; the joys of fellowship and service together remain as a pleasant memory to all who have shared 'the fortunes of war.' " But a lieutenant stationed at Starkville wrote, "You would have almost cried to see the men when they started home last night, ragged, dirty, and with only a few nickels left after paying their bills, or as much of them as they could. It is a terrible disgrace to the state of Colorado."

Governor Ammons summarized developments in a public statement. The strike was being turned over to local authorities. It had cost the state more than $500,000. Not a dollar had been available in the treasury; the entire amount was borrowed. "With a limitation of 4 per cent interest, on indefinite period of payment, and strong opposition both open and secret, we have had to rely upon the patriotism of the people to get the money so far authorized and to protect the credit of the state . . ."

The strike had also ravaged the union treasury. In March 1914 strike benefits were being paid to 20,508 men, women, and children. Among all factions of the struggle, only the companies remained free of money worries. Most of their mines were in operation. Their claimed labor force of 9200 for March was only about 1000 less than for the previous month.

On March 25 John Lawson and John McLennan were out at Forbes and by afternoon had put up a tent. Somebody informed the militia and down it came. Three days later, just before the fateful April began, Judge Jesse Northcutt addressed a public audience with his customary blend of cracker-barrel humor, dire prediction, and straight-from-the-shoulder admonition. Let the workers strike if they wished, but woe betide anybody who denied the judge his rights. Rebellion was in the air. A "string of communes" reached from Walsenburg south to the New Mexico line. Northcutt spoke in the Otto Theater, Trinidad, a few blocks from the jail cells still housing strikers at General Chase's pleasure, and the advertised title of the judge's speech was "Law and Order."

~~~ 13 ~~~

THE TERRIBLE ARBITRAMENT

BY 1914 IT WAS FIRMLY IMPRESSED upon the unprejudiced American consciousness that the world's richest young man was more
concerned with the betterment of humanity than hoarding his
wealth. "Your fortune is rolling up . . . like an avalanche,"
Frederick Gates had been wont to remind John D. Rockefeller, Sr.
"You must distribute it faster than it grows. If you do not, it will
crush you and your children and your children's children." Gates
deserves the credit for conceiving of great corporate philanthropies. Nineteen thirteen had seen the creation under the junior
Rockefeller's presidency of the Rockefeller Foundation with the
commendable aims of disseminating knowledge, relieving hardship, promoting the well-being of mankind at home and abroad.
That same year, as a result of studies and recommendations that
Rockefeller had made while foreman of a grand jury investigating
white-slave traffic and prostitution, the Bureau of Social Hygiene
was founded — and for the next twenty-five years he financed it.

Even the New York *Press*, never too friendly toward the Rockefellers, foresaw a possibility that the world might have to forgive
them their great wealth. "It is about time to stop laughing at John
D. Rockefeller, Jr., because he 'goes to Sunday School,'" said the
paper. "If [it] results in this kind of reform . . . it is time we all
began to go to Sunday School." He led a blameless personal life.
Racehorses, yachts, automobiles, were "foolish extravagances," he
once said. His one expensive hobby was a recently kindled fond-

ness for Chinese porcelains, a pursuit he described in terms which he perhaps hoped could be as accurately applied to himself — "quiet and unostentatious and not sensational." The porcelain collection owned by J. P. Morgan had captured his fancy, and after Morgan's death in 1913 he thought of buying it. Rockefeller may have been pondering how best to make his bid, when he received an invitation to appear before the Congressional investigators and testify on his connection with a company of whose securities his father owned 40 per cent and from which he had not, to his subsequent boundless regret, as yet dissociated himself.

Among the young Rockefeller's widely advertised goals of aid to the wretched and oppressed before 1915, one seeks in vain any specific indication that the recipients might include American workmen. It may not be fanciful to suspect that the very sensitivity of conscience alleged to be the basis of his philanthropy generated a commendable dread of what he might find among the masses from whom his family derived its wealth and therefore precluded any searching inquiry on his part. Although the Rockefeller Foundation, originally endowed with $100 million, was launched with sweeping aims for the improvement of the human condition, they contain no hint of acknowledgment of new problems and manifold distress that had developed everywhere as by-products of the industrial revolution. When at last events diverted Rockefeller's philanthropic impulses from, say, the victims of a natural calamity in the Orient or starvation in Bulgaria to the lot of his laborers in Colorado, there could have been relief behind the alacrity with which he accepted Welborn's and Bowers' assurances that the men had nothing to complain of. But there is not really a great deal left for speculation. Enough documentary evidence exists to furnish a reliable picture of Rockefeller's general views and attitudes on labor as the strike against his company entered its most melancholy phase.

There appeared in a spring 1914 issue of *Popular Science Monthly* what was even for that day an explicitly callous and re-

actionary essay entitled "Capital and Labor." It was written by
Professor John J. Stevenson of New York University and among
the notions dogmatically delivered as verities were these:

> . . . a wife and children cannot be considered in connection with
> the relations of wage earner to wage payer. The only question
> concerns the worth of a man's services. Introduction of other mat-
> ters would so increase the uncertainty of business affairs as to make
> them little better than a lottery. If a man's services are not worth
> enough to secure wages which would support a family, he should
> not marry. He may not complain because the community is unwill-
> ing to have him gratify his desires at its expense . . . One is told
> that in each year 200,000 women in our land are compelled to sell
> their bodies to procure the necessities of life, and that each year
> sees 700,000 children perish because their parents had insufficient
> nourishment . . . if it be true . . . one must coincide that their
> deaths are a blessing to themselves and to the community. Such
> children should not have been born . . . Unskilled labor is merely
> animated machinery for rough work and adds very little value to
> the final product. One E. H. Harriman is of more lasting service to
> a nation than would be 100,000 of unskilled laborers. Without a
> Harriman they would be a menace.

In addition there was a copious display of indiscriminate antiunion ferocity.

John D. Rockefeller, Jr., praised the article as "one of the
soundest, clearest, most forcible pronouncements" he had ever
read and recommended its use in public defense of his company's
position on the labor question.

On the subject of the responsibility of stockholders and directors for labor conditions in the properties they controlled, he subscribed to the prevalent businessman's view that the duties of
stockholders were predominantly concerned with the election of
directors and the director's business was to select honest and capable executive officers who should be left to operate the property
with a free hand. He believed in collective bargaining, though
had difficulty when asked to define it, and professed ignorance on
the subject of unionism. Workers might be expected to have

grievances — "they are human" — but these were best handled by the company officers. A Boston businessman, telling Rockefeller of his plan for a nonunion workers' association that would insure the employer against disaffection among the employees, compared it with paying more for a trustworthy horse than for one likely to attack or desert when needed most. Rockefeller, evidently unoffended by the parallel, replied favorably and said that the labor organization most needed by the country was one that would raise the standard of efficiency and make workers more valuable. About the same time, a letter he wrote to Adolph Ochs, publisher of the *New York Times,* thanking him for a sympathetic editorial, contained a more elaborate statement of views on the ideal labor organization: that which would stimulate a workingman's best endeavor instead of reduce his daily output, advocate the increase of earning power and proportional rewards according to efficiency, and uphold the principle that the interests of labor and capital are mutual.

How Rockefeller visualized his responsibilities as they specifically related to the Colorado Fuel and Iron Company emerged during four hours of questioning mostly by Congressman Martin Foster in Washington, D.C., on April 6, 1914. "What possible value," he had written his father when Foster's invitation came, "any knowledge I may be able to impart may be to this inquiry I do not know. However . . . I felt it wise to accept it without any hesitation."

Foster's tone was polite, the witness self-composed. He represented his father's interest in the company, had done nothing personally to end the strike, but denied taking no more than a passing interest in it. He had not visited Colorado for ten years, nor had he attended a board of directors' meeting since the strike began. Preferring to act on the data secured by competent people — "when I was investigating vice in New York I never talked to a single prostitute" — he did not consider his presence necessary on the strike scene. For information he relied upon officers whose views he would defend as long as he deemed them worthy of his confidence. As far as he knew, the miners of the CFI had no real grievances. He had no idea whether the company had bought guns or hired Baldwin-Felts detectives and knew nothing of the Death Special, but if local law authorities were unable to provide adequate protection for the company's employees its officers had a duty to do so. He did not know whether his company owned saloon buildings, but he reminded the committee that efforts had been advanced in the coal properties to reduce the liquor evil among the workers who, "being largely foreign," drank a lot. He also praised his company's investment in schools and churches. The violence at Forbes was regrettable but, as Sherman said, "war is hell" and this was especially true of civil strife.

As the testimony continued and Rockefeller, probably without intent, registered little more than a coldly impersonal interest in the Colorado situation, Martin Foster's manner grew sharper and more tenacious. In consequence the multimillionaire's poise wavered. His responses then acquired an almost welcome warmth. Foster at one point was charging him with having neglected to find out for himself whether the miners had any grievances or not. Rockefeller started to reply:

"Just the minute that I have the slightest lack of confidence in the man in charge —"

"I know; but you have not done that."

"I have not found it necessary in the discharge of my duty."

"As a director of the company you thought that all that was necessary for you to do was to put your name there —"

"No, sir."

"Wait a minute; I am not through. To put your name on the roster of officers of the company as a director, not even attending a meeting of the stockholders, not even attending the meetings of the directors, but to turn the matter all over to somebody else and say 'Go ahead.' Now, do you not think that your duty as a director goes further than that?"

"We spent ten years testing out . . . one of the men in charge."

"Do you think your duty goes further than that? . . . Don't

you believe that you, looking after the welfare of other civilians of the United States, that somewhat closer relations between officers and . . . these six thousand coal diggers who work underground, many of them foreigners, ignorant and unacquainted with the ways of the country, would be an uplift to them and make them better citizens?"

"It is because I have such a profound interest in these men and all workers that I expect to stand by the policy which has been outlined by the officers, and which seems to me to be first, last and always, in the greatest interest of the employees of the country."

"But you do not regard it as personal to you to look into these matters yourself?"

"Oh, I am giving it constant and close attention."

Later Rockefeller declared that it was costing the company about $1 million "to stand for the principle which we believe is to the ultimate interest of those men."

"And that is to fight the union?"

"That is to allow them to have the privilege of determining the conditions under which they shall work."

"And not that men shall get together and talk over their own interests?"

"They have every right to do that."

"Collective bargaining and sale of their labor — you want to fight that?"

"I do not say that. Not that outside men, who have no interest in them or in their employers, shall come in and impose upon them that organization."

"You are an outsider with respect to Colorado, are you not?"

"I do not live there. I am an outsider except in a representative capacity . . . I am an outsider to the extent of being one who is spending $1 million in helping to look out for the interests of those people."

"And is the man who works to be excluded from going in and looking out for the interests of that class of men?"

"I think that when you help a class of persons you have to

give them the right to say whether they will be helped or not."

"But are the outsiders who invest their money there the only ones?"

"Certainly not; but these men have not expressed any dissatisfaction with their conditions. The records show that the conditions have been admirable. If the men should express themselves as dissatisfied —"

"You have had a strike there within a year?"

"A strike has been imposed upon the company from the outside."

"How can you have a strike without dissatisfaction? They could not make men go out of the mines for nothing."

"They could not make the men go out? Then I do not think you have as much knowledge of the conditions as I have. I — the information that I receive — Black Hand letters, threats of violence to miners' wives and daughters, are the ways which outsiders make men go out . . ."

"And that is the way they brought on the strike?"

"And nothing else."

"All this disturbance and loss of life . . . out there has not been of enough importance . . . to cause you to say, 'Let us have a meeting of the directors' and find out more about it?"

"I . . . have such a warm sympathy for this very large number of men that work for us that I should be the last one to surrender the liberty under which they have been working and the conditions which to them have been entirely satisfactory — to give up that liberty and accept dictation from those outside who have no interest in them or in the company."

"But the killing of people and shooting of children — has not that been of enough importance to you for you to communicate with the other directors, and see if something can be done to end that sort of thing?"

"We believe the issue is not a local one in Colorado. It is a national issue whether workers shall be allowed to work under such conditions as they may choose. As part owners of the property, our interest in the laboring men in this country is so immense, so deep, so profound that we stand ready to lose every cent we put in that company rather than see the men we have employed thrown out of work and have imposed upon them conditions which are not of their seeking and which neither they nor we can see are in our interest."

"You are willing to let these killings take place rather than to go there and do something to settle conditions?"

"There is just one thing that can be done to settle this strike, and that is to unionize the camps, and our interest in labor is so profound, and we believe so sincerely that that interest demands that the camps shall be open camps, that we expect to stand by the officers at any cost. It is not an accident that this is our position —"

"And you would do that if that costs all your property and kills all your employees?"

"It is a great principle."

It was, Rockefeller went on, upon a similar principle that the Revolutionary War was fought. All in all, it was a revealing display. The gaps in Rockefeller's knowledge about the Colorado coalfield were attributable to the kind of information he was relying upon from the Denver officers, but the intensity with which he replied to some of Foster's questions could only have reflected deeply rooted and long-held ideas. He declared that his conscience acquitted him. And if he had had it all to do over again, "I would not know how more conscientiously to perform my duty as a director of this company and representative of a large interest than I have."

The most serious charge to be directed against Rockefeller in due course was that he managed the strike from headquarters at 26 Broadway. This is unsupportable. In December 1913 Starr J. Murphy had written to Bowers proposing that the dispute be investigated by a board of federal judges. Murphy had carefully added that his letter was not to be regarded as an attempt to influence the executives. Bowers rejected the idea. As far as the correspondence shows, this was the only suggestion from New York in the strike period prior to April 1914. No evidence exists indicating an order or even the application of strong pressure, but neither can there be the slightest doubt that the Denver men were encouraged in their course by Rockefeller's expressions of loyalty and approval.

From the standpoint of a multimillionaire, the Rockefeller stake in the CFI was not very large. During the dozen years that John D. Rockefeller, Sr., had owned stocks and bonds in the company he had received an average annual return of only two thirds of 1 per cent on the stock and 6 per cent on the bonds, making a net yearly return of 3½ per cent on the money invested. Allan Nevins has written that the elder Rockefeller regarded the coal mines as red-ink items in a ledger. Not once in the years of his control did the common stock pay a dividend. Even so, it was brought out that the money return to him over the period of roughly twelve years ending in 1914 approximated $9 million. The question was whether the stake was important enough to have imposed a duty upon either Rockefeller to familiarize himself with conditions in the coalfields. Nevins thought that since the elder Rockefeller had approved the choice of L. M. Bowers to handle his affairs out there, he could not be wholly exculpated. But the more direct responsibility rested with his son, Fred Gates, and Starr J. Murphy, all of them directors, none of whom had put the Denver executives under critical scrutiny.

Instead they relied on their one-sided reports. Bowers was, in his own words, Rockefeller's "hired man." He and the company president furnished New York with abundant references to the sins and violence of the unionists, but as far as their letters and telegrams reveal, rarely did they report on countermeasures and only then when it was too late for revocation. At no time did they tell Rockefeller about the machine guns they had bought or the gunmen deputized by the sheriffs Farr and Grisham and salaried with company funds. And had Rockefeller even considered balancing his biased input with a correspondingly one-sided version of events from union leaders, he had foreclosed his chances by committing himself to the Bowers-Welborn policy of recoiling from the slightest gesture or circumstance which might lead to or be mistaken for recognition of the miners' union. The reports from the Boston Building in Denver were composed by men whose self-interest required that Rockefeller believe in the wisdom and fairness of their methods. He received therefore half or less of the whole picture. That he swallowed all he was told without question reflects not so much a woeful gullibility as the corporate habit of depending upon one's administrative subordinates and loyally supporting them under fire. And not to be overlooked is Rockefeller's probable eagerness for reassurance that his company bore no stain of turpitude.

The fairest conclusion may have been that reached by John Fitch, a contemporary journalist whose articles in *The Survey* on the Colorado strike were models of clarity and balance. "To the degree that Mr. Rockefeller did or did not acquaint himself in competent ways as to what was going on in Colorado, we have a measure of his stewardship. To the extent that he backed up his officials in private and public, he increased the responsibility for what transpired in Colorado that was already in large measure his because of ownership."

Unable to foresee how harrowing were the events now imminent in Colorado, Rockefeller failed to grasp last-minute opportunities to avert them. After the hearings he retired to the country for a rest and to acknowledge a flood of congratulatory mail from businessmen praising his performance before the Foster committee. "It was a bugle note that was struck for principle," wired his mother, flustered with pride, and his father rewarded his "splendid effort at Washington" with a gift of 10,000 shares of CFI common stock. A letter from Bowers arrived too, exulting over the failure of "biased political wirepullers to trip you" and concluding, "Now for an aggressive warfare to 1916 and beyond for an open shop." More likely to wince at than reciprocate such bombast, Rockefeller wrote back that it might be a good idea to set up a YMCA in Pueblo for the steelworkers.

His incoming mail that mid-April week also included a private note from Frank Hayes, the UMW vice president, seeking a personal meeting, and almost certainly compelled by the anxious exploration now initiated from Indianapolis for an honorable way out of the strike. It was an opportunity that might have brought peace. But the company's obsessive fear of real or imagined recognition prevailed and Rockefeller, forwarding a copy of the union leader's letter to L. M. Bowers, assured him that "in conformity with the policy adopted by Welborn and yourself, I will make no reply."

In the Colorado coalfields the departure of the investigating committee had left, outwardly at least, an atmosphere of calm. Ugly things had been said at the hearings about the conduct of the Colorado National Guard, and Governor Ammons, privately irritated over the Congressional visitation, had asked General Chase to provide Foster with his own version of events. The general drew up a hasty report telling of the "absolute terror . . . anarchy reigned supreme . . ." that he had found on arrival in the strike zone. Two bodies of men were "ready to fly at each other's throats . . . [but] with the all too meager force at my command I was able, without bloodshed, to occupy this territory, reestablish the constitution, and enforce a sullen peace."

Peace of a sort continued. The process of withdrawing the militia as directed by Governor Ammons was undisturbed. In the middle of the month, on another order from Ammons, Mother Jones was freed — "automatic with the suspension of martial law," in the words of General Chase, who would otherwise have had to produce her before the Colorado Supreme Court three days hence as directed in the habeas-corpus proceedings on her behalf. On April 17 all the militia were gone from the strike zone save thirty-four men of Lieutenant Karl Linderfelt's Company B at Ludlow. According to other militia officers, this unit was selected to remain because, while hated by the strikers, it was the one they most feared. Linderfelt himself was technically no longer in charge of the company. He had been relieved of his command on April 8 and "sent away on recruiting service."

As a protective barrier between the largest of the tent colonies and the richest mines, Company B gave no special comfort to Northcutt's newspaper in Trinidad, which reported that for the first time in five months southern Colorado was defenseless. As if taking the judge's hint, on the night of April 14, over 130 men gathered in the armory at Trinidad and organized themselves into a Troop A. One hundred and twenty-one of them were mine guards, pit bosses, clerks, engineers, and foremen employed by the CFI and Victor-American. The rest were sheriff's deputies and sundry local vigilantes. Playing the chief roles in Troop A's organization were one of Northcutt's newspapermen and Doctor Edwin M. Curry, surgeon from the Victor-American mine at Hastings, who was fond of calling the strikers "outlaws, bums and gunmen." Lieutenant Karl Linderfelt was on hand to administer the oath, after which the men were put under command of Captain Edwin F. Carson, an Englishman whose sixteen years in the British army had included active service with the Seaforth Highlanders against the Dutch Boers in South Africa and an earlier campaign in the Sudan when the famed regiment played its part in the decimation of the Dervishes. Troop A would have no time to select its officers, receive training, earn discipline, or even be issued uniforms and equipment before it went into action.

*

The idea of enrolling mine employees into a state militia unit to replace troops withdrawn by the governor originated either with company officials or General Chase or both in concert. It was never made clear if Governor Ammons was told in advance. Chase could have based his endorsement of the scheme on his professed unconcern with a recruit's pedigree. The general was to admit that as far as he knew, no record was made of an enlistee's background or even citizenship. The raising of Troop A stirred considerable local disquiet as state Senator Helen Ring Robinson discovered when she arrived in the area for a reception given by the Democratic County Committee. Several guests told her of their fear that Troop A had been formed for a sinister purpose. She hurried back to Denver and at 9 A.M. the next day, Saturday, April 18, she was at the governor's door prepared to demand that he do something to head off trouble. But Ammons had left Colorado the previous day for Washington, D.C., where, as a welcome change from strike matters, he hoped to secure an order from the Secretary of the Interior allowing Colorado settlers right of way for irrigation ditches across government lands in the Arkansas Valley.

That same Saturday a letter announcing the debut of Troop A left L. M. Bowers addressed to the junior Rockefeller. "Another favorable feature . . . is the organization of a military company of 100 volunteers at Trinidad this week. They are to be armed by the state and drilled by military officials. Another squad is being organized at Walsenburg. These independent militiamen will be subject to the orders of the county sheriff. As these volunteers will draw no pay from the state, this movement has the support of the governor and other men in authority." When pressed later to say whether he understood from Bowers' letter that the CFI was to pay the volunteer company its salaries, Rockefeller replied, "If that is what the letter states, I must have understood it so."

For once Rockefeller had been told by the "hired man" in Denver of a countermeasure reprehensible and potentially dangerous. He might at least have sought further clarification. But he was, as a personal aide put it, "tired out with the winter's work." Bowers' letter arrived as the aide, at Rockefeller's behest, mailed off a check for $2500 in preliminary payment for the installation of limestone carvings depicting children with baskets to adorn the east façade of the Rockefeller retreat at Pocantico Hills. Any thoughts of the Colorado situation that he had just then could well have focused on Bowers' additional information that the entire union leadership, pinched for funds as never before, was crumbling. Strikers were about to have their relief money cut off and no longer did union representatives encourage them to hold on for ultimate victory. Now they dodged the issue, in some cases even sought to deliberately offend the miners in hopes of making them quit the tents and return to work, thereby lessening the union's financial burden. All these confidential tidbits Bowers ascribed to "reliable sources." But whatever their effect, or that of the news about Troop A, upon John D. Rockefeller, Jr., time had now run out on opportunities for saving the innocents.

The grimmest week in the history of American labor conflicts dawned on a people at first glance quite unlike those of our time. They had not known two world wars. There had been business slumps and stock-market panics but no shattering economic depression. Airplanes in the sky, no longer a novelty, were nonetheless far from commonplace and military experts were still pondering their use in future warfare. Epochal events took place, campaigns and conventions ran their courses, without the intrusion of television cameras or even radio microphones, although more and more were being captured on motion-picture celluloid. But there were surprising similarities between the United States of 1914 and some six decades later. Feminine militancy was strident in demands for liberation from bondage to the whims and presumptions of men. Parents, teachers, and biologists were then as now arguing about the desirability of sex education for the young and already the polemical emphasis was shifting from whether sex should be taught in classrooms to the question of how much. "Tango madness" was supposed to hasten the death of Terpsichore, which today's lovers of dance declare rock music to have done, and the terminology of 1914's morality crusaders attacking "indecent" trends in art, popular literature, and motion-picture theaters was not altogether unlike today's outcries against permissiveness.

In the newspaper columns Lillian Russell regularly revealed her beauty secrets, while other columnists applied their expertise

to the ageless problems of lovelorn youth and housewives besieged by cockroaches. A time traveler from the second half of
the century would have recognized familiar targets though of unfamiliar campaigns. Cigarettes were frowned upon by notables
like Thomas Alva Edison but on grounds that they weakened the
brain. The medical profession was under fire not for charging
high fees but for harboring quacks. There were complaints on all
sides about the rising costs of goods and services, but consumer
groups were unknown and the permanent bane of big manufac-
turers were so-called radical cliques, muckraking journalists, and
trust-busting politicians.

"The great American middle-class is disgustingly serene in the
contemplation of [its] own virtues, and therefore [pays] scant
heed to the great seething mass . . . struggling . . . for economic freedom and a little bit of joy." This observation on the self-
centered complacency of Middle America had nothing to do with
black poverty but was made in 1914 by a federal investigator concerned about the plight of the downtrodden laboring class. Con-
servatives wore little metal flags in their lapels as a public token of
their patriotism and condemned the spreading disregard for "law
and order." As startling as anything that mirrored problems of
our own time was the alarm over drug addiction among school-
children. Two-reel dramas exposing "cocaine's deadly lure to
youth" were distributed to motion-picture theaters and one sociol-
ogist estimated that 60 per cent of New York's children had used
cocaine or opium.

A *New York Times* headline in April 1914 announcing an attack
by "patriots" on antiwar orators would not have looked so out of
place, either, to a visitor from the future. But in this case the
hawks far outnumbered the doves. Although President Wilson resisted infection, popular war fever against Mexico was running so
high he could seek honor only through the threat of force. The
arrest of American marines at Tampico had constituted an indignity to the American flag that could only be erased with an apolo-
getic formal gun salute. When Huerta hedged instead of ordering

one fired, Wilson issued an ultimatum expiring at 6 P.M. the following Sunday, April 19. The President spent that weekend in the West Virginia hills with his family. He was back in the capital at 7:15 A.M. Monday, his manifest sorrow probably as much due to the blatant jingoism of most U.S. front pages as the fatuous arrogance of the Mexican dictator. He had prepared an address for Congress, and later that morning for the first time in history, an American President appeared in person before the legislature to seek prior approval for the employment of the armed forces in whichever way he saw fit.

When Governor Ammons arrived in Washington the war crisis was on everybody's mind. The possibility of a conflict with Mexico was also exciting his fellow citizens back in Denver, where one newspaper forecast that Colorado's militiamen would probably be the first reserve troops called upon because strike duty had conditioned them admirably for camp life and instant hostilities. Before leaving Denver the governor had handed over control of state affairs to his lieutenant governor, Stephen R. Fitzgarrald, who, if he had opened his Rocky Mountain *News* to the editorial page that Monday, might have read: "Slowly, regretfully, honorably, war seems to have come to the United States. All that men could do has been done to maintain peace, and peace has failed. Now there must be the terrible arbitrament of battle and death." The editorial dealt with Mexico. Nobody, certainly not the lieutenant governor, could then have imagined that except perhaps for the reference to honor, before nightfall the words would be more accurately applicable to southern Colorado.

·····14 ·····

LUDLOW

Visualize a rough capital K facing left instead of right. The upper arm is formed by the wagon road stretching northwest across a flat plain to enter the Hastings-Delagua canyon. The lower arm, another crude road, swings southwest along a branch of the Colorado and Southern Railroad to enter the Tabasco-Berwind canyon. The shaft or backbone of the left-facing letter is the Colorado and Southern's main line north and south. Immediately above and to the right of where the arms converge at the shaft stands the union tent colony — in other words, just northeast of the strategic focal point. North of the colony and at intervals of about 100 yards the railroad, or shaft of the letter, passes a pump station, then crosses a steel bridge over a wide east-west arroyo. Some 600 yards south of the focal point, the main railroad line runs past the Ludlow depot with its adjacent saloon, store, and post office, and after another 400 yards skirts a shallow mesa that takes its name from the water tank on its crest.

The monotony of the flat spread of terrain eastward meets only limited relief in the low dust-hued ridge called the Black Hills. To the west, the Spanish Peaks are obscured by the half-barren slopes of the nearer coal-rich hills. Along each arm, on both sides of the shaft and within the angles of this wrong-way K, would ebb and flow the day's events.

Some 500 yards across the railroad tracks from the colonists' gray or white tents stood three brown ones of the Colorado National Guard. Formerly occupied by men of Captain Van Cise's more or less friendly Company K, they now housed twelve troopers of the detested Company B and Major Patrick C. Hamrock, technically in command of the militia force left in the strike zone. Hamrock's main detachment of twenty-two men were stationed about two miles away on Cedar Hill overlooking the coke ovens at Tabasco. And Lieutenant Karl E. Linderfelt was back with his unit.

The lieutenant's presence at Cedar Hill that fateful morning was to be variously explained as a weekend call on his two brothers, both fellow officers, as a visit to the CFI superintendent at Tabasco, and by his own vague account, as an inspection tour of military storage facilities. His wife accompanied him, and her slowness in dressing was subsequently put forth as the reason why he missed the Sunday night train back to Trinidad. At any rate, he stayed overnight at Cedar Hill and the next morning, contrary to later testimony by General Chase that at no time after April 8 was he in charge of Company B, Lieutenant Karl Linderfelt reassumed command at about 8 o'clock, when he received a written message from a woman living at the Berwind coal camp. He ordered it taken down to Major Hamrock.

Of the "Greeks, Montenegrans, Bulgarians, Servians, Italians, Tyroleans, Croatians, Austrians, Savoyards and other South European aliens" listed by the militia as forming most of Ludlow's union population, the Greeks were the doughtiest element to reckon with. A number who had arrived since the strike started were reputed to have fought in the Balkan Wars. They kept to their own block of tents, were truculent showoffs among themselves, and apparently without exception were unhampered by wives or children.

Most of them were deeply religious and throughout Sunday, April 19, they had celebrated with song and necessarily frugal feast the Orthodox Church Easter, which that year fell one week later than the Gregorian holiday. A morning baseball match had been arranged between the Ludlow men and their wives after which the Greeks, several wearing native costume, entertained at dinner. Louis Tikas took photographs and then the women, still attired in sports bloomers, returned to the baseball plot for another game. This time they had spectators: a handful of militiamen.

The banter had been ill-humored and bitter. The women scoffed about how easy it would be to seize the three tents, how if one of them advanced with a BB gun, the militiamen would take flight. The soldiers in turn had advised them to make the most of their holiday today because "we will have the roast tomorrow." This was not meant as the grisly prophecy it turned out to be. Threats of one kind or another were so common on both sides as to become predictable. But every fresh gibe nourished mutual hostility. There was truth in Karl Linderfelt's defensive complaint that the tensions of extended strike duty "wore on them . . . and us, and this constant grinding and picking on a man will get him."

Among the lower ranks on both sides grew a sense of inevitability that one or the other would have to be sacrificed. It was common knowledge that General Chase and certain subordinate officers shared the coal companies' desire to see the union colonies dismantled. Strikers believed the process had already begun with the demolition of the tents at Forbes and, given the first usable pretext, the same fate would be dealt the principal target, Ludlow. On the other side, noncommissioned officers and enlisted men expected a mass attack by the strikers at any moment, followed by a seizure of the mines, expulsion of the strikebreakers, and vengeance wrought upon the mine guards. So much more of a dark hint of conspiracy surrounded the commissioned levels of the militia that it cannot be said how genuinely this possibility was feared by the officers. Certainly the militia force now in the field was outnumbered. It had only to be caught off guard when weapons long secreted by the strikers and believed recently dug up in readiness might be put to swift and bloody use.

Against this background, Major Hamrock on Monday morning read the note relayed by Linderfelt, claiming that the writer's husband, an Italian miner, was being held at the Ludlow colony against his will. Hamrock ordered a corporal and two men to make the necessary inquiries at the tents; when they returned with word from Louis Tikas, the Greek leader and interpreter, that no such man was enrolled in the colony, the major reached for his telephone.

Hamrock was a bluff, Irish-born officer noted for his prowess at rifle tournaments, who in 1898 had helped found a volunteer group of crack shots called the Rocky Mountain Sharpshooters. The Spanish-American War, for which the Sharpshooters were planned, ended before they could distinguish themselves. However, Hamrock was already experienced in wars for the suppression of lesser breeds, having seen active service with the U.S. Army in the campaign against the Sioux uprising that culminated in the massacre at Wounded Knee. In more recent years, when not on National Guard duty, Pat Hamrock was a Denver saloon-keeper.

Now he telephoned Tikas at the tent colony and invited him to a meeting in his own tent. The Greek striker said no. Hamrock had no delusions about the tenability of his position, given trouble. His scant tents were in full view of the colony and all but three of his dozen troopers were some distance off on routine duty or watering their horses. There were close to 150 union tents. Of their 900 or so occupants nearly half were men and of these over 100 were believed to be hardcore Greek fighters. Hamrock's adjutant, Lieutenant Ray Benedict, had the colony constantly under surveillance and through his artillery fieldglasses thought he detected an ominous commotion. Hamrock telephoned for the Cedar Hill troops to be brought up to Water Tank Hill and drilled conspicuously along its crest.

Now his phone rang: Tikas would meet the major at the railroad depot, roughly equidistant between the strikers' tents and his own. Hamrock consented, but a harassed or unsteady quality in the voice of one who, although a Greek redneck, had hitherto impressed him as a "restraining influence" in the colony caused the major to telephone Cedar Hill again. And the expression he used, "Put the baby in the buggy and bring it along," required no decoding. The company machine gun Linderfelt had supervised as mine guard for the CFI was still in his custody. He ordered it loaded in the wagon. With Lieutenant Gerry Lawrence in charge, the party set out at a gallop downhill.

Not much is known of Louis Tikas. Born in Crete and reportedly a college graduate, he had first worked in Colorado as a strikebreaker in the northern mines. He joined the UMW, his bilingual fluency making him an obvious choice for an organizer, and in due course came to the notice of John Lawson, who gave him the vital assignment at Ludlow shortly after the southern miners struck work. Tikas' relatively calm and cultivated manner, easily mistaken for an air of superiority, had the effect of sparks on tinder among men like Karl Linderfelt, unaccustomed to educated wops and rednecks. But except for the impatient and jealous among his own people, Tikas was well-liked by all nationalities in the colony and Captain Van Cise was to recall him as "the greatest single agent for peace during the strike."

Tikas had his toughest work cut out trying to control the warlike spirit that possessed most of his countrymen at Ludlow. He had telephoned Hamrock under extreme pressure from strikers incensed by the bluster of the uniformed trio who had come inquiring after the missing husband. Until they rode in, the day had begun pleasantly. Fresh laundry swayed on the clothesline in a light breeze. Here and there a flag flew. The sky was pale; the ground had softened beneath diminishing patches of snow. Snatches of song and the strains of a mandoline or accordian may have attested to a lingering festive atmosphere after Easter. But all jollity had evaporated during the soldiers' visit and when they left was replaced with clamorous determination to resist with guns any further intrusions.

Only with persuasive effort did Tikas secure a promise from the men not to behave rashly while he conferred with Hamrock. He met the major at 8:50 A.M. and was insisting to him and the woman, then present, that her husband no longer dwelt in the colony, when Lieutenant Lawrence rode up to report the arrival of his advance detail on Water Tank Hill.

This was military formality, hardly necessity, because the mounted guardsmen prancing on the crest were visible from the depot. Most importantly they could be seen by three strikers' wives at the nearby Snodgrass store. The women hastened back to the colony in great agitation and notified the smoldering Greeks, who at this point either forgot their promise to Tikas or interpreted the signs as an imminent attack on the colony. There was a rush for positions of defense. Lieutenant Lawrence, halfway back to Water Tank Hill after making his report, wheeled his horse again and galloped for the depot shouting, "My God, Major, we're in for it." He had seen what neither Hamrock nor Tikas could because of intervening buildings: scores of armed strikers defiling from the colony southeastward across the ball ground, taking up positions in a sand cut along the Colorado and Southeastern tracks, to the right of the reversed K, less than a thousand yards east of the depot and in excellent position from which to deliver fire at the right flank of the twenty or so men on Water Tank Hill.

At the same time, generally unnoticed by militiamen because the tents were in the way, a much larger force of strikers was slipping beyond the northern rim of the colony and ducking into the wide arroyo. Tikas raced back to his tents, waving a handkerchief, screaming for the men to return. They ignored him. Hamrock hurried across the railroad tracks to his quarters and was completing a call to General Chase in Denver when he heard a burst of rifle fire.

It was even more audible to the militiamen on Water Tank Hill at whom it was directed. They pleaded with Lieutenant Linderfelt for permission to fire on the strikers still streaming for the cut and some militiamen may in fact have already pressed their triggers precipitating the strikers' fire. The question of who discharged the first bullet is now unanswerable, but it suited Linderfelt's vanity to await a particular signal from the militia tents near Ludlow that would demonstrate his military initiative. He had fashioned three crude bombs, each composed of eight sticks of dynamite bound with heavy twine and primed at the center stick with two feet of fuse. According to Linderfelt the bombs — "simply a military precaution that any commander would take" — were to be exploded by the Ludlow detail to signal the Cedar Hill force. More likely, as suggested by other officers, they were designed to warn the coal camps in the canyons.

The gunfire from the cut grew hotter. Linderfelt at last ordered his men to shoot back, and a brisk exchange between the Springfield service rifles and machine gun on Water Tank Hill and the strikers' assorted arms, Winchesters predominating, had gone on ten minutes when the three bombs exploded at sixty-second intervals, detonated by Lieutenant Benedict at a safe distance behind the militia tents.

In the union colony Maggie Dominsky's children were just out of bed, half-dressed and unfed. Mary Thomas appeared at the entrance of the Dominskys' tent, her Welsh voice warning of coming trouble and advising immediate flight to the shelter of a pump station and boiler house northwest of the colony, hard against the Colorado and Southern track. The Dominsky children trotted off in Mrs. Thomas' care while their mother raced to the front of the colony and reached her husband's side as Louis Tikas came running from the depot frantically waving his handkerchief. Virginia Bartoloti's husband, John, insisted, over her cries of disbelief, that a machine gun was in action and ushered her and their three children into a hole under the tent floor. There were a number of such pits, of varying breadth and depth, dug under the tents for storage and shelter. The Bartolotis remained thus cramped for several minutes before clambering out again and heading for the pump station. From her tent in the second row of the colony facing south, Alcarita Pedregon, who had got up late, caught a glimpse of the militiamen maneuvering on Water Tank Hill. She went underground with her two infants. Mrs. Ed Tonner, in the final weeks of pregnancy and sweeping the tent floor when the bombs sounded, threw the broom aside, dislodged the floorboards over a hole through which she hustled her five children, and then went in after them.

It was not all panic and confusion. A sense of common danger reinforced the neighborliness which long months of fear and hardship had developed between families of disparate origin and culture. Clorinda Padillo and her four children made room in their pit for the Juanita Hernandez family. Charles Costa's wife and two children and the Valdez family shared Alcarita Pedregon's pit shelter. In James Fyler's tent the paymaster's family had taken to their dugout at the first sound of gunfire, and when the exploding bombs sent terror through the colony Fyler's daughter fainted. Virginia Bartoloti interrupted her own escape to pause at the tent and revive the girl with wine and sugar, then she gathered all the Fylers together with her own children and continued the flight to the pump station.

It was a small structure, quickly overcrowded and soon to be a target for militia bullets. M. G. Low, the Colorado and Southern's pumpman, directed the onrush of refugees to a railroad well north of his house measuring at least twenty feet wide and ninety feet deep, with three interior platforms connected by ten-foot stairways. The steps were rotten and crumbling, the water at the bottom stank, but somebody voiced the philosophy that one might as well drown as be shot and into the well went some seventy women and children.

By 9:30 the firing was general. On the strikers' side it proceeded from the railroad cut in the east, from rifle pits and sanitary trenches John Lawson had ordered dug in the colony months earlier, and from the arroyo north of the tents as far west as the Colorado and Southern steel bridge across it. Return fire came from Water Tank Hill, where Linderfelt had now deployed his men as skirmishers, and from in and under a string of steel railroad cars on the Colorado and Southeastern track.

At about 10 A.M. Linderfelt sent Lieutenant Lawrence and

three men off to the right with orders to dislodge the strikers from one end of the sand cut, at the same time dispatching a second party under Lieutenant Maurice Bigelow directly ahead to intercept any more making for the cut. Bigelow's detail ran into heavy fire and he fell back with a man wounded. Lieutenant Lawrence's sortie got about halfway when a striker's bullet entered Private Albert Martin's throat. The lieutenant applied a first-aid pack and the party retreated carrying the helpless soldier as far as they could until forced to abandon him in a draw. Several attempts thereafter to recover Martin were turned back the moment they were launched.

It was still morning when Linderfelt on Water Tank Hill spotted concentrations of strikers in the vicinity of the pump station and steel bridge about two thirds of a mile up the railroad track. Leaving Lieutenant Lawrence with the machine gun to continue firing on the sand cut, he gathered eight or ten men and led them in a crouching march north along the track. This was the principal military movement of the day: Linderfelt's advance up the shaft of the left-facing K toward the northern steel bridge across the arroyo. Once his men attained the first objective, the railroad depot, they concealed themselves in and around the buildings or behind lumber piles and raked the easterly flats with a steady fire that, aided by the machine gun on Water Tank Hill, dislodged the strikers from the sand cut and forced their retreat into the Black Hills.

The detachment pressed on up the railroad track, firing at the pump station, arroyo, and into the tent colony until their ammunition ran low. Uncertain of plans for fresh supplies, Linderfelt left a detail under command of his brother Ted, who although a captain apparently had no objection to obeying the lieutenant, and returned to the depot. He found Major Hamrock on the point of hanging up after telephoning General Chase in Denver. The major's orders now were to maintain present positions. Reinforcements and approximately 6000 rounds of ammunition were on the way.

Within the tent colony, chickens, dogs, and frightened children added to the racket of the guns. After the strikers were driven from the sand cut, increased fire fell upon the tents, shredding canvas, ricocheting off heavy iron stoves, shattering furniture, mirrors, utensils. Pearl Jolly wore improvised Red Cross armbands. The bullets nevertheless flew at her heels as she ran from tent to tent administering comfort and first aid. Louis Tikas, still a leader despite the failure of his initial efforts to keep the peace, found it necessary to be everywhere — directing the men entrenched in the arroyo, ascertaining that noncombatants were safely underground or evacuated, making repeated stops at the office tent to sprawl below bullet level and telephone John Lawson in Trinidad for help and instructions. Mothers in the holes kept trying, rarely with success, to climb out and get food for their tearful huddled young. Many of the husbands on the firing line or darting from tent to tent were without knowledge of their families' condition or whereabouts. John Bartoloti may have been making for the well where his wife sheltered with their children when four bullets pierced his chest and limbs and he fell, mortally wounded.

The pumpman provided what food and drink he could for the people in the well and any left to spare was carried by Mary Thomas across the bullet-swept ground between his converted boxcar home and the arroyo. She was thus engaged when Charles Costa was fatally hit. The story passed into legend, soon forgotten when legends became unfashionable in union circles, that Costa's last words before expiring in the arroyo were a request that "Union Forever" be sung at his funeral. He died mercifully unaware that his family would never attend it.

Meanwhile, Linderfelt's advance party remained stalled just north of the railroad depot. The relief force promised Hamrock was on its way, men rounded up over General Chase's busy telephone from the coal camps at Hastings, Berwind, and Segundo, and the courthouses and saloons of Aguilar and Trinidad — the warriors of Troop A, L. M. Bowers' "independent militiamen," undrilled and undisciplined, without officers, uniforms or regular arms but imbued — certainly its heavy contingent of mine guards were — with a contempt for the tent population that had crystallized into lethal hate.

Captain Carson, supplied with a CFI mine guard's .45, brought about fifty men. They included some of the area's most notorious labor baiters — sheriff's deputies like the George Titsworths, father and son, the elder a mine guard thirteen years for the CFI, and William Reno's local spy master, Monty Massingdale. They boarded a special train commandeered by Sheriff Grisham in Trinidad. Not for the first time, the Colorado and Southern's divisional superintendent had to intervene because the train crew balked at hauling men to fight the strikers.

The new troop's intimate connections with the CFI had bestowed on its members the military status that accompanies possession of a machine gun. Detraining south of Ludlow soon after 4 P.M., they commandeered a passing automobile to carry the gun and ammunition on up to Water Tank Hill, a peremptory act that unintentionally secured two witnesses, occupants of the car, who would testify later to overhearing the officers talk of clearing out the colonists and burning their tents.

Like the militiamen, the strikers were also looking forward to the arrival of reinforcements. John Lawson had responded to Tikas' urgent phone messages that morning by ordering his aides out to enlist every available volunteer into a relief army. While they were thus engaged, Lawson set out in the union's familiar red tourer with the hired driver, John Barulich, and Mike Livoda. After dropping Livoda off at Suffield, six miles out of Trinidad, to alert the small union colony there, Lawson ran into gunfire south of Ludlow forcing a detour east and north across open prairie. They finally parked behind Frank Bayes's ranch a mile or so west of Ludlow. Proceeding on foot along the arroyo, Lawson was unable to get any closer than the steel bridge, but he had Tikas notified and brought to him. Not all of what passed between the two is known. The Greek leader's report could hardly have been optimistic. As far as he knew the strikers still outnumbered their foe, but the soldiers were superior in weapons and at any moment were bound to be reinforced. The strikers also lacked medical attention. A sympathetic Aguilar physician had reached the steel bridge by way of the Bayes ranch too late to save Big Frank Rubino, an Italian striker shot in the head, and had crawled on south to the well where other wounded had been reported. Once down there with them, the doctor was trapped by the crossfire above the entrance. Lawson is believed to have told Tikas to hold out until the relief force got there. The two then embraced and separated.

By 5 P.M. the strength arrayed against the strikers numbered 177 men. Captain Carson reported to Linderfelt with a case of ammunition that the lieutenant broke open; after distributing the contents, he sent the newcomers on up the track to bolster his advance party. Simultaneously he ordered a messenger to Major Hamrock, now on Water Tank Hill with two machine guns, requesting that they be used to cover the drive. Hamrock ordered the guns swung around to point north and had the range altered to 1000 yards. As he said later, although his main targets were the pump station and steel bridge, he was unable to tell precisely where the bullets fell. The light was failing and he experienced some concern lest he machine gun his own men, but his announced determination with respect to the strikers was to "smoke 'em out." By their own admission, all the principal officers fired into the tents at one time or another and Hamrock was no exception.

The National Guard's official reference to the major and his company-bought machine guns ran, "There was no general wanton mowing down of the tents . . . Major Hamrock tested his range . . . and sent machine gun fire into the first tents . . . it could not be supposed that any women or children or other noncombatants remained in the colony. The women and children had been seen departing early in the morning and it was impossible to believe that the strikers would draw the fire of their opponents from all sides into the colony." Certainly the Colorado

National Guard did nothing to make sure that the tents were unoccupied.

About now, according to one militia report, Private Martin was brought in. Left wounded in a hollow between Water Tank Hill and the sand cut, the militiaman had died. He was also mutilated, but the militia's officers and medical men were to file curiously differing reports on the nature of the mutilations. No two accounts agreed on whether he had been shot in the head at close range or if his face was bludgeoned. "In such a way does the savage bloodlust of this southern European peasantry find expression," ran the official comment of the National Guard, based on the unverified presumption that the strikers had killed a helpless man or desecrated a corpse. Yet there was also disagreement over the time the body was recovered. Nine P.M., according to Lieutenant Lawrence who commanded the detail, but these "atrocities" inflicted upon Martin, "exciting his comrades to a frenzy," would be blamed by the militia's apologists for excesses unquestionably committed two or three hours earlier.

Actually, meaningless killing had got off to an early start. Innocent blood was shed in the middle of the day. Primo Larese, a passer-by on the road to Trinidad, unconnected with either of the warring forces, died when a stray bullet struck him in the head. About 5 P.M. Lieutenant Linderfelt was firing from the freight door at the depot, his rifle aimed into the southeast corner of the tent colony. Through his glasses, he afterward said, he could see eight or ten rifles poking from trenches in that vicinity and tent openings. At the same time Lieutenant Benedict's force, deployed west of the railroad track and augmented by civilian-clothed Troop A men fresh down the canyon from Osgood's mine at Hastings, were firing into the colony as well as at the steel bridge. Some Hastings men who crossed the arroyo and attacked the strikers from the rear were quickly beaten off with two casualties, one fatal. And Captain Ted Linderfelt, advancing "in a series of rushes," fired pointblank at tents in the southwest corner. Beyond question the tent colony was a no man's land under crossfire.

Its trapped occupants included the Snyders, one of the few families unseparated by the battle. William Snyder (no relation to the Baldwin-Felts undercover man Charles Snyder) owned no weapon and had stayed with his wife and six children in a pit beneath a tent that, measuring 16 by 24 feet and partitioned with a curtain, they had been pleased to call home since the first day of the walkout. An apparent lull in the fighting tempted them to venture forth for a meal. The eldest child, Frank, aged eleven, was fetching his baby sister a drink of water when the firing started up again and a heavy bullet flew through his brain. So fiercely did the gunfire resume, then, that Snyder was not allowed to finish the agonizing task of washing his dead son's face. He had only time to fold the boy's arms across his chest before shepherding his family underground again. And when next the Snyders emerged they saw five or six militiamen setting fire to the tent.

Some tents were already burning. The first flared in the southwest corner, where Hamrock's machine-gun bullets were striking, between 5:30 and 6 P.M. There is no evidence that this was deliberately started by militiamen. No systematic investigation was undertaken. The National Guard theorized vaguely that a bullet containing "high explosive material" must have struck the tent or that a stove overturned. Since the stoves weighed as much as 300 pounds or more, this possibility would have required, in Helen Ring Robinson's scoffing opinion at least, nothing less than the blast of a German field gun. Certainly the photographic evidence of the Ludlow devastation suggests that the stoves remained upright. Major Hamrock was at least half a mile from the scene and the light was fading. His subsequently varying testimony that the most advanced troops were no closer than 400 yards, 150 yards, 200 yards from the colony is difficult to take seriously. The men themselves halved Hamrock's lowest estimate, in closer conformity with other evidence that the Linderfelt brothers, Captain Carson, and Lieutenant Bigelow were all engaged as far up the railroad track as to be roughly abreast of the colony's first row of tents.

The nearest tent to them stood, in fact, just across the track
alongside a small, corrugated-iron store and some fifty feet from
the southwest corner of the colony. This detached tent was the
residence of one Bill Borton, the store owner, who kept a coal-oil
stove in it and a popcorn roaster fueled with gasoline. Frank
Bayes, a local rancher and deliveryman for the Continental Oil
Company, had put twenty gallons of bulk coal oil in Borton's tank
that Monday morning. But against the possibility that an accidental fire started in Borton's tent is Bayes's sworn testimony that
the can he kept his gasoline in for the roaster was dry that morning, and that Bayes subsequently recovered the coal-oil tank
undamaged, thus ruling out explosion. Yet Bayes, watching
through binoculars from his ranch a mile or so due west of the
colony, thought it was this tent that first went up in flames.

But the mystery surrounding the cause of the first tent blaze at
Ludlow is less important than the fact that no mystery at all is
attached to the burning of the main colony. This began an hour
or more later. There was very little wind, as Linderfelt was to
inadvertantly admit. Almost in the same breath he declared that
the wind became strong and carried the flames and sparks of "exploding ammunition" from one tent to another, but in truth at
least half a gale would have been needed to bridge the wide
spaces between the tent rows with flames. In any event, no one
ever seriously challenged the National Guard's own findings, influenced as will be seen by a comparatively fair-minded officer,
that "men and soldiers swarmed into the colony and deliberately
assisted the conflagration by spreading the fire from tent to tent
. . . Beyond a doubt, it was seen to, intentionally, that the fire
should destroy the whole of the colony."

As flames and smoke took possession of a canvas community
that twenty-four hours earlier had been the setting for Easter joy,
strikers' families penned up in terror during the battle gathered
what personal effects they could and frantically sought opportunity to flee. The attempt looked to be suicidal. Crossing the open
flat between the tents and the arroyo would mean exposure to the

riflemen along the railroad track, while a southward exit risked running into machine-gun bullets. But to stay among the burning tents was equally unthinkable.

What undoubtedly saved many lives was the timely arrival of a southbound local freight. It rumbled into Ludlow about 7:20 P.M., headlight picking out the militiamen firing across the track. The advancing train served as a temporary barrier between the opposing forces and in the cupola of its caboose a startled rear-brakemen saw not only the gun flashes all along the righthand side of the track, but, looking to his left, scores of women and children staggering from the pump-house buildings, the big well, and rows of burning tents to dash within the shadow of the thirty-six freight cars for the deep arroyo. The brakeman would also swear that he saw a uniformed man in the colony running a blazing torch up the tent sides. More might have been seen had the freight engineer carried out his intention of halting the train on a siding, but militiamen, presumably angered by the interruption and their exposure in the headlight's beam, aimed their rifles up at the engineer and cursed him on his way.

Once in the arroyo the surge of refugees split in two. Some veered off right along its broad bed, making for the Black Hills three miles away. The majority, obeying the counsel of Louis Tikas and other men on the firing line, stumbled westward toward Frank Bayes's ranch less than a mile off. In many cases there had been no time to dress adequately against the April temperature. The pregnant Mrs. Donner, having fled from tent to tent with her five exhausted children and seen invading troops use flaming brooms dipped in coal oil to ignite tents, was clad only in a thin shift, Mother Hubbard apron, and wornout shoes. Long cherished personal treasures were left behind. Mrs. Fyler, the paymaster's wife, kept glancing backward at the burning tents, grieving over childhood mementos left behind. She was to suffer an infinitely more unconsolable loss.

There was, as admitted, "the usual loot . . . clothes, bedding, jewelry, bicycles, tools and utensils were taken . . ." Some of the pillaging had begun even before the victims could leave their tents or crawl from holes of refuge. Juanita Hernandez had seen her husband's accordion stolen; another woman wept as civilian intruders, probably members of Troop A, carried off her sewing machine. Captain Carson, whose undisciplined irregulars were no easier to control than had been Louis Tikas' Greeks in the morning, tried to stop the looting. And as proof that not all the confiscation lacked military justification, from the tent marked *Headquarters, John Lawson* the soldiers took away not only a fresh supply of strikers' underwear but quantities of ammunition in thousand-round boxes.

The Snyders were leaving Ludlow too. Firing had slackened and they headed for the railroad depot, William Snyder carrying his three-year-old daughter on one arm and his dead son over his shoulder. Near the Snodgrass store Lieutenant Karl Linderfelt shone a flashlight in Snyder's face and only after further abuse and harassment, which one hopes the Snyders were too numbed by this time to sense, were they allowed to enter the depot, where they wrapped their boy in a white sheet and began an all-night wait for the train to Trinidad.

The machine-gun fire had tapered off because of a message brought by runner to Major Hamrock that Captain Carson and Lieutenant Linderfelt were about to storm the enemy's position. Now Linderfelt was leading the assault, he and his men shouting battle cries inspired by memories of similar charges against Filipinos and Mexicans. There arose suddenly what Linderfelt afterward described as "the most awful wail." His account, as absorbed into the official militia report, portrays the officers as stunned by this first realization that any women and children had remained in the colony after the battle started. And thereafter the officers appear as gallant rescuers, bullying or carrying a total of thirty-six wretched humans to safety, Linderfelt stalking from the blazing tents with a babe under each arm, Carson chopping away the floor "which was nailed down on these people." There was no subsequent rally of rescued victims — beneficiaries of the militia's chivalry — to attest to all this. Far from being noble deliverers, the troops were said by the National Guard itself to have "ceased to be an army and become a mob." Even so, there is some evidence that a number of soldiers did assist colonists out of the danger zone.

But no would-be rescuers looked in the hole underneath Alcarita Pedregon's tent. It was a pit approximately 8 feet long, 6 feet deep, and 4½ feet wide, the diameter of the entrance hole at the surface little more than 3 feet. The capacity of the pit, including the entrance area below ground, allowed for approximately 350 cubic feet of air space. A few timbers braced the roof. Leading down into the cave, four or five crude steps had been notched in the earth. Here the Pedregons and Costas had cowered since the bursting of Linderfelt's bombs at breakfast time, and later that morning they had been joined by Patricia Valdez and her four children. In other words, for most of the day this pit had been occupied by three women in their twenties and eight children aged from three months to nine years. The arrival of the Petruccis toward evening increased the total number of occupants to fifteen.

Mary Petrucci, aged twenty-four, was a true child of the coal camps. Born to a coal digger in the shadow of the tipple at the Victor-American mine, Hastings, she was raised and schooled on company property and at sixteen married a boxcar loader for a coal company in Walsenburg. They had a boy aged four and two girls, aged two and a half years and six months. A fourth Petrucci child, severely chilled one February morning in 1914 when militiamen for some reason refused the mother admittance to the Ludlow depot, sickened and died the following month.

Mary Petrucci's tent was No. 1 in the southwest corner, front row, and the first, or so it seemed to her, to be set on fire. When the flames curled inside the tent, compelling her to abandon the dugout, she raced to the Pedregons' tent directly behind, crawled near or under the bed above the pit entrance, and worked herself and the children down inside. The entrance hole was left uncovered. The only dangers that the women were aware of were the bullets and flames, and it was agreed that from these the safest place was below ground. There they stayed: Alcarita Pedregon and her two children; the Costas huddled under a single bedcover, Cedilano Costa in an advanced state of pregnancy; Patricia Valdez breast-feeding her three-month-old baby; the Petruccis squeezed up against the clay wall beneath the pit entrance. One or two of the little girls may have clutched homemade dolls.

When the tent overhead began to burn and smoke sank in on them through the open hole, Mary Petrucci grasped her infant tighter and strained upward. But all were too tightly cramped and quickly enfeebled by coughing to effect swift exit or even block the hole against the invading smoke. Then the Pedregons' burning bed collapsed, debris falling over the pit opening. Mary Petrucci slumped back with the baby still on her lap and in a few minutes was unconscious.

Above ground the shooting had become desultory, the gunfire now subordinate to the crackle of the flames consuming the colony. The day ebbed, its quota of sacrifice still to be completed. At an undetermined time, probably after 8 o'clock, Louis Tikas, whose exact location just then must be guessed, received a message summoning him to a section of the arroyo where he found some forty men fatigued and short of ammunition. Hope had all but been given up for the arrival of reinforcements. The strikers did not know that Lawson and a trainload of volunteers packed in five gondola cars, having left Trinidad on the Denver and Rio Grande track, had detrained at Barnes about four miles from Ludlow and were even now approaching on foot. Tikas ordered a retreat into the Black Hills, refusing to leave with his men but promising a quick reunion in the hills to plan a continuance of the struggle. Then he made off in the direction of the burning tents.

According to Pearl Jolly, herself about to take a party of refugees along the draw to the Bayes ranch, Tikas had heard screams coming from the tents and was hurrying to investigate. Pearl Jolly's own escape would have been in the nick of time: Militiamen now gained control of the steel bridge over the draw and thus sealed the westerly exit route. Tikas was also said by some to have decided on surrendering himself in exchange for a cease-fire and an end to the burning. At all events, he disappeared from view somewhere near the bullet-riddled pump house and minutes later Lieutenant Linderfelt near the intersection of the wagon road and the Colorado and Southern Railroad track heard a triumphal cry, "We've got Louie the Greek!"

They had also seized another familiar target for the lieutenant's perverse attentions during the strike months, the paymaster James Fyler. A third captive was never positively identified. All the evidence for what now followed comes from the military side. There were no sympathetic or impartial eyewitnesses. Of the more than fifty men who rushed to the scene when the prisoners were brought before Linderfelt sometime after 9 P.M. in the lieutenant's version, many were intensely prejudiced mine guards and Troop A irregulars. Linderfelt admitted that he cursed the Greek strike leader for failure to stop the conflict. Then Tikas "called me a name any man with red blood in his veins will not stand" and the lieutenant swung his Springfield rifle at the prisoner's head. Tikas' arm came up to take the blow, which fell with such force the stock of the rifle snapped. The slightly built Tikas, his scalp bleeding, did not fall. There were loud cries to hang him. Some went so far as to throw the lynch rope over a telegraph pole. Linderfelt ordered them to behave and turned the prisoners over to Sergeant Cullen, whom he charged with the responsibility for the Greek leader's life. But no sooner was he off down the track to collect men at the depot for a final assault across the flat, when Cullen shoved the prisoners on to a pair of militiamen named Mason and Pacheco, the latter a Mexican. "During this time, the group of men and prisoners at the crossroads were standing erect in the glare of the burning tents; they were not firing but afforded an excellent target to their adversaries." There was a fierce resumption of gunfire from the east. The militiamen, obliged to abandon their prisoners in order to save their own skins, jumped for cover along the western embankment. All three prisoners made an immediate dash for the tents, were caught in the crossfire, and killed.

This was the superficial version offered by the militia. More detailed evidence at the inquest, particularly from the Las Animas County physician who examined the victims, indicated that Tikas had been shot three times in the back and the fact that two of the bullets had passed clear through his body identified them as the steel-jacket type fired from the soldiers' Springfields. The one bullet recovered, fatally damaging lungs and heart before lodging between the ribs, was of the soft-nosed variety not officially issued to the National Guard. Troop A of course was not armed with standard weapons. The stated cause of Tikas' death was internal hemorrhaging. As for the rifle-butt blow, it had left a scalp wound 1½ inches long and deep enough to show bone but had caused no discoverable skull fracture.

James Fyler died from a frontal gunshot wound in the head. When the paymaster's body reached his widow, she accused the militiamen of having looted it of a ring, a gold watch, union documents, and $300 in cash. Little of significance was said at the inquest or anywhere else about the death of the third man.

Scattered firing filled the remaining hours of darkness. Soon after midnight Major Hamrock rode up to the coal camp at Berwind and reported by telegram to General Chase in Denver: The strikers had attacked first, the soldiers had resisted, and when the tents accidentally caught fire, they had risked their lives to rescue women and children. Of casualties on either side his telegram said nothing. Hamrock withdrew the soldiers and their motley allies from combat and they rested, some of them in the railroad depot, their boastful banter about the day's events audible in the baggage room, where the Snyders sat with their five sleeping children and the sixth who would not awaken.

East of Ludlow bands of strikers met up with Lawson and told him the colony was done for. The stragglers and the reinforcements then combined and headed into the Black Hills to mobilize for new moves, reunite with families, or anxiously inquire after the missing. A rancher in the hills heard a woman sobbing all

night long for her lost life's savings, heard also bitter recrimina-
tions directed not alone at the militia but the impetuous and hot-
headed Greeks. To the west of Ludlow, Frank Bayes and his wife
watched their food supplies dwindle as the tired and hungry kept
streaming in long after midnight. And by 5 A.M., at the first glimmer of dawn, militia bullets were streaking near the Bayes ranch.

It may have been the sound of renewed gunfire that stirred
Mary Petrucci half awake in the acrid blackness of the pit under
the smoking embers of the Pedregons' tent. The baby on her lap
was utterly motionless. She reached for the hand of her son beside her and found it cold.

·····15·····

CANYONS OF STRIFE

THE LONG-DISTANCE TELEPHONE had yet to bring the blessings of
direct communication between the western lands and the Atlantic
seaboard. Telegrams composed in haste and with bias gave John
D. Rockefeller, Jr., and the governor of Colorado their first intelligence of the fighting at Ludlow. L. M. Bowers told Rockefeller it
was an unprovoked attack upon heavily outnumbered militiamen,
causing casualties and a fire in the strikers' colony with explosions
that proved the existance of dynamite in the tents. Bowers advised that this information be given to "friendly papers." Rockefeller wired back his regrets over "this further outbreak of lawlessness" and then, there is evidence to suggest, turned his thoughts to
the improvements under way at Pocantico and Mrs. Rockefeller's
objection to the "rather cramped" conditions resulting from a pro-
liferation of gardens, balconies, and terraces.

The news started trickling in to the governor during Monday
afternoon and evening. Learning nothing definite, he sat up all
night at the home of Colorado's Congressman Edward Taylor in
northwest Washington, hoping for denials to some of the more
distressing bulletins. He had left instructions with his lieutenant
governor and General Chase that if the calm in the coalfields
lasted until April 22 the balance of the National Guard should be
withdrawn. But on Tuesday morning, April 21, Washington
newspapers mostly preoccupied with the military moves against
Mexico spared enough column space for other matters to impress
upon Governor Ammons that the calm had been well and truly

shattered. The governor did not then know the half of it, but after another anxious night and for the next twenty-four hours telegrams overwhelmed him.

One from Chase told of a couple of hundred troopers, "half of them recruits," clinging to the Ludlow area in critical need of reinforcement but additional men could not be put in the field unless funds were forthcoming. This meant a special session of the legislature, which only the governor could call for. Stephen Fitzgarrald's wire said much the same. Six hundred soldiers were needed "to avert catastrophe" but were not likely to move without assurance of that special session to guarantee their pay. "We think we had better do it . . ."

Fitzgarrald also reported the coal-camp country as "helpless." More accurately, in those hours immediately following the battle at Ludlow, the situation south of Walsenburg was confused and rumor-ridden. There were stories of massacre and incendiarism by the militiamen, and fears of imminent counterattack by hordes of miners and sympathizers now arming themselves in the hills. Mystery surrounded the disappearance of a number of Ludlow colonists, and the efforts of concerned local citizens to investigate among the ashes were discouraged by Major Hamrock's guns.

The flow of unverified intelligence into the union offices at Denver had a galvanic effect on Ed Doyle, who unleashed a flock of his own telegrams to Colorado congressmen and labor leaders begging them "For God's sake and in the name of humanity . . . to demand of the President of the United States and both houses of Congress to leave Mexico alone and come into Colorado . . . miners, their wives and children, are being slaughtered by the dozen." Without awaiting direction from Indianapolis, Doyle next alerted every union local in the state for defensive action. He phoned Lawson in Trinidad and conferred with William T. Hickey, a leader of the State Federation of Labor who assumed the role of military coordinator. Out went a "Call to Arms" over the signatures of Doyle, Lawson, Hickey, and others. To resist "armed assassins in the employ of coal companies . . . serving under the guise of militiamen" labor unionists were directed to organize armed volunteer companies, sending their rosters and any spare guns to William Hickey in the German-American Bank Building, Denver.

The accurate measure of the bloodshed at Ludlow was still not generally known twenty-four hours after the slaying of Louis Tikas, but retaliation was expected momentarily. "When day breaks there will be 600 to 700 strikers waiting to crush the soldiers," Harvey Deuell had written for the Tuesday morning edition of the Rocky Mountain *News*. The only gunfire before noon consisted of nuisance volleys aimed at Frank Bayes' ranch, interrupting the extra milking chores he had to perform for replenishing the supplies consumed by the refugees crowded in his cellar. The militia at Ludlow had other things to do. When Bayes climbed the windmill tower in front of his ranch and peered through field glasses at a group of tents in the southeast corner of the colony still standing, he saw four or five soldiers methodically set them afire.

East of the ranch Susan Hollearan, the Ludlow postmistress whose father owned the ground leased to the union, had watched the same burning from the depot yards. Then she hurried along to the colony site. For seven months a neighboring community of song and laughter as well as peril and despondency, she found it now a deserted shambles of blackened tent poles, skeletal bedsteads, shards of pottery and glass, scorched floorboards, and charred clothing. The postmistress also found her friend Mary Petrucci wandering in a daze, unclear of the whereabouts of her children, unable to tell how she had got out of the pit or indeed point out its location.

Susan Hollearan discovered Alcarita Pedregon in a similar incoherent state. She put them both on the Trinidad train, aroused Lieutenant Karl Linderfelt, who was sleeping in the depot, and requested an escort to search for the missing children. She had understood the women to say their underground refuge had been in the second row of tents from the rear. Heedless of the scoffing of a few militiamen, she searched anxiously, but the dugouts had caved in or were choked with debris. She returned to her post office and it was some time that Tuesday afternoon when the Pedregon pit was uncovered exposing the bodies of Patricia Valdez and her four children — Elvira, 3 months, Eulala, 8, Mary, 7, and Rudolph, 9; the pregnant Cedilano Costa and her children — Onafrio, 6, and Lucy, 4; the two Pedregon children — Gloria, 4, and Roderlo, 6; the three Petrucci children — Frank, 6 months, Lucy, 3, and Joe, 4.*

Major Hamrock was notified of the discovery but for reasons still obscure took no immediate steps to get the bodies out. That same day Edwin Brake, the state labor commissioner, left Denver for the south to see if reports reaching the capital corresponded with the truth. When his train reached Ludlow twenty-five militiamen boarded the cars boasting, Brake said, of the number of rednecks they had killed. They refused to let him get off the train and he had to carry on to Trinidad. On the other hand, Doctor Edwin Curry, the Victor-American Company physician and a founding member of Troop A, entered the colony ruins that afternoon and visited the death pit. Exactly who was first to see the dead remains a mystery. According to the Colorado Springs *Gazette,* a railroad telephone linesman repairing the broken line stumbled across the dugout, but no other newspaper picked up this story and no linesman ever came forward to testify.

Neither is it known how the news of Ludlow's death pit reached Trinidad. From the experience of the undertakers requested by the union to go out and collect the victims late that night it is safe to assume that it was not through the cooperative offices of the Colorado National Guard. The three "dead wagons" had just passed Cedar Hill when a storm of machine-gun bullets struck the road ahead, killed a grazing calf, and panicked the wagon team. The drivers wheeled and raced back to Trinidad. The dead were

---

* The spelling of the first names may not be accurate in every case. Where the immigrant families were concerned, neither notaries public nor coroner's clerks went to any great trouble to get the names right.

still in the pit Wednesday morning. The corpses of Louis Tikas and the other two prisoners shot near the railroad track also lay where they had fallen, plainly visible to shocked passengers on passing trains.

There is no telling how long this appalling state of affairs would have been allowed to continue if left to Major Hamrock and his superiors. Neither is there much point in speculating on just what the militia authorities had in mind or whether there are genuine grounds for the suspicion afterward circulated that burning or some other form of body disposal was contemplated. Clues are unavailable because the appropriate questions were never asked at any subsequent inquiry. Yet there exists no evidence of base motive, and the obscurity surrounding the discovery of the dead in Ludlow's "black hole," the refusal of the militia detachment to allow prompt and unprejudiced examination or sanitary collection of the victims, may all have been due to nothing more sinister than blind uncertainty or plain funk.

Anyway, the word had got out. Around noon on Wednesday, representatives of the Colorado and Southern Trainmen and Engineers in Rugby, fifteen miles north of Ludlow, wired John Lawson:

> BODIES OF WOMEN AND CHILDREN EXPOSED IN TENT COLONY . . .
> DEATH FROM SUFFOCATION THE CAUSE   PLEASE DO SOMETHING WITH
> THE BODIES FOR GOD'S SAKE FOR THEY ARE HUMAN SOULS AND DE-
> SERVING OF DECENT BURIAL

At noon the same day John McLennan, who had arrived in Trinidad, telephoned an agent of the American National Red Cross with some influence around the Denver statehouse to try and restrain Hamrock's machine gunners long enough for the bodies to be recovered. Not until five hours later was this done, perhaps because the agent, S. Poulterer Morris, felt obliged to tread carefully. He was in the process of securing full accreditation for a Denver chapter of the Red Cross and wanted nothing to go awry at this point. But this organization, still young, with only thirteen years as a quasi-official agency of the United States government, was itself unprepared for the present contingency. The first response from headquarters in Washington, D.C., to Morris' request for guidance — namely, that the Red Cross could not participate in relief operations growing out of labor controversies — was countermanded the following day and explanation given that the fire had, after all, placed the situation on a disaster basis.

At any rate, the undertaker's wagons set out for Ludlow again under a flag of truce and this time Hamrock's guns were silent. McLennan, accompanying the party, was twice arrested by the major's men but this constituted the only harassment. The thirteen bodies in the Pedregons' dugout were separated and extricated, a prolonged and harrowing task, and taken into Trinidad, where an inquest was held six days later. The testimony presented showed unanimity on the cause of death: asphyxiation.

Significance was attached to the time element. If the victims could be shown to have died during the day, responsibility rested with the strike leaders who encouraged them to shelter in the pits. If the fire in some way caused their deaths, then culpability shifted in the direction of the militia. Understandably, after the long delay, no medical evidence was vouchsafed approximating a time of death. Doctor Curry, the coal-company physician permitted at the death site before anyone else, was dogmatic in his assertion that nobody could have lived in the pit all day. Major Boughton had described it as "almost hermetically sealed," but, said Curry, speaking as a "medical expert . . . even if the trap door above the pit were open the thirteen would have died within two hours as their bodies generated such heat that pure air could not descend into the pit." The atmosphere became poisonous after twenty minutes. The children died first. In sum, the oxygen in the chamber had not been sufficient to support the lives of the thirteen and they had suffocated long before the tents caught fire.

This argument presumed that all the victims had been in the pit since morning. Obstinately reiterated by guardsmen of every rank from General Chase down, it was to become an unbelievably fatuous presumption. That the two women who survived did not appear at the coroner's inquest was understandable in the light of their still-numbed state. However, Mrs. Pedregon's affidavit was secured ten days after the destruction of the Ludlow colony. At that time and in all future inquiries conducted by the Colorado National Guard, the dogged assumption was that neither Mary Petrucci nor Alcarita Pedregon existed, that there had been no survivors from the death pit, and as if in furtherance of this design no mention of either woman appears in any published testimony gathered by the guard. The militia's "findings" were an eminently suitable base for the defensive statements put out by the companies, some of them implying knowledge that not even the National Guard had claimed. For instance, E. H. Weitzel wrote in *Coal Age* that the victims were suffocated "by being placed in a cellar . . . and covered over by tight plank boards with mattresses thrown over the floor. This was done by the strikers themselves in their ignorance of natural laws and the women and children were suffocated not by the burning of the tent but by lack of air circulation in the hole in which they were placed by their would-be protectors." Both women who survived testified in 1914 that the pit entrance was uncovered. Mary Petrucci's recollection on this point was still firm in 1971.

The Pedregons' pit was crowded but not overcrowded until the late afternoon. When the tents were set afire and Mary Petrucci and her children entered the pit all were alive. Oxygen deficiency would have approached the lethal point only when the tent burned overhead. The survival of two of the pit's occupants proved that conditions within the pit were not uniformly intolerable for human life and admitted the possibility that incoming smoke accumulated or clung in varying density. The victims were asphyxiated by smoke inhalation. These factors or theories would not have been lost on even the customary hand-picked coroner's jury, though its verdict might have suggested otherwise. In this rare case the jury was not wholly antagonistic to strikers and unionists. John J. Hendricks, the district attorney often found in the miners' corner, directed the questioning of witnesses. And the Las Animas County coroner, B. B. Sipe, may not have thought so highly of the soldiers since he had ridden one of the "dead wagons" turned back by Hamrock's gunners. The coroner's verdict, henceforth ignored by the coal companies and militia as utterly as the fact of the two survivors, found that the victims "came to their deaths by asphyxiation or fire, or both, caused by the burning of the tents of the Ludlow colony and that the fire on the tents was started by militiamen under Major Hamrock and Lieutenant Linderfelt, or mine guards, or both . . ."

The shocked pause following the news of the grim discovery at Ludlow offered an opportunity for wise intervention and quick steps to peace. Then it was gone and the hate flared higher. Conciliation looked now to be impossible and even neutral charity was rewarded with malice. At considerable risk Frank Bayes made trips to Trinidad and various ranches, distributing his refugees. He and his wife returned from one to find their home broken into, furniture overturned, silverware scattered, even a child's savings bank looted, and a canceled check with a warning scribbled on the back:

> *This is to be your pay for harboring the union, cut it out or we will call again.*
>
> B.F. and C.N.G.

Fury swept through the "mobilization camps" in the Black Hills, where several hundred strikers and their allies had been shivering in the absence of camp fires that would have attracted militia bullets. What next occurred in the Trinidad coalfield became mythologized into a coordinated attack by over 1000 strikers along a forty-mile front. It was not that organized and here and there involved political feuding and the settlement of old scores. Communications were not efficient enough for large-scale concerted action. What planning took place was improvised and local. But a large part of the general inspiration for aggressive action flowed from one man — John Lawson.

In the privacy of a hotel room just before going into the Black Hills, he had confessed his inability to control all of his men. Secretly despairing of a situation that had slipped so far out of hand, he rationalized his decisions now on grounds that force must be met by force. His public tone of voice in the days after Ludlow was as militant as that of any of the ideological hotspurs in whose company he had never felt comfortable. "I must decline to state where the strikers secured the guns they used . . . I am sorry they haven't got ten thousand times as many . . ." He blamed the "hellish acts" on John D. Rockefeller, Jr., who "may ease his conscience by attending Sunday School regularly in New York but he will never be acquitted of committing the horrible atrocities . . . We now have the sinews of war backed by guns and ammunition and the faith and financial backing of every union-labor man in the country . . . The murder of men and women at Ludlow . . . has cinched the determination to fight to a finish . . ." When he broke openly with the union in later years remarks like these would be recalled by foes labeling him a publicity-hunting poseur. At the moment of utterance they damned him in the eyes of coal operators while divorcing him further from the pacifistic hierarchy of the UMW. But they stirred the pulses of a tatterdamalion army now swarming through hills and over mesas to burn, wreck, and kill.

*

The Victor-American mine at Delagua was kept working by strikebreakers who could count on no more than fifteen mine guards for their protection. The guards were on watch along the northern ridge above the mine at 5 A.M. on April 22 when 160 strikers, stealing across the hills from Aguilar in the night, launched their first attack. Both sides raced at once for the highest point of the ridge; a mine guard died in the fire fight for its possession. The strikers won and, in one of several subsequent attacks, rushed to within 200 yards of the mine entrance, killing two more guards. Meanwhile, on Cedar Hill near Ludlow, a squad of thirty militiamen under Captain Carson, alerted for the relief of Delagua, waited impatiently for a special locomotive to come and haul them up the Colorado and Southeastern track. It arrived late but the strikers had failed repeatedly to capture the mine and when the train steamed in view with the troops at 7:30 P.M. they retreated along Apishapa Creek.

By now buildings and installations were blazing at six big mines. West of Aguilar at the Empire mine, owned by one of the smaller enterprises, Southwestern Fuel, the stage was set for even worse tragedy than had occurred at Ludlow. The day had begun with sniper fire from the surrounding slopes and, anticipating trouble, the company president, J. W. Siple, had transferred thirty-five mine officials, employees, wives, and children, from offices and dwellings to the shelter of the tipple house. But it was in this vicinity that the strikers attacked in force around midday. Fires were started and, fanned by a light breeze, they spread rapidly. At the same time shots ripped through the wooden walls of the tipple house. William Waddell, the mine superintendent, had hung behind, frantically seeking his young son, unaware that the boy was crouched in hiding with a leg wound up among the rafters of the boiler house. The elder Waddell was looking along the west side of the tipple when a bullet pierced his lungs. The tipple area quickly became untenable and Siple ordered everybody back to the mine. Carrying the wounded superintendent and two or three infants, they groped inside to a distance of about twenty-five yards. Six armed defenders at the mine entrance kept the strikers off, killing three of them, during this retreat. Unable to reach the people in the mine with rifles, some of the strikers scrambled up the hillside and dropped a charge of dynamite down the forty-foot air shaft. It exploded eighty feet from the terrified party in the blackness of the mine and more dynamite was set off on the surface, blowing the fan house to pieces. Yet a third blast at the mouth of the mine where the roof was loosely timbered brought tons of it crashing down. When darkness fell all the buildings of the Empire mine were burning or in ashes, Siple's people were still trapped in the mine, and, since the ventilation fans were destroyed, their air supply steadily diminished.

Word of the thirty-five entombed alive in the Empire mine reached Major Hamrock at Ludlow. But he expected a massed attack on his own position any minute from the Black Hills and he had barely a hundred men with two machine guns to meet it.

These events burdened the communication channels to Elias Ammons' vacated desk in Denver while his substitute, Fitzgarrald, tried in vain to resist the operators' latest importunities. That morning they had conferred with thirty members of the Denver chamber of commerce and all left in a body for the capital set on forcing Fitzgarrald to hurry the troops back into the strike field. Beyond making an agitated effort to arrange a truce through John McLennan, the lieutenant governor hoped to avoid anything in the nature of positive action until Ammons returned. But as J. F. Welborn afterward said, he and his fellow operators applied "heavy pressure" upon Fitzgarrald. General Chase was also very much in evidence with galling reminders that not a militiaman would budge unless somehow assured of his pay. Off now went the telegrams to Ammons in Washington urging an extra session of the legislature. Ammons' reply was a promise to arrange the troops' temporary pay immediately on his return. Fitzgarrald then ordered General Chase once more into the strike zone "with such forces as in your judgment may be necessary to create laws, suppress insurrection and repel invasion."

With United States Marines about to land at Vera Cruz and Washington, D.C., caught up in a jingo fever, Ammons' innocent mission to seek a fair deal for settlers in his state had stood a slim chance for a hearing anyway, and now he put the matter out of his head entirely. The governor left for home, a bald, almond-faced little man with large ears and faltering gaze, whose unimpressive bearing seems somehow to have been inadequately suited to the known facts of his boyhood strength and perseverance and rather more appropriate to the image of pusillanimity in which he was now cast by capitalists and labor unions alike in his beloved state.

United Mine Workers' leaders, 1915: Frank Hayes, United Mine
Workers' vice president, left, and Ed Doyle, Secretary-Treasurer,
District 15. *Library of Congress*

John Lawson, Mother Jones, the aggressive matriarch of the miners' union, and Horace Hawkins, United Mine Workers' attorney. *West Virginia Collection*

General John Chase, Commander of the Colorado National Guard. *Library, State Historical Society of Colorado*

Opposite page: The saber charge along Main Street, Trinidad, January 22, 1914, after General Chase fell off his horse. *Denver Public Library, Western Collection*

Jeff "King" Farr, long-time sheriff of Huerfano
County and protector of the CFI's interests. *Denver Public Library, Western Collection*

John C. Osgood testifying before the Congressional investigating committee, Denver, February 10, 1914. At right, D. W. Brown, President of the Rocky Mountain Fuel Company. *Denver Public Library, Western Collection*

L. M. Bowers, Chairman of the Board, CFI, during the strike. *Library of Congress*

Jack McQuarrie

You had better leave this part of the country, as you are to free with your mouth and God hates a squealer You done fine in Denver but it is the Last chance you will have

Take my advice or Take a Traitors chance

Committie

"Black Hand" letter of warning received by John McQuarrie, formerly a company agent, who testified on behalf of the strikers before the Congressional group. *Library, State Historical Society of Colorado (Dold Collection)*

The crude armored car feared as the Death Special. Note machine gun manned by Baldwin-Felts detectives. *Library, State Historical Society of Colorado (Dold Collection)*

Miners' houses in the town of Primero, about 1910. *Library of Congress*

Elias Ammons,
Governor of Colorado.
Colorado State Archives

John Lawson, strikers' leader, and the Greek interpreter Louis Tikas in the strike field near Ludlow. *Library, State Historical Society of Colorado (Dold Collection)*

Strikers' tent colony near Walsenburg after the great blizzard, December 3, 1913. *Library, State Historical Society of Colorado (Dold Collection)*

National Guard militiamen en route to a battle near Ludlow, probably October 1913. *Library, State Historical Society of Colorado (Dold Collection)*. Below: Coal company guard and two militiamen wait on a loaded car for the approach of union pickets, probably October 1913. *Library, State Historical Society of Colorado*

National Guard officers at Ludlow, April 1914: Lieutenant Karl E. Linderfelt, center; on Linderfelt's right, his two brothers; on his left, Lieutenant Gerry Lawrence and Major Pat Hamrock. *Denver Public Library, Western Collection*

The militia mans a machine-gun post with mine-guard allies at the foot of Water Tank Hill. *Library, State Historical Society of Colorado*

Ludlow tent colony on the eve of its destruction. *State Historical Society of Colorado*

The death pit, where women and children perished. *Denver Public Library, Western Collection*

Ruins of the tent colony, April 1914. Note upright stoves and pits for storage and refuge. *Denver Public Library, Western Collection*

"Ludlow, Colorado, 1914" by John Sloan. Cover for *Masses*, June 1914. *Dartmouth College Collection, gift of John and Helen Farr Sloan, courtesy of the Trustees of Dartmouth College*

Funeral for the martyred Louis Tikas. A line of walking strikers a mile long follows the cortege from the Trinidad business district. Note Colorado Supply Company building, part of the CFI's company store system. *Library, State Historical Society of Colorado*

Balkan-born miners like the guerrilla strikers above attacked Forbes on April 30, 1914. *West Virginia Collection.* Below, mining property still burning after the attack. The body on the tramway track is of the mine's slain blacksmith. *Library, State Historical Society of Colorado*

Frank Walsh, Chairman of the Industrial Relations Commission, 1915. *Library of Congress*

This is the picture of young Frank Snyder, slain at Ludlow, that Frank Walsh thrust before Rockefeller at the Industrial Relations Commission hearings, May 1915. *Library, State Historical Society of Colorado*

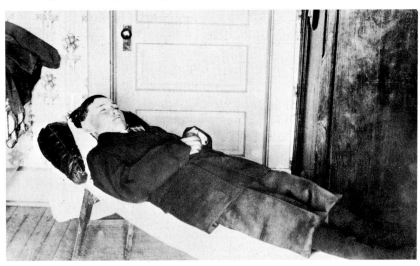

John D. Rockefeller, Jr., after appearing before Frank Walsh. Just behind and on his left, Mackenzie King. *Courtesy of Dr. Joseph Ernst, Archivist of Rockefeller Family Papers, Rockefeller Center, New York*

Mackenzie King, Canada's future prime minister, and the young Rockefeller in miner's garb during their tour of the properties in the fall of 1915. *Courtesy of Dr. Joseph Ernst, Archivist of Rockefeller Family Papers, Rockefeller Center, New York*

The United Mine Workers' monument to the Ludlow dead, shortly after its construction in 1915. The death pit is a few feet in front of it. *Archives, Denver* Post

That impression had also spread beyond its borders. To an appeal Ammons issued earlier for practical solutions to the strike, William Green, secretary-treasurer of the UMW, had retorted with candor that he should have taken a positive stand, demanded that both sides submit all questions to arbitration. What if there were no law on the statute books providing for the assumption of such authority? His boldness would have won such public support neither the operators nor the miners could have resisted. Green had ended: "You can still do it." But Ammons felt otherwise and what worried him once more was the question of how to raise money. His administration owed a total of $1 million, the militia's campaign had cost $600,000 so far, and the troops had yet to be paid for their last three months of service.

On the long journey westward the governor was allowed little respite. Telegrams awaited him at most big stations and even whistle stops. "We beg that you rush troops to Rugby," wired the president of the Primrose Coal Company in Pueblo. "Should be there in eight hours or great loss of life. 375 men, women and children at Primrose camp and we are not prepared to protect them." When his train drew into Harrisburg, Pennsylvania, at about 10 P.M. this awaited him from Sheriff Grisham:

STRIKE SITUATION ABSOLUTELY BEYOND CONTROL . . . THIRTY MEN WOMEN AND CHILDREN NOW AMONG THE DEAD   TIPPLE AT EMPIRE MINE BLOWN UP   ROYAL MINE NOW BURNING . . .

J. F. Welborn minced no words. Delay in suppressing the uprising would be "criminal," and a second telegram from the CFI president reaching Pittsburgh in time for the governor's train painted the situation as "hourly more desperate. Wholesale disaster may occur before midnight. Will you mobilize troops immediately?"

A wrathful labor demonstration and the entire police force augmented by militia units were at Denver's Union Station to meet the train at 8:30 P.M., April 23. The demonstrators were disappointed if they expected to see the governor. Warned of threats to assassinate him, he had left the train a dozen miles northeast, was met by the president of the chamber of commerce, and smuggled into the city by auto. At the statehouse Fitzgarrald greeted him in tears. The lieutenant governor was a Christian Scientist who had spent much of the past three days in prayer or soliciting the prayers of fellow believers. Someone had told him brutally that if all-out war erupted in the coalfields "the state guard would come home in boxes . . . strikers would fall in heaps in the canyons and arroyos." Had that happened while he was acting governor, "I should not have lived three weeks . . ." About half-past ten that night Stephen Fitzgarrald handed over affairs to Ammons, and the governor was once again in the thick of it.

One source of consternation to him was the attitude of sections of the press. Only the tone of the Denver *Express* contained more sorrow than anger. A Scripps publication, it had energetically championed the strike and missed no opportunity to condemn the operators and militia. Foreseeably it regarded the bloodshed at Ludlow as woeful justification for its long prounion crusade. The Denver *Post* and Denver *Republican* had always favored the operators, although not slavishly, and had professed to see no reason except sentimentality why the strikers continued the stoppage. Influential newspapers accurately charged as being "coal company tools" were those with strong circulation in the coalfield counties where the companies' stranglehold on the press had become part of local tradition. The Pueblo *Star Journal*, Pueblo *Chieftain*, Walsenburg *World*, Boulder *Daily Camera*, were operators' mouthpieces no less blatantly than Judge Northcutt's two Trinidad papers, the *Advertiser* and the *Chronicle-News*, whose editor admitted nearly half a century later that he had smothered sympathy for the miners and editorially vilified them because to do so made money for himself and his publisher. These papers, generally speaking, had treated the governor kindly since the advent of the strike. But now the *Daily Camera*, for instance, blamed everything on Ammons' "dilly-dallying," and most upsetting of all was the radical shift of the widely read Rocky Mountain *News.*

During the first months of the strike the paper was published by the former United States senator Thomas Patterson, whose sympathies were for labor but whose advanced age and pacifist inclinations precluded aggressive crusading. In late October 1913 its acquisition by John C. Shaffer of Chicago signified little alteration in editorial policy. Shaffer had no intention of getting involved in Denver's political brawls and on the first day of the coal strike the *News* meekly judged both sides to be acting within their rights. Two months later the paper slid in the strikers' direction by supporting unionism in principle, scrambling back to the middle of the road with a scolding for the UMW's insistence on recognition, and named Governor Ammons, thanks to his "wise and impartial attitude," as the public's best hope for a strike settlement.

Things began to change after the Congressional hearings shed light on ugly conditions in the coalfields, and Shaffer sent William Chenery from Chicago to the Rocky Mountain *News* as an editorial writer. A third important factor was the assignment of Harvey Deuell to cover the strike. Deuell employed the same journalistic mix of emotion and objectivity that Damon Runyon had once effectively blended for the paper. Still Ammons found little in the *News* to complain about. But Chenery had developed instincts for muckraking badly in need of exercise. Only in deference to John Shaffer's satisfaction with the Denver daily's 16,000 circulation and the boss's disposition against upsetting apple carts had he squirmed under self-imposed inhibitions.

Ludlow exploded them. The fact that Shaffer was safely away from the scene vacationing in Europe also helped. Overnight Elias Ammons became a lackey of the coal barons and the leading editorial of the April 22 issue, headed MASSACRE OF THE INNOCENTS, traced a fruitless search for parallels to Ludlow via allusions to the Indian slaughter of frontier families, Villa's barbarities in Mexico, and the "bloodiest page in the French Revolution." But the mine guards and militiamen who pulled the triggers and brandished the torches were not the guilty. "The blood of the innocent women and children rests on the hands of those who for greed of dollars employed such men . . . The world had not been hard upon these; theirs had been a gentle upbringing. Yet they reck not when pecuniary interests are involved. The blood of the women and children, burned and shot like rats, cries aloud from the ground. The great state of Colorado has betrayed them." Woodrow Wilson was passionately supplicated. "Think, Mr. President . . . then, with that vast power which has been committed to you . . . attend to the misery wrought by an anarchistic lust for dollars."

Since the chief executive might not be expected to have the Rocky Mountain *News* readily delivered, a telegram was dispatched pleading with him to "act as promptly and as patriotically as you have met the issue in Mexico. Here in Colorado . . . under the stars and stripes, and in the uniforms of American soldiers, we are murdering people whose principal offense is that they are fighting for a living."

All this was too much for the Denver chamber of commerce, whose members stormed into the Rocky Mountain *News* editorial offices and swore they would withdraw their advertising unless Chenery was silenced and Deuell transferred to some other newsfront. Chenery defied Denver's big business to do its worse, singled out the CFI for special scorn, and declared that the company chieftains could never bulldoze and browbeat the *News* as they had the governor of the state of Colorado. The Denver *Post*, financially Colorado's sturdiest newspaper, allied itself promptly with the *News* and the threat of a boycott diminished. But though Chenery had briefly trebled his paper's circulation with the "Massacre" essay, he had also numbered his days on its editorial staff.

Meanwhile Ammons was hoping for the best from a truce negotiated by Stephen Fitzgarrald and Horace Hawkins, the miners' attorney, which, if Lawson and McLennan carried out their promise to enforce it, would end the shooting in a matter of hours. The other side of the bargain required Chase's troops to proceed no further south than Ludlow. Right then the general had his work cut out to make them so much as leave Denver. He had boasted his ability to put 600 men in the field without delay, and he had issued the call at midnight, April 22. All branches of the Colorado National Guard were to mobilize and entrain for the south. Only 362 answered the summons and 76 men of Troop C, confined to a grimy ill-ventilated armory since their return from the strike zone weeks earlier, answered the general's call with mutiny. Unpaid, hungry and rebellious, they refused to stir until given all their back pay owing. Ironically, Troop C was familiarly known as the Chase Troop because two sons and three other relatives of the general were on its roster. Chase himself finally washed his hands of the mutinous men and, although their captain swore he would drag them to the front in handcuffs if necessary, they were left behind in Denver.

Other elements were lukewarm. Company K of Denver, the "College Company," mustered only 25 men under Captain Van Cise, who had postponed his wedding when first ordered to the strike zone and now had to do so again. General Chase took along two 3-inch field pieces with 220 shrapnel shells but had scarcely enough artillery men to man them. Six locomotive crews were called before a fireman and engineer were found willing to haul the militia. The troop train steamed out of Denver shortly after noon on April 23, two engines pulling twenty-three cars, two of them flatcars carrying the field pieces. A dozen sharpshooters rode in the locomotive and as a pathfinder, a precaution against possibly dynamited or blocked track, two empty steel cars were coupled in front. As soon as the train had departed, Ed Doyle wired ahead, warning strikers everywhere to be on the lookout for its approach. Doyle gave a description of the train, the equipment, and the number of troops it carried, even the serial numbers on the engine, but issued no orders to intercept it. As stated in his telegram, the purpose was to make sure that "these militiamen will not repeat the horrible massacres of Ludlow . . ."

The train rolled very slowly southward, not reaching Walsenburg until after midnight. Here there had been occasional fighting and citizens who had remained in town were in a nerve-wracked state fearing a general attack on the nearby mines. To arm the strikers, more guns and ammunition had been rushed into the combat zone. Racing General Chase's troop train south, William Hickey, E. L. Neelly, Eli Gross, and Don MacGregor rode in a four-car caravan loaded with arms from Hickey's home in Denver. They were driving through rain and sleet south of Pueblo when the leading car skidded off the highway and plunged into seventeen feet of water. While Neelly and Hickey held off inquisitive farmers with their Winchesters, the rest of the party salvaged what they could of the submerged cargo and stacked it in the other cars. They were delayed again later in the journey for want of gasoline, finally obtained after a four-mile trudge to the nearest ranch.

Hickey's guns still got to Walsenburg before General Chase's troops, who were told immediately on arrival that hundreds of strikers were lurking in the hills determined to attack the train as soon as it came into range. Chase tried to phone ahead for confirmation but reliable communication was next to impossible because the sleet storm had felled telephone wires. And meanwhile, about fifteen miles below Walsenburg, the strikers sacking the Empire mine were sorely tempted to avenge Ludlow by allowing all thirty-five property residents bottled up in the mine to perish. A vestige of sanity prevailed. After twenty-one hours of the siege Jess McGuire, an Aguilar strike leader, ventured near the half-sealed mine entrance with a white flag and shouted an offer of release and safe conduct for the women, children, and wounded. This was accepted. Those freed were ushered beyond the danger zone and put on a train to Pueblo. McGuire promised the same treatment to the twenty-eight men left in the mine if they would surrender their guns. They refused and were in the mine as the second night fell. All this occurred before Chase's slow-motion troop train got as far south as Walsenburg.

The following day at dawn it was crawling ten miles beyond the town and approaching Monson, where a branch line forked to the coal properties amid the ancient Indian grave mounds at Pryor and Rouse. Strikers picketing the heights cautiously withdrew as the train approached. Through field glasses they saw a detachment get off and proceed south on horseback until shortly after 11 A.M., when the cavalry dismounted and made for the hills on foot.

According to the stories back in Walsenburg, Chase's troops ought now to be heading into an eighteen-mile gauntlet of gunfire from the hidden strikers. But direct attack on Chase's troops was actually nowhere in the miners' plans. Many of them were armed to the teeth and festooned with ammunition bandoleers, but even among those unimpressed by John Lawson's persuasions as he sped through the hills with news of the delicate truce, the common motivation was to destroy rather than fight. To the ringing of bells at union headquarters in Aguilar calling them to action, the strikers had streamed into the hills throughout the previous night and burned every mine property in their path. Now Chase's troops were coming across fire-blackened camps and company towns but meeting no opposition. And at 3 P.M., when the militiamen closed in on the Empire mine, they found no sign of life. Warned by lookouts of the advancing train, Jess McGuire's guerrillas had fled. Only then, after fifty hours in darkness and worsening air, did Siple and his colleagues come staggering out. At 4:30 troops entered Aguilar. By dusk they had linked up with Hamrock at the truce-imposed southerly limit of their advance. And by nightfall the hills were quiet.

A DILEMMA FOR THE PRESIDENT

THE WEEKEND AFTER THE BATTLE at Ludlow, Captain Philip Van Cise hurried back to Denver profoundly disturbed by what he had learned at the destroyed colony. He sought out Captain Danks, the officer perhaps closest to Van Cise in terms of fairness and civility, and told him of "unbelievable atrocities" committed there and of his determination to inform the editors of the large daily papers. Danks notified Major Boughton and, according to the latter, they deplored the "hot-headedness" of their fellow officer as likely to inflame public sentiment. "Between us we determined to prevent its being done." The pair called on the governor, suggested he appoint an investigating committee, and they "talked Van Cise out of his foolish notion." With Ammons' authority Boughton then tried to telephone General Chase. He was unable to reach him by that means and on Saturday afternoon he sent the general a telegram. It read:

HAVE SUPPRESSED VAN CISE STORY   DO YOUR OWN INVESTIGATING AND PUBLISH REAL FACTS BEFORE ANY OTHERS   SUGGEST DETAIL DANKS, VAN CISE AND SELF   LEAVE AT ONCE   SERIOUS   ACT QUICKLY   GOVERNOR APPROVES

Van Cise said afterward that at Ludlow on the night of April 24 when he told Chase of the evidence he had gathered relating to the death of Tikas, the general's reaction convinced Van Cise that he intended to whitewash the whole affair. Next day Van Cise learned that he had been appointed with Boughton and Danks to a board of inquiry. As reflected in the ambivalent tone of its final report, spite and mistrust burned between the major and Van Cise while Danks oscillated. Boughton ruled that no member of the board should seek testimony unilaterally; it had to be obtained by all three at the same time. Van Cise, aware of his former comparative popularity in the field, knew that witnesses would tell him alone what they would otherwise refuse to disclose and, ignoring Boughton's order, he solicited testimony in secret. For his part, Boughton also conferred privately with Lieutenant Karl Linderfelt and Major Hamrock. Over Van Cise's objections men from Linderfelt's company were not permitted to be questioned individually, and General Chase tried his best to bedevil any serious examination of the freight-train crew.

The most significant achievement of Philip Van Cise's private investigations was the sworn confession of a sergeant in Linderfelt's company that Tikas and the other prisoners were deliberately shot by order of the lieutenant. (Van Cise's charges were formally made at a secret court of inquiry on alleged malpractices in the Colorado National Guard. The hearings, held in August 1915, were never made public.) With Boughton as president of the board it was impossible for Van Cise to inject his discoveries concerning Tikas into the published report, and he had to settle for this much: "The prisoners . . . were shot while running towards the tents. The evidence is conflicting whether they were made to run or tried to escape."

That first weekend after the Ludlow incident Governor Ammons was practically a prisoner in his own statehouse. At nine o'clock on Saturday morning, April 25, over 1000 members of the Women's Peace Association swarmed into the building and began what a later generation would call a sit-in. At first Ammons dodged, refusing to take the invasion seriously, and Stephen Fitzgarrald tried to hold the women off with the excuse that the governor was too busy on the telephone maintaining the peace in the coalfields. But Helen Ring Robinson, in a voice that conceivably reached Ammons in his inner office, cried out, "The women of

Denver summon you . . . do you understand?" A committee of
five swept past Fitzgarrald and confronted the governor with a demand that he telegraph President Wilson for federal troops. He
promised to consider it, and to make sure he did the women settled
in for the day with sandwiches, defiant humor, and hymns. The
committee had dinner in the governor's anteroom while he fled
outdoors for his and were there "like a Nemesis" when he got back
at 6 P.M. Three hours later Governor Ammons wired Washington
for federal troops. Helen Ring Robinson was furnished a copy of
the telegram which she read to the waiting women, who thereupon broke into cheers, sang "Praise God from Whom All Blessings Flow," and dispersed.

As the Denver press reported it, the occasion represented one of
the century's early examples of woman power in action. Although
Ammons and his attorney general, Farrar, were already discussing
the possibility of a troop request, no conclusion had been reached
until "the silent army . . . ordered the state's chief executive to
do their bidding and were obeyed." Whether feminine leverage
was in fact that decisive is questionable and the newspaper account invites doubt by its choice of description of the assembly:
an army, yes, but silent the women were not.

As a matter of fact, pressure for federal military intervention
had been applied not merely to Ammons but exerted upon the
state's Congressional delegation as well, and on April 23 in Washington Colorado's lawmakers and Congressman Martin Foster had
conferred at length with Secretary of Labor Wilson and his assistant, Louis F. Post, regarding the advisability of federal action.
William Wilson agreed at this session to bring the matter up at a
White House cabinet meeting the following morning and to rec-
ommend that troops be furnished if Governor Ammons requested
them. At the same time Foster had suggested the possibility of his
committee returning to Colorado. Newspaper speculation on the
cabinet meeting of April 24 had inspired an oddly worded wire
from Ammons to the White House asking if the cabinet had been
talking about Colorado and wondering whether, if he lost control

of the situation, federal troops might be sent. The President's reply was that the cabinet had met "merely for the sake of information" and he added a broad hint that Colorado ought not to shift the state's responsibility to the federal government.

Woodrow Wilson was under severe physical strain. Telephone calls from State, War, and Navy departments robbed his nights of slumber. (It was during this week that a member of the Senate Foreign Relations Committee, at the White House by appointment, found the President sound asleep on a couch.) Probably more than the nation realized Wilson regretted the fracas with Mexico. Now this domestic crisis had burst on him, all the more exasperating because those who in his opinion might have avoided it showed no zest or initiative for ending it — a crisis that had already taken more American lives than were lost in the fighting at Vera Cruz and that had left, in the words of a protest telegram from an ethnic labor group to the White House, "a far greater blot upon the honor and flag of this country than the trivial occurrence at Tampico."

One year and a month after his inauguration and less than a week after he had sent the marines to Vera Cruz, President Wilson was wholly reluctant to send federal soldiers into Colorado. Like Presidents before and since, he may have considered military usurpation of a state's rights even more abhorrent and politically dangerous than pouring American troops into a foreign land. In addition to the constitutional objections, until the Mexican situation eased, U.S. troops could be ill-spared for other contingencies. Finally, Wilson was acutely mindful of the political risks should the increasingly powerful labor blocs interpret such action as strikebreaking and develop a bias against his administration. At the Friday cabinet meeting he had decided to put the matter off by sending the Foster investigating committee back to Colorado, and as the weekend began he also took action on a suggestion by Congressman Edward Keating that the Rockefellers be challenged directly to help solve Colorado's trouble.

It was a distinctly unpropitious moment for such recourse. The news of Ludlow had sent a wave of anti-Rockefeller feeling across the land. Social crusaders, militant humanists, and muckrakers, as intoxicated with publicity as inspired by a sense of outrage, commanded the rostrums at protest meetings and led the ranks of chanting marchers. Sober demands for inquiry and reform foundered in a flood of savage rhetoric. On Sunday, April 26, on the well-trampled grounds of the Denver statehouse, more than 5000 people massed beneath umbrellas in drenching rain to hear local union representatives brand Ammons and Fitzgarrald as traitors and accessories to infanticide. But the most febrile oratory issued from George Creel and was concentrated on the younger John D. Rockefeller.

It took four decades for Creel to swing from radical left to a position defending Senator Joseph R. McCarthy of Wisconsin, and even then he could still recall without apology how his attack on Rockefeller and the moneyed interests exceeded in vituperation anything else heard on that emotional occasion. Creel's motives that Sunday should be considered against his earlier experiences in Denver. After a disheveled newspaper career, the "carpet bagger from Kansas," as his Colorado foes called him, had in 1910 headed a task force of reformers including Philip Van Cise, Charles Thomas, Edward Costigan, and Josephine Roche dedicated to the rescue of the city's morals. Creel's first objective, the sanitization of Market Street and other red-light thoroughfares, unleashed a groundswell of resentment and its crest rose fast after he became police commissioner in 1912. He managed to infuriate every municipal department and when the mayor finally took his job away from him a combination of political, business, and newspaper interests virtually ran George Creel out of the state.

Now the exile had returned to make the most of Colorado's present distress. It was only a matter of three or four years before George Creel would be stoking the fires of war propaganda against baby-killing Huns. Some of the incitant and sloganeering skills that so fitted him for the Office of War Information he was to head were honed without restraint on the capitol lawn that sodden and windswept Sunday.

> Every prayer Rockefeller utters is an insult to the Christ that died for suffering humanity . . . The martyrs of Ludlow did not die in vain . . . the Rockefellers, who profess Christ in public and crucify him privately, have been unmasked . . . Patriotism is robbed of its power to befool . . . Private ownership of natural resources and public utilities is seen as a thing that corrupts officials, poisons the law and makes murderers . . . These then are Ludlow's challenges to those who sit in the seat of the mighty, wrapping the flag about their profits, putting their assassins in their country's uniforms, buying law and legislators, and crying out against class prejudice even while they draw class lines with a bayonet's point.

It was a bravura performance even for Creel and, rushing in from Union Station just then, Mother Jones came on stage as an anticlimax for the first time in her career. After telling her "boys" to keep cool, go home, and stay out of saloons, she sat down almost meekly.

The demonstration in Denver was an extreme example, but in varying degrees of abuse the name of Rockefeller was being execrated in every part of the country. Having for years enjoyed and benefited from the CFI's preeminence in the state's coal industry, its directorate and executive alike now anxiously sought exits from the limelight. The day of the Denver massed meeting, and while a demonstration organized by Upton Sinclair paraded outside 26 Broadway, the junior Rockefeller wired questions to L. M. Bowers. "How many coal companies are involved in the strike? What proportion of their normal total output does your company represent?" And Bowers, suddenly void of the self-confidence with which he was wont to boast of the company's leadership and influence, complained, "We have been given altogether too prominent a place in this trouble." As if his chronic insomnia did not interfere enough with his rest, the offices in the Boston Building had been kept open night and day since the affair at Ludlow, phones rang constantly, and cots had been brought in so that the weary executives could snatch catnaps.

What the Rockefellers wanted now was to lower their profile in the strike, not enlarge it. Woodrow Wilson's humbly worded wire to the elder Rockefeller that weekend announcing Congressman Foster's imminent return to Colorado ventured, "May I not say to him that you will confer with him before he leaves, in the interest of a peaceful and human settlement of the difficulties . . . ?" And Rockefeller senior answered that he had not been in his office for twenty years, knew nothing of the CFI's affairs, but would arrange for his son to meet Foster in New York.

The telegram was awaiting President Wilson when he returned to the White House from church on that Sunday, and that same morning Governor Ammons' formal request for troops arrived. The governor pleaded inability to increase the strength of his National Guard beyond 650 men and asked for at least a battalion of infantry and a troop of cavalry. To give the request constitutional validity he ascribed the labor war to "an industrial controversy between interstate organizations with headquarters outside Colorado."

That Sunday was no day of rest for President Woodrow Wilson. While he was at worship in the Central Presbyterian Church, Congressman Keating had rounded up colleagues to back Governor Ammons' appeal for troops with their own, and they were waiting sober-faced at the White House gates when Wilson returned. It was an emotional encounter. Senator Charles Thomas, reciting the toll of lives so far in the strike zone, became overwrought and wept. After the deputation had gone, President Wilson summoned Lindley M. Garrison, Secretary of War, but still he did not give the word, although he had pinned his only hope now to the meeting in New York for which Martin Foster left that Sunday night.

Unlike the last occasion when they had met, Congressman Foster asked Rockefeller no uncomfortable questions. What he sought now was an agreement to submit the strike to an arbitration board. Rockefeller, in the new effort to play down his company's role, impressed upon the congressman that the CFI, although controlling one third of Colorado's coal output, was but one of many coal concerns in the southern part of the state. And that afternoon Rockefeller wrote to the President that Foster had been unable to suggest anything which did not involve unionization of the mines or arbitration of that forbidden issue. Either way, as far as the operators were concerned, the question was nonnegotiable.

President Wilson read Rockefeller's words with dismay, not knowing, although he may have guessed, that they were practically those of L. M. Bowers. Told of the forthcoming meeting with the congressman, Bowers had hastened to remind Rockefeller that "any proposition of Foster involving unionizing mines would be almost unanimously refused by the operators of Colorado; also anything he may press for temporary withholding [of] Federal troops would be exceedingly detrimental and unwise." Trinidad was in the hands of strikers and "many fighting Greeks" were being brought in from New Mexico. "Immediate protection should be demanded . . ." President Wilson took no pains to conceal his extreme displeasure from Rockefeller and even managed an oblique slight at the rich man's vaunted altruism. "It seemed to me a great opportunity for some large action which would show the way not only in this case but in many others." Convinced that Rockefeller had slammed the door on the remaining alternative to military intervention, Wilson conferred with his Secretary of War on April 28 and, while the coded telegrams went out from the War Department alerting units for movement to Colorado, he drafted a message to Governor Ammons announcing that "I shall forthwith order the troops . . ."

At the same time Wilson made the mandatory proclamation calling upon all participants in violence to disperse and go home peaceably, on or before April 30. It was asking a lot. The fragile truce was coming apart and within a half-moon-shaped territory about fifty miles long a guerrilla-style labor war now raged on a scale unprecedented in Colorado or indeed anywhere else in the nation.

General Chase's arrival in the Ludlow vicinity with a force of some 400 men had brought the total militia strength to 650. The truce terms prevented him from going as far as Trinidad, now the organizational nerve center of the strikers' forces, and on April 25 it was just as well. The mere sight of a militiaman's olive drab might have transformed mourning and anguish into uncontrollable fury. Feelings were heightened at an early hour when a mysterious fire broke out at the Hall and MacMahon Undertakers' morgue and the caskets of the Ludlow victims had to be carried from the premises into the street to escape the flames. At 9 A.M. the women and children were buried from Holy Trinity Church, directly opposite the Chronicle-News Building from whose second-floor office Judge Northcutt could witness the procession as it left: horse-drawn drays for hearses bearing two black caskets and eleven small white ones, while the church bell tolled as it so often had when dead coal diggers were borne out of the mines.

All that day sporadic gunfire from the hills had concentrated on the Chandler mine six miles south of Canon City. A nonunion miner died and a mine guard lost both arms when a bullet struck the weapon he held and it exploded. At three o'clock the next afternoon, the few defenders having fled, scores of strikers rushed the property to loot offices, sabotage equipment, and destroy mine records. They melted back into the hills before General Chase reached the scene with 200 troops late that night.

Chase had left the Ludlow area in the command of Colonel Verdeckburg, a loyal subordinate since their service together in the Cripple Creek strike of 1903-4. On Monday, April 27, his troops stationed near the ruins of the tent colony had little to do. Attention was focused on Trinidad, where a funeral service was held for Louis Tikas; four armed Greeks in the undertaker's chapel swore an oath of vengeance, pounding ritually on the floor with their rifle butts. A mile-long procession followed the casket down Commercial Street, across the Purgatoire, and on over the hill to the Knights of Pythias cemetery. Still no disturbance interrupted the atmosphere of mourning. It was 7 P.M. when Colonel Verdeckburg received orders from General Chase in Canon City to send a detail of sixty men on the next available train to Walsenburg, where hundreds of strikers were reported to be wrecking the CFI's McNally mine.

The violence at Walsenburg was not exclusively a reaction to Ludlow. Neither was it directed by important union leaders. There is nothing to indicate that John Lawson was involved in the planning; Adolph Germer had gone back to Illinois. Lawson's control of events at this point was at best haphazard. To a telegram from Governor Ammons charging truce violations and demanding to know if he still maintained influence among the strikers, Lawson could only reply that he was doing his utmost and had sent messengers into the hills to stop the fighting. The fragmented guerrilla movement on the rampage from Walsenburg to Trinidad was probably beyond anyone's powers of coordination. Lawson's chances of maintaining his leadership were further complicated by the fact that new candidates, legitimate and pretenders, now vied for local authority. The UMW had sent three fresh organizers to Trinidad, where in addition a second-rank agitator from the East nicknamed "General" John Brown secured the willing attention of local newspapermen with pompous and misleading interviews. Among the Greeks the self-appointed replacement for Louis Tikas was "Little Pete" Katsulis, a roguish boaster with a dislike for union officials because they had passed him over for the job of Ludlow's interpreter in favor of the more stable Tikas. And on the Walsenburg front the role of guerrilla commander was to be assumed, alcoholically according to some, by the former newspaperman Don MacGregor.

In Huerfano County politics and long-festering feuds were as much involved as authentic strike action. The 1912 Democratic landslide had left the local power edifice cracked and crumbling. In a kind of panic-stricken counteroffensive against the mounting challenges to Sheriff Jeff Farr's regime, his lieutenants took to the streets in a fresh wave of physical assaults on reformers and rivals like E. L. Neelly, the hardware merchant who had armed the miners in exchange for their pledge of political support, and Robert Mitchell, editor of the Walsenburg *Independent* and a middle-of-the-road Progressive fated for early assassination at unknown hands. Thus local passions as much as anything else inspired the fighting around Walsenburg.

Here the drama had for its central backdrop the soaring Spanish Peaks. From their snow-streaked altitudes the Cucharas River tumbled to the foothills, curved through the beauteous vale of La Veta, and for a distance of five miles west of Walsenburg it coursed past a series of rich CFI properties. One of them, the Walsen camp, was the company's second oldest and none yielded a larger output. In 1876 when the four generous veins outcropping the river were first mined, the coal had been hauled by ox team to the railroad junction, and the mineral that now traveled in gondola cars over the Rio Grande Railroad came from the same seemingly inexhaustible measures.

Armed strikers of half a dozen different nationalities had been infiltrating the area all weekend. Walsenburg itself was almost deserted. Sheriff Farr and his deputies kept to their courthouse. At 2 P.M. a mob of strikers left the Union Hall north of town and deployed along the Hogback, a mile-long piñon-carpeted ridge stretching west. From this position and other vantage points where the town's dusty environs merged with coal mine property, gunfire opened up on the McNally mine. Thirty mine guards defended the camp. As their rifles banged away in reply, the battle's first fatality was a Polish miner who fell on Seventh Street with a bullet in his head. By nightfall the defenders had been driven from the McNally mine, its bunkhouse, tipple, and shaft house were blazing, and the strikers turned next to the heavily guarded Walsen property.

Seventy-five mine guards took a stand on the slopes of a hill surmounted by the mine's water tank. They had installed a pair of makeshift cannon manufactured in one of the CFI's machine shops, and the muzzle-loaded weapons, each with three-inch bore, roared all night long, hurling improvised missiles aimlessly into the darkness and creating more noise than damage.

The militia detachment from Ludlow arrived in the night to find the Walsen mine besieged, its searchlight still in operation atop a sixty-foot wooden tower, and desultory attacks under way against two more mines, the Robinson and Cameron. The detachment was ineffectual for a number of critical hours because of its small size and some uncertainty over its function in view of the illusive truce. No such indecision hampered the strikers. More of them converged on the Walsenburg district and by daybreak on April 28 were entrenched north and west of town. The death toll had reached seven with an unknown number of wounded, some sprawled unattended on open ground between the Hogback and the smoldering ruins of the McNally mine.

At the Walsen mine 160 strikebreakers reinforced the guards. All day long the echoes of gunfire bounced and clattered through the Cucharas valley. Shortly after 5 P.M. a motorcyclist with a girl on the pillion came racing down the road from Pueblo. A striker on the Hogback took aim and fired. The motorcyclist spun from the saddle mortally wounded and his vehicle somersaulted off the road, injuring the passenger. When another day dawned, the strikers still held the Hogback, defying belated efforts by the sixty soldiers to dislodge them.

When the bad news from the Trinidad field reached General Chase in Fremont County he was unable to respond satisfactorily although his troops had recaptured the Chandler mine. He had found it necessary to divide his forces again, sending half of them an additional 200 miles north on a 40-mph freight-car journey to Boulder County, where the hated Walter Belk, far from having been retired in the interests of peace and supposedly on bond pending further investigation into the killing of Gerald Lippiatt, commanded the mine guards at the Rocky Mountain Fuel's Hecla and Vulcan properties, now surrounded by some 200 strikers. Unknown to Chase, groups of sharpshooters were posted at intervals overlooking the railroad track between Denver and Louisville determined to halt the troops with gunfire. Although the train was shot at several times, two developments foiled the plan and brought the outbreaks north of Denver to an early halt. State Senator Martin Garman, a prolabor legislator who overheard of the intended train ambush, got in immediate touch with John Mc-Lennan and Ed Doyle and, using the senator's automobile when the terrain permitted, they raced from one ambush point to another with pleas for restraint. At the same time William Hickey of the State Federation of Labor, presumably unaware of Garman's peacemaking intervention and driving north with 20 high-power rifles and 10,000 rounds of ammunition in the back seat, was overtaken five miles out by a posse of Baldwin-Felts operatives on wheels and brought back to Denver under arrest.

In Washington, meanwhile, Lindley Garrison had written the President a detailed letter making it clear that Wilson should not concern himself with the merits of either side in the strike but dedicate the entire federal intervention to the speediest possible return of peace to the state. Garrison reminded the President of the "indisputable" fact that the Colorado militia tended to "provoke rather than allay disorder." Acting on the secretary's advice, Wilson directed Governor Ammons to recall the militia as soon as federal forces arrived, since it would be confusing to have two military forces operating under "separate sources of control."

Word that federal units under orders of President Wilson were on their way to occupy the strike zone spread like wildfire throughout the state. To most citizens the news was profoundly welcome, but General Chase and Major Boughton fumed against the humiliating reflection cast upon their ability to preserve order. Coal operators greeted the news cautiously, on guard lest the Wilson administration, too friendly with labor "agitators," seize the occasion to nationalize their properties, a possibility they were prepared to resist as fiercely as they had unionization. Union leaders at Indianapolis expressed relief mingled with hope that stabilized conditions in the coalfield would provide new opportunities to end the strike. Field officials took heart from President Wilson's assurance that the troops would not be used for strike-breaking. But those red-kerchiefed strikers whose vengeful or retributive impulses were yet unappeased reacted with demands for last-minute raids and many were, in any event, too caught up in the momentum of violence for sudden halt now.

At Forbes, the Rocky Mountain Fuel's coal camp between Trinidad and Ludlow, only eighteen of the nonunion miners still working shouldered arms. Halfway up the hill behind the superintendent's office a poorly functioning machine gun was mounted. This comprised the total defense of Forbes and the camp was beyond the militia's southernmost command as dictated by the now tattered truce. Late on April 29 more than 100 armed strikers set out from Trinidad, were joined by groups in the hills, and near 5 A.M. something like 300 guerrilla fighters took position on the canyon heights overlooking the narrow mile-long coal camp at Forbes.

The attackers swept in from the southern end, shooting along both walls of the canyon. The camp's stable boss, in the mule barn feeding the animals, dropped his pail at the crackle of the opening gunfire and ran. The barn was among the first buildings set on fire and thirty-seven mules perished in the flames. Ed Kessler, a Denver carpenter whose wife had recently obeyed a premonition of danger by beseeching him in a letter to come home, raced into a shack for safety, but this was the next structure put to the torch and Kessler never came out alive. The machine gun at the northern end of the property clattered away at a second assault wave leaping down the eastern slopes. Two strikers were killed and then a third, his body tumbling downhill to hit a piñon stump and wedge there, 100 yards above the camp. The destruction intensified.

Strikers swarmed everywhere, dashing oil on the tipple, scales, on the floor of the post office, and in the boiler house, and then applying flame. Some of the attackers shouted, "Remember Ludlow!" Six nonunion miners dragged from the boardinghouse spent a terrifying ninety minutes as half their captors demanded that the scabs be strung up. They were eventually turned loose in the hills. Among those at Forbes not so lucky was a miner named Jack Smith, father of six children, killed while running for an abandoned mine tunnel on the northern slope where the mine superintendent had herded about sixty women and children for safety.

The superintendent, a Scotsman named Bob Nichols, feared himself to be a marked man since it was he who had recommended the dismantling of the Forbes tent colony in February. Now he was on the phone, frantically seeking help from Colonel Verdeckburg at Ludlow. Verdeckburg had been summoned elsewhere and Nichols found himself talking to Major Hamrock, who in turn telephoned Denver for permission to speed troops south of Ludlow to relieve the situation at Forbes. In the statehouse Ammons and Chase conferred, formed the mistaken conclusion that the attacks were a cunningly arranged plan to confuse and scatter the militia, and Major Hamrock was ordered to stay where he was. At Forbes the superintendent could scarcely believe his ears when Hamrock relayed this message. Then he heard nothing more because the telephone line went dead. Bullets tore through Nichols' office. He climbed the hill to the machine gun and found it abandoned, its crank jammed.

Twelve camp buildings were ablaze. In one burning shack four Japanese miners died. Forbes's blacksmith tried to escape the gunfire by riding a coal tram. Bullets chased him. He was struck in the head and his lifeless body rolled off and was left on the tramway. Not counting the strikers' casualties, nine men died at Forbes and the camp was almost totally gutted. Their grim labor done, the strikers collected their own dead and wounded and left the smoke-shrouded canyon at 10 A.M., just two hours before the first federal troops in Colorado, 125 men of the Twelfth U.S. Cavalry from Fort Robinson, Nebraska, reached Canon City.

Colonel Verdeckburg could hear the firing at Forbes shortly before daybreak but he had just received orders for the dispatch of a

strong force north to Walsenburg. The colonel took 18 other officers and 114 enlisted men, and arrived at the battle of Hogback
about 7:30 A.M. He sent a 6-man patrol to scout near the junction
of the Hogback and the Pueblo road, on the strikers' left flank, and
set up his command post on a ridge behind the Walsen property.
He had only just relieved the force of mine guards who had held
the ridge forty-eight hours when a trooper dashed up to report
that the patrol had blundered into a trap and was pinned down.
Verdeckburg responded to this by sending two separate forces
totaling 38 officers and men in a series of alternating rushes to lift
the pressure on his beleaguered patrol. Half the men were soon
falling back under fire and "badly shaken."

Inebriated or not, Don MacGregor knew that by placing outposts at each end of the Hogback and entrenching sharpshooters
behind rocky outcrops along its crest he commanded a natural
fortress. He had mustered 160 rifles not counting those brought in
Hickey's motorcade from Denver. Strutting about his Walsenburg command post in approved guerrilla garb complete with
kneeboots, ammunition bandoleer, and red kerchief, the former
newspaperman acted the part of guerrilla chieftain to the hilt.
Besides having the advantage of an impregnable defense position, MacGregor confronted an unimpressive foe. Verdeckburg,
one of General Chase's favorites, was privately considered by his
other fellow officers to be a dolt.

But more intelligent commanders would have had their work
cut out, given the same attack strength, to dislodge MacGregor's
guerrillas. Fortunately for Verdeckburg, negotiations for a cease-
fire were being pressed in Denver between General Chase and the
miners' lawyer, Horace Hawkins, under an urgency to get the
shooting stopped before the incoming federal troops were faced
with a possible dilemma of having to choose sides in a continuing
battle, an unthinkable addition to Colorado's mortification. The
U.S. cavalrymen in Canon City had found the situation quiet, but
350 soldiers of the Fifth Cavalry had left Fort Leavenworth with
orders for the Trinidad area and were expected within twenty-

four hours. So it was a race against time, but as so often in this bizarre labor conflict, prudence and common sense were rare commodities.

Telephone lines between Denver and Walsenburg were kept humming. Horace Hawkins emphasized to MacGregor that things had gone far enough, that unless he halted the gun play, General Chase would come down there and sweep all his men off the Hogback with heavy artillery. Chase meanwhile had been talking to Verdeckburg and induced the colonel to advise Mac-Gregor by messenger that the National Guard's fire, called off at 1:45 P.M., would be resumed at 3:00 if the strikers refused to lay down their arms. Either Verdeckburg was unaware that his circumstances were hardly appropriate for launching ultimatums or else he was bluffing. The strikers kept firing. They were under orders to hold their position until the flag of the federal troops came into view, and then go home.

At nearly half-past two near the Walsenburg end of the Hogback a private named Miller, in action 150 yards from the strikers' rifle pits, was shot in the face and within seconds a lieutenant was also hit. Accounts differ as to which wounded man was being medically treated — probably Private Miller — but Major Pliny Lester, Verdeckburg's surgeon, was thus engaged or in the act of making for the casualty when a bullet struck him in the left breast. MacGregor's comment on this fatality was that the major had been acting more as combatant than medico. Colonel Verdeckburg's reaction to the bad news from the right of his sector was to send thirty men in a leftward dash to the western edge of the Hogback, which, reportedly unoccupied, invited an outflanking attempt. It proved to be a trap and the men were surrounded near Martin's Lake. By late afternoon at least a dozen dead were counted on the terrain between Verdeckburg's ridge and the Hogback. Major Lester was the militia's only fatal casualty, but of the two forces the colonel's squads and platoons were in the least enviable situation since none could be safely extricated before darkness fell. Lester's body was recovered later that night, looted and with his military insignia torn off. The bloodshed and embarrassment around Walsenburg mercifully ceased shortly after 7 P.M. with more positive orders from Denver, and at 8 the next morning, April 30, some 350 troops of the Second Squadron, Fifth U.S. Cavalry Regiment, detrained at Trinidad.

The first contingents of federal troops in Colorado were not nearly enough to suit Governor Ammons and he asked the Secretary of War for more. Before the end of the opening week in May, the U.S. military presence in the state would amount to 1590 enlisted men and 61 officers.

Garrison did not bind his commanding officers to inflexible policies. He chose rather to issue general directives from Washington, leaving each commander some leeway in applying them to the particular conditions in his zone. He made it clear that no group, including the companies, could expect special privileges. Within hours of the troops' initial arrival Garrison issued a proclamation calling upon all persons not in the military service of the United States to surrender their arms. He ordered a "broad interpretation" of the proclamation, as applying not only to strikers, deputies, and mine guards, but militiamen as well. Privately, Garrison hoped that before his edict became fully operative the Colorado National Guard would have retired from the scene. The secretary also ordered all gun shops and saloons in the strike district closed. Neither was he encouraging the opening of those mines not working because of the strike. "We are having enough difficulty," he told President Wilson, "to maintain things in an equilibrium with the mines that are already running."

The arrival of the federal soldiers in Colorado was accompanied by phenomenal rainstorms. In a heavy downpour on their first day in Trinidad, Major W. A. Holbrook, the commanding officer, sent a detachment to Walsenburg, where just three hours after they had detrained they arrested six members of the Colorado National Guard for looting a saloon on Seventh Street. The strikers finally yielded their arms and came down off the Hogback, as they had been told to do by Don MacGregor before he hurried away.

Shadowed by Baldwin-Felts agents in Denver, MacGregor was to leave there for Chicago. Having, however briefly, tasted command as a guerrilla leader, the former reporter may have hankered for more. Long afterward he was said to have gone to Mexico and fought at the side of Pancho Villa. No published work on Villa mentions him and he was never heard of again.

Colonel Verdeckburg's militiamen evacuated Ludlow and turned that desolate ground over to Troop H of the Fifth Cavalry. May began with no slackening of the rain. The deluge and melting snows transformed the Cucharas, the Apishapa, and the Purgatoire into torrents. Overflowing their banks in places, they raced through blackened coal camps, choked the arroyos, and swirled across the desecrated flats like a pure and cleansing flood.

·····17·····

POST-MORTEMS, PLOTS, AND PUBLICITY

In GENERAL THE NATIONAL DAILIES hung back from the hue and cry against John D. Rockefeller, Jr. Nowhere outside Colorado had the strike been adequately reported. Having all along overlooked or impatiently disapproved of it, most newspapers with comment to spare now contributed little more than displays of their publishers' prejudices. As expected, Hearst's New York *American* gave the multimillionaire an editorial scolding. Of the strike itself Hearst's newspaper readers knew next to nothing, so crammed were the regular columns with chauvinistic propaganda, cartoons bestializing Huerta, and protracted copy from the Vera Cruz "front." The *New York Times*, monotonously enamored of the Rockefellers, deplored the militia's "horrible blunder" at Ludlow but threw maximum blame on the strike organizers. The New York *Sun's* Mexican dispatches left scant room for news from the Colorado coalfield or indeed anywhere else and with shameless inconsistency ran an editorial that attached greater significance to the labor war than to U.S. foreign policy.

In Washington, D.C., the newspapers took no editorial stand on the strike or its bloodshed and gave it grudging column space. The strikers were attacked in the Chicago *Tribune;* the San Francisco *Chronicle* stooped to topical insult by calling them no better than Mexicans. The Milwaukee *Journal* felt that at the bottom of the conflict was the "brutal and heartless" treatment of miners by the CFI. And thoughtfully, the Kansas City *Star*, recalling how Rockefeller had told Congressman Foster that he would sacrifice his investment before yielding to the strikers' demands, reasoned that "No 'principle' of distant corporation owners that invokes homicide and paralyzes the dominant rights of the public in industry can survive in law or public opinion."

In contrast to the meager or lackluster press coverage, the Colorado struggle was intensively probed and dramatized by most leading magazines of the moderate-to-left spectrum. Even a partial list of names that bylined the choicer pieces — Charles Edward Russell, John Reed, Max Eastman, Eugene Debs, Lincoln Steffens, George Creel, Walter Lippmann, Upton Sinclair — reads like an honor roll of the early century's progressive to radical thinkers and activists. But they were the literary elite. A good deal of the prose was raw and ham-fisted. Similarly the verse. The socialist periodical *Appeal to Reason* ran a poem about John D. Rockefeller, Jr., that ended:

> . . . as long as he has the cash to spend, it's easy the people
>   to fool,
> As long as he builds a cottage or two and teaches Sunday
>   School.
> The toadies fawn, and the lickspittles kneel,
> He's worshipped by all the freaks,
> While the bodies of little children are burned 'neath Colorado's
>   peaks.
> And this skulking, sanctimonious ass, this breeder of crime
>   and hate,
> With the greed of a jackal and a heart of brass,
> Whines, "Nothing to arbitrate."

This sort of thing reached a wider and more appreciative audience than far better poetry is accustomed to: *Appeal to Reason* boasted a readership of more than half a million.

With rather more restraint, another socialist publication, the New York *Call*, deplored the nation's absorption with Mexico: "It is unfortunate indeed that the working class of the country has . . . allowed itself to be diverted by a foolish and trivial imbroglio with a foreign power from the only really vital question that now confronts it — the struggle with its masters." *The Masses* vigorously championed the cause of the miners, its brilliant cartoon illustrators specializing in the art of horrifying impact: in one, an agonized miner stands before his burning tent, wife and infants dead at his feet; in another, Rockefeller washes the blood off his hands. *The Masses'* editor, Max Eastman, reported on a tea party he gave in Trinidad, Colorado, to study the reaction of upper-class groups to the Ludlow "massacre." His abhorrence of them was apparently confirmed. A railroad superintendent's wife had remarked that strikers, like cattle, should be exterminated. A Presbyterian minister's wife consigned coal miners to perdition because they were unfamiliar with the Christmas story. Eastman concluded that the militiamen were not to blame for the events of April 20 but "the gentlemen of noble leisure who hired them . . ."

Most of the popular magazines, as all those of labor and radicalism, weighed Rockefeller without ceremony and found him incurably wanting. *Harper's Weekly,* which had published a score of articles on the strike, vilified him in cartoons and, yielding to a kind of trend, juxtaposed his hapless testimony before the Foster committee with what occurred at Ludlow only a fortnight afterward. The Rockefellers' lifelong contributions to Christian endeavor, mocked now as hypocrisy, were defended only in loyal sections of the religious press. The *Central Christian Advocate* blamed everything on revolutionary plotters — "in Las Animas County . . . the commune has leaped to its feet" — and suggested the assignment of missionaries trained in foreign tongues to save the souls of Colorado's debased miners. When they did not skirt the Colorado tragedy altogether, most of the clerical journalists, following the line of Denver ministers whose pulpiteering went no further than the exhortation of both sides to replace violence with "the golden rule," condemned or pitied the miner for his heathenry.

After such pharisaic copy it may have been refreshing to turn to commercial and industrial journals unequivocally opposed to strikes and strikers and read, for instance, *Coal Age's* frank defense of operators and militiamen: "It is not those men who should bear the brunt of our condemnation but these aliens who have brought us a new glimpse of the Middle Ages and have disgraced our orderly civilization by their unwanted crimes." *Coal Age* heartily recommended deporting the lot of them.

Ludlow afforded graphic emphasis to all that the muckrakers had been saying. Although a popular reaction against corporate tyranny showed signs of stirring even before Ida Tarbell's exposures of Standard Oil, the public by and large had remained too tolerant of moneyed oppression to suit both genuine reformers and professional agitators. Ludlow was their godsend, and the impulsive resort to typewriters and the open streets produced such a fulmination of incandescent journalism and sidewalk militancy that in the emotional exhilaration of a class war seemingly consummated and long-courted publicity finally won, the true causes and nature of the strife in Colorado were often lost sight of.

Upton Sinclair did his utmost to saddle John D. Rockefeller, Jr., with direct responsibility for the strike and all its sorrows. In articles and speeches, vituperative outlines of the multimillionaire's iniquities were followed by matter-of-fact speculation upon suitable punishment. After due consideration, thrashing Rockefeller or putting him to death was rejected in favor of the "social chill," which took the form of mournful picketing with crepe armbands outside his Broadway office, his places of worship, and in Tarrytown around the gates of Pocantico Hills, to whose seclusion Rockefeller had retreated after the meeting with Martin Foster on April 27. Here he was said to be confined with a cold following an afternoon's golf in the rain.

Behind the shield of his publicized indisposition Rockefeller attended to several pressing matters. For one thing, he discussed the events with his father, probably a fruitless exercise since the elder Rockefeller's unchanging opinion of labor organizations was that "the real object of their organizing . . . is . . . to do as little as possible for the greatest possible pay." Also, to correct what he called "inaccuracies" published after the conference with Foster, the younger Rockefeller enlisted Starr Murphy's aid in the composition of a statement to the effect that the CFI had met the miners' most important demands in advance of the strike. The basis for this claim was of course L. M. Bowers' reassuring letters of the previous fall, but three days after its publication a letter appeared in the New York *Evening Post* that Starr Murphy, manning the office at 26 Broadway in Rockefeller's absence, read with a frown. The writer made the point that the company's "concessions" were nothing of the sort but only pursuant to Colorado statutes of law.

Meanwhile for John D. Rockefeller, Jr., sick or not, April 30 had been a busy day, in part as a result of the anxiety among the UMW chieftains in the Merchants Bank Building, Indianapolis, to end the strike as speedily as possible. The bellicose anger greeting the news from Ludlow had served only to interrupt, not banish, their growing defeatism. A telegram from Frank Hayes to Ed Doyle swearing "we are with you to the end" (words once used by Rockefeller to the Denver officers) and raising the threat of a nationwide strike — "half a million miners have heard the death cries from Ludlow" — had been followed by a sober statement from William Green, who as UMW secretary-treasurer knew better than Hayes or anyone else how critical the union's finances were. Green had grown irritable with men in the field who persistently failed to appreciate the difficulties at headquarters. After wiring Doyle $15,000 to care for the wounded, bury the dead, and rebuild Ludlow's tent colony, costly but unavoidable expenditures, he was still getting requests from him for money with which to purchase guns.

Doyle was also apparently oblivious of the fact that officers at Indianapolis had lost a good deal of faith in District 15's officials and were prepared to write off Colorado as an expensive lost cause. There were other fronts more important: Ohio, for instance, where operators and miners were in deadlock since the last week of April, and the Industrial Workers of the World, following the custom of the old and no longer potent Western Federation of Miners, was seeking to weaken the UMW before its members by accusing it of having no stomach for a strike. Should a walkout become inevitable in Ohio while the one in Colorado dragged on, the UMW would be at wits' end to finance it.

The union veered toward bankruptcy. The coal mines in Colorado were being run, anyway, by scabs, more of whom would arrive with the summer months. Union president John White determined that the strike be ended with all speed and, although Frank Hayes added "as gracefully as possible," it was with little grace that he now backed away from his own brave words to Doyle about a general strike. Then came the first major indication of the pessimistic mood at Indianapolis: William Green's public statement denying that unionization was a barrier to negotiations, since unionization was not the question in contention.

Martin Foster had seized this opportunity to wire Rockefeller asking if he would now talk with the unionists on that basis "and stop the killing of men, women and children? I strongly urge you to do so . . ." Received April 30, the telegram was promptly forwarded by Rockefeller to Welborn and Bowers, who conferred at once with other Colorado operators then issued a statement over twenty signatures declaring their refusal to meet the unionists and blaming the UMW alone for "the terrible reign of disorder and bloodshed." At the same time, following discussions over his bedside telephone with Starr Murphy in New York, Rockefeller had resumed efforts to dissociate his name from unsavory developments. (The multimillionaire's earnestness in this regard could scarcely have been sharper had he known that even as he composed a statement for publication, Representative Keating in Washington was dictating a telegram to the Denver unionists stressing a need now to keep the spotlight on John D. Rockefeller, Jr.) References to the strife in Colorado as "Rockefeller's War" the financier described as infamous — had not John Osgood recently announced that the Victor-American Company would refuse to recognize the United Mine Workers no matter what turn the CFI's policy took?

Recognition, Rockefeller's published statement went on, was the only stumbling block. Governor Ammons had said as much in his letter of November 27, 1913, containing proposals for a settlement which the operators had accepted and the miners rejected. Rockefeller may have forgotten that this was the occasion of which J. F. Welborn had written him, "we reached no understanding . . . we wanted none," but the present circumstance was too urgent for it not to be recalled and put to good use. So a second telegram went out that day from Pocantico Hills to Denver with a strong recommendation that the November business with Ammons be resurrected to the company's advantage with suitable logic and emphasis, the object being to identify the source of all the trouble that had occurred since as the strikers' rejection of the governor's proposals.

The success of this stratagem to isolate the recognition issue and thus pin the blame squarely on the strikers depended upon public acceptance of CFI claims that the company had voluntarily granted the other demands, claims effectively punctured by the chance correspondent in the *Evening Post* during the first week in May. But the telegrams and statements produced by Rockefeller and Starr Murphy had been issued. Hurriedly Murphy sent the newspaper clipping to Bowers with a request for explanation.

L. M. Bowers had been in an euphoria of renewed confidence. Not unaware of the UMW's financial embarrassment, the operators had confronted Congressman Martin Foster with staunchly closed ranks, indicated that they had all the miners they needed to operate the mines, and showed if possible less disposition to negotiate than ever. The congressman had given up and departed. Bowers' mood changed with the arrival of Murphy's letter, when for once his characteristic bluntness deserted him. The *Evening Post* letter, he told Murphy in reply, was "misleading in some respects plus half the truth in others . . . our legal department has furnished me some hurried notes . . . I will say in this connection that [the legal department] did not know that there had ever been such a law passed and if Mr. Welborn or any of our other officials knew it, it had slipped their minds, or I should not have emphasized this point as I have done . . ." As if aware that his words were awkwardly inadequate, Bowers ended with a testy reminder that nobody in the Boston Building was getting much rest these days, or had time to spare for disputing statements of "the score or two of representatives of yellow newspapers and muckraking magazines" who had descended upon Denver in droves.

Among those Bowers had in mind was assuredly Upton Sinclair, who had conceived the audacious idea of having a group of Ludlow women and children, escorted by reputable Colorado citizens, journey across the nation, stopping at principal cities for purposes of publicity, and finally reaching the White House to tell President Wilson in person what had happened at the tent colony. His twofold purpose, as he later described it, was to stir the American conscience and secure President Wilson's intervention in the dispute on the side of the strikers. Along with George Creel, reported by one of Creel's friends as "having the time of his life over the strike situation," Sinclair raised $2000 at a mass rally on the statehouse grounds, but Judge Ben Lindsey, whom he wished to lead the proposed expedition, at first balked with excuses — a busy calendar, the delicate state of his wife's health, the alertness of local enemies plotting his downfall. Sinclair lost no time arguing. He gathered together a dozen of the judge's friends and, Sinclair later recalled, they practically drove him out of town. Sinclair stayed behind to take advantage of publicity breaks.

Deceptively dapper but mousy-looking, Benjamin Barr Lindsey possessed the kind of intrepidity without which he could never have so often propounded heretical theories and delivered scandalous judgments. A child-labor abolitionist and father-confessor to juvenile delinquents, the future prophet of companionate marriage at whose own wedding to a pretty socialist the word *obey* was omitted, Judge Lindsey of Denver walked with controversy. It did not abandon him on his cross-country tour with the women of Ludlow.

Mostly the gossip was concocted by old foes including coal operators who had never forgiven him for his public calculations that from 1910 to 1913, 622 children had been left fatherless by Colorado mine accidents, the majority at CFI properties. Also, citizens were genuinely wrought up over the national discredit cast upon their state, as at one railroad stop after another Lindsey furnished the press with horror stories of the strike, not all of them strictly accurate. In Denver the judge's party was maligned as a traveling harem. So gross were the insinuations that when Lindsey's wife heard of them in Chicago, she became ill and suffered a miscarriage. L. M. Bowers entered into the spirit of the thing with letters alerting the younger Rockefeller to the approaching group's "web of falsehoods." Talk of a possible meeting between Lindsey and Rockefeller had got back to Bowers, and he was determined to prevent one. Characteristically, his pen ran away with him. Rockefeller found himself reading of Judge Lindsey's consortion with harlots and of how the late Louis Tikas had once been a white slaver.

Continuing eastward — "as recklessly courageous a thing as I have ever seen," Walter Lippmann wrote of the mission — Lindsey found time to make his bid for a personal interview with John D. Rockefeller, Jr. The judge meant well, but his solicitations were self-defeating. Accompanied by implications that the financier was un-Christian or at best blindly stupid, they practically invited the reply from Rockefeller's secretary terming "your letter . . . of such a character as to make any conference with you impossible." When word of this got to Denver, it did not faze Upton Sinclair, who had told Lindsey if his private overtures were rejected to follow up with action forcing Rockefeller into making public ones. The miners' wives must be shepherded to Rockefeller's office, to his town and country residences, and be turned away each time. "The harder we pound Rockefeller," Sinclair had written, "the surer we are of winning."

Lindsey's party arrived at Washington on May 20 and was received the next day at the White House. Mary Hannah Thomas had brought her children along and President Wilson held one baby briefly while listening to the tales of Ludlow. In New York two days later Lindsey announced that he had given up hope of meeting Rockefeller, who was still at Tarrytown, indoors mostly while his children drove daily with the governess. Neither did Lindsey take his entourage to Tarrytown as Sinclair had directed, but Mary Thomas and Pearl Jolly picketed 26 Broadway until an assistant told them that Mr. Rockefeller would see nobody on the Colorado matter and resented being made its "goat." The two women were also star attractions at a climactic mass meeting in New York's Beethoven Hall, where Rockefeller's name was cursed and the audience reacted emotionally to melodramatic hyperbole like that of the union official, nowhere near Ludlow during the battle, who shouted, "Over every tent where a baby was burned to death flew an American flag!"

Subsequently reviewing the expedition East, Lindsey, George Creel, and Upton Sinclair agreed that it had paid off well in publicity for "the cause." Sinclair left Colorado with the judge's parting advice to do for coal miners what *The Jungle* had done in the stockyard industry. In due course, *King Coal* was published and widely praised. Certainly there were desirable results of the publicity trip. Amid all the emotion and sensation, however, one member of Lindsey's itinerant party had scarcely uttered a sound, seemingly unaware of what was taking place about her: the childless Mary Petrucci, enveloped in mourning, mutely unconsolable, her mind still unhinged.

Meanwhile, as chief executive of Colorado, Elias Ammons was keenly distressed over the bad name his state was receiving and was being urged from all sides to do something about it. The governor's ordeal had not ended with the arrival of federal troops. President Wilson, patently annoyed that the special session of the

Colorado legislature had not been called for earlier than May 4, had directed him to impress the members with the "imperative necessity" of restoring Colorado's sovereign power. The special session turned out to be at least impassioned. "Colorado is cruelly wronged and undeservedly shamed," cried Senator John I. Tierney, one of a handful of forward-looking legislators, "since neither party to the conflict is of the state, being absentee landlords on the one hand and on the other . . . polyglot, exploited foreigners . . . Colorado is . . . paying the price of a national stupidity that has permitted the private exploitation of natural resources, and has bred a powerful and unscrupulous group of financiers who seek their wealth in special privilege instead of honest industry . . ."

Governor Ammons' demand for authority to compel the arbitration of strikes came to naught when Attorney General Fred Farrar ruled that such legislation did not fall within the scope of the present special session. Senator Harvey Garman, a faithful Democratic machine supporter until now, called regretfully on Ammons to resign. "Someone . . . has led him astray. His heart is not in what he is doing . . . in his unfortunate physical circumstances he has no wise, strong men to advise him . . ." However, a resolution demanding the governor's resignation was defeated.

Early on May 16 Lindley Garrison, anxious to pull the troops out of Colorado at the earliest safe moment, read an item in the New York *Sun* that made him jump. The Colorado legislature had voted to adjourn without considering any bill or resolution to end the strike. The Secretary of War immediately scribbled a note to Woodrow Wilson: "This is what I have been fearing. Can you, if not too late, wire Ammons to put him and the legislature on notice regarding your feelings . . . ?" At once the President sent off one of his sternest communications. Disturbed by news of the contemplated adjournment, he had to remind the governor that "my constitutional obligations with regard to the maintenance of order in Colorado are not to be indefinitely continued by the inaction of the state legislature . . . I cannot conceive that the state is willing to forego her sovereignty or to throw herself entirely upon the government of the United States and I am quite clear that she has no constitutional right to do so when it is within the power of her legislature to take effective action."

Ammons wired back that the President had been misinformed. The legislature, far from being inactive, had provided for a million-dollar bond issue to clear the militia's indebtedness and passed resolutions permitting the governor to close saloons and prohibit the carrying of firearms. In other words, the militia would go back into the strike field to maintain order, something labor leaders swore would mean civil war, while nothing was to be done to force a settlement of the strike. According to the Rocky Mountain *News,* the special session had been dominated by the CFI and the Democratic old guard. From the outcome, it must certainly have appeared so. And there was also widespread belief, backed by some circumstantial evidence, that Governor Ammons tried to withhold release of the President's embarrassing rebuke to him until after the legislature adjourned. When it finally leaked out, Senator Tierney shouted in the legislature at the governor, "How much stronger a spur do you need? What more stinging lash must crack over your shoulder?"

A flood of telegrams descended upon the statehouse and the White House opposing the return of the militia as an act of sheer lunacy. Even Ammons had to admit the likelihood that violence would only break out all over again, and a week or so after the special session had ended he wrote asking the President to have patience with Colorado — "a new state" — and keep the federal soldiers in the field for the time being. His hopes for their early withdrawal now swiftly evaporating, Woodrow Wilson asked Garrison to have some of the troops discreetly check the ability of the state militia to carry out proper police action. The President could not resist making a dig at General Chase. "I dare say they can find this out better than we could through the extraordinary Adjutant General if we applied to him."

Chase's legal counsel right then was eastbound as Governor

Ammons' emissary to secure what the governor called a wider publicity of the facts. There is evidence that the idea was conceived before Judge Lindsey's party set out, but its officially implied intention was to offset the kind of unflattering impression of Colorado sowed by the judge wherever he went. Major Edward Boughton's arrival in New York coincided with the Lindsey group's departure for home. And as became astonishingly evident, Boughton's trip for refurbishing Colorado's tarnished image was incidental to the real purpose of rescuing that of the Colorado Fuel and Iron Company. For one thing, a letter of introduction to Starr Murphy from L. M. Bowers defined the major's mission as being at the request of the governor and attorney general of the state "backed financially by ourselves and one or two of the other operators . . ." Bowers had thought it best to let the agitators "blow off their hot air until the public became tired, and then we would begin a conservative and carefully planned campaign of publicity." Boughton was also equipped with a letter from Ammons to Elbert Hubbard proposing that the author of "A Message to Garcia" and other reactionary tracts talk with the major. This scarcely enhanced the objectivity of Boughton's motives, especially since Hubbard was about now privately dunning John D. Rockefeller, Jr., for money to distribute his magazine, *The Fra,* buttering his chances with such stated opinions as "a good many of the [Colorado] strikers are poor, unfortunate, ignorant foreigners who imagine that . . . they are fighting for liberty."

In New York the major went straight to 26 Broadway and met Jerome D. Greene, one of the New York directors of the CFI and secretary of the Rockefeller Foundation. And when he confessed a shortage of ideas on how to give the East a better understanding of Colorado's strike problem, the visitor was told that he should speak with Ivy Lee.

All at once, publicity seemed to be on everybody's mind. Rockefeller gave it a great deal of thought. Occupying an unsavory spotlight was in no sense a picnic. To a friend he had confided that the first two weeks in May were most trying, for no man liked to be publicly and unfairly pilloried. Besides uncomfortable, it was hazardous. The time bomb which exploded in a tenement building on Lexington Avenue, killing four members of the IWW, was believed intended for Rockefeller's town house and IWW hotheads still lurked about Tarrytown, under the surveillance of Burns detectives hired to guard the multimillionaire's family. But aside from personal considerations it was a matter of "our duty as individuals and stockholders and directors to get the facts before the public." Rockefeller had turned for suggestions to Arthur Brisbane, the Pulitzer and Hearst newspaper editor sometimes called "master of the commonplace." And Brisbane had recommended a master of propaganda.

Ivy Ledbetter Lee was at least an artful verbalist, presently waging a publicity campaign to gloss over the higher freight rates sought by eastern railroad magnates. Lee was to describe his success in aiding the railroads as an exercise in the "art of getting believed in." For suitable models in this endeavor he cited Henry VIII of England and Kaiser Wilhelm II of Germany. After the Pennsylvania Railroad's president had been persuaded to loan out Lee's services on a part-time basis, the CFI hired the publicist for $1000 a month, paid by the senior Rockefeller. It was not Lee's first association with coal bosses: In 1906–7 he had worked for eastern anthracite operators.

Major Boughton's need of publicity ideas confronted Lee with his first challenge in his new job, but the manner in which he met it had already been outlined in a long memo Brisbane had sent Starr Murphy on June 2, suggesting a presentation of the facts in a manner acceptable to the governor of Colorado and if possible over his signature. It should be sent to every newspaper in the country and would be followed by a series of advertisements that "all ought to be sent out as statements by the governor . . ." Issuing from the state's chief executive as a formal defense of the state against unjust attacks, the campaign was bound to command attention. The material going out over the governor's signature would be composed by Ivy Lee, whom Brisbane thought ideally suited for the job.

Lee conferred privately with Major Boughton in the latter's hotel room at the Waldorf-Astoria and improved on the Brisbane plan by adding the President of the United States to the mailing list for the statements ghostwritten by the CFI's publicist and signed by the governor of Colorado. Even Boughton developed doubts about the scheme, though whether ethical or practical is not clear. He asked Lee to go ahead and draft the kind of letter he had in mind. Boughton, meanwhile, would contribute a memorandum of his own view of the situation as part basis for the draft. When John D. Rockefeller, Jr., learned of what was afoot it occurred to him that he also had material which Lee might deem helpful. Evidently he found nothing obnoxious about an official representative of the governor of Colorado, supposedly assigned to make public the facts of a labor dispute, collaborating with the publicity agent of business interests directly involved to perfect a plan that would in effect deceive the President and the American people.

When it all came out Rockefeller belittled his contribution as having been the rough draft of a statement to the press that for some reason he had never used. (It was in fact derived from the Colorado National Guard's official denials of a "massacre" at Ludlow without mentioning, however, the deliberate burning of tents described in the same report.) On June 10 Rockefeller wrote Lee a letter that would subsequently serve to discompose him. "Several points in my memorandum . . . could well even more appropriately be used in the letter from Governor Ammons to President Wilson which you are proposing to prepare . . ." Lee wrote back next day that the matter was of foremost importance. In due course his finished draft was forwarded to Boughton, now back in Denver, with a suggestion that the final statement be addressed "To the American People" and distributed all over the United States.

Fashioned by so highly touted a craftsman at influencing public opinion, the draft was a decidedly unsubtle composition defending the Colorado militia as noble heroes, extolling the probity of the coal companies, and condemning the strike leaders as desperate rogues or ungrateful foreigners. Rockefeller never saw the finished piece, Ivy Lee seemed to have had second thoughts about it, and Major Boughton, for undisclosed reasons, failed to pass it along to Governor Ammons. But whether it was a fair monument to Ivy Lee's skills is beside the point. The significance of all that designing was to be publicly interpreted as dramatic evidence of the multimillionaire's disdain for Colorado state authorities and his lofty assumption that they would do his bidding.

Major Boughton's eastern tour prevented him from attending an incredibly squalid and farcical military tribunal. Although the report of the Ludlow investigating commission made up of the officers Boughton, Danks, and Van Cise blamed the Greeks for firing first and had a lot to say about Balkan "atrocities," it included at Van Cise's insistence charges that Major Hamrock had turned a machine gun on the colony, that militiamen had deliberately spread the fire, and that Lieutenant Karl Linderfelt was chiefly responsible for the antagonism that led to the fighting. Thus it was by no means a thorough whitewash of the National Guard, and there is reason to believe that Governor Ammons and General Chase thought of suppressing it. The report reached the newspapers anyway and its recommendation for a general court-martial required action. But a court-martial could itself be used effectively by those determined on a whitewash, and a few officers, including Danks and Van Cise, pointedly avoided any part in the proceedings after their superiors told them that the object was to "take care of their own," to safeguard the accused against civil trial on the principle that a man's life could not be put in jeopardy twice in the courts.

The military court convened in the officers' quarters of the state rifle range at Golden, west of Denver. Newspapermen were admitted. There was a confusing implication at the outset, with or without intent, that no accurate estimate was possible of the number of officers and enlisted men to be tried. All told, in the space of the next fortnight, the trials of ten officers and a dozen men were completed. The officers of the court, including the president and judge advocate, were all cronies of General Chase. None of the mine guards who had served in the militia during the Ludlow fighting was numbered among the accused. All the evidence was *ex parte,* except in the case of one witness, John Lawson, subpoenaed after union officials decided to ignore what they considered a trumped-up show with exoneration prearranged. Testimony often conflicted but no cross-examination of witnesses was conducted and inconsistencies were left hanging. Questions were transparently leading, answers flagrantly hearsay, and irrelevancies were introduced and lingered upon for the only discernible purpose of maligning the strikers.

Mayor Hamrock, unguarded and armed with a six-shooter, was first to be tried. When the proceedings got into their stride he wore full regalia and a sword. To the sixty-two charges and specifications alleging murder, arson, manslaughter, looting, and larceny, Hamrock pleaded not guilty and he waived counsel. The theme of his defense was that he and his men fired only when attacked. No one seriously questioned it. Medical evidence was vouchsafed by the militia's medical officers and Doctor Curry of the Victor-American Company: The women and children in the pit had died hours before the tents caught fire. No one asked about the two women who had survived, whether or not the pit had been sealed, or how the doctors could be so sure that all the victims had been in the hole since early morning.

The court's plan was to try all the men at once and the officers likewise, except Hamrock and Lieutenant Karl Linderfelt, who faced an additional charge of assault with a deadly weapon. Lieutenant Edwin Carson, unconvinced that the present procedure would foreclose the possibility of a later trial in civil court, asked to be tried apart from the others, whereupon similar requests came from his fellow officers. The applications were granted. Less than half a day was devoted to each trial. Carson alone, perhaps because he had spent half his life in the British army, pleaded justification for anything he did at Ludlow in the traditional finality of military orders. "It was not up to me to question or ask the reason why."

At precisely the time that news of Judge Ben Lindsey's party in the East was capturing Denver headlines, the military court unexpectedly introduced a new defendant, Lieutenant Linden B. Elliott. The significance was made unbelievably obvious. Although the same charges of murder, arson, etc., were leveled at Elliott, the questioning almost exclusively centered on foul curses he allegedly had overheard Pearl Jolly and Mary Thomas — the pair whose antiguard candor was then getting bounteous publicity — teach Ludlow's children to shout at the militiamen. The court had to be cleared before the coy lieutenant could be induced to repeat the words, and they turned out to be all the familiar polysyllabic barrack-hut obscenities. Asked next if an underground tunnel had connected Pearl Jolly's tent with Louis Tikas', Elliott replied that none was needed, so close together were the tents. After plumbing these preposterous depths the court finished with Elliott, hurried through the trials of ten enlisted men at once, and then turned to Karl Linderfelt.

Linderfelt admitted striking Tikas with a rifle, conceded such conduct was unsoldierly, and added, "but any man who curses me has got the same thing coming." Major Hamrock was recalled to the witness chair and testified that depending on the grain of the wood, the stock on some Springfields could be broken with a very light tap. The veteran rifleman was handed Linderfelt's Springfield. He ran his experienced eye over it, invited the officers to see how the oil had worked its way into cracks, and would stake his life on its having long been defective.

Everybody was acquitted. The verdict in Linderfelt's case was stated with such curious ambiguity that the court might have saved itself further self-defilement by saying nothing. It found Lieutenant Linderfelt guilty of committing an assault on Louis

Tikas with a Springfield rifle "but attaches no criminality thereto. And the court does therefore acquit him . . ."

The National Guard had exonerated itself of Ludlow's guilt. Now the effort to affix that guilt firmly upon the union leaders went ahead in earnest. The drive was launched and directed in clandestine fashion by a formidable alliance of coal companies, local political machinery, the Baldwin-Felts Detective Agency, and the facilities of the office of the state attorney general. At the instigation of Judge Jesse Northcutt in Trinidad, a grand jury had been assembled to investigate the strike outrages. The twelve men, Sheriff Grisham's selections, consisted of three former employees of the Colorado Fuel and Iron Company, three deputy sheriffs who had fought against the strikers, and six local merchants who relied on coal-company patronage for their livelihood. Fred Farrar, state attorney general, launched the secret inquiry in person at Trinidad on June 23, 1914.

During the recent turbulent months Farrar, an old-guard Democrat, had trod lightly, avoided alienating labor by either staying clear of the governor's controversial decisions or vaguely implying disapproval of them. At the same time, aware that he was the coal operators' best bet for spiking union guns under the guise of asserting law and order, Farrar quietly courted their financial and political influence. After he returned from Trinidad to Denver, his assistant, Frank West, took over direction of the Las Animas grand jury investigation and, as amply shown in their private correspondence, the objective of securing indictments against strike leaders was coupled with one of consolidating voter strength for Farrar's reelection in the coming fall.

Seeking evidence to support indictments, the grand jury used bribery, intimidation, and the exploitation of interunion squabbles and jealousies. Northcutt cooperated actively, supplying names of prospects who, suitably "sweated," could be persuaded to talk. Little Pete Katsulis worked off his grievance against John Lawson by furnishing testimony that placed Lawson in the firing line during the battle of October 1913. Little Pete's reward was a job in a CFI mine. One effective method that the assistant attorney general hit upon for scaring local strikers and thereby loosening tongues was to ride about Trinidad and Aguilar in what he referred to in correspondence with Farrar as "the old gunboat," in other words the Baldwin-Felts Death Special, with Walter Belk and a couple of Sheriff Grisham's more menacing deputies also aboard. Soon West was able to inform the attorney general that if the jury indicted all the Aguilar miners against whom he had collected evidence the town would be depopulated. The investigation spread its net to Pueblo, where the CFI obliged by rounding up witnesses, and on July 12 West took pleasure in reporting a falling-out among the unionists, panic in the Greek ranks, and the imminence of a general stampede to confess.

All this time Frank West had his boss's political fortunes in mind. He had been careful not to sow suspicions that his errand in Las Animas County was political, but he need not have worried. The grand jurors made it easy for him by asking for his assurance that the indictments they had determined upon would be prosecuted to the end. West neatly replied that the only thing to possibly prevent it would be Fred Farrar's retirement from office before he could secure verdicts. The jurors took the hint and immediately pledged all political support.

On August 29 the grand jury made its report:

> The evidence produced before us clearly shows that the crimes were committed by armed mobs, acting in pursuance of well-defined, carefully matured plans, having for their object the destruction of property and human life. These mobs were composed of members of the United Mine Workers of America and their known sympathizers . . . The organization through its officers in Colorado bought the guns and ammunition and directed criminal activities . . .

The planned insurrection was unintentionally financed by the members of the UMW and other labor organizations outside Colorado, whose money therefore had been collected under false pretenses. Accompanying the report were indictments of 124 labor leaders and union members, and high on the list was John Lawson — accused of murder, assault with intent to kill, arson, and conspiracy in restraint of trade.

There is no evidence that John D. Rockefeller, Jr., even knew about the grand jury's investigation until the published news of its indictments. He had been engaged in the campaign above ground, so to speak, furthering the publicity program master-minded by Ivy Lee. From June to September at about weekly intervals a series of bulletins supposedly put together by the coal operators but edited by Ivy Lee and printed at his Philadelphia office were circulated to congressmen, governors, editors, journal-ists, college presidents, professional leaders, and church ministers. The bulletins carried the title *Facts Concerning the Struggle in Colorado for Industrial Freedom* and a second series was planned for the winter.

Rockefeller had suffered probably greater mortification than anyone suspected as a result of his exclusive faith in the informa-tion sent him from Denver. Adding Ivy Lee to the payroll augured no great improvement, since the publicist's function was to receive the same biased or inaccurate material that Rockefeller had been getting. Lee did not go beyond his sources. A good deal of what he sent out in the bulletins consisted of secondhand stuff about Mother Jones's bawdy past, the number of men still at work in the mines (with no allowance made for recently arrived strike-breakers), and reprints of grossly partisan articles, reports, and sanctimonious sermons. The first pamphlet reproduced a letter which non-CFI operators had written to President Wilson deplor-ing the attack on Rockefeller. A letter from Governor Ammons to the Boulder *Daily Camera* chiding fellow citizens for not suffi-ciently honoring "the brave boys of the National Guard" formed the basis for another bulletin.

One of the least reliable sources tapped by the operators for material to go into Lee's tracts was the Denver Women's Law and Order League, a group formed to counterract the Women's Peace

Association and whose membership was dominated by wives of coal managers and National Guard officers, including John Chase. The league had been busy manufacturing statements of its own. Among those faithfully repeated by Ivy Lee, one contended that "no machine gun was at any time directed against the [Ludlow] colony," a fiction which not even Major Hamrock had tried to get away with.

Ivy Lee, who boasted of being concerned only with facts, let a number of blunders or deceits slip by him. One of his bulletins reproduced the Doyle-Hickey-Lawson "Call to Arms" after Ludlow as "A Call to Rebellion" and another displayed quotes from a sermon delivered by the Reverend Newell Dwight Hillis, a prominent Brooklyn minister who said quite falsely in the pulpit that the operators were "perfectly willing to recognize the union." Lee found another quotable divine in the Reverend A. A. Berle of Cambridge, Massachusetts, whose own pamphlet *The Colorado Mine War* described the strike as an "invasion of the State by bloodthirsty agitators." A collection of clergymen and college deans sent an open letter to Secretary of Labor William Wilson fuming against union leaders, whose perfidy had prolonged the strike. This too went into Lee's bulletins, the Rockefellers shortly thereafter donating $100,000 each to the University of Denver and to Colorado College, whose dean and president respectively had been among the signatories.

Rockefeller himself was constantly on the lookout for material to go into Lee's *Facts*. His submissions to the publicity wizard were on the order of prejudiced pieces from *Coal Age* and the reactionary sentiments of John J. Stevenson, the New York University professor who had extolled capitalism in the May 1914 issue of *Popular Science Monthly*.

The biggest boner circulated in what Rockefeller liked to call "a broad educative campaign of publicity" appeared in the August 25 issue of the bulletin and was intended to discredit the UMW leadership. Salaries and expenses paid to Frank Hayes over the period of one year were boldly displayed as for nine weeks. Different methods of juggling the figures gave similarly false versions of incomes drawn by John Lawson, John McLennan, and Mother Jones. Who in the Boston Building arrived at these fraudulent calculations is not known, but the facts, obvious to anybody taking the trouble to check the periodic report of the UMW secretary-treasurer, were quickly brought to the attention of J. F. Welborn and he wired Lee right away. Lee replied by advising Welborn to insert an appropriate errata slip in each copy, but by then the Denver office had mailed out hundreds of bulletins. A consequence of all this was that radical journals took to calling Lee a paid liar and dubbed him "Poison Ivy." Presumably unabashed, Lee journeyed to Colorado, discovered that there was "no safety valve for the men to get petty grievances out of their system," and suggested that some such machinery might "take the wind out of the union sails." He also advised Rockefeller that the company's propaganda literature should go into the homes, where women would see it, because "women are voters in the state and their influence is important."

It must have been this sort of private counsel from Lee that Rockefeller believed to be something special. No one paying the publicist $1000 a month merely for the *Facts* could have thought he was getting his money's worth. Indeed, if the publicity campaign for the CFI was all one had to go by, it would be a mystery to see just how Ivy Lee was anything but overrated. The Rockefellers might have done better by hiring someone from the other side like Creel or Sinclair or even Walter H. Fink of Denver, District 15's publicity director, who managed to infuse the right degree of credibility into his emotional account of the tragedy at Ludlow and by nationwide circulation secured its permanent designation in labor historiography as a *massacre*. The union also put out its own series of pamphlets with the title, *The Struggle in Colorado for Industrial Freedom,* deliberately close to that adopted by Lee for his bulletins but written in moderate language and probably more factual — its first issue was based on statistics from the U.S. Bureau of Mines showing the danger to life and limb in Colorado's coal mines.

Although Ivy Lee's campaign for the CFI fell short of being illustrious, he was rewarded the following year with a full-time position on Rockefeller's personal staff and a directorship in the company. Lee protected the Rockefeller name almost to the day he died in 1934, and thereafter the office he founded continued to aid John D. Rockefeller, Jr., until the latter's death in 1960. After those shattering events in Colorado, Rockefeller's image was indeed to be restored with polish, not by a publicity prodigy from the railroad interests but by an unemployed labor expert from Canada, fretful, self-exiled, and so near destitution as to appear on the very edge of panic.

﹎18﹏

THE CANADIAN

WILLIAM LYON MACKENZIE KING's educational background included study under Thorsten Veblen at the University of Chicago and Frank Taussig of Harvard, educators deeply concerned with the complexities of the new industry in relation to labor and society. Later he spent some time in England listening to Sidney and Beatrice Webb and the Fabians. By the age of twenty-five, when he was invited into the Canadian Ministry of Labor, King had gained considerable insight, mostly theoretical, into social problems of the new age and secured a reputation for sympathetic expertise in the field of organized labor while prudently eschewing union militancy. In 1909 he became Canada's Minister of Labor. During this tenure he drafted the Industrial Disputes Investigations Act based in part on the mystical theories of a Quebec bishop and legislative trends in countries overseas. Neither the new law nor the young minister was able to quiet Canada's labor ferment, and nearly 200 strikes raged from early 1910 to the fall of 1911, when the Laurier administration was defeated at the polls. King lost his government post and his parliamentary seat. His private ordeal began that winter.

Responsibility for his parents' livelihood (he also had a brother in ill-health) and his own failing circumstances burdened his mind to the point of mental anguish. According to a critical biography of Canada's great statesman, this phase of his life "permanently conditioned his thinking about money . . . was at the bottom of his life-long caution about money matters, excessive concentration on the necessity to make adequate provision for the future." He read of a railroad strike in Britain and it maddened him that "with the kind of ability I have and service I might be rendering" he was instead poor and idle.

The occasional lectures he gave in the United States were not of much help. "Public life hereafter must be a closed opportunity to me," he wrote gloomily in March 1913, money worries compounded now by a stillborn love affair. His apprehensions grew obsessive, he seemed to fear himself trapped in an excruciating paradox. He had so much to give, was so esteemed an authority on labor that the new United States Commission on Industrial Relations (itself on the verge of an intoxicating career) sought his views on the subject. Yet this notability was bringing him neither wealth nor contentment and on May 12, 1914, a month after his appearance before the Commission, he mourned privately, "How terribly broken down on every side is the house of life around me . . ."

Deliverance was at hand. King had spoken at the Harvard Commencement Dinner in 1909 and agreeably impressed Professor Charles W. Eliot, the university's venerable president and one of the leading academic thinkers meditating on the accelerating class conflict. At the same time, King had met Jerome D. Greene, then Eliot's secretary. On June 1, 1914, the Canadian received a rather mysterious telegram from Greene, now head of the Rockefeller Foundation, inviting him to New York for discussion of a major project under Foundation auspices. That same day Professor Eliot wired King his opinion that what the Foundation contemplated offered an "immense" opportunity. "You might greatly serve all white race industries and show the way to industrial accord . . ."

An amplifying letter from Greene disclosed that a program of economic and social studies with possible bearing on labor problems had been in the minds of Foundation planners but if, as influential industrialists, they could work out improvements in management-labor relations "on a basis compatible with sound finance," greater social service might result than any to be rendered through the Foundation's strictly philanthropic expenditures.

According to Rockefeller's associate and biographer, Raymond B. Fosdick, the financier's thinking on the Colorado strike was now in a process of profound change. He had come to realize that the facts did not necessarily square with Bowers' and Welborn's point of view, that automatically blaming union agitation for labor unrest was self-deluding, that the important thing now was to get at the underlying causes of the miners' dissatisfaction. For this purpose he badly needed the help of someone with objective experience in the field of industrial relations and at this moment Mackenzie King made a providential entrance. The Canadian himself came to believe that the establishment of his association with Rockefeller was by no means an accident of chance. And they took to each other immediately. Rockefeller declared himself "seldom . . . so impressed by a man at first appearance." The rapport was permanent; they were to become close as brothers.

They first met in the town house on West 54th Street. Starr Murphy and Jerome Greene were also present. The conversation dealt almost wholly with Colorado. Rockefeller, stating his company's opposition to unionization, asked if King could come up with some form of representation plan within the company whereby employees could air their grievances. Greene went into broader detail in a letter to King on June 9 envisaging "some organization or union . . . [affording] to labor the protection it needs against oppression and exploitation while at the same time promoting its efficiency as an instrument of economic production." A month later King again heard from Professor Eliot, who with Greene had recommended him for the proposed Foundation study. The proffered post was "the most important work which the civilized world offers." Obviously there was a difference in focus. The utopian vision exciting Eliot in the seclusion of Harvard was not precisely the inspiration for the repeated offers King received from 26 Broadway, where less sublime motivations involved a need (despite Ivy Lee's efforts) to still the public outcry against Rockefeller and hopes of getting the coal mines back in 100 per cent operation.

About now a close female friend acknowledged to King that Rockefeller's job opportunity certainly promised a means of banishing all his financial worries, but he must be on his guard against an attempt to buy him. King's invalided brother, coincidentally in a Denver sanitarium, worded it more strongly: No business arrangement with the "interests" could possibly withstand "your clear-cut conscience" indefinitely and would brand him forever in the eyes of the laboring classes. "The very heart of the CFI has to be changed, and millions of dollars sacrificed by them before things will be right in the sight of God."

It would not have been improper for King to argue with his conscience as well as his brother that those very millions might be harnessed to noble causes of labor reform, but a letter written on August 4 made evident that for all the grandiose talk in which others were indulging about solving industrial problems on a universal scale, John D. Rockefeller, Jr., at least was chiefly interested in finding some method of palming off on his miners alternative inducements to those offered by the unions. The coal mines were quiet, he told King, production was up to 80 per cent, ample for present business purposes, but the tent colonies still stood, "a constant menace." He quoted his advisers on the only two ways to restore normal conditions: for the UMW to leave Colorado alone or for the development of a system providing the employees with opportunities for collective bargaining, discussion of grievances, and "any other advantages, which may be derived from membership in the union." And again Rockefeller appealed for Mackenzie King's help.

The day he received this letter the Canadian had something else to think about. The European war had begun and Canada was in it. King wrote back to Rockefeller that patriotic duty would oblige him to stay on in Ottawa at least until the end of the emergency session of parliament. But King was out of office, his services not automatically required, and his astute mind found opportunity to size up the war in relation to the problem perplexing Rockefeller. Only two days after the mammoth slaughter began in Europe, King, though not yet on Rockefeller's payroll, furnished him with six pages of theory on its present and future potentials for the benefit of America's capitalists and the confusion of her labor unions. Written by one who had encouraged an impression of himself as a friend of organized labor, the letter deserves attention. Among those presently "embarrassing" the Colorado situation "there are many foreigners who may feel compelled to return to Europe." After hostilities cease, "thousands of men and their families in the Old World are going to seek further employment here in the New. In certain industries it is going to be easy for employers to find all the labor they desire, and unions will be confronted with a new problem." Under the war-created stimulus to immigration the unions would "change their policy," laying less stress on recognition. Working conditions would comprise the issue, and the alliance and loyalty of laborers could be secured by big companies that raised standards of pay and work hours on their own initiative. Here, it seemed to King, was the key to solution of the Colorado dilemma. In the same letter he outlined his proposals for boards of conciliation on which employers and employees were represented to deal with grievances and working conditions.

In the middle of August the trustees of the Rockefeller Foundation meeting at 26 Broadway resolved to appoint Mackenzie King director of an investigation into problems of industrial relations. About now Rockefeller received a letter from Frank Hayes suggesting an exchange of views for ending the strike. In conformity with the policy established by the Denver officers, he did not answer it. Rockefeller had bright hopes of King pulling that feat off and in letters to Denver he proposed a secret tour by King of the coal properties, touted the Canadian's plan, and portrayed him as possessing a positive genius for settling labor disputes through his knowledge, experience, and a knack of getting men of every rank to trust him.

The response from Denver was cool. Welborn thought that King's boards of conciliation would weaken the operators in the eyes of the men and be tantamount to an executive admission that grievances existed in the first place. Bowers feared the plan would somehow be claimed by the union as recognition and that socialist papers would lampoon the mineowners for grasping at eleventh-hour face-saving schemes. To move an inch from their stand now that "defeat seems certain for the enemy" would be folly. The UMW was bankrupt, its leaders at swords' points with each other because of their Colorado fiasco, and the thing to do now was sit tight until victory.

Ivy Lee, in Denver to reestablish confidence in the credibility of his propaganda sources, also demurred. The situation locally, he confided to Rockefeller, was too delicate for King's visit just now. Stalwart unity no longer existed among the operators — John Osgood, with his stubborn and fossilized ideas, was a particularly troublesome handicap. "There is real work . . ." wrote Lee, "missionary work . . . to be done." Rockefeller replied that he understood, and now began efforts on the part of the officers in New York to convert the Denver managers to a more progressive view of industrial relations. Welborn in time would be won over. Bowers, no less inflexible than Osgood (whom the CFI chairman happened to detest) was beyond salvation. In any event, the early attempts to modernize the thinking in Denver were feeble. The officers who favored an unyielding line found an unexpected ally when Starr Murphy arrived in Colorado and, primed with intelligence about the UMW's financial hardship, declared for a fight "to the finish" with all talk of reforms postponed until the union had capitulated. Murphy probably wrote in the additional knowledge, also acquired in Denver, of the continuing effort to discredit John Lawson and other strike leaders by putting them behind bars.

President Wilson, meanwhile, took new steps to end the strike.

He was unaware of Rockefeller's aspirations to pacify the coal camps with management-employee conciliation boards. He may not have known either how obsessively some of Rockefeller's team wanted to force the UMW into unconditional surrender. Wilson's earnest wish was to get the federal troops out of Colorado. Also he was made to feel uneasy by information from the Department of State that the violence in Colorado was a potential cause of complications with foreign governments. Both Italian and Austro-Hungarian ambassadors were demanding protection for nationals in the American coalfields and claiming damages where deaths had occurred. (By contrast, the British vice consul in Denver, after rejecting a complaint of illegal arrest from Mary Thomas, self-righteously assured Attorney General Farrar that British subjects flouting U.S. laws could expect no sympathy from him.)

Martin Foster's return to Colorado had proved fruitless. The operators had been in no mood for lectures or mediation attempts on the part of one whose previous visit was to embarrass them with questions. So Foster had gone, and next to arrive in Denver were a pair of would-be mediators. appointed by Secretary of Labor William Wilson. One of them, Hywel Davies, was president of the Kentucky Mine Operators Association, a retired coal operator and therefore warmly welcomed by J. F. Welborn as a natural advocate of company interests. The other, W. R. Fairley of Alabama, had once been a member of the executive board of the UMW. The two spent their summer in Colorado, Fairley concentrating on the operators, Davies working on the miners.

They did so against a background of continuing brittle peace in the Trinidad coalfield. The federal troops had settled in for a longer stay than foreseen. Disarmed and denied access to saloons, the irresponsibles on both sides were neutralized. It was also part of the policy developed by the President, his Secretary of War, and the officers in the field, that only those mines operating at the time of the Ludlow battle would be allowed to continue or reopen operations. No new miners other than Colorado residents who voluntarily applied for work at the mine offices could be hired by these companies and the importation of strikebreakers was strictly forbidden. Letters to the War Department from Welborn and Osgood strenuously protesting this policy met with Garrison's cool reply that he anticipated no change in it. The federal occupation of Colorado was in general executed with such tranquilizing skill that mineowners, politicians, unionists, church leaders, and foreign envoys joined in petitioning Woodrow Wilson to keep the troops where they were.

The President was acutely sensitive to his constitutional limitations, thus ever alert for new opportunities to force Governor Ammons into reassuming his responsibilities. As summer waned he reminded the governor of the early onset of a Colorado winter. Snowstorms began in September, shelter for men and animals would have to be arranged, and aside from the additional costs to the administration it would all but advertise an intention to keep the soldiers in Colorado indefinitely. Wilson could not believe that this is what the great state of Colorado would permit. The troops had been put into Colorado on the understanding that their stay would be short "and I doubt my constitutional right to keep them there indefinitely." Ammons replied that it was a matter of money. He gave Wilson some statistics: little more than a quarter of the state was taxable. "You may be surprised to know that nineteen-twentieths of our taxable revenues come from one-twelfth of the state." In less detail he also blamed the European war, but the bonds he hoped to float would take care of future peace-keeping costs and the President need have no doubt that he would be notified the moment Ammons saw his way clear to agree on the removal of the soldiers.

The President's exasperation was relieved by word from Denver that his appointed mediators had drawn up a tentative basis for adjustment. Recognition formed no part of it. The plan called for a three-year truce during which the state mining code would be rigidly enforced. Strikers found not guilty of violating the law were to be rehired. Each mine would have its own grievance committee selected by the miners. Grievances not settled by the committees would be referred to a three-man arbitration board named by the President of the United States. On September 5 Woodrow Wilson submitted the Fairley-Davies truce plan to the officers of the three largest Colorado coal companies and the international officers of the UMW. The strike's "many serious stages," Wilson wrote in an accompanying letter, had turned it into a national problem. The new proposals had his strong endorsement, he hoped they would be considered by both parties "as if you were acting for the whole country . . . I beg that you will regard it as urged upon your acceptance by myself with very deep earnestness." The first reply came swiftly from the union leadership and signified approval, subject to a special convention of Colorado miners.

On the morning of September 15, ninety-six miners representing the locals of District 15 gathered in the Trades Assembly Hall at Trinidad to be confronted with realities. Frank Hayes, in contrast with his clarion oratory of a year ago in the cause of unionization and enjoined now by the International Executive Board of the UMW to end the strike with all seemly haste, talked defeat and raised the threat of withdrawn strike funds. It was an ignominious function the vice president had to perform, although logic was certainly on his side. He could have told his audience how the union had poured nearly $4 million into Colorado since the northern walkout in 1910, how during the latter months it had been found necessary to borrow $875,000 to continue the struggle. The difficulty of raising enough money through assessment of union members was compounded by a steady drain in membership from 377,682 in 1913 to 311,786 two years later. And the miners in Ohio were on strike. All this Hayes might have stressed to the sober-faced men of the Trinidad field, but perhaps he had not the heart. It was enough to admit that naught could avail against stubbornness backed by mountainous wealth. "You are not fighting a few independent capitalists," he told his silent audience, "but you are fighting John D. Rockefeller and his associates.

You can strike from now until doomsday, and if that man makes up his mind to spend his money, you will be in the same condition that you are in today."

Ed Doyle and John Lawson spoke and were all for continuing the strike. But W. R. Fairley took the floor to urge acceptance of the proposal as written with nobody trying to "cross a T or remove a dot." The outcome became inevitable when Mother Jones got up to join those who had changed their tune, and she framed her words to make rejection of the truce plan a repudiation of "a type of statesman we have not had since . . . Jefferson and Lincoln." The proposals were approved by an almost unanimous vote. Frank Hayes managed to keep his voice steady as he declared the union's position "immeasurably strengthened." And the conference adjourned on a forlorn note of bravery, as the miners broke into their Colorado strike hymn, "Union Forever."

Instead of the peace Woodrow Wilson now anticipated he was made to realize just how intractable Colorado's coal managers could be. They had no intention of accepting the plan in its present form. Arbitration boards made up of Presidential appointees reflected too great a threat to their power. Neither were they prepared to take back all strikers found not guilty of legal violations. Delaying unequivocal reply to the President's appeal, they cast about in private for some means to counter the truce plan without fanning the anti-Rockefeller sentiment that Ivy Lee and Mackenzie King were then applying their fertile minds toward reducing. By making the Fairley-Davies plan public, the President had placed the coal bosses in what Starr Murphy, writing to Welborn, called "a delicate situation," one he hoped the executives would handle with their customary discretion, avoiding both contact with the union and appearances of obstinacy likely to offend the public. Not being all that hopeful, Murphy followed up a few days later with suggested counterproposals for President Wilson.

Welborn considered them. The most essential feature would require the company to unite with its employees in creating a committee for the discussion of ideas and grievances, guaranteeing the worker not only against molestation from outside the company but offering him protection against unfair treatment from within. As far as Welborn and his colleagues could perceive, Murphy's "permanent and impartial body" was nothing less than one of Mackenzie King's "boards of conciliation." Welborn merged the more harmless of the lawyer's ideas into the reply he and Ivy Lee were drafting for the White House and left this one out.

Starr Murphy, a brilliant, warm, and conservative lawyer to his associates, had been doing his best to produce ideas for improving the morale of the coal miners. At one point he thought a good plan might be to set up contests of efficiency in some particular line of work, the winner to be awarded a free trip to Denver. This suggestion no doubt got short shrift. Welborn was busily preoccupied with preserving the corporate image and, as he told Starr Murphy with noteworthy candor, it was "an extremely difficult task to present a situation like ours so that it will command understanding and sympathy from the public."

During this period, the junior Rockefeller and his New York staff continued to react nervously to the pressure of public opinion. On September 16 Murphy sent Welborn editorial clippings about the truce offer, noting how often they made the point that the parties either accept President Wilson's proposals or suggest alternatives. Wilson enjoyed widespread popular affection. The union showed signs of going along with his wishes. Mine management was in danger of being left wearing the villain's black hat, it seemed to Murphy. "A mere refusal to do anything would be disastrous." When this news reached Welborn, the letter he had composed jointly with Ivy Lee was en route to the White House.

It was a rebuff. The truce plan was brushed aside as a foolish attempt to buy a temporary peace with lawless agitators. Welborn also told the President that a superior plan based on practical experience was under development, a vague reference designed either to stall or remove the sting of outright rejection.

The only thing resembling a plan in the Rockefeller camp just then was what Mackenzie King envisaged and had already been turned down by the operators as at least premature.

Welborn's letter represented the attitude solely of the CFI. Acting on strong hints from New York, that company now charted its own course. D. W. Brown and John Osgood had assumed leadership of the other companies, forty-eight of whose operators joined them in rejecting the President's proposals. Their reply not only exceeded Welborn's in length but far outmatched it in vituperation against organized labor. And at this point, what Woodrow Wilson thought of the Colorado coal oligarchy could only have been expressed in blistering language.

They had tried his patience sorely with their tactics. At the same time, they had grossly humiliated the UMW officers who had sacrificed the principle of unionization to accept the truce plan on the assumption that the companies would follow suit. What the mineowners had done instead was dash salt on grievous wounds. Now President Wilson heard from union leaders, furiously wondering how long such arrogance would be tolerated; since the UMW was still paying out more than $30,000 a week in strike benefits, the rage in the Merchants Bank Building was mixed with desperation. All President Wilson could do now was hope the operators would change their minds or rapidly produce the alternative plan hinted. Even Hywel Davies found their attitude inexcusable. Could they not see that negotiations on the President's proposition offered the best hope for "the assurance of peace, prosperity, possibilities of forgetfulness and a period of goodwill [meaning] larger dividends to the employer, more work to the employee . . . and the saving of the state of Colorado from bankruptcy?"

They could or would not. It was a moment long overdue for stern direction by the CFI officers in New York, but in a letter to Welborn on October 5 suggesting a management-labor committee at each mine property at least to see that safety laws were observed, Starr Murphy added weakly, "I am merely thinking out loud." Perhaps Murphy still privately leaned to the hard-nosed views he had expressed during his Denver visit. At any rate, Welborn wrote back that he had thought along the same lines but the idea "came too near meeting one of the strikers' demands as expressed through their so-called truce proposal presented by the President." Extreme caution was necessary, Welborn went on, to avoid implanting a feeling among the men that their employers were alarmed or that they were entitled to some representation heretofore nonexistent. Meanwhile, Welborn concluded, Murphy's thoughts "out loud" were always welcome at the Boston Building.

By mid-October the President had given up hope of the operators' relenting. UMW spokesmen called upon the government to take over the mines. The American Federation of Labor urged placing them in the hands of receivers. Wilson was not sure he had the constitutional authority to take these steps, although he did consider the possibility of closing down the mines. Governor Ammons quickly protested that no such action was necessary, adding the unintentionally alarming intelligence that the Colorado National Guard would shortly be ready to reassume its duties in the strike field.

This was the moment in which Mackenzie King formally accepted the offer to direct a Rockefeller Foundation study of the problems of industrial relations, which the public was told "in spirit and method . . . will be like that carried on by the Rockefeller Institute for Medical Research and other inquiries instituted by the Rockefeller boards . . . in no sense will the investigation be local or restricted, or carried on with particular reference to an existing situation, or for that matter, with reference to conditions in any one country . . ." At one point the Foundation acknowledged the impossibility of a purely objective study: "The Rockefeller Foundation is . . . a large owner of corporate securities, and in that capacity is itself directly concerned in maintaining harmonious relations between the companies in which it is enterested and their employees." Yet — "in so far as Mr. King's inquiries have to do with industrial controversies, his attitude will be that of a physician who investigates the nature and causes of the pathological conditions with which he has to deal, with a view, if possible, to the discovery of effective remedies." Detectable beyond the ambiguity was the purpose of emphasizing King's role in the vision of Professor Eliot and others, that is, as a scientific investigator diagnosing problems on a worldwide scale. Any suggestion of his role as industrial adviser to a large employer of labor currently beset by an urgent labor crisis was muted or concealed. King was to say, also for public consumption, that he had scarcely commenced his duties in October when his attention was drawn to Colorado's "canyons of strife" and he entered his task with a desire to visit localities that served to illustrate existing needs. "Colorado very naturally suggested itself as one." As shown in King and Rockefeller's correspondence, Colorado was in fact a central topic of discussion from the start of their association in early summer and the Canadian's tour of the coal properties was broached as an idea weeks before he publicly enlisted with the Foundation.

Mackenzie King felt he was worth $15,000 a year in his new post. He cited offers he had rejected in the past and a risk he now ran of sacrificing his political career. Rockefeller replied that any figure below $10,000 was not contemplated, but he could not remunerate work for the Foundation on the same basis as if for business. The final offer was $12,000, which King accepted.

*

Winter approached with the Colorado coal operators sticking to their guns. Ideas involving grievance committees or boards of conciliation or arbitration remained unwelcome. As Welborn insisted with complete sincerity, "No commission, no matter how impartial, would be as competent as the natural managing officers of a company to say how its properties should be operated." The strike continued, the union leaders now acutely mortified. Nothing stirred at the White House in their interest, and the uncompromising mood in Denver was reinforced by political developments in the operators' favor.

In July the board of county commissioners in the strike zone, with the connivance of representatives of coal companies or at their express command, had adjusted the boundaries of certain election precincts to conform with the fences about each of several closed coal camps. As later described by appalled judges of the state Supreme Court, "thus each election precinct was . . . placed exclusively within and upon the private grounds and under the private control of a coal corporation, which autocratically declared who should and who should not enter . . ." Everything and everyone in these election precincts was owned by the company. "The polling places were upon the grounds, and in the buildings of these companies; the registration lists were kept within the private offices or buildings of such companies, and used and treated as their private property. Thus were the public election districts and public machinery turned over to the absolute domination and imperial control of the coal operators . . ." The precinct boundaries were patrolled by mine guards. Democratic candidates, including E. L. Neelly, running for sheriff of Huerfano County against Jeff Farr, had to call upon federal soldiers for escort to and from the polls. The election judges were company employees, and miners who lived on the properties and knew no English cast company-dictated votes. The closed precincts, the "fraudulent and infamous prostitution of the ballot" — all in the name of what counsel for the coal companies, with presumably a straight face, pleaded as "industrial necessity" — constituted a brazen major effort to counter new political trends and maintain the Republican grip on county offices. It succeeded in Huerfano County, where Jefferson Farr's victory was announced with a majority of 329 votes.

In Denver the coal operators' choice as gubernatorial candidate against the old liberal reformer Thomas Patterson was an obscure lawyer and temperance crusader named George A. Carlson. Without difficulty the drift of campaign dialogue was steered from labor troubles, of which many Colorado citizens were tired of hearing, to Carlson's forte, prohibition. Sentiment against liquor ran strong in the state and was subscribed to heavily by the CFI, not only by virtue of the Rockefellers' devotion to temperance causes but because company executives were delighted to find that since the federal troops had closed all saloons in the strike district, coal production figures had soared. The operators sent 150 men into the wards to campaign for a prohibition amendment to the state constitution.

The coal operators also came out strongly for Fred Farrar, then in the process of directing the Las Animas grand jury to secure indictments against John Lawson and other strike figures. There was no place in their scheme of things for the wretched Elias Ammons, but they were determined to reelect his Democratic-machine attorney general. When L. M. Bowers was later asked if the prohibition issue had not been used to gain acceptance of a "law and order platform . . . designed to aid in the ruthless persecution of strikers and union officers," he acknowledged that "it all interlocked together." Apparently so: Carlson defeated Patterson handily. Edward Costigan, running on a Progressive ticket, ran a poor third. Referring to the only prominent Democrat to win, J. F. Welborn explained to Rockefeller why his victory was to be applauded. "Mr. Farrar . . . the only reliable force for law and order in the statehouse, has been very actively engaged . . . in connection with the work of grand juries in the various coal counties where indictments have been brought against those who participated in the rioting." Rockefeller's reply expressed his gratification. And so elusive or shadowy are the indications of the multimillionaire's innermost feelings on any of the woeful events in the Trinidad coalfield, from the needless mine accidents to the carnage at Ludlow and the havoc done to justice and constitutional rights in his industrial domain, that one can only guess his reaction had he known — it must be presumed he did not — that the Las Animas grand jury had met at the behest of a CFI-owned judge who thereupon assisted its investigation, that Baldwin-Felts men and equipment were used to intimidate witnesses, and that the company's influence in support of Fred Farrar's reelection had all the appearances of payment for services rendered, namely the final expunction of the union effort in southern Colorado.

*

Months had passed since the presentation of the Fairley-Davies proposals. The UMW leaders could wait no longer. A meeting was arranged with President Wilson at the White House for November 19. Again Wilson was pressed to seize the mines and again he pleaded lack of constitutional authority. Frank Hayes quietly told him that the union had reached the end of its financial resources. The President was beseeched to appoint the proposed mediation commission as allowed for in the truce plan, thus giving the union leaders something of substance to accept honorably and call off the strike in a face-saving manner. This Wilson agreed to do in the form of a public statement. It was released on December 1. The President had harsh words for the mineowners' intransigence, but unable to force them into submission, neither could he withdraw the troops and leave the situation to settle itself. Despite the operators' rejection of the plan of temporary settlement, he had decided to appoint the commission his proposal contemplated, and "thus at least create the instrumentality by which like troubles and disputes may be amicably and honorably settled in future." He named Seth Low, president of the National Civic Federation, Charles W. Mills, a manufacturer, and Patrick Gilday, the president of Pennsylvania District 2 of the UMW.

This afforded the exit the union had so desperately sought. Copies of Woodrow Wilson's statement went out to each Colorado local along with the International Executive Board's wan words of comfort.

We deem it the part of wisdom . . . to terminate the strike . . .
All lovers of liberty and believers in fair play between man and
man must admire the heroic struggle of the Colorado miners
against the great wealth and influence of Rockefeller and his
associates. We believe that our people have not died in vain . . .
We recognize no surrender . . .

On December 7, 1914, the Colorado delegates voted unanimously
to obey their leaders and end the strike. It officially ended three
days later, and in Frank Hayes's words, "thus passed into history
one of the greatest conflicts ever waged by any body of workers on
this continent."

*

Hundreds of out-of-work miners were suddenly bereft of strike
benefits. Many had no place to go. Some clung to their tents for a
time with their families. Others drifted out of the state. Those
who had long endured hardship faced an even bleaker winter of
uncertainty and privation. In the shadow of the fabled hills, tents
came down, were folded, and then were gone.

Gone, too, after another month, were the federal soldiers, after
closing out the most successful police action by federal troops in
American labor history. Lindley Garrison issued a well-deserved
tribute: "Injected in the midst of an inflamed populace, lately in
open conflict, they restored and maintained order. Their poise,
justness, absolute impartiality and effectiveness . . . commended
them to all." Garrison himself merited compliments for insisting
on a fair course. According to a student of Presidential intervention in civil strife, "the federal government had never before exercised such extensive powers over an area as it did in southern
Colorado. The power of the United States Army and federal government was projected into the vacuum left by the virtual collapse
of a discredited local government."

The chief function of the three-man commission selected by the
President had been to provide a loophole for the UMW. Its subsequent and generally superficial report noted that the "one dis-

turbing element in the industrial situation" after the strike was the indictment of hundreds of miners. Frank Hayes recalled that "it seemed to be the purpose of the operators, when the strike was concluded, to railroad as many of our men into the penitentiary as possible." Not only had the union been confounded and beaten in Colorado, with the freshly triumphant Fred Farrar determined to secure convictions it had now to be degraded. Once more the mineowners appeared to be undisputed masters of the situation, indeed of the state. There was considerable relief in 26 Broadway, too, tempered by caution against rocking the boat.

"Our feeling here," Rockefeller wrote Welborn, "is that, the strike being over, it will be to the wishes of all connected with the fuel company to introduce as rapidly as expedient the various progressive steps in such a plan as your further thought will suggest, looking to the prevention of possible recurrence at any time of the disorder and loss resulting from the recent strike." But before action on such good intentions or even the semblance of a victory celebration at the Denver Club could seriously begin, the outgoing Elias Ammons was joining governor-elect Carlson in a frantic appeal to President Wilson, for the sake of the state and newborn labor peace, to keep the Industrial Relations Commission out of Colorado. If John D. Rockefeller, Jr., in New York believed that with the abject defeat of the UMW, followed by a conciliatory attitude on the company's part toward innovation in labor practices, nothing substantial stood in the way of early restoration of his peace of mind, he was never more sadly mistaken.

THE COMMISSION

THE UNITED STATES COMMISSION ON INDUSTRIAL RELATIONS owed its existence to the tempest of hate and intolerable frustrations that during the first decade of the century shook or imperiled every industrialized state in the union. The killing of Idaho's former governor by a homemade bomb, the dynamiting of the Los Angeles Times Building, the furtively planted explosives and combustibles that derailed trains, burned property, destroyed innocent lives — these were the symptoms of labor revolt and industrial disorder that had inspired a concerned group of thinkers and social reformers to interrupt President William H. Taft's celebration of Christmas week, 1911, and urge the formation of a federal commission to explore origins and prescribe remedies. After due debate Congress gave the necessary authorization on August 23, 1912, and one of the first matters to engage Woodrow Wilson on entering the White House the following year had been the selection of nine members "who have before them," wrote Walter Lippmann, "the task of explaining why America, supposed to have become the land of promise, has become the land of disappointment and deep-seated discontent."

The President based his choices mostly on the recommendations of the Secretary of Labor, but it was a note from his Secretary of the Treasury, William G. McAdoo, extolling the candidate's vigor, capacity, and acceptability to labor, that decided him to place at the helm of the new commission Francis Patrick Walsh of Missouri.

The son of a laboring family no stranger to poverty, Walsh studied law between long hours as a railroad water boy, was admitted to the bar at the age of twenty-five, and thereafter specialized in legal defense of underdogs. After successfully defending Jesse James, Jr., against charges of train robbery, based less on firm evidence that kinship with the slain outlaw, Walsh quickly acquired fame. Sports-loving, with a boxer's build, Frank Walsh, the Missouri Progressive, received the stamp of confirmation from the conservative President Taft as red, white, and blue all-American, but his foes, numbered usually in capitalist circles, called him a faker, a demagogue, and an "expert in mare's nests." Walsh was a cynical realist with compassion to spare only for the oppressed, a lawyer without brief for judicial poise, for whom the discomfiture of witnesses he disliked took precedence over the elicitation of facts.

The other eight members of Walsh's panel included the first woman to serve on a federal commission. She was Mrs. J. Borden Harriman, Daisy to associates, a wealthy Wilsonian Democrat genuinely anxious to do more about labor problems and social ills than repeat the year-round futility of pondering them from the remoteness of winters spent in fashionable Fifth Avenue town houses and summers on the Hudson.

The Industrial Relations Commission had given Colorado its unheralded attention throughout most of 1914. George Creel was in close gear with the Commission, doing occasional publicity work and supplying members with notes on what he had witnessed or imagined. Walsh had five more or less skilled investigators in the field after Ludlow, including George P. West, who was to write the Commission's final sensational report. Creel seems not to have been hired on a permanent basis, his credentials perhaps diminished by prejudices too blatant. "The High Cost of Hate," an article he wrote for *Everybody's,* was savage enough to fan some hate itself, besides broadly implying that the author had been a denizen of the tent colonies, a warrior of the arroyos.

In October 1914, when it became known that the Rockefeller

Foundation planned to invest vast sums in the study of industrial relations, Walsh reacted at once to the threat of competition. The sweeping investigation supposed to be directed by Mackenzie King had ostensibly the same goals as the federal group's program. Walsh's opinion of the moneyed classes based on lively experience identified the real purpose behind the Rockefeller Foundation's sudden interest in industrial ills: to drown out the Commission's work and "subvert the truth about labor." Frank Walsh already had his sights set on the Rockefellers. He had ordered a full-scale investigation of their philanthropic activities and eagerly anticipated a face-to-face encounter with the younger John D. To head off the Foundation's study, the Commission's research director, Charles McCarthy, got in touch with Rockefeller and indulged in the liberties of candor granted old college chums — McCarthy had attended Brown University with the multimillionaire and played halfback on the football team he had managed. Among other things, Rockefeller was admonished to shrug off the influence of the "men who are simply wooden" surrounding him. McCarthy did not immediately inform Frank Walsh of his private communication with the enemy's camp, an omission destined to have upsetting consequences for him. In any case, his letter failed to alter minds at 26 Broadway, and now Walsh had ordered full speed ahead to probe Rockefeller's responsibilities in connection with the tragedy of the Colorado coalfields.

During its first year in business the Commission had created no big splash, but "if we have a good hearing [in Denver]," Walsh wrote to a colleague on November 16, "it will stamp our Commission with success." Two weeks later President Wilson received the Ammons-Carlson wire pleading with him to block Walsh's visit. The President was just as anxious that nothing be allowed to disturb the fragile labor peace. Characteristically avoiding overt interference, he scribbled a memo directing his private secretary to see if Daisy Harriman could be persuaded to get the Denver hearings called off. Just then, however, Mrs. Harriman's husband died.

When she could properly attend to her affairs again it was too late. The Commission had gone to Denver without her and convened on December 2.

In fairly rapid succession Walsh took public testimony from Colorado's two governors, lame duck and elect, as well as state mining officials and coal company executives. J. F. Welborn was kept in the witness chair nearly three days while Walsh drew his admission of the purchase of guns and disclosures pertaining to compensation settlements the CFI had paid out that year. The Denver hearings were "corking fine," Walsh reported to an aide. Yet more thrilling sessions were in store for him. John Lawson and Ed Doyle brought to his hotel room a copy of the telegram Rockefeller had sent Welborn on April 30 recommending a way to confute the strikers. A telegrapher whose "heart beat for Ludlow" had taken the message off the wire in Ohio or Indiana and slipped it to the UMW officials. Welborn, confronted by a triumphant Walsh brandishing the copy, admitted its authenticity. He was immediately served notice to produce all the correspondence that had passed between the Boston Building in Denver and 26 Broadway, New York, during the strike. The Commission left Denver with heads beginning to shake over the tactics and manner of its chairman, whose glee at the prospect of sifting those letters and telegrams and of grilling John D. Rockefeller, Jr., struck at least the conservative commissioners as bordering on the fanatic.

On the other side, the "railroading" rushed ahead. Following the indictments engineered by Attorney General Fred Farrar in the coal counties, scores of officials had been arrested, minor figures with the prominent exception of John Lawson, backbone of Colorado unionism in the view of many coal operators and therefore the prize catch. He stood charged with the killing of John Nimmo, mine guard, near Ludlow on October 25, 1913.

The intensive preparations to win a conviction included an unedifying struggle to influence two potential prosecution witnesses, James Fyler's widow and son, an anguished and disillusioned pair following the death of the paymaster at Ludlow. A report spread that promise of financial aid from Lawson had induced them not to talk. The combined forces of Farrar's office, company attorneys, and Baldwin-Felts detectives swung promptly into action. The widow was pestered with offers of a lifetime job running the boardinghouse at Berwind. Her son, one of the accused in the county jail, signed the required statement after a lengthy visit to his cell by the Baldwin-Felts agent Walter Belk. At the same time, Albert Felts notified the assistant attorney general that Jess McGuire, the Aguilar strike leader who had led the attack on the Empire mine, was among the embittered recently cut off the union payroll and he, too, was ready to talk. By the end of January 1915, William T. Hickey and Eli Gross, the Denver unionists, were added to the list of indicted and the total of warrants issued for strikers charged with murder and arson exceeded 150.

The mass arrests and inevitable consequences of renewed bitterness in the coalfield had yet to make any impact at 26 Broadway, where, under Mackenzie King's guidance, discussions were proceeding on how discreetly but effectively to reduce the inflexibility in distant Denver. As the new year began, the Canadian had to confess that the company officers were still "sensitive" to his reform suggestions. Only J. F. Welborn showed recognizable signs of softening. Fortunately for their stupendous success in business, the Rockefellers had never shrunk from demanding sacrifices. The way Rockefeller later explained it, Lamont Montgomery Bowers was "not ready to go forward into the new day." So the multimillionaire summoned him to New York and spent an unforgettable four hours trying to secure his amicable retirement from the Colorado Fuel and Iron Company.

When Mackenzie King received an account of the interview he marveled at Rockefeller's courage and tact. Bowers boiled with rage, knowing it would be the talk of Denver that he had been put "in cold storage" because he obstructed the appeasement policies of the Rockefellers' new advisers, but he was given no choice. With less than a week to Rockefeller's scheduled appearance before the Walsh Commission, Bowers resigned from his company posts and his seat on the board of directors was filled by Ivy Lee.

At 10 A.M. on January 25, the Industrial Relations Commission began public hearings in the New York City Hall under the crystal chandeliers of the former Board of Estimate room. At least half the onlookers in the pewlike seats were ideologically or professionally hostile to corporate business personalities, but curiosity as much as anything accounted for the presence of so many wobblies, socialists, radicals, and reformers. Seldom did they get the chance to see on public display the powerfully rich targets of their daily objurgations. John D. Rockefeller, Jr., took his seat with the same self-composure as when he had appeared before the Senate committee, but in other respects things promised to be different. Where Martin Foster, who had a medical practice in Olney, Illinois, would aim steadily for the truth like a doctor with an unerring probe, Frank Walsh on occasion became an inquisitor, going after it with a blowtorch.

Also, Rockefeller was better prepared this time, having had Mackenzie King coach him for the witness chair and school him in the elementals of putting himself across as a well-meaning fellow. Rockefeller's opening statement, a King composition, reiterated the extent to which stockholders and directors of a corporation were responsible for labor and social conditions within its domain. The directors did not shape managerial policies. These were the province of the officers, whose efficiency was measurable by the harmony and good will they were able to maintain between the company and its employees. The charge that he dictated the policy of refusing to recognize the union was abhorrent. He believed in the right of labor to organize for the advancement of its legitimate interests just as capital combined for the same object. Questions of recognition or nonrecognition of the union were functions of the management, not the stockholders or directors. "The decision of the officers with respect to the recognition of the union was reached without any consultation or communication with me, and I had no knowledge of their decision until after the strike had been declared."

It was now, during the questioning led by Frank Walsh, that Rockefeller repeatedly dodged efforts to pin him to specifics by pleading limited experience, insufficient study, or total ignorance. On the subjects of work hours, house rents, the scrip system, company stores, political corruption, and the employment of private detectives, he registered angelic innocence. Only when the topic of his company's resort to a publicity campaign came up did he expound freely. Large corporations had traditionally maintained silence, a policy grown unwise since the public was entitled to know about big concerns. Hence the hiring of Ivy Lee. Then the questions resumed, but no matter how impatiently or from what angle they were hurled, the mutimillionaire without a trace of guile always had his guard up.

It was a new image, altogether disarming and probably more successful than King had dared hope. Rockefeller evinced relish in it. When he strode into City Hall the next morning he reportedly objected to the police barrier separating him from well-wishers, then sought out Mother Jones with a handshake and an invitation to visit his office. She accepted, disclosing that she had never believed he knew what "those hirelings out there were doing. I can see how easy it is to misguide you." Rockefeller smilingly reproved her for throwing compliments and she responded with "I am more inclined to throw bricks." The bantering exchange, in full view of the press and Mother Jones's admirers, was guaranteed to excite King as an unexpected and magnificent stroke.

The second day's hearing began and again Walsh failed to score. Speaking in courteous, inoffensive tones, Rockefeller shrugged off question after question with a disclaimer of knowledge, a plea of inadequate background, a regretful admission of no formed opinion. It almost always worked. Rockefeller faltered just once, when Walsh led him into criticism of the checkoff system by which union dues and fines were deducted before the worker received his pay.

"I should think," said Rockefeller, "that any company would

somewhat hesitate to deduct from the wages of its men in the interest of some other institution. Just a passing thought."

Walsh refused to let it pass. "Why? Why would they hesitate if a man agreed that it should be deducted from his wages?"

"Well, I do not know why they should take it upon themselves to make payments on his behalf, but then it is a matter on which I ought not perhaps to have introduced myself . . ."

Walsh would not drop it. "Are you aware . . . that the Colorado Supply Company has such deductions made from the wages of the men covering bills at their store?"

"I am not familiar with the details of the management."

"Were you familiar with the fact that by that system . . . money to pay for the conduct of the hospitals for your company is raised? . . . that in some properties the camp's water is sold to the inhabitants, the cost collected by a checkoff system?"

Rockefeller was not familiar. He had no knowledge.

But whatever losses in new-found esteem this stumble may have produced, they were recouped by a convincing display of repentance as Rockefeller revealed that his views on a director's moral responsibilities had undergone substantial change. Something was fundamentally wrong in the Colorado coal properties. Events there had aroused his conscience. He sought no defense of the indefensible and asked only fairness. No one was perfect. "I should hope," he replied to a final question from Commissioner Austin B. Garretson, "that I could never reach the point where I would not be constantly progressing to something higher, better — both with reference to my own acts and . . . to the general situation in the company. My hope is that I am progressing. It is my desire to."

Commissioner Garretson: "You are, like the church says, 'growing in grace'?"

"I hope so. I hope the growth is in that direction."

Rockefeller's concluding remarks brought forth a round of sympathetic applause.

The next day Mother Jones spent ninety minutes with Rockefeller at 26 Broadway amply registering remorse for the malignity she had heretofore expressed for him. Now that she saw the kind of man he really was she no longer held him responsible for the evils in the Trinidad coalfield, and she began to lay plans for his complete conversion through the means of motherly talks. At Mackenzie King's prompting Rockefeller also invited union officials, including Doyle, Lawson, and Hayes, to his office — "clean-cut fellows" he called them — and Hayes responded by confessing that he had misjudged the multimillionaire, who ought now to be properly restored in public opinion. Some of the commissioners added their voices to the chorus of vindication. Garretson, a Railroad Brotherhood chief, said that laboring men had been misled into condemning Rockefeller, and Daisy Harriman, revising her view of him as a "psalm-singing, cold-blooded capitalist," now declared him "intensely human." Altogether it was a successful pioneer essay in public relations and image-making, much of the credit owing to Rockefeller himself, whose sons were to admit that at propitious moments he could indeed charm the birds from the trees.

Not everybody was taken in. Frank Walsh's determination to publicly pillory the multimillionaire waxed fiercer than ever, and he was already casting about for fresh opportunities. Upton Sinclair, alarmed by the wave of defections, wired Mother Jones to resist Rockefeller's witchery. "We are sure you will not let yourself be overcome by the odor of the American Beauty Rose." She shook off enough of the spell to warn Rockefeller that he had better not "fool my boys." And foremost among the unbeguiled was John Lawson, endangering the outcome of his forthcoming trial, not to mention his fragile standing with the union, by continuing to declaim against the mineowners.

"Out of [Rockefeller's] mouth," Lawson told the Industrial Relations Commission, "came a reason for every discontent that agitates the laboring classes in the United States today . . ." Philanthropies? "It is not their money that these lords of commercialized virtue are spending, but the withheld wages of the American working class . . . Health for China, a refuge for birds, food for the Belgians, pensions for New York widows, university training for the elite, and never a thought of a dollar for the thousands . . . who starved in Colorado."

Developing a special dislike for the union leader, Mackenzie King confided to his diary that if there ever was ground for refusing recognition to an organization, Lawson's testimony on the witness stand before the Industrial Relations Commission would have afforded it.

*

Once, before the Senate committee investigating the strike, John D. Rockefeller, Jr., had prided himself on being "too sensible" to seek the facts of a dispute on the spot. Now inspired by King's unbounded faith in "the personal relation in industry" he proposed visiting Colorado for the first time since 1903. Welborn made known his reluctance to take responsibility for the financier's life in the former strike zone and King went out in advance. The Canadian spent a good deal of time on Welborn's farm as well as in the Boston Building, and the company president, agreeing that the old policy of controlling legislatures was wrong, determined now to sever the company's liaisons with politics. Welborn also acknowledged that too little attention had been paid to workers' welfare. This too he promised to remedy. Meanwhile, personal abuse having given way to plaudits, and with his company both solvent and in a mood for self-improvement, Rockefeller showed signs of slipping back out of public gaze again. King reacted to the symptoms of relapse with a letter on February 9 from Denver. "You will have to lead, have to be the example whether you will or no . . . Circumstances for which you are not responsible have identified part of your future, part of your life, with Colorado . . . You can withdraw from that field altogether, or you can make it an object lesson to the world, but you cannot maintain an attitude of neutrality . . ."

While in Colorado, the Canadian was in a position to learn in detail of the CFI's original impetus behind the drive to jail Lawson and other unionists. One cannot be sure that he did, but evidence of continuing company manipulation or involvement in the legal activity was pronounced. Already the seven strikers brought to trial for the ambush murders at La Veta had been acquitted, largely because the attorneys for the defense never allowed the jury to forget that CFI lawyers were assisting the prosecution. In John Lawson's case an initial victory was scored when a Denver judge under no coal operator's thumb ruled favorably on the petition Horace Hawkins and Edward Costigan had filed for dismissal of the Farrar indictments on grounds that the grand jury had been hand-picked. The attorney general avoided having to answer this charge by withdrawing all the indictments. But the jubilation of the union lawyers was short-lived. Resorting to the permissable substitute for grand jury indictment, Farrar went back into Trinidad District Court on February 15 and filed a "direct information" charging Lawson and ten others with Nimmo's murder.

The signs of conspiracy accumulated. The "information" bore the signature of the deputy sheriff whose party had shot up the Forbes tent colony as a preliminary to the debut of the Death Special. New in office, Governor George Carlson appointed Granby Hillyer of Lamar as judge for the Third Judicial District, which embraced Las Animas County. Hillyer, a notoriously prejudiced attorney for coal companies, was also a law partner of the assistant attorney general, Frank West, who had ridden up and down the coalfield in the Death Special scaring Greek miners into betraying one another. And West was selected by Fred Farrar to direct the prosecution in Lawson's trial.

The first strike case to go before Judge Hillyer was Louis Zancanelli's trial for the murder of the Baldwin-Felts detective George Belcher. It ended with a hung jury on March 26 and a new hearing started five days later, Zancanelli's chances reduced to vanishing point now by the presence of Jesse Northcutt, still at the beck and call of the CFI, Victor-American, and Rocky Moun-

tain Fuel but designated in court as "special prosecutor" to assist
Frank West. Hillyer ordered jurors drawn from open venire instead of the jury box and the venire was provided by the company-
controlled Las Animas County sheriff. CFI mine guards served as
court bailiffs. The jurors took scant trouble to hide their prejudices and Judge Hillyer allowed one of them to remain despite
affidavits from the union lawyers showing him to have wagered on
the outcome of the first trial — "there would be a hung jury or a
hung dago." The jury deliberated, if the word can be seriously
applied in this case, twenty-four hours before returning the expected verdict of guilty. Zancanelli was sentenced to life imprisonment at hard labor.

By contrast, the four strikers charged with the death of Major
Lester during the fighting at Walsenburg were acquitted, their
trial having been moved on the petition of the defendants from
Huerfano County to Castle Rock, where agriculture not coal was
king and the jury of four stockmen and eight farmers reached its
verdict on the first ballot. However, when Horace Hawkins
sought a change of venire on behalf of John Lawson, Bob Uhlich,
and the others — a total of 162 men had been named in forty-two
informations — Judge Hillyer denied the petition.

One week before the trial's scheduled opening, Judge Northcutt
sent a representative to the rooming house in Denver where Mary
Thomas now lived with Mack Powell's widow. After taking the
women to a motion-picture show, the judge's agent offered them
$1500 if they would testify against John Lawson. They sent him
packing. Similar errands for the prosecution forces were more
successful. By April 21 when Lawson's trial began in the Las
Animas County courthouse the hostile witnesses ready to testify
included union turncoats and some of the strike war's bitter bereaved, in addition to undercover men of the Baldwin-Felts
Agency.

Mackenzie King developed the notion that the course of the Industrial Relations Commission as directed by Frank Walsh became, in willful disregard of how the other commissioners felt,

intimately connected with the trial of John Lawson. Walsh hoped
to influence affairs in Colorado by reopening the battle with Rockefeller, trapping him into admitting that he favored Lawson's conviction or, should he indicate otherwise, mocking sentiments of
sympathy as hypocritical. King also harbored an alternative belief that Walsh needed to persuade the public, as he had failed to
do in January, that the conduct of the Rockefeller interests in Colorado from the start fully justified the extreme countermeasures
charged against Lawson and his friends.

Certainly the desire to cast Rockefeller in a bad light and Lawson thereby in a better one motivated Walsh to a great extent that
spring, but King could not know how irresistibly Walsh was also
compelled by a mischievous instinct for manufacturing sensation
and maddening critics. After some of the eastern newspapers had
deplored his methods at the January hearings he wrote to a friend,
"I am glad you understand how thoroughly I enjoyed my New
York 'panning.' In fact, I am busy at the present moment devising
ways other than the old-fashioned standard one for 'making the
wildcat wild.'" Walsh was then in the process of single-handedly
crushing a revolt within the Commission. Daisy Harriman and
other worried members were still deploring their headstrong
chairman in murmurs behind his back, but his research chief,
Charles McCarthy, foreseeing a publicity carnival ahead under
Walsh's present policies, had come out openly for a drastic shift in
budgeting priorities and advocated maximum research and an end
to public hearings. At once Walsh alluded to the letter McCarthy
had written to Rockefeller before the Denver hearings. He accused him of attempted double-dealing, then ordered him to give
the research staff two weeks' notice and quit. McCarthy headed
back to his native Wisconsin "so sick with pain that I did not notice I had been fired."

Basil M. Manly, the Commission's new research director,
shared Walsh's predilections for the scandalous and had no sooner
begun to sift and analyze the batches of subpoenaed CFI strike

correspondence when his attention was seized by letters of "tremendous significance." Walsh agreed with him when he saw the material and like Manly was of the immediate opinion that Rockefeller must be given an opportunity to explain publicly. As Manly wrote to the chairman, "I am not sure that the papers are not tired of Bowers, King and Lee, but Rockefeller is, of course, always front page news."

Neither Manly nor Walsh was disposed to keep the letters confidential until Rockefeller could be summoned to discuss them. Manly was all for the chairman making their contents public in a speech he planned to deliver in Cincinnati. The impact would be greater, Manly thought, than if released at a press conference. But Frank Walsh, assuredly mindful of Lawson's trial, which had begun in Colorado the day Manly had mailed off his exciting news, decided on instant action through the Kansas City *Star* — "it has an immense circulation." On April 23 Walsh called the reporters into his Kansas City office and announced that for all Rockefeller's pious talk of keeping hands off the strike, he had been in reality its chief strategian, had exercised personal influence even in the statehouse at Denver, and presumed to dictate letters over the governor's signature intended for the President of the United States. To prove his charges, Walsh quoted liberally and lingeringly from letters written by and to Rockefeller, Bowers, Welborn, and Ivy Lee.

Perhaps at no other time in his life was John D. Rockefeller, Jr., so stunned and aggrieved. The spring had got off to a bad start. Mackenzie King had prepared the groundwork in Colorado for an unprecedented good-will tour of the properties, set for March, but Rockefeller's mother had died and his departure was postponed. In April, doubts about the visit coinciding with the first anniversary of the Ludlow conflict were resolved and new train tickets bought for the middle of the mouth. But the trip was again called off when Rockefeller's father-in-law, Nelson Aldrich, was taken ill and died April 16. Now had occurred the "wholly indefensible" publication of his private correspondence, to be surely followed by a second and probably more grueling collision with Frank Walsh.

At John Lawson's trial, meanwhile, no attempt was made to show that he had actually fired the fatal shot. Instead the prosecution held him responsible by virtue of his leadership at Ludlow on the day of the shooting. Against this oblique thrust Horace Hawkins, a resourceful lawyer in the Darrow tradition of applied courtroom acumen and humanitarian appeal, could do little beyond whittling the credibility of Frank West's witnesses. In his final address to the jury Hawkins declared, "You could not hang a yellow dog, or a known sheep-killer, on the testimony of such men . . . Your children's children will tell with pride of your verdict in this epochal case, and they will frame you in their hearts as men who stood like a bulwark for American liberty." On May 3 when Lawson was found guilty Hawkins at once demanded thirty days in which to prepare a motion for a new trial.

Mackenzie King reacted to the news of Lawson's conviction with an unpleasant stiffness. Welborn had supplied details. "Apparently there were eleven [jurors] for hanging and one for life imprisonment," King wrote in his diary. "This verdict will be a surprise to everyone. At the same time, having seen conditions as we have, one cannot but feel that it will prove a wholesome thing for the community. It shows that at last lawlessness has to reckon on the possibility of condemnation in the courts . . ." He warned his multimillionaire employer to expect Walsh's questions to be aimed at convincing the public that the attitude of the Rockefeller interests justified a new trial for Lawson and the annulment of his conviction.

Certainly the union leader and Frank Walsh were in contact. The moment he heard of the verdict Walsh rushed off a letter asserting his confidence in Lawson's innocence. Lawson wrote back May 15, "It is not myself Rockefeller desires to crush, but the hopes and aspirations of every man and woman who toils in this great country." Four days later in an overheated hall of the

Shoreham Hotel, Washington, D.C., where the Industrial Relations Commission began its new round of hearings, John D. Rockefeller, Jr., sat waiting to testify, looking rather lonesome, one observer thought, and as if resigned to the fact that this time Frank Walsh was determined to force him through an unprecedented ordeal.

Rockefeller took the stand at 4 P.M. in a room packed to suffocation. He was on the defensive from the start, pointing out that the letters and telegrams between New York and Denver signified not absentee control of the strike situation but merely support for the company officers. Frank Walsh mocked or ignored his explanations and introduced the subject of Lawson's trial. One of the jurors who convicted the unionist had exclusive sales privileges in CFI camps. Grounds for a new trial, Walsh suggested, and demanded to know if the financier would intercede in Lawson's behalf. There was an unmistakable implication now of a proffered deal, Rockefeller's promise of aid for Lawson finding its reward in softer treatment in the witness chair before Frank Walsh. Rockefeller resisted it and the questions grew fiercer.

In reference to his enthusiasm for the Professor John J. Stevenson article extolling capitalism, excoriating labor, and insulting the poor, twice Rockefeller said the poor would never read it and he protested the unfairness of quoting from it out of context, only to flinch under Walsh's sharp retort that how he chose to conduct the questioning was none of Rockefeller's business nor anyone else's. Stevenson had said that labor-union principles were no better than those of Indian thugs. "Now," asked Walsh, "if the members of the labor unions were not thugs or murderers, and you knew it, and Ivy Lee sent that out, was it not a palpable suggestion to him to do something that would poison the wells of public information . . . ?"

"I resent the implication . . . I utterly repudiate the motive."

Some discerned a frightening quality now about Frank Walsh's preoccupation with Rockefeller. That evening, embarrassed Commission members met in executive session and issued a joint complaint against their chairman's blustering severity. They were wasting their efforts. Next morning Walsh announced defiantly that he would run the hearings his own way, at nobody's dictation. He grilled the multimillionaire all day, chagrin probably among his various motivations because furtherance of his tactics to impress Rockefeller into the cause of saving Lawson from jail or worse was now decisively shut off. Walsh had asked if the fact that deputized gunmen paid with Rockefeller money testified against Lawson was not enough to warrant the multimillionaire going to Colorado and interceding for a new trial. Rockefeller was ready, armed with a statement Mackenzie King had hurriedly written emphasizing the impropriety of expressing public opinion on criminal proceedings still before the courts. The Canadian had outwitted Walsh, who was not likely to forget it.

Now, however, he could take it out on Rockefeller. At times the pair seemed locked, even trapped, in an intensely personal duel. Once they engaged in a heated running debate which ended with mutual accusations of falsehood. For hours without interruption Walsh was the only interrogator. The other commissioners remained stonily silent. Daisy Harriman, according to the New York *Sun*, sat in her place "with flushed cheeks and compressed lips and fanned herself with a vigor not altogether due to the weather." George Creel described Rockefeller as a pitiable figure writhing and perspiring under the chairman's merciless barrage, and Creel's word on this occasion need not be doubted because the impression of Rockefeller as an ashen-faced victim of savage interrogation was recorded by more controlled pens. Newspapers were to attack the exhibition as "debasing the Commission's work," "irresponsible and preposterous badgering." Walsh himself wrote afterward, "I turned the young man inside out . . ."

At one stage in this process he referred to a postcard, just received from the parents of Frank Snyder, who was "shot through the head while caressing his little sister" at Ludlow. One side of the card was a shocking photograph of the dead boy. Walsh thrust it before Rockefeller's eyes with a single brutal question. "Do you care to look at it?"

"You have described it," Rockefeller replied quietly, "and I see what the picture is."

Cruel as Walsh seemed in his handling of Rockefeller, in retrospect it was almost as if the performance was a warming-up for his bout with Mackenzie King two days later. Repeatedly the Canadian was driven into the mortifying necessity of having to resolve contradictions or otherwise explain his own words. King was painfully conscious of his handicaps: As an alien he could not appear too hostile toward an institution of the country wherein he now earned a living, and he also had to be on guard against finding himself depicted as Rockefeller's lickspittle, "to be used later to my disadvantage in public life."

Walsh questioned him penetratingly about his plan for grievance boards in the mining industry, trying to trip him into confessing that the real purpose was to keep out the UMW. Never was King in greater peril of losing his reputation as a friend of organized labor. At least once he blurted out as much. While dodging Walsh's efforts to pin an antiunion badge on him, King also tried to retaliate in kind: Rockefeller was seeking to use his wealth for the improvement of mankind and "I humbly submit, Mr. Chairman, that no one who strives to destroy an effort of that kind, to frustrate it, is a true friend of labor."

Unimpressed, Walsh queried King about his Colorado visit. King refused to discuss it, until the suppositions that formed the burden of Walsh's persistant questions at this juncture led to a picture of King hobnobbing with the coal operators and avoiding a meeting with the miners. King declared angrily, "I do not intend to let the impression go abroad that I avoided seeing anyone, not for one minute. If the [union] president and secretary and treasurer . . . were interested in seeing me, they knew exactly where I was staying . . ."

All Colorado wanted now, King testified, was to let bygones be bygones. Walsh countered that what the people wanted were the facts, and this inspired the following exchange:

Mackenzie King: "Well, do you mean that everyone in the United States wants to know exactly?"

Walsh: "No, but they must know . . . so that these deplorable conditions will never occur again."

King: "The way to do it is to get hold of the forces controlling the situation . . ."

Walsh: "Is there any force in the American people — ?"

King: "We are playing in words."

Walsh: "No, I am not. Is there any force to control the Rockefeller interests in Colorado to do the right thing if they are not doing the right thing, except the ordinary people of America?"

King: "If you are speaking of the immediate force, and the immediate influence, I think that the conscience of Mr. John D. Rockefeller, Jr., is more powerful on that, and will effect social justice in Colorado quicker than any other single force . . ."

Walsh: "You think that the will and conscience of Mr. Rockefeller in bringing proper conditions . . . in Colorado is more powerful than the will and conscience . . . of the people of the United States?"

King: "No . . . I don't put it that way at all. You asked me what factors could do the most in Colorado."

Walsh: "Pardon me; I didn't ask you that. I asked you if it was not necessary for all the people . . . to get a knowledge of what was taking place . . ."

Nothing would avail, King replied, without the will and intention of the man with most influence and power there.

And that was Rockefeller, the chairman broke in at once. "If the heart and will of the whole country was at work bringing decent and just conditions in Colorado —"

King: "That is a different question."

Walsh: "Well, put it yourself . . . Put it any way you want."

King: "I assume the purpose of the Commission is to get the truth, not to distort or pervert evidence that is given?"

Walsh: "Will you please answer my question? There is nothing that you can say that is going to irritate me."

King: "We are talking today to the American people, and I don't intend to allow you to distort or pervert anything that I may say."

Walsh: "And I don't care how insulting your attitude may be toward me. I am going to pursue the same course that I did in my examination of your employer . . . I am going to insist on your answers. You have given your opinion of me here, but I have not given my opinion of you."

King: "I have no doubt you will do it."

Walsh: "Indeed I will. But I would like to have you answer my questions without any further comment, if you will, with regard to how I am doing my work or personal characteristics."

Except for certain testimony volunteered on labor conditions in Puerto Rico, the Industrial Relations Commission's public hearings closed with an appearance by LaMont Montgomery Bowers. Following so swiftly upon the tempestuous sessions with Rockefeller and Mackenzie King, the former CFI board chairman's performance, contrite and crest-fallen, ended the Commission's public life almost on a note of bathos.

Bowers looked strained and agitated. Perhaps Frank Walsh was himself exhausted by now, or content that the peak of publicity had been reached. He allowed Bowers to run on. The system in Colorado had been pernicious and damnable. The reason Bowers had supported prohibition in the state was to help stamp out saloons, sheriffs like like Jefferson Farr, and "political bossism." The strike? He had nothing to do with it, had shut it from his mind, so bad was his insomnia that "excitement of that kind" would have prostrated him. Ludlow? Bowers covered his eyes at the mention of it, then fluttered his hands helplessly. "It was a sickening, disgusting, disgraceful piece of work . . . I wish I could forget everything about it."

*

The remarkable fact about the Industrial Relations Commission is that its ideals conquered its weaknesses and brought forth public good. Congress had empowered it to "inquire into the general conditions of labor in the principal industries of the United States" and "to discover the underlying causes of dissatisfaction in the industrial situation." The achievement of the latter goal would have required a superhuman agency, but the Commission could not help pursuing the former even when uppermost motives were detectable as a thirst for publicity, the obligations of scheming, or just plain rancor. Frank Walsh even at his most spiteful acted out of sincere convictions that Rockefeller and his kind were the villains for whose greed or thoughtlessness the downtrodden paid in misery and life itself. Daisy Harriman, unashamed when friends chided her for having turned "radical," defended the Commission's role for having brought Rockefeller "close to the terrible drama for which, because he was Capital, he was in the last analysis responsible."

Mrs. Harriman was one of the three commissioners who objected to the tone of the final report, composed by George P. West, one of Basil Manly's investigators. The language she deemed to be incendiary and revolutionary, likely to exacerbate passions and defeat the Commission's hopes for improving relations between capital and labor. She was forgetting that its primary function had been the gathering and evaluation of facts. It was impossible to deny that the voluminous wealth of data brought to light by the Industrial Relations Commission, added to the findings of the Congressional committee and innumerable lesser boards of inquiry, along with the regular announcements of engineered indictments and indiscriminate jailings, constituted indeed what the West Report described as the "infamous record in Colorado of American institutions perverted and debauched by selfish private interests . . . anarchism stripped of every pretense of even the chimerical idealism that fires the unbalanced mind of the bomb thrower . . . anarchism for profits and revenge."

◆◆◆ 20 ◆◆◆

THE BLOODSTAINED LESSON

THE SMALL MOTORCADE on the main highway north of Trinidad turned west along the wagon road to Ludlow and paused briefly near the Colorado and Southern Railroad crossing. A CFI official in the first car with John D. Rockefeller, Jr., and Mackenzie King pointed out the site where the tent colony had stood, now a forlorn expanse in the pale morning sunshine. A black cross fashioned out of two railroad ties marked the location of the pit in which the thirteen had died.

The automobiles wheeled left, continued on past the railroad station and Water Tank Hill to enter the canyon, halting at the Berwind coal town. Rockefeller lunched on beefsteak, beans, and mashed potatoes with Berwind and Tabasco miners in the boardinghouse. Afterward miners' children sang and the multimillionaire, addressing them, spoke fondly of his own five sons and a girl. Then he walked around the camp, inspected the half-finished clubhouse, the new cottages going up to replace old redwood frame houses, visited the school, the company store, and the homes of about thirty miners. No trace of shyness or awkwardness marred his itinerary and everyone who met or respectfully approached him was the immediate recipient of his smile or cordial remark. Later, in a private memorandum, Rockefeller recorded that the miners and their families looked happy and contented. He was especially pleased to see little gardens blooming, which showed "what could be done."

Thus, on September 20, 1915, began his tour of the Trinidad coalfield's eighteen CFI mine properties.

The next day at the Frederick mine west of Trinidad it was decided that he would enter the shaft and swing a pick. Weitzel bought him a two-dollar suit of overalls from the company store. Once at the coal face in the almost total blackness Rockefeller informed the startled diggers that he and they were partners. On his way out he embarrassed a mule driver with searching questions about the animal's raw and chafed hide. Next he was taken to the Segundo coke ovens and that night slept at Primero. Two days later at the Walsen property, an elderly miner who had been with the company twenty-two years came up to him and humbly inquired about the chances of a pension when he retired. Rockefeller's jocular response was that they would probably both go on pension about the same time.

At Sopris, Rockefeller had ordered the construction of a bandstand, and he had done the same at Primero. Moving north to Cameron — "the most attractive camp . . . exquisite views . . . I have not seen a neater tipple" — he was conducted to the schoolroom, where entertainment was staged in his honor. For those who remained after the songs and recitations the four-piece band provided dance music. Mackenzie King suddenly selected a partner and joined the swirl of dancers for "The Hesitation Waltz," whereupon Rockefeller turned politely to his hostess, the mine superintendent's wife, and a murmur of excitement swept the schoolhouse as they also took the floor. Before the evening was done Rockefeller had danced with every miner's wife or sweetheart present, more than twenty women, and he ordered not only a bandstand for Cameron but a dance pavilion to go with it.

❋

Thereafter a lot would be heard from Rockefeller about clasped hands, common partnership, and the harmony of interests, as in speech and writing he strove to promote "the personal relation in industry." It was another extension of his deep-seated Christian principle, one for which he had by bold example set the theme in the Colorado coal region, and he was duly applauded in the *New York Times* as "a mighty good mixer." However, he had no more gone to Colorado exclusively for revealing himself to the miners than for polishing up on his waltz. Although Mackenzie King was to admit having "something to do with the dance at Colorado," that novel display was but part of a campaign to put across the Industrial Representation Plan, which King had gradually worked out in conjunction with company officials and directors, Rockefeller included. King himself now tended to stay clear of the limelight, and the plan soon acquired Rockefeller's name.

He outlined it in Pueblo on October 2, 1915, before CFI officials and workers' representatives. As finally adopted, it provided for the election of two men to represent the miners at each mine, or one for every 150, and they would meet annually with an equal number of company officials. The coal camps would be organized into five districts; district meetings would be scheduled every four months. Joint committees would discuss health, sanitation, mine safety, recreation, and education. Standardized provision was made for the election of check-weighmen. Periodic tours by a representative of the company president would insure the maintenance of harmony throughout the CFI's chain of properties.

The plan included clauses forbidding discriminatory practices against workers or job applicants who were past or present members of a union. For the settlement of grievances, avenues of appeal would be available all the way up to the company president and, if necessary, to the Industrial Commission of Colorado, an institution legislated into existence in the wake of the strike and modeled on one of Mackenzie King's ideas.

Polls were quickly taken. The executives in Denver voted unanimously for adoption of the plan. The miners' approval was signified by announced results of a secret ballot: 2404 out of 2846 votes had been cast in favor. For unspecified reasons, the votes of about 2000 miners were not canvassed.

In theory at least, the Rockefeller Plan was a major if not giant step forward and, as anticipated, it stole some of the UMW's thunder. Organized labor reacted to publicity given the experiment with jeers and skepticism, and it was variously decried as a pseudo-union, a company tool offering workers only the illusion of collective bargaining, a hypocritical pretense of granting what was in reality withheld. It was a device for restoring Rockefeller's reputation and it sapped the spirit of independent labor. It was paternalism's latest and most pernicious guise.

Paternalism was what Rockefeller in fact felt constrained to oppose publicly and privately. Confident of the success of his company plan, he no longer feared the blandishments of unionism among the miners and had declared the CFI an open camp, all but inviting union organizers to roam wherever they pleased. This had caused consternation in company headquarters and E. H. Weitzel sent a candid protest to New York. Did not Mr. Rockefeller realize that most of the miners were as children, easily duped and in need of constant protection? Strengthened by a timely word of advice from Mackenzie King not to waver, Rockefeller wrote back that Weitzel's attitude was paternalistic and "paternalism is antagonistic to democracy."

So was machine politics, a subject on which he made no recorded comment. Even as he and his entourage had journeyed from camp to camp fraternizing with labor, the machine through which his company had for so long maintained political dominion in the coal counties apparently claimed another victim. Since Jefferson Farr's latest victory at the polls, Robert Mitchell, Canadian-born editor of the Walsenburg *Independent*, had been quietly furnishing undercover federal investigators with evidence of corrupt election practices in Huerfano County. Reaching home one Sunday evening, Mitchell was shot to death in the act of opening his front door by someone waiting inside the house. Sheriff Farr, blaming burglars, put a bloodhound on the trail, which led a posse fruitlessly through miles of underground passages at the Walsen mine, which Rockefeller had visited the previous week.

Positive hopes for an improved way of life in the coal baronies had been raised as a result of the new enlightenment exemplified by the Rockefeller Plan. These were seriously jeopardized now only so long as John Lawson remained behind bars for a murder no one had said he actually committed. Granby Hillyer had denied Lawson a new trial even as the state Supreme Court considered a petition from Horace Hawkins to prevent the prejudiced judge from hearing any more strike cases. Judge Hillyer sentenced Lawson to life imprisonment and the strike leader shared a cell with Louis Zancanelli, their nightly prison guard the deputized detective Walter Belk, who was himself under indictment for the slaying of Gerald Lippiatt. Once more the protests echoed across the land, their common theme bracketing John D. Rockefeller, Jr., with John Lawson. If the strike chieftain was culpable in the death of a mine guard he had never set eyes on, did not Rockefeller, whose money had been used to employ murderous gunmen, bear similar responsibility for their victims at Ludlow and elsewhere?

Rockefeller may have suffered the disquieting sense that such sentiments were not all that far removed from logic and fair play, and now J. F. Welborn was believed to favor a new trial or amnesty for Lawson. On October 4, Rockefeller visited Governor Carlson at the statehouse in Denver. Speculation flew at once that all 400 strike cases including Lawson's were about to be dropped, but Rockefeller had no more than hinted such an appeal during the interview with Carlson, confining himself to expressions of personal hope for harmony on Colorado's labor front. No matter what the muckrakers said, Rockefeller's wish was not infallibly command in the Denver statehouse. Were Ammons still governor, things might have been different, but Carlson, at least on this occasion, preferred to heed his legal counsel, Fred Farrar, and his military adviser, General Chase. Ignoring strong suggestions that the CFI would be happy to see the indictments set aside, the governor on October 7 announced his intention of letting the prosecutions take their course.

Two days later Lawson was free anyway on $35,000 bond put up by Thomas Patterson and a Denver merchant worried over possible effects of prolonged labor bitterness on the state's commercial future. Significantly, the UMW made no contribution to the bail amount. Its policy was to shoulder Lawson's defense expenses, but ways were already being explored to freeze him out of the union. To the various jealousies and antipathies held for John Lawson in the Merchants Bank Building in Indianapolis was added the fact that he had come to symbolize in sections of the national press persecuted unionism at bay before capitalist might. While footing his legal bills, the union made a transparent effort through its publications to diminish his stature from that of prominent protagonist to a mere incidental. Rockefeller's war was with the union, not any one member of it, and the union must be considered as on trial. Repeatedly the word went out to the rank and file: in all published accounts of the legal developments, for John Lawson read the UMW. And those who had never forgiven Lawson his old cronyism with Tom Lewis, the renegade former president, assured each other that as soon as the union had done its duty by John Lawson he would be ousted.

Other notables of the strike came in for union disfavor. Adolph Germer was forced to defend himself against a storm of innuendo that portrayed his conduct during the strike as craven or immoral. (Thereafter Germer was fiercely involved in the union's every major power struggle; he became a sidewalk casualty during one of the intramural battles of the 1930s.) The anarchist Bob Uhlich, unwelcome in the union after his acquittal for the murder of Mack Powell, vanished from the labor scene. Ed Doyle, of whose impetuosity and lively imagination the union hierarchy had long despaired, talked himself out of the UMW at the International Convention in January 1916. He charged the national officers with having betrayed Colorado's miners and traded off the strike for a Presidential commission, thus ridding themselves of a costly struggle while protecting their own lucrative positions. Some of Doyle's former comrades joined William Green and Frank Hayes in calling him an ungrateful liar and he was silenced on the convention hall floor by the pounding gavel and thunderous voice of the presiding officer, John L. Lewis.

Early that summer the first legal blow of measurable impact fell upon the operators' political control of their mineral-rich territories. The Colorado Supreme Court, after sifting evidence supplied by federal investigators, threw out the entire vote of the Huerfano County coal-camp precincts in the 1914 election, declaring Jefferson Farr's victory invalid and E. L. Neelly the rightful sheriff. Boss Farr marched out of Walsenburg Courthouse with a final show of defiant bombast befitting one who had reigned fifteen years. (He died suddenly four years later, his legacy to the county being oft-told legends and a postal hamlet bearing his name.) Frank Walsh, meanwhile, hurried off a letter to Rockefeller reporting Farr's downfall and demanding to know, since his company was implicated in the court's 10,000-word account of wholesale election fraud, what he intended to do about it. Rockefeller, on vacation, replied that he no less than Walsh was disgusted by the offenses described but felt sure that such conditions could not exist in camps where the Industrial Representation Plan was now in effect.

If the collapse of the Farr regime in southern Colorado failed to cast any disturbing echoes as distant as Seal Harbor, Maine, it affected the thinking in Denver, where businessmen profiting from the first real labor peace in twenty years now pressured Carlson's administration to stabilize it. With the approach of another election, the steady growth of labor's voting strength had not gone unappraised. Strategies in the statehouse had, perforce, to be adjusted. Carlson and Attorney General Farrar now decided that it was politically expedient to start quashing the indictments against the miners, and by late summer most of the court dockets in the state had been cleared of strike cases.

John Lawson's was not one of them. The shadow of lifelong imprisonment still hung over him, but he was busy these days fighting to maintain a position of influence in the UMW. At the end of the year devoted miners elected him president of District 15, while Ed Doyle was named to Lawson's old post on the International Board. The union heads in Indianapolis countered this development by suspending District 15's charter on grounds that the union branch was unable to support itself. The international officers seized control of its affairs, moved its headquarters to Pueblo, and Lawson and Doyle were left out of the picture.

In April 1917 a new state attorney general — Farrar and Carlson had been defeated at the polls — filed a brief confessing error in the case of John Lawson. The state Supreme Court, taking note of the extreme prejudicial circumstances surrounding the trial, unanimously reversed his conviction. The state high bench also freed Louis Zancanelli and no further steps were taken to try him. Altogether, 408 striking miners had been charged with felonies, principally murder. Most never got to court. There were four convictions, all overturned because of irregularities during trial. On the other side, except for the National Guard's court-martial, which defies serious consideration, no attempt was made to bring anyone to legal account for the tragedy at Ludlow. The only Baldwin-Felts detective to appear in court was charged with a prestrike crime. The trial was brief, and with Granby Hillyer on the bench and Jesse Northcutt defending, Walter Belk's acquittal was no more than a formality.

On April 20, 1917, crowds flocked to Ludlow. The UMW had bought forty acres of ground around the death pit and planned a fine monument. Speeches were made in assorted tongues. John Lawson dropped flowers into the hole and a band played "Nearer My God to Thee." Lawson, no longer of importance in the UMW, still carried his union card and had found work underground in a northern coal mine. At Ludlow that day thoughts were focused on the martyrs for unionism who had died in the tent colony. One week later the tears flowed for a heavier toll. An explosion 7000 feet inside the Hastings mine across the flats from Ludlow cremated and entombed 121 miners. This latest installment of the sum payable in the human scrip that coal unremittingly demands was itself soon eclipsed by the casualty figures from the holocaust in which America, with bands playing and flags flying, had just officially decided to plunge.

*

Colorado's agony in 1913–14 was no isolated phenomenon. In retrospect certain novel factors, including geographic isolation, frontier aspects, and the concentration of immigrant labor, give the episode a special flavor. Although unequaled in bitterness and strife, it was in essence a manifestation of the social instability and labor turmoil affecting all America. No major lasting reforms led directly from the conflict. When it ended, Frank Hayes called it an inspiration for the creation of a bigger, brighter labor movement. Others foresaw that by riveting national attention on the issues at stake in southern Colorado the strike would somehow contribute to the growth of political and economic democracy in America. The passage of time justified none of these prophecies decisively, and if Ludlow was a milestone in labor history the message engraved upon it is forever blurred by the bloodstains.

One can assert that what happened at Ludlow produced the Industrial Representation Plan. Bitterness in Colorado's coalfields diminished, but no permanent peace had been achieved. During the next seven years there were an equal number of strikes, four involving the CFI. Late in 1921 when the company wiped out previous wage increases and the miners struck, martial law again governed the Trinidad coalfield, and this time tent colonies were forbidden by order of Patrick Hamrock, former commanding officer of the militia at Ludlow and now the state's adjutant general. Six years later the IWW incited miners in the northern and southern fields to come out, and at the Rocky Mountain Fuel's Columbine mine near Lafayette state-police guns killed five picketing wobblies. The UMW, detesting the militant organization, played no part in this dispute, its goal now to gain recognition not by wanton threats and stoppages but persuasiveness and a conciliatory façade.

The union's patience was not to go unrewarded. The Rockefeller Plan served as a halfway house on the road to complete unionization. It brought the miners tangible gains in welfare, medical care, housing, recreation, and education, but these were blessings bestowed by the management, in the old paternalistic way. In no sense were the employees' representatives allowed powers of decision. What was often called The Colorado Plan, denoting systems of works councils and company unions, was tried out in its varied forms in other branches of industry during the 1920s, but in 1933 the plan was abandoned by the CFI after a majority of miners declared by ballot that they favored an independent union. That same year the company negotiated its first genuine collective-bargaining agreement with the UMW, and in 1935 the Wagner Act effectively outlawed the practice of company unions.

Before then the CFI had all but foundered. Railroaders were a vanishing breed; demand for the rails of whose superior quality Bowers had once boasted dwindled to zero. At the same time, the tapping of natural gas had cut into the firm's coal earnings. Moreover, business competition had acquired a significant new dimension. In 1928 Josephine Roche, an ardent crusader for social and industrial reform, had inherited the controlling stock in the Rocky Mountain Fuel Company, and she put her progressive beliefs into practice, signing a contract with the UMW and increasing the miners' salaries. Thus the company attracted the most skillful workers and its output rose. In 1931 worsening business forced further wage cuts and the precipitation of a price-cutting war on the CFI. The Rocky Mountain Fuel Company weathered it, but following a default in bond-interest payments, the CFI was placed in federal receivership.

The approach of war and national defense needs put the CFI back on its feet. Rockefeller interests still controlled it until the eve of Christmas 1944, when they sold out to a Wall Street syndicate led by the investor Charles Allen, Jr. The only coal mine at present operated in Colorado by what is now the CFI Steel Corporation is located west of Trinidad in the Purgatoire Valley. Giant concrete silos with rapid-loading facilities have replaced the old tipple structures, and forty-car unit trains haul the coal direct to the company's Pueblo steel plant at a rate of 4000 tons a day.

◆

No one can gauge what effect the coalfield struggle of 1913–14 had upon the lives and characters of those directly involved. Their destinies might have been the same if they had never heard of Ludlow. Frank Hayes, after all, drank heavily before ever coming to Colorado. The contempt with which former comrades regarded him for his role in the strike's ignominious conclusion possibly aggravated his addiction. The old socialist fire had drained from him, not involuntarily perhaps but of necessity if he wished to keep his job in a union electing to purge itself of Marxists and militants. At any rate, it was of no avail to Hayes. Lacking the taste or talent for managing a cumbersome, strife-torn union, in 1918 he was inadequate as its president even when sober. His vice president drew inspiration not from liquor but visions of power. John L. Lewis' partisans have themselves admitted that if he did not actually aid and abet Hayes's excessive drinking, he did little to discourage it. Lewis was in truth president of the UMW long before Hayes, desperately seeking a cure, quit office and active union work. Hayes remained likable, maintained his flair for simple poetry, even served a term as lieutenant governor of Colorado in 1937 with Elias Ammons' son Teller as governor. The union kept him on its payroll, but in 1948 when Hayes died, alone and a bachelor, President John L. Lewis and the other international officers were reportedly immersed in wage negotiations and unable to attend his funeral.

John Lawson's acceptance of a post as employment agent for the Victor-American Company in 1917 was generally acknowledged as his complete severance from the labor movement, but his most useful service was performed during the eleven years he worked with Josephine Roche as vice president of Rocky Mountain Fuel. In this capacity he wrote a union contract that re-flected the principle on which the company's new policy was based, one recognizing that "the men employed are as much an essential factor in the industry as the capital invested in it, and have independent rights in the determination of working and living conditions." But for all the concessions Lawson was now able to win for labor — more than he had ever managed to wrest as strike leader — miners could no longer accept him in unqualified brotherhood. He was also director in a coal companies' insurance firm, its attorney Frank West, the former assistant attorney general who had prosecuted Lawson for murder. Compounding the irony, West was succeeded in this post by Lawson's defense counselor, Horace Hawkins. A sequel perhaps more to be expected than those shifts in allegiance was the appointment of Fred Farrar, on leaving the state attorney general's office, to the post of chief counsel for the Colorado Fuel and Iron Company.

Not much has been written of the events culminating in the Ludlow "massacre" without emotion and distortion — the mine guards are all thugs, the militiamen trigger-happy rabble, the coal operators heartless profiteers. Yet the more one ponders, the harder it is to delineate heroes and villains. Ignorance and braggadocio affected the strikers to a reckless degree, and the motivations of their leaders were not unfailingly altruistic. So many of the influential characters on both sides were strait-jacketed by principles and prejudices whose worth could never have survived exposure to open debate and joint scrutiny. No impasse in labor history cried out more for the succor of free discourse and face-to-face communication.

There were enough extenuating circumstances to go around. One suspects that Governor Ammons' physical deficiencies had a damaging impact on unfolding events. And if L. M. Bowers, contrary to his testimony, did not suffer insomnia so badly that it kept him on the sidelines, certainly his perceptions were jaundiced by old-fashioned modes and theories. J. F. Welborn's sole fault may have been naive but stubborn fidelity to a business concern and the tenets on which he believed its success was based. In later years, when his wealth evaporated with the company's fortunes, he endured simultaneously financial loss, the death of his wife, his own collapsed health, and assorted domestic strains with unyielding fortitude. Even Karl Linderfelt and Patrick Hamrock were soldiers whose conduct at Ludlow ought not to be condemned without reference to the squalid campaigns in which each man had reached his military maturity.

"The Colorado strike was one of the most important things that ever happened to the Rockefeller family." John D. Rockefeller, Jr.'s words to Raymond Fosdick were taken to mean that no event had so opened his eyes to the sins of industry in that era. What we are asked to believe, and no positive reason speaks to the contrary, is that this labor tragedy is what it took to impress the richest young man in the world, a professed and tutorial Christian, with the reality of the Christian ethic of common brotherhood. In other words, Ludlow taught him more than he could ever have imparted to the pupils in his weekly Bible Class. Equally important to his moral and intellectual expansion was the fact that he had escaped the influence of old-fashioned capitalist-Christians like Frederick Gates and heeded the shrewder, more pragmatic counsel of associates like Raymond Fosdick, probably the first in Rockefeller's circle to recognize some truth in the charge leveled by organized labor that the Industrial Representation Plan was a form of counterfeit.

Rockefeller assigned his most generous credit to Mackenzie King: "No other man did so much for me. He had vast experience in industrial relations and I had none. I needed guidance. He had an intuitive sense of the right thing to do." When King retired from politics after his lengthy tenure as Canada's prime minister, Rockefeller presented him with a seventy-fourth birthday gift of $100,000 worth of shares, and the following year the Rockefeller Foundation issued a grant of $100,000 to assist him in the preparation of his memoirs.

The role of the state National Guard in the coalfield war

strengthens the temptation to seek modern parallels. If the over-reaction of the National Guard at Kent State, Ohio, did not invite comparison, the sense of history repeating itself is almost eerily stirred by the similarity between the circumstances of John D. Rockefeller, Jr., in self-seclusion at Pocantico Hills as the militia ravaged Ludlow, and — less than six decades later and closeted within the same family retreat — his son withholding personal intervention as the New York National Guard guns blazed at the Attica state prison. But caution must be exercised. Whatever the deficiencies of today's National Guard, no fair comparison can be made with the Colorado militia of 1914. With the establishment of the Army of the United States in 1920, the National Guard, along with the Regular Army, became a basic component of the federalized defense organization. The general revision of procedures included new recruiting methods. As General Chase had felt no compunction about revealing, recruitment under his administration took no account of pedigree, background, character, or even nationality. It was no harder for criminals to join the militia's ranks than the college boys who were part of Van Cise's Company K.

Colorado's state militia was thoroughly discredited before the end of 1915. The War Department in Washington had no use for it, particularly after Chase failed to explain satisfactorily the disappearance of $12,000 worth of federally loaned equipment. That same year a secret court of inquiry in Denver weighed charges of drunkenness, graft, and incompetence directed by Philip Van Cise against Chase and his satellites. The general resisted efforts to dislodge him until forced to resign in 1916. He died two years later of pneumonia.

Since the Bureau of Mines began compiling statistics in 1910 — the year of Starkville and Primero — 80,400 men have died in American coal mines. No one gathered statistics on the rate of disabling injuries until 1930; since then the figure has exceeded 1,500,000. Coal mining remains the most dangerous of all industrial occupations. The dust that baffled Bowers' "experts" with its terrifyingly explosive quality has yet to be safely controlled. There is a harrowing comparability between mine disasters of his day and those of our own. According to the Bureau of Mines' investigators, illegal blasting practices — the shot-firing of earlier coal-mining generations — and excessive concentration of dust caused an explosion in Kentucky at the close of 1970 that killed 38 miners.

The indifference displayed by some of today's mineowners is reminiscent of that charged against the operators of a less enlightened era. In 1970 a major West Virginia firm, anxious to resume operations after a disaster and discontinue investigation into its cause, offered widows $10,000 each if they would agree to the sealing up of their dead, that part of the mine to be monumented as "a kind of cemetery."

The insidious peril of pneumoconiosis — "black lung" — surely prevalent but unsuspected at the time of Ludlow, adds at least 1000 to the annual mine fatality count in Pennsylvania alone. The lethal properties of coal dust are greater than anything dreamed of by industrial researchers sixty years ago. Yet in measurable concern over pneumoconiosis the United States lags thirty years behind the British. Among American coal miners the mortality rate from diseases of the respiratory system is twice that in Great Britain. Only nine of our twenty-three coal-mining states specifically provide workmen's compensation for black-lung victims, although there are 125,000 of them, active and retired miners. Not until recently have federal standards been set for permissible dust levels in U.S. coal mines and adequate law enforcement is unlikely. The complaint of 1913's coal-mine inspectors that they lacked staff and facilities for regular and comprehensive mine inspection is echoed by today's federal mine-safety officials.

The U.S. Mine Safety Act was passed in 1969, the year Americans reached the moon. Nothing had been done on a national level to protect coal miners from roof falls, gas and dust explosions, fires, and crippling lung diseases since the day the Wright brothers arrived at Kitty Hawk. So much has remained unaltered.

Now, as then, the miners' union shakes under the pressures of internal discord, but now its scandals and intrigue are under scrutiny from without. It is still one of the most powerful trade unions in the nation, but the multiplying cracks in the monolith may prove irreparable. Coincidentally, the industry may face an unprecedented boom. Ecology and high costs have darkened the once bright future forecast for nuclear fuel. Oil and gas resources are shrinking. Foreign demands for U.S. coal have soared. New mines are being drilled deep into the punished earth or stripped from its surface. Old mines have been reopened. Men and machines brought out 600 million tons of coal from U.S. mines in 1971 and a figure of 700 million is predicted for 1975.

The great expansion of the coal industry will exact its toll in human life and misery. Sacrifices will result from the same kind of greed and moral insensibility that led to Ludlow. And if, in justice to the innocent dead, we are constrained to seek meaning in what befell there, perhaps it is timely to settle for "the kinship of humanity" that Rockefeller insisted the tragedy had taught him, the most familiar yet disregarded of all lessons, that whether we choose to be or not, each one of us is his brother's keeper.

SOURCES AND
ACKNOWLEDGMENTS
BIBLIOGRAPHY

SOURCES AND ACKNOWLEDGMENTS

THE TRAGEDY AT LUDLOW impressed the separate imaginations of the authors long before they met. In 1953 groundwork for the present book was firmly established when George S. McGovern submitted a dissertation on the strike to the graduate school of Northwestern University in partial fulfilment of the requirements for his Ph.D. His personal gratitude to his professors of American history at Northwestern goes without saying, and it is unnecessary to repeat in entirety the acknowledgments accompanying the dissertation. However, an expression of lasting appreciation is due Professor Arthur S. Link, who suggested the topic and who, by salting praise with vigorous criticism, inspired the student in the most effective possible way.

The preliminary research of any writer conscientiously presuming to re-create events of a not-too-distant past is bound to include personal interviews. In the present case, discharge of this routine obligation brought an unexpected and rather moving bonus. Beyond the customary goals of acquiring fresh insight or corroborative information, the writers on more than one occasion found their sense of involvement further kindled by the manifestations of feeling which their questions apparently evoked. The pride, for instance, of the eighty-six-year-old former union paymaster as he sang his interviewer a few lines of "Union Forever" in a second-floor room of the Columbian Hotel, which still stands in Trinidad. And in Denver one crisp spring afternoon, the labor organizer of sixty years ago who took a Winchester down off the wall to show his visitor handled it with a sudden ominous fervor, for all the world as if reminiscence had melted away his years and the weapon, plucked from retirement, must serve once more against Baldwin-Felts thugs who had returned to lurk outside in the quiet side street.

It is not possible to credit individually everybody who helped in the preparation of this book. Some of the names selected are of private persons, others represent organizations whose staffs combined courtesy with willing aid. Since all are equally deserving of the authors' thanks, the following list obeys no order of priority. Mrs. Adolph Germer, Rockford, Illinois; Mary (Thomas) O'Neal, Hollywood, California; Mary Petrucci, Joliet, Illinois; Joyce Covey, Denver, Colorado; Enid T. Thompson, Librarian, State Historical Society, Denver, Colorado; Alys Freeze, Head of Western History Department, Denver Public Library; Dolores C. Renze, State Archivist, Denver, Colorado; Mrs. Edward Keating, Washington, D.C.; John A. Brennan, Curator, University of Colorado Library, Boulder, Colorado; Larry Cantwell, Archivist, Denver *Post*, Denver, Colorado; Robert F. Welborn, Denver, Colorado; Clement G. Bowers, Maine, New York; Roy P. Basler, Manuscript Division, Library of Congress, Washington, D.C.; Professor Morris F. Taylor, Trinidad State Junior College, Trinidad, Colorado; J. William Hess, Curator, West Virginia University Library, Morgantown, West Virginia; Barron B. Beshoar, Denver, Colorado; Justin McCarthy and Rex Lauck, *United Mine Workers Journal*, Washington, D.C.; Charles S. Vigil, Denver, Colorado; Michael Livoda, Denver, Colorado; A. R. Mitchell, Curator, Old Baca House, Trinidad, Colorado; Dr. Joseph W. Ernst, Archivist, Rockefeller Family Office, Rockefeller Plaza, New York, New York; John Horsman, Starkville, Colorado; M. Chambers, Archivist, Catholic University, Washington, D.C.

*

The original material drawn upon consisted in part of official documents and private correspondence previously overlooked by scholars or not available for study. Printed sources included the bound volumes of the Industrial Relations Commission's hearings and those of the Congressional committee investigating the strike. These were employed so habitually throughout the work that a detailed chapter by chapter explanation of sources would weary the reader. The following remarks are proffered as general guidance.

Camp and Plant, indispensable study material for anybody seeking examples of industrial paternalism, served as partial basis for Chapter 1. The financial columns of New York and Denver newspapers were utilized, as were the private papers of John L. Jerome. The Iowa Crowd possibly deserve a book to themselves. For all his bluster, John L. Osgood was an enigmatic entrepreneur. One hopes that Professor Howard L. Scamehorn of the University of Colorado, presently completing a history of the Colorado Fuel and Iron Company, will have seen the founder's papers in company vaults and be able to shed more light on his character.

Testimony gathered by the federal and Congressional investigators proved a rich source for study of the life led by immigrant miners and their families in the company towns. Headway in following the stormy course of the United Mine Workers during the period 1903–1915 would have been impossible without frequent reference to the minutes of miners' conventions, back files of the *United Mine Workers Journal,* and union correspondence in the separate manuscript collections of John Mitchell and Adolph Germer. The metal workers' strike at Cripple Creek, signaling General Chase's debut in the labor wars, has been well chronicled. A valuable Chase scrapbook, donor unknown, is steadily moldering in the Department of Labor Library, Washington, D.C. Useful information was provided on the subject of Greek immigration to the American West by Helen Z. Papanikolas. Raymond Fosdick's biography of John D. Rockefeller, Jr., generally unimpaired by bias considering the author's long association with his subject, had obviously to be consulted for our survey of the multimillionaire's background and upbringing. So had Rockefeller's private correspondence. Material on the prevalence of detective agencies in United States labor affairs was found among the incomplete and scattered unbound records of the Industrial Relations Commission.

One of the by-products of today's feminist liberation movement appears to be an interest in the buried history of women as agents for social change. Mother Jones has become target for several research projects, the most active of them centered in West Virginia, where her legend flourishes most. Caution is necessary. Such oft-quoted assessments as Clarence Darrow's ". . . the most forceful and picturesque figure of the American Labor Movement" imply no guarantee of a corresponding strength of influence within that movement, and students should not be surprised to find that the irrepressible old lady could bore or irritate big labor as much as she enraged any capitalist. As for her early history, it remains as elusive as the niche she should occupy in that of organized labor. The new researchers have yet to verify even her age. Almost assuredly she died at least two years shy of the hundredth birthday that she and a nation of well-wishers, including John D. Rockefeller, Jr., had already celebrated. For our treatment of Mother Jones we examined impressions recorded privately by both her detractors and admirers, the few letters she left, her inadequate autobiography, and contemporary articles.

From Chapter 7 on, the quoted correspondence between Rockefeller's headquarters in New York and the CFI officers in Denver is taken from the volumes of the Industrial Relations Commission hearings. President Wilson's part in the strike is traceable in the Woodrow Wilson Papers in the Library of Congress. The solicitations from spies cited in Chapter 12 were found in a packet marked INTELLIGENCE among the papers of Ed Doyle.

Piecing together the events at Ludlow on the day of the principal tragedy necessitated the comparison of often conflicting accounts, but enough salient details corresponded to fashion an acceptably sturdy framework for the narrative. Letters, telegrams, affidavits, inquest reports, and the state militia's version made up the bulk of the source material. The surviving occupant of the death pit was persuaded to contribute some (she can never share all) of her inescapable memories. The trial by court-martial of the Colorado militia for murder, arson, and looting was covered spottily by the local press at the time. When, for the present work, appropriate steps were taken with a view to examining the official record, the Records Office of the Colorado Department of Military Affairs curiously denied that either Lieutenant Karl Linderfelt or Major Pat Hamrock was court-martialed. Fortunately, a copy of the voluminous proceedings complete with charges, specifications, testimony, and verdicts was found among the papers of Governor Ammons' attorney general, Fred Farrar, at the Denver Public Library. This latter collection also cast important light on the motives and practices involved in the grand jury investigation which resulted in the mass indictment of the strikers.

For the chapter dealing with Mackenzie King we consulted published biographies of the Canadian statesman and correspondence subpoenaed by the Industrial Relations Commission. The bound volumes of the Commission's hearings are substantially the basis for Chapter 19, with valuable augmentation furnished by items in the Frank Walsh Papers in the New York Public Library.

BIBLIOGRAPHY

MANUSCRIPTS AND ARCHIVAL SOURCES

Elias Ammons Papers, Division of State Archives, Denver, Colorado.

Ray Stannard Baker Collection, Library of Congress, Washington, D.C.

George A. Carlson Papers, Division of State Archives, Denver, Colorado.

Colorado National Guard, Record of the Court-Martial of Sergeant C. E. Taylor, Captain Edwin F. Carson, Lieutenant R. W. Benedict, et al., Military District of Colorado, May 11, 1914. Adjutant General's Office, National Guard Headquarters, Denver, Colorado. (Copy of the proceedings in the Frederick M. Farrar Papers.)

Colorado National Guard, Report: Cripple Creek Campaign, Adjutant General's Office, National Guard Headquarters, Denver, Colorado.

Edward P. Costigan Papers, Library of the University of Colorado, Boulder, Colorado.

Edward L. Doyle, Private Manuscript Collection, Western History Department, Public Library, Denver, Colorado.

Frederick M. Farrar Papers, Western History Department, Public Library, Denver, Colorado.

Adolph Germer Collection, State Historical Society, Madison, Wisconsin.

John L. Jerome Papers, State Historical Society, Denver, Colorado.

Mother Jones Correspondence, Catholic University, Washington, D.C.

Edward Keating Collection, Library of the University of Colorado, Boulder, Colorado.

John R. Lawson Collection, Western History Department, Public Library, Denver, Colorado.

Benjamin B. Lindsey Papers, Library of Congress, Washington, D.C.

John Mitchell Papers, Catholic University, Washington, D.C.

Thomas M. Patterson, The Strike in Colorado, ms in the Western History Department, Public Library, Denver, Colorado.

Rockefeller Family Archives, Rockefeller Center, New York, New York.

U.S., Justice Department Archives, Dispute Case File: Colorado Coal Strike, Washington, D.C.

U.S., Labor Department Archives: (1) Proceedings of Las Animas, Colorado, County Coroner's Inquests, April 1914, with affidavits; (2) Miscellaneous Correspondence of the U.S. Industrial Relations Commission; (3) Ethelbert Stewart Correspondence, Washington, D.C.

U.S., War Department Archives, Adjutant General's Office, File 2154620, Washington, D.C.

Colonel Edward Verdeckburg, Record Book, Division of State Archives, Denver, Colorado.

————, Report of Colonel Edward Verdeckburg to the Adjutant General, State of Colorado, May 9, 1914, ms in the Division of State Archives, Denver, Colorado.

Frank P. Walsh Papers, Manuscript Division, New York Public Library, New York, New York.

J. F. Welborn, Statement by Mr. Welborn Regarding the Coal Strike of 1913–1914, ms in the Western History Department, Public Library, Denver, Colorado.

U.S. GOVERNMENT DOCUMENTS

U.S., Bureau of Mines, Albert H. Fay, comp., "Coal Mine Fatalities in the United States, 1870–1914," *Bulletin* 115 (Washington, D.C., 1915).

U.S., Bureau of Mines, F. W. Horton, comp., "Coal Mine Accidents in the United States and Foreign Countries, *Bulletin* 69 (Washington, 1913).

U.S., Congress, *Congressional Record,* 63rd Cong., 2d sess., 1914, LI.

U.S., Congress, House, *Industrial Disputes in Colorado and Michigan, Hearings before the Committee on Rules,* 63rd Cong., 2d sess., 1913.

U.S., Congress, House, *Conditions in the Coal Mines of Colorado, Hearings before a Subcommittee of the Committee on Mines and Mining,* 63rd Cong., 2d sess., 1914, 2 vols., pursuant to H. Res. 387.

U.S., Congress, House, *Brief of the Coal Mining Operators: Conditions in the Coal Mines of Colorado, Hearings before a Subcommittee of the Committee on Mines and Mining,* 63rd Cong., 2d sess., 1914, pursuant to H. Res. 387.

U.S., Congress, House, *Brief for the Striking Miners: Conditions in the Coal Mines of Colorado, Hearings before a Subcommittee of the Committee on Mines and Mining,* 63rd Cong., 2d sess., 1914, pursuant to H. Res. 387.

U.S., Congress, House, *Reply Brief for the Striking Miners: Conditions in the Coal Mines of Colorado, Hearings before a Subcommittee of the Committee on Mines and Mining,* 63rd Cong., 2d sess., 1914, pursuant to H. Res. 387.

U.S., Congress, House, *Appendix to Reply Brief for the Striking Miners: Conditions in the Coal Mines of Colorado, Hearings before a Subcommittee of the Committee on Mines and Mining,* 63rd Cong., 2d sess., 1914, pursuant to H. Res. 387.

U.S., Congress, House, Committee on Mines and Mining, *Report on the Colorado Strike Investigation,* made under H. Res. 387, 63rd Cong., 3rd sess., 1915, Doc. 1630.

U.S., Congress, House, *Labor Difficulties in the Coal Fields of Colorado,* 64th Cong., 1st sess., 1916, Doc. 859.

U.S., Congress, Senate, Commissioner of Labor, Carroll D. Wright, comp., *A Report on Labor Disturbances in the State of Colorado, from 1880 to 1904,* 58th Cong., 3rd sess., 1905, Doc. 122.

U.S., Congress, Senate, *Industrial Relations: Final Report and Testimony Submitted to Congress by the Commission on Industrial Rela-*

tions, Created by the Act of August 23, 1912, 64th Cong., 1st sess., 1916, Doc. 415, VII–IX.

U.S., Congress, Senate, *Final Report of the Commission on Industrial Relations, Including the Report of Basil M. Manly and the Individual Reports and Statements of the Several Commissioners,* 64th Cong., 1st sess., 1916, reprinted from Doc. 415.

U.S., Congress, Senate, *Report of the U.S. Coal Commission,* 68th Cong., 2d sess., 1925, Doc. 195.

U.S., War Department, *Annual Reports, 1914–1915* (Washington, 1914, 1916).

West, George P., United States Commission on Industrial Relations, *Report on the Colorado Strike* (Washington, 1915).

COLORADO PUBLIC DOCUMENTS

Colorado Adjutant General, *Biennial Report,* 1912/1913–1914/1915 (Denver, 1913, 1915).

Colorado Adjutant General, *The Military Occupation of the Coal Strike Zone of Colorado by the Colorado National Guard, 1913–1914, Report of the Commanding General to the Governor for the Use of the Congressional Committee, Exhibiting an Account of the Military Occupation to the Time of the First Withdrawal of the Troops in April, 1914* (Denver, n.d.).

Colorado Attorney General, *Biennial Report, 1913–1914* (Denver, 1914).

Colorado Bureau of Labor Statistics, *Twelfth Biennial Report, 1909–1910, Thirteenth Biennial Report, 1911–1912,* and *Fourteenth Biennial Report, 1913–1914* (Denver).

Colorado Bureau of Mines, *Thirteenth Biennial Report* (Denver, 1914).

Colorado Special Board of Officers, *Ludlow: Being the Report of the Special Board of Officers Appointed by the Governor of Colorado to Investigate and Determine the Facts with Reference to the Armed Conflict between the Colorado National Guard and Certain Persons Engaged in the Coal-mining Strike at Ludlow, Colorado, April 20, 1914* (Denver, 1915).

Colorado State Board of Immigration, *Year Book of the State of Colorado, 1920* (Denver, n.d.).

Colorado State Geological Survey, *Bulletin* 6 (Denver, 1913).

Colorado State Inspector of Coal Mines, *Fourteenth Biennial Report, 1909–1910, Fifteenth Biennal Report, 1911–1912* (Denver, n.d.).

Colorado State Inspector of Coal Mines, *Annual Report,* First–Fourth, 1913–1916 (Denver, 1914–1916).

Colorado Supreme Court, *John R. Lawson, Plaintiff in Error vs. The People of the State of Colorado, Defendant in Error, Error to the District Court of Las Animas County in the Supreme Court of the State of Colorado, No. 8730.*

Las Animas County, *Coroner's Record and Accounts,* 1913–1914, Coroner's Office, Trinidad, Colorado.

PERIODICALS

(In addition to leading national and Colorado newspapers, the following periodicals and proceedings were consulted.)

Appeal to Reason, 1913–1916.

Churchman, 1913–1915.

Coal Age, 1913–1916.

Collier's Weekly, 1913–1915.

Congregationalist and Christian World, 1914–1915.

Everybody's Magazine, 1913–1916.

Harper's Weekly, 1913–1916.

Independent, 1913–1916.

Literary Digest, 1913–1916.

Masses, 1913–1916.

Metropolitan, 1913–1915.

Nation, 1913–1916.

New York Call, 1913–1915.

New York Christian Advocate, 1913–1916.

Outlook, 1913–1916.

Pearson's Magazine, 1914–1916.

Survey, 1910–1916.

United Mine Workers Journal, 1913–1916.

Proceedings of the . . . Annual Convention of the United Mine Workers of America, 1910–1912.

Proceedings of the . . . Annual Convention of the Colorado State Federation of Labor, 1913, 1915–1916.

Proceedings of the . . . Biennial Convention of the United Mine Workers of America, 1914, 1916.

ARTICLES

(in periodicals not previously listed)

Ammons, Elias M., "The Colorado Strike," *North American Review,* CC (July 1914).

Baker, Ray Stannard, "The Reign of Lawlessness: Anarchy and Despotism in Colorado," *McClures,* XXIII (May 1904).

Cannon, Harry, "Use of Federal Troops in Labor Disputes," *Monthly Labor Review,* LIII (September 1941).

Fuller, Leon W., "Colorado's Revolt Against Capitalism," *Mississippi Valley Historical Review,* XXI (December 1934).

Hubbard, Elbert, "The Colorado Situation," *The Fra,* XIII (August 1914).

Porter, Eugene, "The Colorado Coal Strike of 1913: An Interpretation," *The Historian,* XII (Autumn 1949).

Roche, Josephine, "Seeking a New Era in the Industrial Relations of Colorado," *American Federationist,* XXXVI (November 1929).

Rockefeller, John D., Jr., "Labor and Capital — Partners," *Atlantic Monthly,* CXVII (January 1916).

———, "There's a Solution for Labor Troubles," *System,* XXX (August 1916).

Seligman, Edwin R. A., "Colorado's Civil War and Its Lessons," *Leslie's Illustrated Weekly Newspaper,* CXIX (November 5, 1914).

———, "The Crisis in Colorado," *The Annalist,* III (May 4, 1914).

BOOKS

Adamic, Louis, *Dynamite* (New York, 1931).

Adams, Graham, *The Age of Industrial Violence 1910–1915: The Activities and Findings of the U.S. Commission on Industrial Relations* (New York, 1966).

Beshoar, Barron B., *Out of the Depths: The Story of John R. Lawson, a Labor Leader* (Denver, 1942).

Coleman, McAllister, *Men and Coal* (New York, c. 1943).

Creel, George, *Rebel at Large* (New York, c. 1947).

Eastman, Max, *Enjoyment of Living* (New York, 1948).

Ferns, H. S. and B. Ostrey, *The Age of Mackenzie King: The Rise of the Leader* (London, 1953).

Fosdick, Raymond B., *John D. Rockefeller, Jr.: A Portrait* (New York, 1956).

Gaynor, Lois Marguerite, "History of the Colorado Fuel and Iron Company and Constituent Companies, 1872–1933" (unpublished Master's Thesis, University of Colorado, 1936).

George, Russell D., *Geology and Natural Resources of Colorado* (Boulder, 1927).

Glück, Elsie, *John Mitchell, Miner: Labor's Bargain with the Gilded Age* (New York, c. 1929).

Goodykoontz, Colin B., ed., *Papers of Edward P. Costigan Relating to the Progressive Movement in Colorado, 1902–1917,* University of Colorado Historical Collections, IV (Boulder, 1941).

Hafen, LeRoy R., *Colorado: The Story of a Western Commonwealth* (Denver, 1933).

Keating, Edward, *The Gentleman from Colorado: A Memoir* (Denver, 1964).

Langdon, Emma F., *The Cripple Creek Strike: A History of Industrial Wars in Colorado, 1903–4–5; Being a Complete and Concise History of the Efforts of Organized Capital to Crush Unionism* (Denver, c. 1904–5).

Lindsey, Ben B., and Harvey J. O'Higgins, *The Beast* (New York, 1910).

McDonald, David J., and Edward A. Lynch, *Coal and Unionism: A History of the American Coal Miners' Unions* (Indianapolis, c. 1939).

McGregor, A., *The Fall and Rise of Mackenzie King: 1911–1919* (Toronto, 1962).

Nankivell, John H., *History of the Military Organizations of the State of Colorado, 1860–1935* (Denver, 1935).

Nevins, Allan, *John D. Rockefeller: The Heroic Age of American Enterprise* (New York, 1940).

Parton, Mary Field, ed., *Autobiography of Mother Jones* (Chicago, 1925).

Perlman, Selig, and Philip Taft, *Labor Movements* (New York, 1935).

Rastall, Benjamin McKie, *The Labor History of the Cripple Creek District: A Study in Industrial Evolution,* (Madison, 1908).

Rich, Bennett Milton, *The Presidents and Civil Disorder* (Washington: The Brookings Institution, 1941).

Rochester, Anna, *Labor and Coal* (New York, c. 1931).

Rockefeller, John D., Jr., *The Colorado Industrial Plan* (n.p., 1916).

———, *The Personal Relation in Industry* (New York, c. 1923).

Selekman, Ben M. and Mary Van Kleeck, *Employees Representation in Coal Mines: A Study of the Industrial Representation Plan of the Colorado Fuel and Iron Company,* Industrial Relations Series (New York: Russell Sage Foundation, 1924).

Sinclair Upton, *The Brass Check: A Study of American Journalism* (Pasadena, n.d.).

——, *King Coal* (New York, 1917).

Wendt, Lloyd and Herman Kogan, *Bet a Million! The Story of John W. Gates* (Indianapolis, c. 1948).

INDEX

INDEX